M

Th
a

CULTURAL TOURISM IN EUROPE

Dedication

Voor Caro

Stel op het strand: 'als het morgen regent, zullen we dan een paar lekkere kathedralen gaan bezichtigen?' Peter van Straaten

Cultural Tourism in Europe

Edited by

Greg Richards

Department of Leisure Studies
Tilburg University
PO Box 90153
5000 LE Tilburg
The Netherlands

CAB INTERNATIONAL

CAB INTERNATIONAL
Wallingford
Oxon OX10 8DE
UK

Tel: +44 (0)1491 832111
Fax: +44 (0)1491 833508
E-mail: cabi@cabi.org

CAB INTERNATIONAL
198 Madison Avenue
New York, NY 10016-4314
USA

Tel: +1 212 726 6490
Fax: +1 212 686 7993
E-mail: cabi-nao@cabi.org

A catalogue record for this book is available from the British Library,
London, UK

ISBN 0 85199 104 1

First printed 1996
Reprinted 1997

Printed and bound in the UK by Biddles Ltd., Guildford and King's Lynn

Contents

Contributors   vii

Preface   ix

PART 1: Cultural Tourism in Context

1 **Introduction: Culture and Tourism in Europe**   3
  G. Richards

2 **The Scope and Significance of Cultural Tourism**   19
  G. Richards

3 **The Social Context of Cultural Tourism**   47
  G. Richards

4 **The Economic Context of Cultural Tourism**   71
  C. Gratton and G. Richards

5 **The Policy Context of Cultural Tourism**   87
  G. Richards

PART 2: National Analyses

6 **Cultural Tourism in Belgium**   109
    W. Munsters

7 **Cultural Tourism in Denmark**   127
    A.-M. Hjalager

8 **Cultural Tourism in France**   147
    M. Bauer

9 **Cultural Tourism in Germany**   165
    P. Roth and A. Langemeyer

10 **Cultural Tourism in Greece**   183
    H. Kalogeropoulou

11 **Cultural Tourism in Ireland**   197
    G. O Donnchadha and B. O Connor

12 **Cultural Tourism in Italy**   215
    J. van der Borg and P. Costa

13 **Cultural Tourism in The Netherlands**   233
    G. Richards

14 **Cultural Tourism in Portugal**   249
    H. de Carvalho Curado

15 **Cultural Tourism in Spain**   267
    C. Maiztegui-Oñate and M.T. Areitio Bertolín

16 **Cultural Tourism in the United Kingdom**   283
    M. Foley

17 **European Cultural Tourism: Trends and Future Prospects**   311
    G. Richards

Index   335

Contributors

Michel Bauer, *LTA, Université de Savoie, PO Box 1104, 73011 Chambéry Cedex, France.*

Maria Teresa Areitio Bertolín, *Estudios de Ocio, Universidad de Deusto, Apartado 1, 48080 Bilbao, Spain.*

Paolo Costa, *CISET, University of Venice, Riviera San Pieto 83, 30030 Oriago di Mira (VE), Italy.*

Hermíno de Carvalho Curado, *SAGEI, University of Aviero, Campo Universitário, 3800 Aveiro, Portugal.*

Malcolm Foley, *Glasgow Caledonian University, Park Drive, Glasgow G3 6LP, UK.*

Chris Gratton, *School of Leisure and Food Management, Sheffield Hallam University, Pond Street, Sheffield S1 1WB, UK.*

Anne-Mette Hjalager, *Advance/1. Science Park, Gustav Wieds Vej 10, 8000 Aarhus C, Denmark.*

Helene Kalogeropoulou, *TEI Larissa, 41110 Larissa, Greece.*

Alfred Langemeyer, *Fachhochschule München, Am. Stadtpark 20, 81243 München, Germany.*

Conceptión Maiztegui-Oñate, *Estudios de Ocio, Universidad de Deusto, Apartado 1, 48080 Bilbao, Spain.*

Wil Munsters, *Faculty of Hospitality Management, Hogeschool Maastricht, PO Box 3900, 6202 NX Maastricht, The Netherlands (and Centre for Postgraduate Studies of the University of Limburg, Diepenbeek, Belgium).*

Brian O Connor, *School of Business and Social Studies, Tralee Regional Technical College, Clash, Tralee, Country Kerry, Ireland.*

Gearoid O Donnchadha, *School of Business and Social Studies, Tralee Regional Technical College, Clash, Tralee, Country Kerry, Ireland.*

Greg Richards, *Department of Leisure Studies, Tilburg University, PO Box 90153, 5000 LE Tilburg, The Netherlands.*

Peter Roth, *Fachhochschule München, Am. Stadtpark 20, 81243 München, Germany.*

Jan van der Borg, *CISET, University of Venice, Riviera San Pietro 83, 30030 Oriago di Mira (VE), Italy.*

Preface

The research project on which this book is based began to take shape in 1991, when the European Association for Tourism and Leisure Education (ATLAS) was given financial support by DGXXIII of the European Commission for a transnational study of European cultural tourism.

The basic reason for establishing the ATLAS Cultural Tourism Project was that very few comparative data then existed on European cultural tourism. Previous studies had tended to cover individual cultural tourism markets, or were generalized conceptual studies. The lack of data was problematic, as the European Commission had designated cultural tourism as a key area of tourism development in Europe in 1990. Without basic data on cultural tourism at European level, it is difficult to implement or to evaluate the implementation of cultural tourism policies. The ATLAS Cultural Tourism Project was therefore designed to provide comparative transnational data on cultural tourism, which would serve as a basis for the analysis of cultural tourism developments and trends across Europe. Although this was originally envisaged as a fairly limited project, the problems associated with organizing a transnational project and collecting and analysing comparable data ensured that the project extended far beyond its original scope.

Assembling a transnational research team from ATLAS institutions in most of the (then) 12 European Community member states posed few problems. At the initial project meeting, however, it soon became clear that differences of culture and language (the Dutch have no word for 'heritage', for example), had produced very different ideas of what cultural tourism meant. Because we wished to produce something which would be of practical as well as academic value, however, we decided to cut the Gordian Knot and define cultural tourism in both 'conceptual' and 'technical' terms. This was perhaps an artifical division, but it did allow us to combine basic data collection with more reflective research on the nature of cultural tourism in different areas of Europe. It also meant that the research could be truly transnational, with common data collection methods applied at a European level, rather than individual national approaches. Hopefully this book reflects our original desire to combine integrated research techniques with the individual national or regional perspectives which are contributed by the transnational research team.

As in all such projects, thanks are due to a large number of individuals and organizations who contributed in different ways to its successful completion. The project would not have been possible without 'pump-priming' funding from DGXXIII of the European Commission, and I am particularly grateful to Matthais Will and other members of the Tourism Unit of DGXXIII for the advice and encouragement that they have given the project over the years. A large number of people have been involved in the data collection, analysis and other aspects of the project work. Particular thanks must of course go to the project team members who have made written contributions to this book, and who made monumental efforts to produce material according to the specifications and the deadlines. A number of other individuals who worked on the project have not appeared in this book as authors, but have still made an important contribution to the research project. Thijs van Vugt, Luisa Aires, Visi Pareda Herrero, and Fred Coalter all helped to organize data collection, and con-tributed to the original research design. Thijs was also co-author of the original report on which the case study in Chapter 13 is based. The research team at the Centre for Leisure and Tourism Studies at the University of North London, and in particular Janet Bohrer, helped to ensure that the data collation and analysis went as smoothly as was humanly possible. The German cultural tourism company, Studiosus, were kind enough to sponsor the initial presentation of the results of the research at ITB in Berlin in 1993. Particular thanks must go to Klaus Vetter, Marketing Director of Studiosus, who also provided material for the original version of the case study presented in Chapter 9 of this volume.

This book would probably not have seen the light of day, however, without the work of my wife, Carolina Bonink. Carolina worked as a researcher on the project during 1992 and 1993, and was largely responsible for coordinating the data collection process. She also devised the data collection instrument for the survey research, and produced an innovative analysis of cultural tourism in the UK and The Netherlands, which helped to inform many of the chapters produced in this book.

Carolina's most important contribution, however, was in persuading me to move from the UK to The Netherlands, where the supportive environment provided by the Department of Leisure Studies at Tilburg University ensured that the text could be produced in a reasonable timescale. Moving to what the

British still largely refer to as 'Europe' has also ensured that the book has less of an Anglo-centric flavour than would otherwise have been the case. I have tried to support the concept of European unification in the text, by ensuring that all currencies are quoted not only in national units, but also in ECUs (converted at prevailing rates on 1 February 1995). Even we British will have to get used to the idea eventually. I have, however, tried not to add to the profusion of Euro-jargon, and the title 'European Union' is used as far as possible as a blanket term for the European Union, the European Community and other possible variations. The Commission has also been referred to as the 'European Commission' throughout. Even if these terms are not totally historically acurate, they do have the virtue of consistency.

Greg Richards
Tilburg
August 1995

CULTURAL TOURISM IN CONTEXT 1

Introduction: Culture and Tourism in Europe

1

G. RICHARDS

Department of Leisure Studies, Tilburg University, PO Box 90153, 5000 LE Tilburg, The Netherlands

If we had to do it all again, I would start with culture.

Jean Monnet

INTRODUCTION

The cultural heritage of Europe is 'one of the oldest and most important generators of tourism' (Thorburn, 1986), and it retains its central role in the European tourism industry to this day. According to the European Union, 'tourism, and especially cultural tourism in a broader sense, . . . deserve priority attention' as policy areas (Bernadini, 1992). Cultural tourism has become recognized as an important agent of economic and social change in Europe. Politicians now refer to cultural heritage as 'Italy's General Motors' (Fanelli, 1993) or as 'the oil industry of France' (Mosser, 1994).

The dramatic metaphors attached to the rapid growth of tourism and cultural consumption are appropriate. The cultural and tourist industries appear to be advancing in all European nations and regions, occupying the spaces vacated by manufacturing industry, and claiming strategic city centre locations (Corijn and Mommaas, 1995). Cultural consumption has grown, and tourism is an increasingly important form of cultural consumption, encouraged and funded by local, national, and supranational bodies. This reflects the change from an era when production drove consumption, to the consumer society where consumption drives production. By attracting that most mobile of consumers, the tourist, cities, regions and nations can secure the consumption power necessary to fuel their productive capacity.

The cultural tourism market in Europe is therefore becoming increasingly competitive. A growing number of cities and regions in the European Union are basing their tourism development strategies on the promotion of cultural heritage, and the number of cultural attractions is growing rapidly. Traditional cultural attractions such as museums and galleries are having to reassess their role as the pressure to generate visitor income intensifies, and the need to compete with a new generation of commercial tourist attractions grows. The opening up of new cultural tourism destinations in Eastern and Central Europe will add to the growing supply of distractions for the European cultural tourist in future.

On the global stage, Europe has long enjoyed a dominant position in international tourism and the cultural industries. However, just as manufacturers are facing growing global competition, so Europe can no longer be complacent about its leading position in the cultural tourism market. Europe is losing market share in the global tourism market as a whole (Brent-Ritchie *et al.*, 1993), and it is also facing growing competition in the sphere of cultural production and consumption.

The culture and tourism industries are now growing fastest in those areas which used to be on the margins of global production. A growing number of tourists are forsaking the Mediterranean beaches for the palm-fringed delights of Asia and the Caribbean. The manufacture of CDs and much other cultural software is now dominated by East Asia. Countries in these former peripheral regions are also beginning to compete with Europe in traditional 'high culture' markets. Examples include the moves by Singapore to literally 'buy into' the international art auctions market, and the creation by the Taiwanese government of a $365 million cultural foundation to underpin the island's fast growing art market (Robertson, 1993).

There is no doubt that culture is an important tourism resource in Europe, and that maintaining the competitiveness of the European tourism product is vital. However, a number of questions surround the use of cultural resources by tourists. Who are the tourists who use these cultural facilities? Why do they engage in cultural tourism? How great is the demand for cultural tourism? What elements of culture attract cultural tourists? Whose culture is being consumed by the cultural tourists? Few previous studies have attempted to answer these basic questions.

One important obstacle to supplying the answers to such questions is the lack of data on cultural tourism. The identification of cultural tourism as a growth market in Europe has been based more on assertion than hard information, and more on isolated observations than systematic analysis. It has therefore been difficult to demonstrate just how important cultural tourism is in Europe, just how fast it is growing, or to identify the reasons why it has grown. This book attempts to provide some of the basic data required to make an informed analysis of European cultural tourism, its causes, its significance, and its impact.

This book further aims to analyse the meanings and significance of cultural tourism in a rapidly changing Europe. In doing so, it examines cultural tourism within the context of the major social, economic and political processes which have influenced its development. The rest of this introductory chapter therefore examines the causes and implications of the growth of tourism demand and cultural supply in an historical context. An introduction to the structure of the book is provided at the end of the chapter.

GROWTH OF CULTURAL TOURISM DEMAND

Tourism and culture have always been closely linked in Europe. Europe has always been an important destination for those attracted by its rich cultural and historic legacy. Roman 'cultural tourists', for example, steeped themselves in the culture of civilizations more ancient than their own, such as Greece and Egypt (Feifer, 1985). Subsequent medieval tourists were mostly pilgrims, and laid the foundations for some of the modern 'cultural itineraries', such as the pilgrim route to Santiago de Compostella in northern Spain.

The origin of the word 'tourism' is usually attributed to the Grand Tour, which originated in Britain in the seventeenth century (Hibbert, 1969; Feifer, 1985). Towner (1985:301) defined the Grand Tour as:

> A tour of certain cities and places in western Europe undertaken primarily, but not exclusively for education and pleasure.

Most of the early Grand Tourists were aristocrats for whom a trip to continental Europe was often a coda to a classical education. Usually in the company of a tutor, they would spend two or three years travelling through France, Italy, Germany, Switzerland, and The Netherlands, often visiting sites connected with classical culture. The cities of Italy in particular were considered the 'prize' to be won by Grand Tourists struggling over the Alps.

During the 1780s the nature of the Grand Tour began to be transformed by the growth of the British middle class, and a resulting shift of Grand Tourists from a predominance of landowners to the professional middle classes (Towner, 1985). This change also reduced the educational aspect of the Tour, with less university-educated tourists, and less tutors accompanying their pupils. The spatial pattern of the Grand Tour also changed, from the 'Classical Grand Tour' which concentrated on the culture of the ancient classical world and the Renaissance, to the 'Romantic Grand Tour', with more attention devoted to romantic views of urban and rural scenery. Feifer (1985) suggests that the Romantic approach was promoted by aristocrats who 'were already so highly steeped in culture that they looked for something beyond high culture', usually in the form of 'exotic pleasures' and 'imaginative experimentation'.

Thus the emphasis of the Tour shifted away from the educational aspects of culture towards culture as a source of pleasure and entertainment.

The eighteenth century expansion of the Grand Tour marked a shift away from precapitalist, ahistorical conceptions of cultural production, where influences from outside the dominant culture were not considered worthy of consideration (Negrin, 1993) to the bourgeois notion of the universal aesthetic of cultural manifestations. This modern view of universality allowed European culture to absorb and evaluate cultural products from different cultures and epochs with reference to aesthetic form as an homogenizing principle. Whereas Medieval 'tourists' were largely bound within a Roman Catholic cultural tradition, for example as pilgrims to Santiago de Compostella or Rome, the Grand Tourists were able to perceive the products of different periods and communities as contributing in different ways to the inevitable progress of European culture.

At the same time as a growing number of Grand Tourists were collecting cultural experiences across Europe, cultural artefacts from all corners of the globe were being gathered together and organized for public consumption in the first museums. The advent of museums in Europe during the eighteenth and nineteenth centuries was the most physical manifestation of the bourgeois idea of the universality of culture. Museums were organized to demonstrate the progress of human artistic and industrial achievement, the pinnacle of which was represented by the products of Modernity (Horne, 1984). Museums were not the only markers of progress. Tourists in nineteenth century Paris were also shown through factories and the sewer system (MacCannell, 1976). This early form of industrial tourism was supposed to underline faith in progress, in sharp contrast to the growth of industrial tourism in the 1980s, which was arguably designed to cash in on nostalgia for past industrial achievement (Shaw, 1991a). As the 'Project of the Museum' took hold in Europe, however, the placing of objects in museum displays became important signifiers of their cultural significance, and the museum increasingly became the centre of cultural tourism endeavour.

The identification of particular cultural products as objects of tourist consumption also dates from the same period. The American historian Daniel Boorstin deplored the

> relatively recent phenomenon of the tourist attraction pure and simple. It often has no purpose but to attract the interest of the owner or of the nation. As we might expect, the use of the word 'attraction' as 'a thing or feature which "draws" people; especially any interesting or amusing exhibition' dates only from about 1862. It is a new species: the most attenuated form of a nation's culture. All over the world now we find these 'attractions' – of little significance for the inward life of a people, but wonderfully saleable as a tourist commodity.
>
> (Boorstin, 1964:103)

The availability of museums, exhibitions, and other cultural manifestations for public consumption helped to boost tourism. The expanding middle class market for travel during the nineteenth century prompted pioneers such as Thomas Cook to offer the first 'package tours' to European destinations such as Italy and Greece in the 1860s. The focus of most of Cook's early packages was cultural, enabling his predominantly middle class clients to exercise 'their absurd pretensions to be in places abroad that they have never dreamed of aspiring at home' (quoted in Swinglehurst, 1982:48), rubbing shoulders with the aristocratic remnants of the Grand Tour.

Cultural motives for travel therefore continued to be relatively important in European tourism up until the First World War. During the inter-war years, however, there was a significant growth in domestic tourism in northern European countries, stimulated by the advent of paid holidays. Much of this tourism was based on seaside resorts or rural destinations, and was designed to provide rest and relaxation in the short respite then allowed from work. Before the Second World War, tourism was still basically a privilege for a minority. In the UK, for example, only 30% of the population took an annual holiday at all in the 1930s.

After the war, a long period of unbroken economic growth in Europe stimulated a consumer boom, which in turn led to greater and more varied tourism consumption. Initially, international tourism flows in Europe were predominantly from north to south, with tourists from the relatively prosperous countries in north-west Europe seeking the cheap sun on Mediterranean beaches. The appearance of mass international tourism in Europe during the 1960s was based largely on standardized products offered by tour operators based in northern Europe. There was little consideration of culture *per se* in these products, except for the idealized national cultures which many tourists were experiencing for the first time. The idea of creating packages with culture as a central element was largely confined to the Germanic markets, where a number of specialist 'study tourism' operators appeared during the 1960s (see Roth and Langemeyer, Chapter 9 this volume). In terms of size, however, these cultural tourism operators remained dwarfed by the sun, sea, and sand production giants.

As the European tourist market matured in the 1970s and 1980s, however, it began to be increasingly segmented into different niche markets. Tourism products were segmented by time (winter sun holidays), by user group (youth, senior citizens), by destination (tour operators specializing in individual countries or regions), and by travel motivation (e.g. activity holidays). For the mass market operators, culture was something inherent in the product, rather than a niche market in itself. Increasing market segmentation did, however, create new opportunities for specialist cultural tourism operators.

By the late 1970s, tourism had grown into a major global industry, and increasing attention was being paid to both the positive and negative consequences of tourism development (Mathieson and Wall, 1982). Tourism policy began to be taken more seriously, as Governments recognized the in-come and job creation potential of tourism, and also became concerned about the possible adverse impacts of mass tourism on culture and the environment. Individual tourists, tired of fighting for increasingly scarce space on Mediter-ranean beaches, began to seek less-crowded alternatives, often with cultural attractions in place of sun and sand. The convergence of tourist demand for more cultural short breaks, and the need for cities to replace lost manufactur-ing jobs created a 'new' market in urban short break holidays in Europe, many of which were based on cultural attractions (Law, 1993).

Over the years tourism consumption patterns have changed dramatically. Tourism has developed from an elite pursuit to a basic leisure need of the masses, and arguably the world's biggest source of employment. At the same time, consumption of all forms of culture has expanded, as the democratization of culture and the growth of the middle class have opened up 'high' culture to a wider audience. As tourism and cultural consumption have grown, so the relationship between tourism and culture has also been transformed.

Until relatively recently, the development of tourism and culture was rela-tively independent. The number of 'cultural tourists' was small, and tourist consumption of cultural facilities during their travels tended to be incidental to the main function of cultural institutions of serving the needs of the local population. Cultural institutions also tended to be elitist in outlook, and saw visitors as an unwanted diversion from their main job of conserving or produc-ing cultural goods. Today, however, museums and other cultural institutions are throwing open their doors to visitors and actively competing with other leisure attractions for their custom and expenditure. An examination of the forces shaping cultural provision will help to identify the reasons for this change.

THE GROWTH OF CULTURAL PRODUCTION

Just as tourism was originally the preserve of the wealthy, so cultural produc-tion was historically controlled by and aimed at the elite. The twentieth cen-tury, however, has witnessed a dramatic growth in the variety and availability of cultural products, which Toffler (1964) dubbed the 'cultural explosion'. The change from private amusement to public spectacle in cultural consumption can best be illustrated through the development of the museum in Europe.

Before the late eighteenth century, collections of art and other cultural products were basically the private property of princes and nobles (Negrin, 1993). As a result of the French Revolution, however, art collections belonging to the royal family and the church were confiscated. The conquests of Napoleon later ensured that works from royal collections throughout Europe joined the French works already assembled in the Louvre, the first national museum in Europe. The Louvre was soon emulated by other national museums such as the Prado in Madrid and the Altes in Berlin. Whereas private collections were based largely on the personal taste of the owner, these new public museums were designed to provide comprehensive collections spanning all epochs and cultures. 'Underlying this comprehensive assemblage of cultural artifacts was the notion of world culture. European culture in the nineteenth century saw itself as a universal culture, valid for all times and peoples' (Negrin, 1993:100).

This modernist concept of the expanded relevance of the past, and the desire to assemble collections which underlined the inevitable progress of history towards the superiority of the present (Horne, 1984) was responsible for the first wave of expansion in cultural production. In the UK, the 1845 Museums of Art in Corporate Towns Act gave an initial impetus to the establishment of local museums (Shaw, 1991b). Much of the early expansion of cultural provision in urban areas was due to philanthropic donations by wealthy industrialists or fund-raising by cultural associations (Bevers, 1993). However, the long-term support of the new cultural institutions in most cases quickly devolved to the state. The early growth of cultural policy based on public museums, galleries and libraries usually had an educational function, aimed at introducing high culture to the masses.

Changing patterns of leisure time availability also shaped views on how that time should be spent. In the nineteenth century, 'free time' among the working classes was viewed as a potential threat to social stability. Various attempts were therefore made to ensure that the working class used their time in constructive ways. The promotion of 'rational recreation' was seen as a weapon against idleness, 'one of the central metaphors of moral degeneration in a bourgeois society' (Rojek, 1993:32) in the nineteenth century. Idleness was attacked mainly through voluntary sector initiatives, such as the Lord's Day Observance Society (1831), which Rojek argues helped to organize leisure according to middle class values. One of these values was the importance of 'high' culture, as embodied in the Art to the Poor scheme operated in London's East End in the 1880s.

Such initiatives helped to solidify distinctions between 'high' culture, which was considered an acceptable use of leisure time for the masses, and 'popular' culture, unacceptable manifestations of which were often suppressed (Corijn and Mommaas, 1995). Efforts to democratize high culture and promote access for the working class were founded in the belief that exposure to suitable forms of high culture would help to educate the masses, and help to create a feeling of national identity and solidarity. The educational role of culture was largely responsible for the significant increases in cultural funding which occurred in many European states after the Second World War.

A second wave of expanded cultural production was created from the 1960s onwards through the recycling and recombination of cultural forms which arguably marked the transition from modernity to postmodernity. Postmodernity not only recycled the past, it also expanded the range of time periods which were considered to form part of our historic heritage. As David Lowenthal (1985:44) has observed, whereas it was 'formerly confined in time and space, nostalgia today engulfs the whole past', so that 1930s Art Deco or 1950s juke-boxes can be considered as part of the 'heritage', whereas museums had formerly looked towards the Renaissance or antiquity for their historic justification (Walsh, 1991). In addition to the burgeoning cultural production stimulated by recycling the past and historifying the recent past, postmodernism has also been marked by the emergence of new interest groups and specialized markets. Museums can therefore abandon the modernist project of universality, in favour of market segmentation and themeing.

[The result has been a second 'museums boom' in Europe. Table 1.1 illustrates the recent origin of many museums in Britain. Even though the first expansion of museum supply in the second half of the nineteenth century was fairly rapid, the museums boom of the last 25 years produced an unprecedented increase in museum supply from an already high base. This trend was present throughout Europe from the 1970s to the present. Figure 1.1 shows that the number of museums in both Western and Eastern European countries

Table 1.1. Growth of museums in the UK, 1860–1989.

Year	Total number of museums	% increase	%/annum
1860	90		
1880	180	+100	5.0
1887	217	+21	3.0
1963	876	+303	4.0
1984	2131	+143	6.8
1989	2500	+17	3.4

Source: After Law (1993) and Walsh (1991).

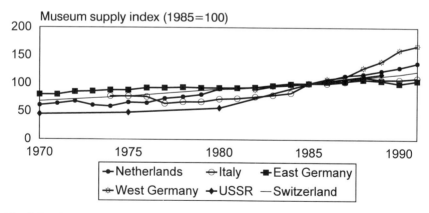

Fig. 1.1.   Museum supply in selected European countries, 1970–1991 (source: ATLAS database).

increased substantially during the 1970s and 1980s. Growth in museum supply has been evident in all areas of Europe, but seems to have started slightly earlier in north-western Europe. Museum growth was also encouraged by Communist regimes in Eastern Europe during the 1980s, although arguably with different motives from their western counterparts.

The disintegration of the notion of a Universal European Culture, rather than delivering a death blow to the museum, has provided a cultural stimulus for the expansion of cultural manifestations. A single museum can no longer claim to contain the essence of European culture. A diverse range of museums and art galleries is required to reflect the increasing fragmentation and integration of cultural products based on both 'high' and 'popular' culture (see Richards, Chapter 3 this volume).

The growth of specialized museums alongside the general collections enshrined in the national museums and galleries has been one of the major forces behind the expansion of museum supply in Europe. Examples of new specialist museums can be found in London (Museum of the Moving Image, Theatre Museum, Design Museum), in Brussels (Cartoon Museum), in Amsterdam (Sex Museum, Pianola Museum, Cannabis Museum) and many other cities across Europe.

As MacDonald (1992:163) has observed, the 'new' museums have partly been created as a response to the deficiencies of the old:

> The failure of mainstream museums (to reach a wider audience) is one reason why we are seeing growing numbers of specialized museums designed for specific audiences, such as children, indigenous peoples and specific ethnic communities.

The rapid growth in the number of museums has opened a new debate about precisely what type of institutions ought to be considered as 'museums'. In the UK the Museums and Galleries Commission has introduced a new registration system with strict qualifying criteria. The effect of this is likely to be a reduction in the number of 'museums' in the UK from about 2500 to around 2000 officially registered establishments (Eckstein, 1993). In the Netherlands, the Director of the Dutch Museums Association (NMV) suggested in 1993 that new criteria should be established to stop 'ego-tripping collectors' from setting up 'silly museums' with no professional basis. He cited the establishment of the Mata-Hari Museum and the Cigarette Lighter Museum as examples. This is a clear plea for the preservation of professional control over the establishment of museums. It does, however, make the point that the diversity and provenance of 'museums' has changed rapidly in recent years, as new market opportunities have been identified, and new interpretations of the role of museums have begun to compete with the old.

The same forces of modernity which led to the creation of the museum led later to the increasing designation of 'historic monuments' across Europe. Modernity implied a vast expansion of the past that was considered relevant to the present (Negrin, 1993), and structures and buildings from all ages acquired relevance at the same time. The number of listed monuments has grown substantially in most EU states since the 1960s (Ashworth and Tunbridge, 1990) and is still growing. The number of listed monuments in France grew by 27% between 1980 and 1991, and in The Netherlands there are currently an estimated 15,000 monuments awaiting official listing.

It can be argued that modernity not only created the project of the museum through expanding the relevance of the past, but also sowed the seeds of destruction of the national entities and ideologies which originally supported the project. The detachment of national museums from their original supporting role as instruments of national ideology is today symbolized by some national museums being placed outside direct government control, as in The Netherlands (see Richards, Chapter 13 this volume). In searching for a new role, museums are looking both to develop as an educational resource for local communities and as providers of commercial leisure products for both residents and tourists. The demands of tourists for more cultural attractions and the need of cultural attractions to attract more visitors have therefore converged rapidly in recent years.

CONVERGENCE OF TOURISM AND CULTURE

Because the basic forces driving the expansion of tourism and cultural consumption are so similar, it is not surprising that mass tourism and mass cultural consumption have coincided in the late twentieth century. In spite of reservations about the potential negative impacts of tourism on culture (see Richards, Chapter 3 this volume), it seems that tourism and culture are inseparable. As Leo van Nispen, Director of the International Council on Monuments and Sites (ICOMOS) put it: 'culture and tourism are destined once and for all to be together' (quoted in Groen, 1994:25).

The basic argument presented in this book is that the convergence of tourism and cultural consumption is not coincidental, and that cultural tourism cannot be understood as simply a 'new' market trend (Myerscough, 1988). The growth of cultural tourism can better be explained as a consequence of wider social and economic trends which mark either the period of 'late modernity' or 'postmodernity', depending on the terminology you prefer (Harvey, 1989).

A more detailed consideration of the impact of these social and economic changes on culture and tourism is presented in Chapters 3 and 4 of this volume. Important elements of these changes which relate to the development of cultural tourism, however, include increasing de-differentiation between previously separate social and economic spheres, such as culture and economy and tourism and culture, and the apparently contradictory trends towards globalization and localization.

An important consequence of these changes is that 'the expansion and deepening of commodity markets has witnessed the transfer of the logic and rationality of commodity production to the sphere of consumption and culture' (Britton, 1991:453). The consumption of tourism and culture is now organized by the 'tourism industry' (Smith, 1988) and the 'cultural industries' (Shaw, 1991b; Wynne, 1992). The resulting changes in the organization of production have created a whole new breed of attractions and intermediaries who supply culture specifically for tourist consumption, a phenomenon dubbed the 'heritage industry' by Hewison (1987). These changes also have significant implications for existing cultural attractions.

As cultural provision shifts increasingly into the market, the test of 'success' for existing cultural institutions can no longer be a purely aesthetic one. It is not sufficient for an art exhibition or a museum display or a theatre performance to be a critical 'success'. Cultural manifestations increasingly need to justify themselves in quantitative terms, such as the number of visitors or income generated. These quantitative performance indicators are equally important for institutions which operate in a wholly commercial environment and for public-funded organizations which have to demonstrate the effectiveness of subsidy. Cultural and arts institutions are therefore becoming increasingly concerned about the cultural audience and its needs. The audience for culture also needs to be broadened if visitor numbers and income are to grow.

Attempting to increase visitor numbers almost inevitably means attracting tourists. Tourists are needed for a number of reasons. The stubborn refusal of audiences for most forms of high culture to grow through subsidy-driven 'vertical equalization', to all social classes (Bevers, 1993) or the more recent policy of 'culture-spreading through market mechanisms' (Brouwer, 1993) means that increased geographic market penetration is required. Often this is achieved through popularizing the product, giving rise to charges that 'some museums are becoming little more than glorified theme parks, running the risk of sacrificing their standards of scholarship and curatorial integrity for the sake of attracting ever increasing numbers of visitors' (Eckstein, 1993:450). In spite of these concerns, the evidence suggests that the cultural audience remains stubbornly elitist (see Richards, Chapter 2 this volume). It has also now been recognized that the cultural audience in all areas, whether urban, suburban or rural is relatively limited (Verhoeff, 1994), and urban and rural centres alike have to attract visitors to support cultural provision. As more competition for this elite audience appears, therefore, cultural attractions have to look increasingly further afield, and many can no longer survive on local audiences alone. In London, for example, it has been estimated that overseas tourists account for 32% of all West End theatre audiences, and in the absence of tourism, many theatres would close (Quine, 1993).

At the same time that reductions in the level of public funding are forcing many cultural attractions to increase visitor revenue, changes in funding structure in some countries are also forcing cultural institutions to become more market-orientated. In the UK, The Netherlands and Italy, for example, national museums and art galleries are being given more control over their own expenditure. That freedom has a price in terms of greater accountability for how funds are spent through the development of accounting procedures and performance indicators. As one of the most important performance indicators will inevitably be visitor numbers, attracting more tourists will be an important means of improving the performance of an attraction.

Using culture as a vehicle for tourism development and promotion is also becoming an important element of public policy (see Richards, Chapter 5 this volume). A notable development is the transformation of former productive spaces into areas of cultural tourism consumption. Industrial and heritage tourism is being used to transform derelict former manufacturing areas into tourism consumption centres, and agricultural land and buildings taken out of production are used for 'green tourism' or folk heritage centres. The development of cultural tourism in both traditional centres of high culture and in former industrial centres to some extent reflects the 'spatial fixity' of tourism (Urry, 1990) which ties tourism development to locally available cultural resources, and the impact of localization, which is reflected in a growing interest in local cultures.

Such social, economic and political changes are forcing publicly funded cultural institutions to join commercial producers in the search for increased visitor numbers and admission income. As the national analyses in this book show, this trend is repeated in all areas of Europe, and extends to both urban and rural environments. The growth of cultural tourism can therefore be viewed as a consequence of both increased tourism demand, and the growing supply of cultural attractions. The demands of economic restructuring have forced cultural attractions to be more dependent on visitor markets in general, and tourists in particular. As cultural markets become increasingly globalized, so competition between cultural attractions for a share of the cultural tourism market will also intensify. The following section gives an overview of the structure of the book, and explains how these arguments are developed.

STRUCTURE OF THE TEXT

Many studies which deal with 'Europe' are little more than collections of individual national analyses, with the integration provided only by summary overviews of the issues presented. This book attempts to take integration a step further, because it is based on work undertaken for an integrated European Cultural Tourism research project run by the European Association for Tourism and Leisure Education – ATLAS (see Richards, Chapter 2 this volume). The research was established on the basis of common definitions of cultural tourism, and the collection of comparative data on cultural tourism consumption and production in 11 EU countries. Although the book concentrates largely on the EU, links with other areas are made where possible.

The book attempts to provide an analysis of the forces shaping cultural tourism at European level, by analysing in Part 1 broad socio-economic and political trends in relation to cultural tourism. Part 2 focuses on the development, management and marketing of cultural tourism at national level.

Chapter 2 covers the basic concepts and definitional issues surrounding cultural tourism, and uses this as a basis for analysing the significance of cultural tourism in Europe. Defining cultural tourism is difficult, not only because of the broad meaning of the terms 'culture' and 'tourism', but also because of the changing role of cultural tourism itself. An exploration of the European Cultural Capital designation, for example, illustrates how the event has shifted from being a cultural celebration to becoming a significant economic event.

Chapter 3 examines the theoretical bases for the study of cultural tourism. Because of the complex nature of the subject matter, this inevitably draws on a wide range of sources, including mainstream sociology, art sociology, geography, etc. As well as considering the factors shaping cultural tourism consumption, the impact of tourism on culture is also briefly considered.

An overview of the economic context of cultural tourism is presented in Chapter 4. Emphasis is given to the funding for cultural infrastructure and production, and the changing role of state, market, and voluntary sectors in cultural provision. The growing emphasis on commercial provision of culture, and the convergence of commercialized culture and commercial tourism is illustrated through an examination of funding policies in different countries. Chapter 4 concludes with an examination of the economic impact of cultural tourism, in terms of income generation and job creation.

Part 1 concludes with an examination of cultural tourism policies in Chapter 5. Policy development is analysed at European, national, regional and local scales, and an attempt is made to identify the links between different policy levels and between different geographic areas. Particular emphasis is given to European policy developments, and policy relating specifically to cultural tourism is placed in the wider context of EU tourism and cultural policy.

Part 2 of this volume presents individual national chapters, all of which were written by authors working in the countries concerned, and most of whom have been directly involved in the ATLAS European Cultural Tourism research programme.

The chapter authors were given a fairly free hand in determining the content of their chapters, to better reflect the diversity of approaches to cultural tourism in the EU. Every chapter follows a similar format, however, in order to facilitate comparisons between nations. The basic elements found in each chapter include an analysis of policy frameworks for cultural tourism, an analysis of cultural tourism supply and demand, and case studies and examples which reflect the development, marketing or management of cultural tourism in that country. Each national chapter provides illustrations of some of the European trends and issues identified in Part 1 of the book, but the national chapters also underline the essential national and regional differences which contribute to the cultural diversity of Europe.

The final chapter provides an overview of some of the arguments developed in the national chapters, and develops an analysis of likely future trends in the development of cultural tourism in Europe.

REFERENCES

Ashworth, G.J. and Tunbridge, J.E. (1990) *The Tourist-Historic City*. Belhaven Press, London.

Bernadini, G. (1992) Tourism and cultural tourism in EC policy. In: Provincie Friesland, *Cultural Tourism and Regional Development*. Leeuwarden, pp. 3–5.

Bevers, T. (1993) *Georganiseerd Cultuur*. Dick Coutinho, Bussum.

Boorstin, D. (1964) *The Image: a Guide to Pseudo-events in America*. Harper and Row, New York.

Brent-Ritchie, J.R., Hawkins, D.E., Go, F. and Frechtling, D. (1993) *World Travel and Tourism Review, Vol. 3*. CAB International, Wallingford.

Britton, S. (1991) Tourism, capital and place: towards a critical geography of tourism. *Environment and Planning D: Society and Space* 9, 451–478.

Brouwer, R. (1993) Het nieuwe Rotterdam: de kunst, het beleid, de zorg en de markt. *Vrijetijd en Samenleving* 11, 31–43.

Corijn, E. and Mommaas, H. (1995) *Urban Cultural Policy Developments in Europe*. Council of Europe, Strasbourg.

Eckstein, J. (1993) Funding the cultural sector in the UK. *Boekmancahier* 18, 449–467.

Fanelli, F. (1993) Our museums are Italy's General Motors. *The Art Newspaper* 33, 6–7.

Feifer, M. (1985) *Tourism in History. From Imperial Rome to the Present*. Stein and Day, New York.

Groen, J. (1994) De werelderfgoedlijst van UNESCO: grillig en willekeurig. *De Volkskrant*, 19 February, 23.

Harvey, D. (1989) *The Condition of Postmodernity*. Basil Blackwell, Oxford.

Hewison, R. (1987) *The Heritage Industry: Britain in a Climate of Decline*. Methuen, London.

Hibbert, C. (1969) *The Grand Tour*. Putnam, London.

Horne, D. (1984) *The Great Museum*. Pluto Press, London.

Law, C.M. (1993) *Urban Tourism: Attracting Visitors to Large Cities*. Mansell, London.

Lowenthal, D. (1985) *The Past is a Foreign Country*. Cambridge University Press, Cambridge.

MacCannell, D. (1976) *The Tourist: a New Theory of the Leisure Class*. Macmillan, London.

MacDonald, G.F. (1992) Change and challenge: museums in the informational society. In: Karp, I., Kreamer, C.M. and Lavine, S.D. (eds) *Museums and Communities: the Politics of Public Culture*. Smithsonian Institution Press, Washington, pp. 158–181.

Mathieson, A. and Wall, G. (1982) *Tourism: Economic, Physical and Social Impacts*. Longman, Harlow.

Mosser, F. (1994) Monuments historiques et tourisme culturel. Quel projet pour quels publics? *Cahiers Espace* 37, 23–27.

Myerscough, J. (1988) *The Economic Importance of the Arts.* Policy Studies Institute, London.

Negrin, L. (1993) On the Museum's Ruins: a critical appraisal. *Theory, Culture, Society* 10, 97–125.

Quine, M. (1993) Theatre audiences in Britain: a continuing research programme. *Journal of Arts Management, Law and Society* 23, 225–239.

Robertson, I. (1993) Taiwan: fast track development. *The Art Newspaper* 33, 31–37.

Rojek, C. (1993) *Ways of Escape: Modern Transformations in Leisure and Travel.* Macmillan, Basingstoke.

Shaw, G. (1991a) Culture and tourism: the economics of nostalgia. *World Futures* 33, 199–212.

Shaw, G. (1991b) Growth and employment in the UK's culture industry. *World Futures* 33, 165–180.

Smith, S.L.J. (1988) Defining tourism: a supply-side view. *Annals of Tourism Research* 17, 581–602.

Swinglehurst, E. (1982) *Cook's Tours: the Story of Popular Travel.* Blanford, Poole.

Thorburn, A. (1986) Marketing cultural heritage: does it work within Europe? *Travel and Tourism Analyst* December, 39–48.

Toffler, A. (1964) *The Culture Consumers: a Study of Art and Affluence in America.* St Martin's Press, New York.

Towner, J. (1985) The Grand Tour: a key phase in the history of tourism. *Annals of Tourism Research* 12, 297–333.

Urry, J. (1990) *The Tourist Gaze: Leisure and Travel in Contemporary Societies.* Sage, London.

Verhoeff, R. (1994) High culture: the performing arts and its audience in the Netherlands. *Tijdschrift voor Economische en Sociale Geografie* 85, 79–83.

Walsh, K. (1991) *The Representation of the Past: Museums and Heritage in the Post-modern World.* Routledge, London.

Wynne, D. (1992) *The Culture Industry.* Avebury, Aldershot.

The Scope and Significance of Cultural Tourism   2

G. RICHARDS

Department of Leisure Studies, Tilburg University, PO Box 90153, 5000 LE Tilburg, The Netherlands

INTRODUCTION

What does 'cultural tourism' mean? The term is widely used, and also widely misunderstood. Academics and policy-makers have been quick to identify cultural tourism as a growth market, without seriously considering what that market consists of. In order to examine how significant cultural tourism is in Europe, we first need to have a definition of the term.

Cultural tourism is a problematic concept, however, because it consists of two elements, 'culture' and 'tourism', which are in themselves difficult to define. Most attempts at defining cultural tourism agree that it consists of the consumption of culture by tourists, but this approach introduces new problems. What kinds of culture should be included within the scope of cultural tourism? Does a visit to a museum turn an entire holiday into a cultural tourism experience? Are tourists who engage in cultural consumption actually culturally motivated? This chapter examines the problem of defining cultural tourism, and the changing nature of the relationship between culture and tourism.

DEFINING CULTURAL TOURISM

Much has been written about the problems of defining both tourism and culture as separate terms. Williams (1983), for example, cautions that culture is 'one of the two or three most complicated words in the English language'.

©1996 CAB INTERNATIONAL.
Cultural Tourism in Europe (ed. G. Richards)

When 'culture' and 'tourism' are put together to form 'cultural tourism', the problems of definition multiply.

Tourism

Tourism is perhaps an easier concept to deal with than culture, because the complexities involved are usually interpretive rather than value-laden. Tourism definitions can be either conceptual, trying to describe what tourism is, or technical, which enable the volume and value of tourism to be measured (Smith, 1988). Conceptual definitions can be very wide ranging indeed. For example, the Tourism Society in the UK defines tourism as:

> The temporary short-term movement of people to destinations outside the places where they normally live and work, and activities during their stay at these destinations; it includes movement for all purposes, as well as day visits and excursions.

> (Quoted in Holloway, 1985:2–3)

There has been considerable debate in recent years over technical definitions, because these have tended to vary from one country to another, making international comparisons difficult. The World Tourism Organization (WTO) definition as amended in 1993 is now widely accepted, however, and is also applied by the European Commission (1995). The WTO definition of tourism includes

> the activities of persons during their travel and stay in a place outside their usual place of residence, for a continuous period of less than one year, for leisure, business or other purposes.

> (World Tourism Organization, 1993)

The WTO definition also makes a distinction between 'tourists', who stay at least 24 hours at their destination, and 'excursionists' who travel for less than 24 hours. In the current research we follow this general convention by referring to all those visiting cultural attractions as 'visitors', and to those staying overnight as 'tourists'. It should be recognized, however, that the definitions of tourism and the methods of measuring tourist flows may vary considerably from one country to another in Europe, and the individual national chapters in this book should be read with this in mind.

Culture

Culture is a more complex concept, as evidenced by the extent of the debate over the term. Tomlinson (1991:4) notes that hundreds of definitions of 'culture' exist, 'which would suggest that either there is a considerable amount of confusion . . . or that "culture" is so large an all-embracing a concept that it can accommodate all these definitions'. There is a sense of culture as a complex whole, which provides an organizing concept for the widely varied 'ways of life'. Trying to define 'culture' in a single broadly acceptable definition therefore produces a level of generalization which renders the act of definition useless.

The solution proposed by Tomlinson and others is not to seek an all-embracing definition of what culture is, but rather to concentrate on the way in which the term is actually used. Williams (1983) identifies three broad categories of modern usage of the term: (i) as a general process of intellectual, spiritual and aesthetic development; (ii) as indicative of a particular 'way of life'; and (iii) as the works and practices of intellectual and artistic activity. Over time, there has been a shift in meanings attached to the word in general usage, away from the former and towards the latter two categories. Two basic uses of the term 'culture' can therefore currently be identified in the academic literature: *culture as process* and *culture as product*.

Culture as process is an approach derived from anthropology and sociology, which regards culture mainly as codes of conduct embedded in a specific social group. As Clarke (1990:28) puts it, culture 'designates the social field of meaning production', or the processes through which people make sense of themselves and their lives. The boundaries of social groups, and therefore cultures, are variable, and can cover a nation, tribe, corporation or those pursuing specific activities. We may therefore talk about the culture of a specific country, or a culture of mass tourism (e.g. Urry, 1990). The culture as product approach derives particularly from literary criticism. Culture is regarded as the product of individual or group activities to which certain meanings are attached. Thus 'high' culture might be used by some to refer to the products of famous artists, whereas 'low' culture might refer to TV soap programmes.

The product and process approaches to culture rarely overlap. However, in the field of tourism, there has been a certain degree of integration between the two terms. Culture as process is the goal of tourists seeking authenticity and meaning through their tourist experiences (MacCannell, 1976; Cohen, 1979). However, the very presence of tourists leads to the creation of cultural manifestations specifically for tourist consumption (Cohen, 1988). In other words culture as process is transformed through tourism (as well as other social mechanisms) into culture as product. The resulting cultural products need not be devoid of all meaning as a result of their isolation from their original social context. Cohen argues that some cultural products developed for tourists may over time attain 'emergent authenticity', and be accepted as 'authentic' by both tourists and cultural producers alike. A clear challenge posed in defining cultural tourism, therefore, is to conceptualize both the cultural products presented for tourist consumption, and the cultural processes which generate the motivation to participate in cultural tourism.

Cultural tourism

MacCannell (1976:25) refers to 'cultural productions', a term which refers not only to the process of culture, but also to the products which result from that process. MacCannell identified tourism as the ideal arena in which to investigate the nature of such cultural production, and the notion of cultural tourism perhaps takes this idea to its logical conclusion.

However, the range of cultural products alone is vast, and the term 'cultural tourism' has been used to describe the consumption of art, heritage, folklore, and a whole range of other cultural manifestations by tourists. Such is the range of possible uses of the term, that no single widely accepted definition of cultural tourism has yet emerged (Richards, 1993).

A review of existing definitions of cultural tourism by Bonink (1992) identified two basic approaches. The first, the 'sites and monuments' approach, concentrates on describing the type of attractions visited by cultural tourists, and is clearly related to a product-based definition of culture. This approach is very useful for quantitative research on cultural tourism, since it is relatively easy to identify, count and interview visitors to cultural attractions. On the other hand, it tends to yield a relatively narrow view of the activities and motivations of cultural tourists, because it restricts the analysis to specific sites. A typical list of the types of sites or attractions which are considered to attract cultural tourists is provided by ECTARC (1989):

1. archaeological sites and museums.
2. architecture (ruins, famous buildings, whole towns).
3. art, sculpture, crafts, galleries, festivals, events.
4. music and dance (classical, folk, contemporary).
5. drama (theatre, films, dramatists).
6. language and literature study, tours, events.
7. religious festivals, pilgrimages.
8. complete (folk or primitive) cultures and sub-cultures.

These features are clearly orientated towards a concept of cultural tourism as 'high culture', and towards the consumption of cultural products, rather than involvement in cultural processes. A similar approach is taken by Munsters in his typology of cultural tourism attractions and events (see Munsters, Chapter 6 this volume).

The second approach might broadly be termed the conceptual approach. As with tourism in general, conceptual definitions of cultural tourism attempt to describe the motive and meanings attached to cultural tourism activity. For example, cultural tourism is defined by McIntosh and Goeldner (1986) as comprising 'all aspects of travel, whereby travellers learn about the history and heritage of others or about their contemporary ways of life or thought'. In other words, cultural tourists learn about the products and processes of other cultures. On the other hand, Wood (1984) sees 'the role of culture as contextual, where its role is to shape the tourist's experience of a situation in general, without a particular focus on the uniqueness of a specific cultural identity', in contrast to ethnic tourism, which has 'a direct focus on people living out a cultural identity whose uniqueness is being marketed for tourists'. In other words, Wood argues that where ethnicity is the product, we are dealing with ethnic tourism rather than cultural tourism. These types of approaches illustrate that conceptual definitions can be useful in focusing attention on why and how people engage in cultural tourism, rather than simply how many cultural tourists there are. Conceptual definitions of cultural tourism are therefore more clearly process-based.

The problems of integrating the technical and conceptual approaches to cultural tourism definition are exemplified by the use of two definitions of cultural tourism by the WTO (1985). The 'narrow definition' includes 'movements of persons for essentially cultural motivations such as study tours, performing arts and cultural tours, travel to festivals and other cultural events, visits to sites and monuments, travel to study nature, folklore or art, and pilgrimages'. Although this 'narrow' definition attempts to broaden the sites and monuments approach by adding other cultural manifestations as tourism goals, it is still essentially a checklist of cultural activities undertaken by tourists. It is significant that the activities mentioned, as in the ECTARC list, are predominantly associated with 'high' culture. The 'wide' definition, in contrast, covers 'all movements of persons, . . . because they satisfy the human need for diversity, tending to raise the cultural level of the individual and giving rise to new knowledge, experience and encounters'. This extremely optimistic conceptual approach is however of little use for definition purposes, because it provides no basis for distinguishing what cultural tourism actually is.

The problem of defining cultural tourism was one of the major stimuli for the launching of the Cultural Tourism Research Project by the European Association for Tourism and Leisure Education (ATLAS) in 1991 (more details of which can be found below). The approach adopted by the ATLAS Cultural Tourism Research Project was as far as possible to encompass process and product-based approaches. A product-based definition was considered to be necessary for the measurement of cultural tourism, whereas a process-based conceptual definition was also needed to describe cultural tourism as an activity. The definition adopted at the outset of the ATLAS Research Project (Bonink and Richards, 1992) was based largely on the definition used by the Irish Tourist Board (ITB) in their study of cultural tourism resources for the EU. The ITB definition is 'Cultural tourism is travel undertaken with the intention, wholly or partly, of increasing one's appreciation of Europe's cultural resources' (Irish Tourist Board, 1988:3). This basic definition was expanded and later refined in the light of research findings from the ATLAS project. The current ATLAS definitions are as follows:

Conceptual definition: 'The movement of persons to cultural attractions away from their normal place of residence, with the intention to gather new information and experiences to satisfy their cultural needs'.

Technical definition: 'All movements of persons to specific cultural attractions, such as heritage sites, artistic and cultural manifestations, arts and drama outside their normal place of residence'.

Both of these definitions are compatible with the Tourism Society definition of tourism, and can be used to deal with both day tourists and overnight stays. The most important difference between the technical definition and the conceptual definition is that the latter considers the motivation of tourists as central. The ATLAS research has supported the contention of the GEATTE (1993) report for the European Commission, which suggested that a 'learning element' is the central distinguishing feature of cultural tourism. As Crompton (1979) has suggested, 'cultural' motives for tourism include the search for 'novelty' and 'education'. Although Schouten (1995) doubts that the expressed desire of cultural tourists has much connection with real 'learning', research into the motives of self-defined cultural tourists in the UK, The Netherlands and Spain tends to confirm the importance of learning and novelty-seeking as motives (Van 't Riet, 1995). Depth interviews with tourists visiting cultural attractions indicated that education was an important motive for 42 of the 45 respondents, whereas 29 indicated that novelty was a key motive (Table 2.1). The use of the learning motive as a definition of cultural tourism is also in line with the German concept of *studienreisen* (Narhsted, 1993). The learning motive also allows some distinction to be made between casual visitors to cultural sites, and tourists with specific cultural motives, who might be considered as the 'specific cultural tourists' (Irish Tourist Board, 1988) or 'culturally motivated tourists' (Bywater, 1993).

Although such distinctions may appear straightforward, the rapid pace of social and cultural change and the progressive de-differentiation of social life is making the application of such definitions increasingly difficult. The following section discusses some of these problems in more detail.

The changing nature of cultural tourism

Not only are 'tourism' and 'culture' difficult concepts to define, but the meanings attached to these concepts are constantly changing. At one time, boundaries between concepts such as 'culture' and 'economics', between 'high' and 'low' culture, and even 'culture' and 'tourism' might have seemed relatively easy to draw. It might, for example, have been relatively easy to draw up an acceptable list of cultural facilities which could be included in the orbit of cultural tourism. Most people might have agreed, for example, that a visit to

Table 2.1. Motivations of tourists visiting Burgos Cathedral (Spain), Nottingham Castle (UK) and Paleis Het Loo (Netherlands).

Motive	No. of respondents		
	Burgos	Nottingham	Paleis Het Loo
Education (self)	14	14	14
Education (children)	–	3	1
Novelty	10	11	8
Imagine life in history	4	8	6
See things in reality	5	5	4
Relaxation and pleasure	4	3	5
Exploration and evaluation of self	3	3	5
Compensating lack of cultural offer at home	5	2	4
Aesthetic experience	2	1	8
Interest in architecture/art	5	1	3
Escape from perceived mundane environment	1	6	–
Enhancement of kinship relationships	–	3	2
Facilitate social interaction	–	4	–
Exchange information with others	1	1	2
Social 'obligation' to visit cultural attractions	1	1	1
Interest in royal houses	–	–	3
Part of work or study	1	–	1
Religious motive	1	–	–

Source: Van 't Riet (1995).

the Uffizi Palace in Florence was cultural tourism, whereas a visit to Blackpool Pleasure Beach was not.

In recent years, however, notions of culture and tourism have undergone significant change, as notions of such distinctions have begun to blur. The disappearance of traditional divisions between the realms of production and consumption, and between the cultural and the economic are examples of what MacCannell (1993) has identified as the collapse of the distinction between means and production. Former production spaces have now been given over to consumption, as in the case of former coal mines turned into museums and visitor centres. For MacCannell, therefore, all tourism is a cultural experience. Urry (1990) takes this argument one step further, by arguing that tourism *is* culture. In the new culture of tourism, specially created consumption areas have been created, which are designed to aid tourists in their search for authenticity and meaning. Such areas have been labelled 'escape areas' by Rojek (1993), who identifies four categories of escape area: 'black spots', 'heritage attractions', 'literary landscapes' and 'theme parks', at least the first three of which (and some would argue all of which) have clear links with cultural tourism.

The growing incorporation of culture into tourism as a basic commodity for tourist consumption, is a change which has led many authors to suggest that the current growth of cultural tourism is something 'new', and qualitatively and quantitatively different from the cultural tourism of the Grand Tour. Narhsted (1993) for example, has suggested that cultural tourism is essentially a postmodern phenomenon, the origins of which are very recent. In Germany, he argues, the use of the term 'cultural tourism' can be dated to reunification in 1990. The idea of cultural tourism as a 'new' form of tourism is also taken up in the influential study of arts tourism in the UK by Myerscough (see Gratton and Richards, Chapter 4 this volume) and has been linked to the growth of the 'new tourism' by Poon (1993).

As indicated in Chapter 1, however, cultural tourism is far from being a completely new phenomenon. What has changed is the extent of cultural tourism consumption, and the forms of culture being consumed by cultural tourists. As Wynne (1992) has suggested, one of the hallmarks of postmodern consumption is the disintegration of distinctions between 'high' and 'low' or 'popular' culture. As these distinctions disappear, so the scope of cultural tourism expands to include elements which previously would not have been considered 'cultural' (such as popular music, modern design or match museums). As distinctions between 'culture' and 'tourism' or 'everyday life' also begin to erode, so cultural tourism can also come to include activities such as simply 'soaking up the atmosphere' of a destination, or sampling the local food. In this way, cultural tourism begins to encompass the passive consumption of culture on holiday, as well as actively seeking 'high' culture through a visit to a museum or a classical concert. As the boundaries between 'high' and 'popular' culture fade, so the consumption of popular entertainment, such as the 'end of the pier show' at Blackpool become part of the cultural tourism sphere as well (Hughes and Benn, 1994).

A further consequence of the integration of high and low culture is the fact that it is now increasingly difficult to determine the boundaries of the cultural sphere of social and economic activity. In the past, high culture was regarded as being synonymous with culture, and this meant that culture could effectively be kept free of commercialism through public sector funding for high culture. As high and low culture become less distinct, however, the aesthetic basis for subsidizing certain cultural forms is eroded, and it becomes increasingly hard for high cultural forms to resist commercialization. The cultural and economic spheres of society are therefore becoming increasingly hard to separate. The effect of this is being seen in the convergence of economic and cultural policy (see Richards, Chapter 5 this volume), the economic justifications required for cultural development, and the growing convergence of tourism and culture.

Cultural tourism is therefore changing, both in terms of the way in which tourists consume culture, and in the way in which culture is presented for tourist consumption. Culture is now becoming an essential element in tourism policies at all levels, from the European Union down to the individual municipality. Perhaps what is essentially new about this wave of cultural tourism development, however, is the fact that culture is now primarily being promoted for economic, rather than cultural ends. An example of how this change has manifested itself at European level is provided by the following case study of the development of the European Cultural Capital event.

THE CHANGING ROLE OF CULTURAL TOURISM: THE EUROPEAN CULTURAL CAPITAL EVENT

A prime example of the changing definition and role of cultural tourism in Europe is provided by the European Cultural Capital event. The idea of designating a different city each year as 'Cultural Capital' of Europe was launched in 1983 by Melina Mercouri, Greek Minister of Culture. The idea was adopted by the European Community in 1985, when Athens became the first European Cultural Capital.

The origins of the Cultural Capital event were arguably purely cultural. The event was designed to 'help bring the peoples of the member states closer together' through the 'expression of a culture which, in its historical emergence and contemporary development, is characterized by having both common elements and a richness born of diversity' (European Commission, 1985). The aims of the event were basically twofold: first to make the culture of the cities accessible to a European audience, and second to create a picture of European culture as a whole (Corijn and Van Praet, 1994). However, as the event has developed, it has been used in different ways by the cities, either to support, extend or challenge the original Cultural Capital Concept.

Corijn and Van Praet (1994), in their review of the history of the Cultural Capitals, highlight the way in which different cities treated the designation. Athens, for example, concentrated on big foreign names, and ignored ancient Greek art. Florence highlighted its own historic importance, and Amsterdam projected itself as a European art city. Berlin was criticized for having an elitist approach, whereas the event was hardly visible among the normal cultural bustle of Paris.

The turning point for the Cultural Capital event came with the designation of Glasgow in 1990. Glasgow, unlike its predecessors, was not a capital city or one of the established 'cultural destinations' of Europe (van der Borg, 1994). Glasgow won the nomination against competition from other British cities largely on the basis of promised commercial sponsorship and the fact that it planned to use the event to stimulate urban regeneration and to boost the image of Glasgow as a cultural city. This approach apparently fitted the UK government's emphasis on public–private sector partnership, although the role of the public sector was eventually more high-profile than the government cared to admit (Todd, 1988).

The Glasgow event had an impressive range of cultural activities, including big names such as Pavarotti, and an equally impressive budget. The argument for this approach was that the investment would be repaid directly through tourist expenditure, and indirectly through improvements in the image of the city and increased economic investment. The staging of an event concentrating on international, rather than local, culture aroused opposition from some local groups, who felt either that the money could have been better spent on basic services such as housing, or that the event should have been more culturally representative of Glasgow itself (Boyle and Hughes, 1991). The event was an economic success, however, producing a net economic benefit to the city of between £32 and £37 million (ECU 40–ECU 47 million), mainly as a result of tourist expenditure (Myerscough, 1991).

Although the immediate successor to Glasgow, Dublin, adopted a relatively low-key approach to the event, the whole Cultural Capital process has taken on a new function since 1990. Glasgow highlighted the potential to use the event as a vehicle for economic development and image-building. The number of candidates for the nomination has substantially increased, as cities vie to attract an event which is now viewed as a tool for economic regeneration rather than a purely cultural manifestation. Madrid in 1992 was used as a part of a wider Spanish image-building campaign, which included hosting EXPO 92 in Seville and the Olympic Games in Barcelona in the same year.

Corijn and Van Praet (1994) argue that Antwerp used the event in 1993 to rejuvenate the city, although in a slightly different way from Glasgow. The Antwerp event concentrated more clearly on the creative arts, and this generated criticism that it was too elitist. Even so, the event attracted an estimated 7.5 million to 10 million additional tourists to the city, injecting an estimated ECU 437 million into the local economy.

Lisbon, Cultural Capital in 1994, was arguably a capital city in need of economic and cultural rejuvenation. The Portuguese economy is the weakest in the EU, and investment in culture is minimal compared with other European capitals. Although the Cultural Capital event was seen as an opportunity by some, it was characterized as 'a burden in difficult times' by Lisbon's Mayor, Jorge Sampaio (Adolf, 1994:1). The Lisbon event attracted an extra 1.5 million tourists during the year. Luxembourg is hoping for a similar tourism boost in 1995.

Copenhagen, the city chosen as the last of the original cycle of 12 EU Cultural Capitals, was in a position to review the experience of the other capitals before deciding on the shape of its own event (see Hjalager, Chapter 7 this volume). The Copenhagen analysis identified five levels of event:

Level 1: a summer festival (Athens 1985, Florence 1986, Paris 1989). A number of artistic events, primarily based on heritage. No international marketing. Short planning period, no long-term investment and few sponsors.

Level 2: an all-year festival (Amsterdam 1987, Dublin 1991, Madrid, 1992). Focus still on fine arts, with national performances supplemented with a few international events. Fairly good quality, but lack of penetration because of planning gaps and lack of international marketing. Little investment, financial base primarily local.

Level 3: an art city (Berlin 1988, Antwerp 1993). Well planned and managed international artistic programme running over a whole year. Strategies to stimulate artistic production. Professional, centralized management, with finance from the city, supplemented by substantial sponsorship.

Level 4: a cultural capital year (Glasgow 1990). A more comprehensive programme based on a broader concept of culture. Many international highlights. Social, popular and economic structures included in the concept, with a view to creating long-lasting improvement in the image of the city. Long-term planning and management with participation of local groups. Financing from a broad spectrum of private and public sources.

Level 5: a cultural capital (Copenhagen 1996). Development of a long-term strategy for the development of a cultural capital and improvement of the image of the city. Planning horizons extend beyond 1996. The involvement of the local population and the business community is crucial, as is the stimulation of educational initiatives and cultural networks. The Cultural Capital concept involves the whole metropolitan region, with a separate environmental strategy and new infrastructure. Funding from a wide range of sources.

It is perhaps predictable that the planners of Copenhagen '96 should place themselves at the pinnacle of a developmental pyramid with respect to the Cultural Capital event. Their analysis does show, however, the way in which later festivals have tended to be more concerned with long-term economic and social benefits, rather than the short-term cultural focus of early events. This change is reflected not simply in the way in which the event is staged, but also the types of cities chosen to stage the event. In the early years, the event was purely limited to established cultural capitals, but the event is now increasingly being used as a vehicle for regional economic development by cities with far less accumulated 'cultural capital'.

A review of the cultural capital events by Myerscough (1995) demonstrates the way in which the event has evolved over the years (Table 2.2). As the event has become established, so expenditure has tended to rise. Almost three-quarters of the total estimated expenditure for the Cultural Capital events (£169 million, ECU 215 million) was accounted for by the five years from 1990 to 1994. The balance of expenditure has also shifted away from central government, which covered 88% of the costs in Athens, towards local government and commercial sponsorship. This reflects the growing use of the event for regional development goals, and the increased emphasis on public–private sector partnership by most European governments. An analysis of attendances at art exhibitions, however, indicates that attendances at organized events

Table 2.2. European Cities of Culture, 1985–1999.

Year	City	Country	Budget (MECU)	% public sector funding
1985	Athens	Greece	7.7	90
1986	Florence	Italy	24.4	91
1987	Amsterdam	Netherlands	3.3	76
1988	Berlin	Germany	27.0	98
1989	Paris	France	0.6	100
1990	Glasgow	UK	60.0	83
1991	Dublin	Ireland	8.6	68
1992	Madrid	Spain	57.9	76
1993	Antwerp	Belgium	17.6	73
1994	Lisbon	Portugal	29.5	80
1995	Luxembourg	Luxembourg		
1996	Copenhagen	Denmark	100.0	
1997	Thessaloniki	Greece		
1998	Stockholm	Sweden		
1999	Weimar	Germany		

Source: After Myerscough (1995).

have not grown significantly. Glasgow was the only city to generate significantly more exhibition visitors than its predecessors, partly because of the large
number of events staged. The average attendance per exhibition in Glasgow
was actually half that in Dublin the following year, in spite of the feeling that
'Dublin 1991 was an opportunity not fully embraced' (Myerscough, 1995).

The success of the Cultural Capital event has spawned other cultural
events throughout Europe. These include the designation of other cities by the
EU to host a 'cultural month', and regional initiatives, such as the cultural city
programme launched in the Province of Zuid Holland in The Netherlands (see
Richards, Chapter 13 this volume).

The European City of Culture event is a useful example, because it underlines some of the key issues surrounding the development and marketing of
cultural tourism in Europe. These issues can be summarized briefly as the
motive for promoting culture, the cultural subject, and the cultural audience.

1. Motives for promoting culture: The 'culture' of the European City of Culture
has undergone a clear change in the past decade. What started as a purely
'cultural' event, designed to promote the ideal of a common European culture,
has become a vehicle for regional economic development.
2. The cultural subject: The localization of the City of Culture event has in turn
focused increased attention on exactly what sort of culture should be promoted.
In Glasgow, for example, there was considerable debate about the programme,
which many felt gave too much emphasis to international, high profile events
and artists, and too little attention to local culture (Boyle and Hughes, 1991).

The content of most of the City of Culture events is clearly orientated towards 'high culture' rather than local 'popular culture'.

3. The cultural audience: The high culture focus of the event is clearly aimed at attracting an upmarket audience. In most cases this means tourists, rather than locals, who bring no new sources of income into the area. If tourists are the target audience, then a generalized, globalized cultural product needs to be offered, which makes few concessions to the cultural needs of the local population (Ashworth, 1992).

The City of Culture event internalizes many of the tensions common to cultural tourism development in Europe, including the dialectic oppositions between culture and economy, 'high' and 'popular' culture, local and global cultures, and transnational, national and regional policies.

The analyses of cultural tourism presented in this book will attempt to illustrate these oppositions in a variety of contexts. Although cultural tourism is widely interpreted as being synonymous with high cultural forms, we will attempt to demonstrate how high culture and popular culture are increasingly being integrated in cultural tourism development and marketing. Attention will also be paid to the growth of certain forms of popular culture as the object of cultural tourism.

THE CURRENT SIGNIFICANCE OF CULTURAL TOURISM IN EUROPE

As cultural tourism becomes more important in economic terms, and more high profile in political terms, a growing number of nations and regions in Europe are using cultural tourism as an integral part of tourism and economic regeneration strategies (see Richards, Chapter 5 this volume). Assessing the significance of cultural tourism in Europe is, however, complicated by the problems of definition outlined at the beginning of this chapter, and the lack of cultural tourism data on a European scale. This section provides a review of the evidence currently available, and tries to place the growth of cultural tourism in a wider context.

One of the first attempts to assess the importance of cultural tourism on a European basis was the research undertaken by the Irish Tourist Board (1988) on behalf of the European Commission. This study estimated that there were almost 35 million international cultural tourists in the European Union in 1986, of whom at least a third came from outside the EU. The study distinguished between 'general cultural tourists' (31 million), who visited cultural attractions as part of a general holiday trip, and 'specific cultural tourists' (3.5 million) with a specific cultural motive for travelling. However, these figures were based on 'guesstimates' obtained from national tourist boards, and are therefore highly approximate. The study also produced an inventory of significant cultural tourism resources, which was achieved by listing attractions mentioned by Baedeker, and then inviting amendments from national tourist offices. The study did not claim that the resulting list of over 3000 cultural sites was exhaustive or representative (Italy alone estimates it has over 2000 cultural attractions, ENIT, 1992) although it was thought to contain the 1000 or so most significant cultural attractions in the EU. One of the key problems identified in the study was the lack of any consistent definition or recording system for cultural tourism data in the member states.

In spite of the lack of precise data on European cultural tourism, many observers seem convinced that demand is growing. A large number of tourism studies have identified cultural tourism as a major future growth area both in Europe and elsewhere (Januarius, 1992; Zeppel and Hall, 1992; Boniface and Fowler, 1993). Bywater (1993:30) for example states 'there is little doubt that cultural tourism is a major market and one that is steadily increasing'. The World Tourism Organization has estimated that cultural tourism currently accounts for 37% of all tourist trips, and that demand is currently growing by 15% a year, although it is not clear on how this estimate was derived (Bywater, 1993). Middleton (1989) has argued that a belief in the 'motivating power' of heritage has sometimes caused marketeers to believe that demand for cultural tourism is growing, even when demand is falling.

In the absence of hard information on cultural tourism, however, rational policy formation is difficult. It was in an attempt to address some of the inadequacies in European cultural tourism data that the ATLAS Cultural Tourism Research Project was established in 1991 with the help of funding from the Tourism Unit of DGXXIII of the European Commission (Bonink and Richards, 1992).

The ATLAS Cultural Tourism Project

The ATLAS Cultural Tourism Research Project aimed to establish a transnational database which could provide comparative data on cultural tourism trends across Europe. The project started in 1991 with 10 members in 9 EU states, and has since expanded to cover 11 EU member states. ATLAS is the European Association for Tourism and Leisure Education, which had more than 100 members in 18 countries in 1994 (Bonink et al., 1994).

The original aims of the ATLAS project were to:

1. Devise definitions of the nature and scope of cultural tourism;
2. Collect data on cultural tourism visits to European attractions;
3. Assess the profile and motivations of cultural tourists;
4. Develop case studies of cultural tourism management.

The research undertaken in 1992 and 1993 included a review of definitional issues (Bonink, 1992), a survey of the supply of cultural attractions and attendance in the European Community, and interviews with over 6300 visitors at 26 attractions in the EU. The countries covered by the original visitor research were France, Germany, Greece, Ireland, Italy, The Netherlands, Portugal, Spain, and the United Kingdom. The research was undertaken by universities in the countries concerned, all of whom are members of the ATLAS consortium.

The most important feature of the research was that the data were collected on a transnational basis, rather than simply being a collection of nationally based surveys. The methods of data collection, the choice of sample sites and the sampling criteria were all agreed on a transnational basis before the research commenced. The emphasis on site-based surveys ensured that a high proportion of those interviewed were cultural tourists. It also allowed a comparison to be made between the cultural consumption of people in their own country and as tourists in other European countries. The site-based survey also ensured that tourists from outside the EU were represented. In order to provide a fairer reflection of the distribution of cultural visitors across Europe, the figures on foreign tourists were weighted according to the level of foreign tourism in each survey country in 1992.

The data collection therefore followed the meso-scale research approach advocated by Murphy (1992). This is based on the integration of on-site surveys to capture information about the consumption of specific products and regions by tourists. This approach has the advantage that it can be used to compare the behaviour of tourists transnationally, without the need to compile samples representative of national populations. The ATLAS survey did not, therefore, attempt to obtain a representative sample of all cultural tourists in Europe. Such data would have to be based on a sample of all tourists, not just cultural visitors. The practical problems involved in assembling a transnational analysis of cultural tourism in Europe are dealt with in detail by Richards and Bonink (1992).

The following sections summarize some of the important transnational findings of the research. Analyses of surveys on a national and a regional basis can be found in the chapters in Part 2.

The visitor surveys, conducted at 26 sites in nine countries (Table 2.3) indicated that the major source markets for international cultural tourists were the USA, the UK, Germany, France, and Spain. Almost two-thirds of foreign cultural tourists came from within the EU. The respondents had a high level of educational attainment, with over 20% having some form of postgraduate education. In contrast to the widespread idea that cultural tourists tend to come from older age groups, the survey found that over 30% of visitors were aged between 20 and 29 years (Fig. 2.1). Younger visitors were even more important in particular major cities, such as Amsterdam, where over half the visitors were under 30 years old (Richards and Bonink, 1994). Although it can be argued that the summer survey period boosted the proportion of students among cultural visitors (20%), this overall age distribution is consistent with

Table 2.3. ATLAS cultural tourism research – survey site profile.

Site	Location	Country	Interviews
Chateau de Blois (HB)	Blois	France	200
L'abbaye de Cluny (HB)	Cluny	France	199
Pompidou Centre (AC)	Paris	France	199
Neue Pinakothek (G)	Munich	Germany	200
Altes Museum (Mus)	Berlin	Germany	201
Porta Negra (M)	Trier	Germany	200
National Art Gallery (G)	Athens	Greece	186
Archaeological Site (A)	Dion	Greece	179
Archaeological Museum (Mus)	Thessaloniki	Greece	181
Muckross House (HB)	Killarney	Ireland	828
St Patrick's Rock (HB)	Cashel	Ireland	109
Palazzo Ducale (HB)	Venice	Italy	609
Rijksmuseum (Mus)	Amsterdam	NL	291
Van Gogh Museum (Mus)	Amsterdam	NL	314
Museu de Arte Moderna (Mus)	Porto	Portugal	198
São Francisco (HB)	Porto	Portugal	200
Torre dos Clérigos (M)	Porto	Portugal	197
Avila (M)	Avila	Spain	200
Mosque (M)	Cordoba	Spain	200
Prado Museum (Mus)	Madrid	Spain	200
Art Museum (G)	Bilbao	Spain	120
Museum of Childhood (Mus)	Edinburgh	UK	208
People's Story (HC)	Edinburgh	UK	97
Urquhart Castle (M)	Inverness	UK	196
St Paul's Cathedral (M)	London	UK	201
Victoria and Albert Museum (Mus)	London	UK	403
Total			6316

Site codes: M, Monument; Mus, Museum; G, Art gallery; AC, Arts centre; A, Archaeological site; HB, Historic building; HC, Heritage centre.

other surveys of heritage attraction and museum visitors in Europe (Bourdieu and Darbel, 1991; Merriman, 1991; Ministère de la Culture, 1991; Schuster, 1993).

Given the fact that the ATLAS definition of cultural tourism is based on cultural motivations, a key question posed in the survey was the extent to which the visitors had travelled specifically to visit a cultural attraction. When asked how important the cultural attraction they were visiting was in their decision to travel, almost 60% said it was 'important' or 'very important' (Fig. 2.2). A combination of cultural attractions may also be sufficient to persuade tourists to choose a specific destination, rather than simply visiting an attraction as part of a holiday. Over 20% of tourists said that cultural attractions had

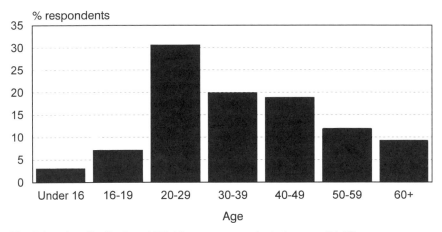

Fig. 2.1.   Age distribution of ATLAS survey respondents (source: ATLAS survey, weighted data).

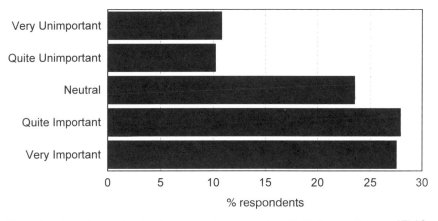

Fig. 2.2.   Importance of cultural attraction in decision to visit destination (source: ATLAS survey).

been 'very important' in determining their choice of destination for their previous holiday.

The ATLAS research findings also seem to support the distinction between 'specific' and 'general' cultural tourists made in the Irish Tourist Board report (1988). A narrow definition of specific cultural tourists could be taken as tourists who had travelled specifically to visit the cultural attraction, and who said that the attraction was 'important' or 'very important' as a motivation for their choice of destination (Bonink and Richards, 1992). Using this definition, 9% of all tourists could be identified as 'specific cultural tourists'. This is higher than the estimated proportion of specific cultural tourists in the 1988 study,

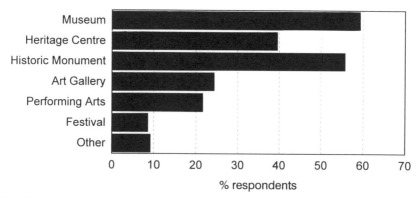

Fig. 2.3.   Type of attractions visited during stay (source: ATLAS survey).

but these data are based on visitors to cultural attractions, which will tend to inflate the proportion of culturally motivated tourists identified. Specific cultural tourists tend to be more highly educated, travel more frequently, and are more influenced by cultural attractions in their choice of destination.

When asked about their total consumption of cultural attractions during their trip, respondents indicated that they were more likely to visit museums (59% of respondents) or historic monuments (56%) than other types of cultural attractions. There was a noticeable difference in the level of visits to the usually more accessible heritage sites (museums, monuments, heritage centres) than to performing and visual arts attractions (Fig. 2.3). Again specific cultural tourists were far more likely to make multiple cultural attraction visits during their stay than other visitors.

The specific cultural tourists were found to be not only more frequent consumers of cultural attractions than other groups, but they had a high level of total tourism consumption, particularly in terms of short holiday trips. Over 40% of specific cultural tourists had taken at least one short holiday (three nights or less) in the previous 12 months, compared with 22% of all cultural visitors. A high frequency of short-break holiday participation is considered by many to be one of the hallmarks of the cultural tourist (Gratton, 1990; Faché, 1994). This certainly seems to be the pattern for foreign tourists, particularly those travelling within Europe. As Table 2.4 indicates, the average length of stay for most European tourists was less than six nights, even though these surveys were taken during the summer. Tourists from outside Europe tended to be staying for a relatively short period in each country visited, but were usually staying in Europe for three weeks or more.

Cultural tourism consumption by the ATLAS survey respondents seemed to be characterized by a high degree of continuity between 'everyday' leisure consumption and consumption patterns while on holiday. The vast majority of

Table 2.4. Length of stay for foreign tourists by country of origin.

Country of origin	Nights in country of survey location	Nights away from home
Austria	5.9	13.4
Belgium	4.3	9.2
Denmark	5.6	11.9
France	5.3	9.7
Germany	5.6	11.6
Greece	5.0	7.3
Ireland	3.8	7.8
Netherlands	6.0	12.4
Norway	4.9	15.7
Sweden	9.5	15.3
Switzerland	4.1	9.0
Eastern Europe	7.0	17.2
Brazil	3.1	25.5
Canada	8.3	23.0
Mexico	4.8	20.0
USA	6.6	21.5
Australia	11.5	41.9
Japan	4.5	23.0

Source: ATLAS Survey (1992).

cultural visitors indicated that visits to cultural attractions on holiday were a reflection of cultural visits made in their home country or region. In an earlier study of cultural tourism, Hughes (1987) had noted that 'it is not clear that those within the socio-economic and demographic groups most likely to participate in the 'high arts' are also those most likely to participate in the high arts on tourist trips'. The evidence collected in the ATLAS research suggests that across Europe as a whole, high levels of cultural consumption at home are likely to be reflected in high levels of cultural consumption on holiday. More important still is the fact that cultural consumption is also likely to be related to employment in the cultural industries.

The proportion of specific cultural tourists connected with the cultural industries was 29%. This is more than double the level of cultural employment among general cultural tourists who did not make a trip to the destination for cultural reasons (13%). There was also a clear link between the sector of employment within the cultural industries and the tourism consumption of respondents. Those with a job in 'heritage' for example, were more likely than other respondents to visit museums and heritage centres on holiday, and employment in the visual or performing arts was also correlated with a higher level of visits to visual or performing arts attractions on holiday. The level of cultural industry employees from all countries engaging in cultural tourism appears to be far higher than the general level of employment in cultural occupations (see Gratton and Richards, Chapter 4 this volume).

Further research conducted by ATLAS in Amsterdam (Roetman, 1994) suggests that these specific cultural tourists can further be distinguished on the basis of cultural capital. Roetman found that visitors to a Mondriaan exhibition who had specific cultural motives, also had a high degree of cultural capital relating to the work of Mondriaan and other painters of his genre. In general, however, the level of cultural capital of tourists was lower than that of local residents. This matches the findings of Verhoeff (1994) that frequent culture consumers tend to live in city centre locations in The Netherlands, and also supports Ashworth's (1992) contention that tourists require a more globalized cultural product than local residents.

Patterns of cultural tourism consumption will therefore vary according to location. A comparison of the different ATLAS survey sites indicates that some sites are predominantly used by tourists, and others appeal more to local residents. The proportion of tourists (day and overnight), for example, varied from more than 95% for sites in Spain (Cordoba, Avila), France (Paris), Italy (Venice) and Ireland (Muckross), to less than 40% for sites in Portugal (Porto) and Spain (Bilbao). In general, sites connected with the arts and high culture attracted more tourists, and heritage sites connected with popular (or local) culture tended to attract more regular, local visitors. This is also reflected in the importance of the attraction as a motivation for travel. The sites which provide the strongest motivation for travel are 'must-see' sites such as the Doge's Palace in Venice, or isolated sites which are basically stand-alone attractions (e.g. Avila). Individual cultural attractions in major cities, such as St Paul's Cathedral in London, are unlikely to attract people on their own, but function as one part of a complex of attractions which motivate people to visit.

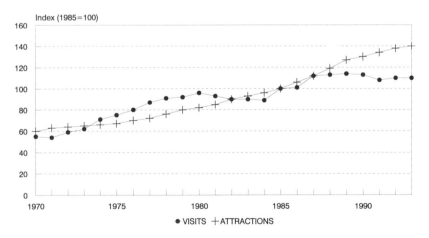

Fig. 2.4. Cultural attraction supply and demand in Europe, 1970–1993 (source: ATLAS database).

⌐A further aim of the ATLAS research was to analyse the development of cultural tourism demand over time.⌐ Examination of cultural attraction attendances in Europe indicates significant growth over the last 20 years (Fig. 2.4). However, it seems that much of the growth has been stimulated by the growing supply of attractions, as more and more cities and regions have climbed aboard the cultural tourism bandwagon. This suggests that cultural tourism can be a double-edged sword – it can certainly stimulate a growth in tourism to particular regions, but the growing number of destinations trying to develop cultural tourism means that competition for the cultural tourists will get even stronger, and in some areas average attraction attendances are falling. This is partly a reflection of the fact that the market for many cultural attractions is still relatively up-market, and therefore relatively small. Based on the ATLAS surveys and data on cultural attraction attendances in the EU, Richards and Bonink (1994) estimated that the current cultural tourism market in the EU accounted for about 25 million specific cultural tourist trips in 1992. As a proportion of all international tourist trips in the European Union, this was equivalent to about 11% of all tourism trips. This estimate is higher than figures from national surveys. In Ireland, for example, about 4% of international tourists might be considered as specific cultural tourists (see O Donnchadha and O Connor, Chapter 11 this volume). In the UK, about 5% of domestic tourists indicated that culture was the main purpose for their holiday trip (see Foley, Chapter 16 this volume). An estimated 8% of all German tourists are cultural tourists and in The Netherlands 8% of all inbound tourists cited cultural heritage as their primary motive (see Richards, Chapter 13 this volume). Foreign visitors to Greece indicated that antiquities (9%) or a combination of antiquities and climate (18%) were a main motive for their visit (Buckley and Papadopoulos, 1986).

Culture can, however, be far more important as a general, or secondary motive for tourism. The ATLAS research indicates that general cultural tourists in fact account for the majority of tourist visits to cultural attractions. Research on wider samples of tourists indicate a similar pattern.

Table 2.5.   Heritage activities of overseas visitors in Britain, 1990.

	% participated	% important in decision to visit Britain
Visiting heritage sites or exhibits	55	42
Visiting heritage sites/castles/monuments	51	37
Visiting artistic or heritage exhibits (museums, art galleries, heritage centres)	40	30
Watching performing arts (theatre, cinema, opera, ballet)	24	19

Source: British Tourist Authority (1990).

Table 2.6.   Factors attracting Japanese visitors to Europe, 1994.

Factor	% respondents
Visiting art galleries and museums	23.1
Local sightseeing	21.6
City sightseeing	18.9
Shopping	13.5
Theatre, concerts	3.9
Hiking, mountaineering	2.9
Visiting friends and relatives	2.5
Eating at leisure	2.1
Rest and relaxation	1.8
Skiing	1.3
Playing golf	0.2
Other	8.2
Total	100.0

Source: European Travel Commission (1994).

For example, the British Tourist Authority (BTA) overseas visitor survey has regularly monitored the motivations of overseas visitors coming to Britain. Over half of the visitors interviewed in 1990 had visited a heritage site, and 42% indicated that some form of heritage attraction was important in influencing their decision to come to Britain (British Tourist Authority, 1990). Table 2.5 indicates that more tourists visited heritage sites than were influenced by heritage sites to visit Britain. In common with the ATLAS survey, the BTA research indicates that performing arts are a much less important motivation for overseas tourists than heritage attractions. Other BTA research indicates that the level of cultural motivations has not increased in recent years. In 1989 41% of overseas visitors indicated that historic sites were an important influence on their decision to visit Britain, compared with 44% in 1985 (British Tourist Authority, 1989). In Denmark, it is estimated that 3.4 million foreign tourists, or 35% of the total, visited a museum during their stay (see Hjalager, Chapter 7 this volume). A study of travel motivations of Japanese tourists shows a similar pattern (Table 2.6), with over 23% of respondents indicating that art galleries and museums were the most important reason for visiting Europe (European Travel Commission, 1994).

There is little doubt, therefore, that tourists are important consumers of cultural attractions throughout Europe. There is also some evidence to suggest that tourists have accounted for a growing proportion of cultural visits over the past 20 years. In many countries there is a strong relationship between tourism growth and the level of cultural attraction visits (see Kalogeropoulou, Chapter 10 this volume, for example). There is far less evidence, however, that cultural tourism is expanding as a proportion of tourism demand as whole. In

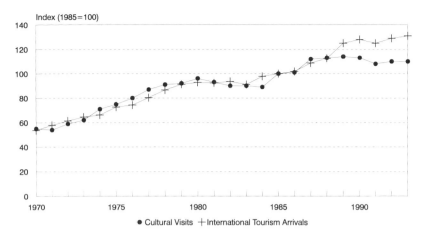

Fig. 2.5.   Cultural visits and international tourism (source: ATLAS database).

Germany, for example, the proportion of holiday-makers giving culture as their primary travel motivation exhibited little change between 1983 and 1991 (Studienkreise für Tourismus, 1991). When the growth in cultural visits is compared with the growth in total international tourism demand, for example, it is clear that the rise of cultural tourism closely parallels the increase in international tourism trips (Fig. 2.5). Although no direct link between the two figures can be made, it does suggest that cultural tourism is not growing any faster than many other sectors of tourism. In some cases, there is actually evidence to suggest a proportionate decline of cultural tourism. In Britain, for example, the proportion of domestic tourists indicating cultural tourism as their main purpose for a holiday trip fell from 10% of all trips in 1989 to 6% of all trips in 1993 (British Tourist Authority, 1994). The suggestion that a recent increase in the demand for culture is the cause of cultural tourism growth is not therefore supported by the available evidence.

An analysis of the growth of cultural attraction supply also tends to indicate a much longer history of increasing interest in culture than recent studies of cultural tourism suggest. A comparison of the growth of cultural tourism demand and cultural attraction supply indicates that there has also been a close relationship between supply and demand over the past 20 years (Fig. 2.4). Since the late 1980s, however, the growth of cultural tourism attractions has actually outstripped the growth in demand, as measured by cultural visits. The downturn in demand for cultural attractions may in part be ascribed to the adverse economic conditions which have affected Europe since the late 1980s. In many countries this has led to a decline in tourist arrivals, which in turn will affect many major cultural attractions. There is also evidence to suggest that cultural visits by local residents and day tourists have also fallen in many areas.

The image of cultural tourism as a dynamic, recession-proof new market segment may have to be reassessed in the light of these developments.

There are also signs that the rise and fall of cultural consumption is not just a Western European phenomenon, but that the same trends are repeated elsewhere. A similar pattern is found in many Eastern European countries, where the supply of cultural attractions and cultural attendances also grew rapidly during the 1970s and 1980s. Visits to museums in the USSR, Czechoslovakia, Hungary, Poland, and Romania grew by 54% during the 1970s, and a further 13% in the 1980s. However, the supply of museums also grew by 29% in the 1970s and by 65% in the 1980s. The number of visitors per museum therefore grew by almost 15% in the 1970s, but fell again by almost 32% in the 1980s. The evidence currently available also suggests an absolute fall in cultural audiences after the democratization of Eastern Europe in 1990. In Poland, for example, the proportion of the population visiting museums fell from 26% in 1988 to 23% in 1992, and theatre attendees fell from 22% of the population to 15% over the same period (Falkowska and Koprowska, 1992). In Germany, the result of reunification was a substantial and sustained drop in museum visits from 1990 onwards in eastern Germany, and stagnation in museum attendances in western Germany. As Jung (1994) has suggested, falling cultural consumption in Eastern Europe reflects the diminished role of the former intelligentsia.

The average attendance at cultural attractions in many European countries has therefore fallen in the last five years. Although this may in part be attributable to the effects of recession on tourism, it also needs to be recognized that the cultural tourism market is becoming increasingly competitive, and cultural attractions must fight for a share of the tourism market, not only with other cultural attractions, but with other tourist attractions as well.

CONCLUSION

One of the few areas of certainty in cultural tourism is the difficulty of defining it. Few studies are agreed about what the 'cultural' element of cultural tourism should encompass. Research indicates that the number of tourists visiting cultural attractions and events has grown significantly throughout Europe. However, the traditional view of cultural tourism as equivalent to high culture attractions such as museums and monuments is now being challenged by a new generation of 'popular' culture attractions created by the heritage industry. The growth in the number of cultural tourists is not keeping up with the growth in cultural attractions, however. Although the ATLAS cultural tourism research has revealed a hard core of specific cultural tourists who have specific cultural motives for visiting cultural attractions, there is little evidence to suggest that the general cultural tourism market is growing any faster than the tourism market as a whole. To understand why the current mismatch between cultural supply and demand has emerged, the following chapter analyses the important social factors underlying the development of cultural tourism.

REFERENCES

Adolf, S. (1994) Lissabon: is de Fado voorbij? *NRC Handelsblad* 24 February, Week-agenda, p.1.

Ashworth, G.J. (1992) Heritage and tourism: an argument, two problems and three solutions. In: Fleischer-van Rooijen, C.A.M. (ed.) *Spatial Implications of Tourism*. Geo Pers, Groningen, pp. 94–104.

Boniface, P. and Fowler, P.J. (1993) *Heritage Tourism in 'the Global Village'*. Routledge, London.

Bonink, C. (1992) *Cultural Tourism Development and Government Policy*. MA Dissertation, Rijksuniversiteit Utrecht.

Bonink, C., De Jong, W. and Sanders, N. (1994) *ATLAS Courses Handbook 1995*. European Association for Tourism and Leisure Education, Tilburg University, Tilburg.

Bonink, C. and Richards, G. (1992) *Cultural Tourism in Europe*. Centre for Leisure and Tourism Studies, University of North London.

Bourdieu, P. and Darbel, A. (1991) *The Love of Art: European Art Museums and Their Public*. Polity, Cambridge.

Boyle, M. and Hughes, G. (1991) The politics of 'the real': discourses from the Left on Glasgow's role as European City of Culture, 1990. *Area* 23, 217–228.

British Tourist Authority (1989) *Overseas Visitor Survey*. BTA, London.

British Tourist Authority (1990) *Overseas Visitor Survey*. BTA, London.

British Tourist Authority (1994) *UK Tourism Survey 1993*. BTA, London.

Buckley, P.J. and Papadopoulos, S.I. (1986) Marketing Greek tourism – the planning process. *Tourism Management* 7, 86–100.

Bywater, M. (1993) The market for cultural tourism in Europe. *Travel and Tourism Analyst* 6, 30–46.

Clarke, J. (1990) Pessimism Versus Populism: The Problematic Politics of Popular Culture. In: Butsch, R. (ed.) *For Fun and Profit: The Transformation of Leisure into Consumption*. Temple University Press, Philadelphia, pp. 28–44.

Cohen, E. (1979) A phenomenology of tourist experiences. *Sociology* 13, 179–202.

Cohen, E. (1988) Authenticity and commoditization in tourism. *Annals of Tourism Research* 15, 467–486.

Corijn, E. and Van Praet, S. (1994) Antwerp 93 in the context of European cultural capitals: Art policy as politics. Paper presented at the Conference on City Cultures, Lifestyles and Consumption Practices, Coimbra, 15–16 July 1994.

Crompton, J. (1979) Motivations for pleasure vacation. *Annals of Tourism Research* 6, 408–424.

ECTARC (1989) *Contribution to the Drafting of a Charter for Cultural Tourism*. European Centre for Traditional and Regional Cultures, Llangollen, Wales.

ENIT (1992) *Istituti di Antichita' ed Arte dello Stato, Anni 1984–1991*. Rapporto no 3.

European Commission (1985) *Resolution of the Ministers Responsible for Cultural Affairs Concerning the Annual Event 'European City of Culture'*. Doc. 7081/84, 4 June, Brussels.

European Commission (1995) *The Role of the European Union in Tourism*. DGXXIII, Brussels.

European Travel Commission (1994) *Annual Report*. ETC, Paris.

Faché, W. (1994) Short break holidays. In: Seaton, V., Jenkins, C.L., Wood, R.C., Dieke, P.U.C., Bennett, M.M., MacLellan, L.R. and Smith, R. (eds) *Tourism: the State of the Art*. Wiley, London, pp. 459–467.

Falkowska, M. and Koprowska, T. (1992) *Cultural Life of Polish People 1992, Initial Report*. Institute of Culture, Warsaw.

GEATTE (1993) *Le Tourisme Culturel en Europe*. DGXXIII, European Commission, Brussels.

Gratton, C. (1990) Consumer Behaviour in Tourism: a Psycho-economic Approach. Paper presented at the Tourism Research into the 1990s Conference, Durham, England, December 1990.

Holloway, J.C. (1985) *The Business of Tourism*. MacDonald and Evans, Plymouth.

Hughes, H. (1987) Tourism and the arts: a potentially destructive relationship? *Tourism Management* 10, 97–99.

Hughes, H.L. and Benn, D. (1994) Entertainment: its role in the tourist industry. Paper presented at the Leisure Studies Association annual conference, Glasgow.

Irish Tourist Board (1988) *Inventory of Cultural Tourism Resources in the Member States and Assessment of Methods Used to Promote Them*. DG VII, European Commission, Brussels.

Januarius, M. (1992) A sense of place. *Leisure Management* 12, November, 34–35.

Jung, B. (1994) For what leisure? The role of culture and recreation in post-Communist Poland. *Leisure Studies* 13, 262–276.

MacCannell, D. (1976) *The Tourist: a New Theory of the Leisure Class*. Macmillan, London.

MacCannell, D. (1993) *Empty Meeting Grounds: the Tourist Papers*. Routledge, London.

MacIntosh, R.W. and Goeldner, R. (1986) *Tourism: Principles, Practices, Philosophies*. Wiley and Sons, New York.

Merriman, N. (1991) *Beyond the Glass Case: The Past, the Heritage and The Public in Britain*. Leicester University Press, Leicester.

Middleton, V. (1989) Marketing implications for attractions. *Tourism Management* 10, 229–234.

Ministère de la Culture (1991) *Développment Culturel*, no. 90.

Murphy, P.E. (1992) Data gathering for community-orientated tourism planning: case study of Vancouver Island, British Columbia. *Leisure Studies* 11, 65–79.

Myerscough, J. (1991) *Monitoring Glasgow*. Glasgow City Council.

Myerscough, J. (1995) *European Cities of Culture*. Glasgow City Council, Glasgow.

Narhsted, W. (1993) Von der Kulturreise zur Reisekultur? *FVW International* 1/93, 25–26.

Poon, A. (1993) *Tourism, Technology and Competitive Strategies*. CAB International, Wallingford.

Richards, G. (1993) Cultural tourism in Europe. In: Cooper, C.P. and Lockwood, A. (eds) *Progress in Tourism, Recreation and Hospitality Management*, Vol. 5, pp. 99–115.

Richards, G. and Bonink, C. (1992) European cultural tourism: myth or reality? Paper presented at the LSA/VVS conference 'Internationalisation and Leisure Research', Tilburg, December 1992.

Richards, G. and Bonink, C. (1994) Cultuurtoeristiche vraag neemt in snel tempo toe. *Recreatie en Toerisme* 4(6), 34–35.

Roetman, E.E. (1994) *Motivatie in Retrospectief: een Onderzoek Naar Motivatie Voor Cultuuroerisme Tijdens de Mondriaantentoonstelling te Amsterdam.* MA dissertation, Tilburg University.

Rojek, C. (1993) *Ways of Escape: Modern Transformations in Leisure and Travel.* Macmillan, Basingstoke.

Schouten, F. (1995) Improving visitor care in heritage attractions. *Tourism Management* 16, 259–264.

Schuster, J.M.D. (1993) The public interest in the art museum's public. In: Gubbels, T. and van Hemel, A. (eds) *Art Museums and the Price of Success: an International Comparison.* Boekmanstichting, Amsterdam, pp. 45–60.

Smith, S.L.J. (1988) Defining tourism: a supply-side view. *Annals of Tourism Research* 17, 581–602.

Studienkreise für Tourismus (1991) *Reisanalyse.* Studienkreise für Tourismus, Starnberg.

Todd, J. (1988) Involving the private sector, or exploding the myth of private sector leadership. Paper presented at the Enterprise in the Inner Cities conference, Barbican, London, October.

Tomlinson, J. (1991) *Cultural Imperialism: a Critical Introduction.* Pinter, London.

Urry, J. (1990) *The Tourist Gaze: Leisure and Travel in Contemporary Societies.* Sage, London.

van der Borg, J. (1994) Demand for city tourism in Europe. *Annals of Tourism Research* 21, 832–833.

Van 't Riet (1995) *Back to Basics: an Analysis of Tourist Motivations for Visiting Cultural Attractions.* MA Thesis, Programme in European Leisure Studies, Tilburg.

Verhoeff, R. (1994) High culture: the performing arts and its audience in the Netherlands. *Tijdschrift voor Economische en Sociale Geografie* 85, 79–83.

Williams, R. (1983) *Keywords.* Fontana, London.

Wood, R.E. (1984) Ethnic tourism, the state and cultural change in Southeast Asia. *Annals of Tourism Research* 11, 186–197.

World Tourism Organization (1985) *The State's Role in Protecting and Promoting Culture as a Factor of Tourism Development and the Proper Use and Exploitation of the National Cultural Heritage of Sites and Monuments for Tourism.* WTO, Madrid.

World Tourism Organization (1993) *Recommendations on Tourism Statistics.* WTO, Madrid.

Wynne, D. (1992) *The Culture Industry.* Avebury, Aldershot.

Zeppel, H. and Hall, C.M. (1992) Arts and heritage tourism. In: Weiler, B. and Hall, C.M. (eds), *Special Interest Tourism.* Belhaven Press, London, pp. 45–60.

The Social Context of Cultural Tourism　　3

G. RICHARDS

Department of Leisure Studies, Tilburg University, PO Box 90153, 5000 LE Tilburg, The Netherlands

INTRODUCTION

The historical analysis of the development of cultural tourism in Chapter 1 traced some of the broad social trends which have influenced the growth of culture as an object of tourism. However, such a general analysis runs the risk of glossing over the complex web of social interactions which underpin the growth of cultural tourism. This chapter examines in more depth some of the major social trends which have been linked to the growth of cultural tourism in Europe and elsewhere.

The bulk of this chapter deals with causes – those factors which have stimulated the growth of cultural tourism. The final section deals with the social and cultural effects of cultural tourism – the impact of cultural tourists on the destinations they visit.

CULTURE AS AN OBJECT OF TOURISM

From a sociological perspective, cultural tourism can be viewed as one aspect of the overall question of cultural consumption. Cultural consumption has been extensively studied, not only as a part of general sociological enquiry, but also in specialist fields, such as art sociology and leisure sociology (Bevers, 1993).

Sociological analysis of cultural participation has identified a number of key variables which can to a large extent explain differences in cultural consumption between individuals. The basic variables identified include

education, income, occupation, and age (Ganzeboom, 1989; Bourdieu and
Darbel, 1991). The effects of these basic variables on cultural consumption and
behaviour are most famously summarized in Bourdieu's concept of cultural
competence, or 'cultural capital'.

Bourdieu (1984:2) argues that in order to understand or appreciate cultural products, people must attain the cultural competence, or capital, which
allows them to recognize and interpret those products: 'a work of art has
meaning and interest only for someone who possesses the cultural competence, that is, the code, into which it is encoded'. Cultural competence, or
capital, is generated through upbringing, education and other forms of sociali-
zation. The possession of cultural capital is demonstrated through consumption, and those forms of consumption in turn act as a form of distinction, which
can define both the individual and membership of a specific social group.

The class struggle, according to Bourdieu, is a battle for control of scarce
cultural, economic and social resources. He argues, for example, that the
increase in educational participation in 'the schooling boom' is the result
of intensified competition between social groups for academic qualifications.
As more people obtain a particular academic qualification, however, the value
of that qualification is devalued as it becomes more common. This drives
'groups whose reproduction was mainly or exclusively achieved through education to step up their investments so as to maintain the relative scarcity of
their qualifications and, consequently, their position in the class structure'
(p. 133). Because education is one of the primary vehicles for attaining cultural
capital,

> Generally increased schooling has the effect of increasing the mass of cultural cap-
> ital which, at every moment, exists in an 'embodied' state. Since the success of the
> school's educative action and the durability of its effects depend on how much cul-
> tural capital has been directly transmitted by the family, it can be presumed that
> the efficiency of school-based educative action tends to rise constantly. (p. 133)

Class factions seek to distinguish themselves from each other in all areas of life,
including education, occupation, and location, as well as through the consumption of commodities. These commodities include not only cultural products and activities, such as museum visits, but also tourism experiences.
These different elements of distinction are combined to create a certain culture
or milieu, or what Bourdieu terms 'habitus', which forms the basis for the
reproduction and differentiation of social classes.

Bourdieu's analysis was based on empirical data collected in France in the
1960s, including a specific study of visitors to art museums (Bourdieu and
Darbel, 1991). It is not surprising, therefore, that Bourdieu's work has often
been used to analyse cultural consumption. In recent years, the increasingly
close links between culture and tourism have also led to a growing interest in
Bourdieu's analysis in the tourism literature (Errington and Gewertz, 1989;
Munt, 1994).

Bourdieu's concept of cultural capital has been tested and extended through a number of subsequent empirical studies. In The Netherlands, data on cultural consumption from the Central Bureau for Statistics (CBS) were used by Knulst (1989) to chart the major changes in cultural consumption in the Dutch population over a 20-year period. Knulst found that visits to museums and monuments had increased substantially, largely due to improved levels of educational attainment. The audience for the performing arts, however, had remained far more restricted. Knulst attributed this difference to the greater amount of cultural capital required for arts participation as opposed to the relatively populist displays offered by museums. A series of studies by re-searchers based at the University of Utrecht (Ganzeboom, 1989; Verhoeff, 1994) have demonstrated that cultural participation remains largely restricted to higher income, highly educated groups, which also tend to be concentrated in major cities, close to centres of cultural production.

In the UK, the work of Merriman (1991) has also indicated the predomi-nantly upmarket nature of museum visiting. His research indicated that museum visitors came predominantly from higher socio-economic groups, and also have a high level of participation in other cultural activities, such as theatre, opera, classical concerts, and ballet. Merriman also argues that museums effectively separate the population into two groups: those who have sufficient cultural capital to perceive museums as a leisure experience, and those who do not.

An important implication of Bourdieu's concept of cultural capital is that people need to accumulate knowledge about art and culture in order to be able to participate effectively. Lack of cultural capital therefore becomes a barrier to participation. The most effective means of increasing participation is to raise general levels of cultural capital through education. The studies by Knulst and Ganzeboom indicate that increasing levels of participation in higher education are one of the most important causes of increased cultural participation in The Netherlands. This is a link which is also confirmed by the high level of cultural tourism participation among students identified in the ATLAS cultural tourism surveys (see Richards, Chapter 2 this volume). In contrast, direct attempts at broadening cultural participation through economic subsidies have proved largely ineffective (Bevers, 1993).

Recent studies have developed the concept of cultural capital still further. Harvey (1989) contends that cultural capital is also an attribute of place. In order to attract investment capital and the spending power of the middle class, regions now differentiate themselves by emphasizing the aesthetic qualities of material commodities and services which represent symbolic capital. Examples of this can be found in the trend toward establishing cultural facilities as part of an economic development strategy (see Gratton and Richards, Chapter 4 this volume). Extending Harvey's argument, Zukin (1991:28) regards culture as 'both the property of cultured people and a general way of life', and that whereas culture in the former sense is a mark of distinction, as suggested by

Bourdieu, in the latter sense culture constitutes 'an inalienable product of place'. The cultural products of place are in effect a physical form of cultural capital ('real cultural capital'), which Zukin contends is just as important as symbolic forms of cultural capital.

> On the supply side, cultural consumption creates employment for a self-conscious critical infrastructure (and lower-level service personnel), and is in turn created by its labor. Cultural consumption contributes to capital accumulation, moreover, by enhancing profits on entrepreneurial investment in production and distribution. And . . . cultural consumption has a positive effect on capital accumulation in real estate development. Cultural goods and services truly constitute real cultural capital – so long as they are integrated as commodities in the market-based circulation of capital. (p. 260)

Investment in real cultural capital becomes attractive not just because, as Harvey suggests, it increases the rate of capital circulation, but also because of

> the inelasticity of demand for certain cultural goods and services that are now deemed essential, at least by the richest stratum of the population with an increasing share of income.

> (Zukin, 1991:266)

Investment in cultural capital therefore has a significant impact on the organization of space. The transformation of downtown areas by gentrification, the creation of 'festival marketplaces' (Harvey, 1989) or the implanting of theme parks in rural areas is driven by the requirements of capital accumulation. The arguments advanced by Harvey and Zukin regarding 'real cultural capital' are important for the study of cultural tourism. Real cultural capital forms a vital link between explanations of cultural consumption, as advanced by Bourdieu, and production of the supply of cultural tourism attractions, as indicated by Harvey. In order to fully understand the conditions under which European cultural tourism has developed, therefore, we need to analyse the social conditions which determine the consumption of cultural tourism, and the economic processes which govern its production. In general, the social aspects of cultural tourism are dealt with in this chapter, and economic aspects in Chapter 4. A strict division is, however, not only undesirable but also impractical. The following sections of this chapter examine first the factors influencing cultural consumption, then influences on cultural production, and an attempt is made to analyse the link between cultural consumption and production in the context of cultural tourism.

PARTICIPATION IN CULTURAL TOURISM

As we have seen in the case of cultural participation in general, participation in cultural tourism is also strongly related to possession of cultural capital. In the case of tourism, however, the direct economic cost of participation, and the opportunity costs involved in time spent travelling means that cultural tourism requires a higher level of investment than many other forms of cultural consumption. As Linder (1970) has argued from an economic perspective, and Bourdieu has argued from a sociological perspective, 'the market value of time . . . increases as one rises in the social hierarchy' (Bourdieu, 1984:282). The convergence of relatively high time and income investment requirements in cultural tourism participation should therefore be reflected in a strong social stratification of cultural tourists.

This section examines the relationship of cultural tourism consumption to key variables of socio-economic status, available leisure time, education, and age, and then goes on to examine further issues with an influence on the social production and reproduction culture, including globalization, localization and the geographic distribution of cultural resources.

Education

The original definition of culture as the act of cultivation (Williams, 1983) underlies the strong link between education and culture made by the original Grand Tourists (see Richards, Chapter 1 this volume). The subsequent growth of the education system has provided arguably the most effective means for transmitting cultural capital (Bourdieu, 1984). The link between tourism and culture in education is still a strong one. The growth of language schools, which offer a taste of local and national cultures alongside language tuition, is one sign of this.

Studies of cultural participation have consistently identified education as one of the primary determinants of cultural participation. For European museums, Schuster (1993:50) argues that 'the difference in participation rates across educational levels is greater than across income levels, indicating that education is a better predictor of an individual's probability of participation'.

In the UK, museum attendance was found to be much higher among those who continued their education beyond the age of 19 (58%) than among those leaving education at 16 (25%). A similar gap exists in Sweden between those with a high school diploma (54% museum attendance) and those with only compulsory schooling (18%) (Schuster, 1993).

American research has also confirmed that education is the strongest single influence on cultural participation. Heilbrun and Gray (1993) remark '(T)hat education is, in fact, the single most important factor determining arts participation has been verified by statistical analyses'. The difference in participation between high and low education levels in the USA is five times as great as the difference in participation by income level.

The expansion of educational opportunities in Europe over the past 30 years has therefore been one of the major factors in stimulating the growth of

Table 3.1. Frequency of museum visiting among the French population.

	% of group visiting museums		
	1973	1981	1988
Upper class and professions	56	60	61
Middle class	48	49	43
Workers	25	24	23

Source: Donat and Cogneau (1990).

cultural tourism. In Amsterdam, a comparison of visitors attending the Rembrandt exhibitions held in 1969 and 1992 showed that the educational level of visitors, already high in 1969, had grown substantially by 1992. At the first exhibition 18.5% of visitors had a university education, compared with 32% in 1992 (Bruin, 1993). Individuals with a high level of education, and also those in higher education therefore form an important audience for cultural tourism. The ATLAS research, for example, found that 20% of respondents interviewed at cultural attractions were students.

Socio-economic status

Cultural participation has always been closely linked with socio-economic position. People from higher social classes in general have greater access to the means of cultural tourism participation (such as higher levels of income and mobility) as well as having the cultural capital necessary to facilitate participation.

In his review of museum attendance in Europe, Schuster (1993) concludes that participation rates are much greater among higher socio-economic groups and professionals. Merriman's (1991) analysis of museum visiting in the UK indicates a strong class stratification, and studies of museum visiting in France tend to support this analysis. Although the proportion of the French population in the higher socio-economic groups visiting museums has increased since the early 1970s, the proportion of working class visitors has actually fallen (Table 3.1). Another national survey of French cultural participation indicated an even greater class divide in art museum visiting in 1989, with higher professionals (73%) being far more likely to visit art museums than intermediate professionals (57%) or unskilled labourers (30%) (Ministère de la Culture, 1989).

Because socio-economic status is strongly related to the possession of cultural capital, social stratification will tend to be even greater for cultural forms which require a high degree of cultural competence for participation. As Bourdieu (1984:273) observes as one moves from avant-garde concerts or plays, museums with a high transmission level and low tourist appeal . . . to spectacular exhibitions, major concerts or the 'classical' theatres, and finally to the boulevarde theatre and variety shows, the rate of representation of the different fractions distributed in order of decreasing cultural capital and increasing economic capital – . . . tends to change systematically and continuously, so that the hierarchy of the fractions distributed by their weight in the public tends to be inverted.

This explains, therefore, why the audience for art museums, which generally require a relatively high level of cultural capital from their audience, are more strongly stratified by social class than other museums. Surveys of visitors to an exhibition of early works by the Dutch artist Mondriaan in Amsterdam in 1994 tend to support this strong link between socio-economic status, cultural capital, and cultural tourism participation (Roetman, 1994).

Surveys in the UK have indicated that the audience base for museums and heritage is much broader in social class terms than the audience for the visual or performing arts (Bonink, 1992). This also provides one explanation for the finding of the ATLAS cultural tourism research that consumption of heritage attractions by tourists is far greater than arts attractions.

Occupation

There is growing evidence that cultural participation, in general, and cultural tourism, in particular, are particularly strongly developed among people with occupations related to culture. For example Bevers (1993:214) reports that 50% of visitors to the Stedelijk Museum in Amsterdam are artists, and that in America 70% of visitors to galleries of modern art are people 'with a professional interest' in art.

This pattern partly reflects the growing importance of culture as an area of employment. In the UK, for example, it is estimated that as many as 671,000 jobs depend directly or indirectly on the cultural industries – equivalent to 2.8% of the UK workforce (Shaw, 1991). Taylor (1987) has estimated that 150,000 artists live and work in the New York region (for more detailed analysis of the relationship between culture and employment, see Gratton and Richards, Chapter 4 this volume).

The importance of cultural occupations for cultural consumption is demonstrated by the ATLAS cultural tourism research. Almost 20% of all cultural visitors interviewed had an occupation which was related to the cultural industries, and among specific cultural tourists, the level of culturally related occupations reached 29% (Richards, 1996).

The consumers and producers of culture, therefore, are often the same people. Those who work in the cultural industries are not only important as direct consumers of cultural products, but also as pathfinders and interpreters for the passive consumers of culture who prefer their culture delivered at home through the media. The media is also playing an increasingly important role in shaping cultural tourism consumption. Reports of exhibitions and perform-ances in other countries now appear regularly in newspapers and art ma-gazines, and cultural attractions feature prominently in television travel programmes.

The role of these 'new cultural intermediaries' in influencing taste and therefore purchasing patterns, is part of their struggle to appropriate particular scarce resources for their own use, and convert these into economic capital.

Leisure time availability

The growth of leisure time availability has arguably expanded opportunities for tourism and cultural consumption in the twentieth century. As paid holiday entitlements also became the norm in postwar Europe, it also became increas-ingly possible to combine cultural activities with tourism. As Scitovsky (1976) has suggested, the greater availability of leisure time in Europe is one of the reasons why cultural participation has tended to be greater there than in the United States.

Leisure time is not evenly distributed across Europe, however. Working hours per year tend to be highest in southern Europe and the UK, and shortest in The Netherlands and Germany (Gratton, 1995). There is evidence to suggest that there will be a convergence of leisure time availability, and holiday entitle-ment as a result of the Single Market (Gratton, 1992). The expansion of leisure time has already produced a qualitative change in time use. One of the most notable trends in the northern European holiday market in the last decade has been the growth of short-break holidays (trips of three nights or less). As total holiday entitlement has expanded, so people are supplementing their main annual holiday with a number of additional short breaks (Faché, 1994).

The growth in short-break taking is considered by many to be a major stimulus for cultural tourism, particularly in urban areas (Law, 1993). The ATLAS cultural tourism survey revealed that over 25% of all respondents were on a short break (three nights or less away from home). In the shoulder seasons (spring and autumn) this proportion would probably be much higher.

Although it has been argued that the expansion of leisure time has been a factor in promoting cultural tourism, there are growing signs that leisure time availability for many in northern Europe is actually falling. As Juliet Schor has demonstrated in her book *The Overworked American* (Schor, 1991) the desire to raise levels of consumption has resulted in a fall in leisure time, as people in employment have had to work increasingly hard to accumulate goods and services. This phenomenon is now being observed in countries such as The Netherlands and the UK. The expansion of working hours, coupled with grow-ing unemployment, has produced a growing gulf between the relatively time poor and money rich (those with jobs) and the time rich/money poor (the non-working population). This trend has also arguably stimulated more cultural tourism, as time-poor, money-rich consumers enjoy more short break trips to major cultural centres.

The greying of Europe

Europe is ageing. In the three decades up to 1990, the number of people aged over 60 in the European Union grew by 50%, while the population as a whole only rose by 17% (Davies, 1995). It is widely assumed that older people have a greater interest in the past, in history and culture in general. The expanding senior citizen market is therefore seen as a prime source of expansion in cultural tourism demand (Berroll, 1981).

Evidence from The Netherlands indicates a greater degree of cultural motivation for older tourists. Interviews with foreign tourists in 1988 revealed that 'museums, historic buildings and cities' were a motivation to visit for 29% of tourists under 30 years old, compared with 33% of tourists aged 30–45, and 39% of those aged over 45 (Nederlands Bureau voor Toerisme, 1988). Although the proportion of culturally motivated tourists tends to increase with age, however, younger people often form a higher proportion of the total tourist population. The Dutch research, for example, indicated that while tourists under 30 accounted for 30% of all culturally motivated visitors, only 26% were aged over 45.

This point is made even more strongly by the ATLAS cultural tourism research. Of all cultural visitors interviewed in the ATLAS survey 44% were aged under 30, and 42% of tourists interviewed were less than 30. This pattern is caused by the higher participation rate by young people in tourism. Although it can be argued that the summer interview period was likely to increase the proportion of young tourists in the ATLAS sample, it is clear that younger tourists form an important element of the cultural tourism market. This is one of the reasons that Studiosus, the leading German cultural tourism tour operator, has begun to target programmes specifically at young people (see Roth and Langemeyer, Chapter 9 this volume). The potential of the youth market is set to increase still further in future, as the decline in the numbers of young people will begin to reverse after the year 2000 (European Travel Commission, 1995).

THE CREATION OF A NEW CULTURAL ELITE?

It is clear from the above analysis of social variables that many of the factors affecting cultural tourism consumption are interrelated. In general, cultural tourists can be characterized as having a high socio-economic status, high levels of educational attainment, adequate leisure time, and often having occupations related to the cultural industries. In broad terms, the growth of such a group of consumers can be linked to the rise of the 'service-class culture' in postindustrial societies.

In postindustrial economies high standards of living ensure that material needs can be met through goods consumption. Increased consumption can therefore be invested in leisure services, and the search for distinction can be increasingly based on cultural capital accumulation. Bourdieu (1984) identifies different factions within the expanded middle class who compete with each other for position and status. The 'new bourgeoisie' is high on economic capital and cultural capital, and consumes exclusive travel products and ecotourism. In contrast, the 'new petit bourgeoisie' or 'new cultural intermediaries', are lower on economic capital, and therefore must professionalize tourism consumption practices in order to create employment opportunities for themselves. Munt (1994) argues that struggles for cultural and class superiority between these factions are responsible for many of the cultural and structural features of modern tourism consumption, such as the distinction between 'traveller' and 'tourist' and the spatial differentiation exemplified in tourism development 'off the beaten track'.

Similar groupings within the middle class have been identified in relation to cultural consumption and heritage tourism (Urry, 1994). These patterns of consumption have led some authors to suggest that we are witnessing the emergence of a 'new middle class' or a 'service class' (Featherstone, 1991; Munt, 1994). Walsh (1991:127) argues that the service class is a phenomenon which emerged in Britain in the 1980s, marked by participation in 'modes of consumption which enhanced their movement away from dull inconspicuous forms of consumption, towards a consumption of signs which many saw as being signs of difference and distinction'.

In contrast to the old cultural elites, the new cultural elite of the service class is based on a greater diversity of consumption, usually organized in globalized niche markets in which the major consumption spaces are metropolitan city centres. The service class is therefore also often seen as the vanguard of gentrification of inner city areas (Zukin, 1991). It is certainly true that there is an increasingly affluent, increasingly mobile and international community within Europe. In Amsterdam, for example, there are 50,000 foreign residents in a population of 700,000, and 50% of the population have lived in the city for less than 8 years (Bevers, 1993). This group has in fact already been the target of another cultural tourism programme created by the German specialist operator Studiosus (see Roth, Chapter 9 this volume). Studiosus packaged cultural tours in Italy and Greece for an international audience in an English-language brochure launched in 1993.

The consumption patterns of the service class entail a constant search for new experiences and sources of stimulation which help to distinguish the participant from the crowd. As Bourdieu (1984:249) puts it the sense of good investment which dictates a withdrawal from outmoded, or simply devalued, objects, places or practices and a move into ever newer objects in an endless drive for novelty, and which operates in every area, sport and cooking, holiday resorts and restaurants, is guided by countless different indices and indications.

Those in search of distinction will automatically steer away from products and places which have become 'popular', and seek out novel forms of symbolic distinction. One could argue that such forces are behind the growth of city-based short breaks at the expense of the crowded Mediterranean beaches, for example, or the decline in Europe's market share of world tourism as more European tourists go in search of more 'exotic' holiday destinations.

This analysis suggests that the rise of cultural tourism is strongly linked to rise of the new service class, and postmaterialistic forms of consumption. As postindustrial societies develop, and more individuals seek to distinguish themselves through cultural capital acquisition, the level of cultural tourism might be expected to increase. As was suggested in Chapter 2, however, cultural tourism consumption is not just dependent on consumption patterns, but also on the relationship of consumption to cultural production. The following section examines the way in which the production and distribution of cultural resources has influenced and been influenced by the rise of cultural tourism.

THE PRODUCTION OF CULTURAL RESOURCES

The tendency of capital to seek geographic locations which maximize the rate of capital accumulation (Harvey, 1989) has had important implications for the geography of cultural tourism in Europe. Wealthy regions have always created material displays of their wealth and power through the construction of impressive buildings or monuments. In the Renaissance, however, political leaders discovered the advantages of using the high cultural forms associated with antiquity to justify their own position. The artistic and architectural creativity of the north Italian cities in the sixteenth century, Claval (1993) argues, was in part stimulated by Italian princes anxious to secure power in an uncertain political climate. Claval also contrasts the monumental capitals of Baroque cities with the more spartan capitals of Calvinist countries. Amsterdam, the archetypal Calvinist city, today suffers from a lack of major monuments to attract tourists in comparison with Paris, London or the Italian cities (Table 3.2).

Both the origin and the subsequent survival of such relics depends on the mode of capital accumulation. As Lynch (1972) remarked, environments rich in historic remains often follow a specific pattern. Once markedly prosperous, they then suffered a rapid economic decline, which discouraged further development and therefore preserved them to some extent in their original

Table 3.2.   Cities with more than ten cultural attractions listed in the European Union inventory of cultural tourism resources.

	International	National	Regional	Total
Belgium				
Antwerp	2	5	8	15
Bruges	3	7	9	19
Brussels	2	9	10	21
Ghent	1	5	9	15
Leuven	2	3	5	10
Denmark				
Copenhagen	2	13	9	24
France				
Paris	9	47	28	84
Rouen	–	7	3	10
Greece				
Athens	4	10	2	16
Ireland				
Dublin	4	8	11	23
Italy				
Bologna	1	2	7	10
Florence	13	11	3	27
Milan	6	5	6	17
Naples	1	3	13	17
Palermo	1	2	7	10
Perugia	–	1	10	11
Ravenna	1	2	7	10
Rome	22	30	51	101
Siena	2	3	8	13
Netherlands				
Amsterdam	3	7	3	13
Portugal				
Lisbon	2	8	12	20
Spain				
Barcelona	1	6	9	16
Madrid	3	8	1	12
Seville	3	8	–	11
Toledo	4	7	5	16

Table 3.2.   *Continued*

	International	National	Regional	Total
United Kingdom				
Cambridge	2	6	6	14
London	8	20	16	44
Oxford	5	4	2	11
York	1	6	3	10
West Germany				
Berlin	4	8	20	32
Bonn	–	2	13	15
Dusseldorf	–	3	9	12
Hamburg	–	2	9	11
Mainz	1	4	5	10
Munich	4	12	8	24
Stuttgart	–	6	7	13

Source: Irish Tourist Board (1988).

form. A good example in northern Europe is Bruges, where the houses of rich medieval textile merchants were left unaltered after the wool trade in Flanders declined, leaving Bruges with an historic city centre which now attracts over 2 million tourists a year (see Munsters, Chapter 6 this volume). The cultural richness of the northern Italian cities owes much to their economic decline between 1600 and 1800 (Dunford and Perrons, 1983), which preserved the material legacy of the Renaissance from subsequent ravages of economic development.

Analysis of the spatial distribution of major cultural tourism resources indicates the continuing importance of medieval and Renaissance cities in the European cultural tourism industry. The European cultural tourism inventory compiled by the Irish Tourist Board (1988) indicates that concentrations of cultural attractions are found mainly in capital cities and important cities dating from the fourteenth to sixteenth centuries (Table 3.2). Thus Flanders accounts for four of the five Belgian cities with more than ten attractions in the inventory, and northern Italy has six cities with more than ten attractions. In The Netherlands, Denmark, Greece, Ireland, and Portugal, only the capital cities can muster more than ten listed attractions. In France, which has the greatest total number of listed attractions, Rouen is the only city outside Paris which has more than ten listed attractions, which indicates the influence of centralization in France on the distribution of cultural resources.

The cities which feature most prominently in the EU Cultural Inventory are to a large extent the same cities that van der Borg (1994) identifies as 'European cultural capitals'. Van der Borg's analysis, based on tour operators' programmes, in turn matches the classification of Bianchini and Parkinson (1993), based on cultural policies, of 'cultural capitals'.

Claval (1993) explains the concentration of cultural resources in the European 'cultural capitals' as a spatial distinction between 'high' and 'popular' culture. He argues that 'high culture' consumption is based on reading and writing, contrasted to the oral and visual tradition of popular culture. The vast collective memory of the museums and libraries of capital cities established the conditions for the concentration of high culture, and the art collections and architecture which make them so attractive for cultural tourism. All the indications are that the areas which accumulated considerable 'real cultural capital' during the Renaissance and during the formation of modern nation states, have continued to benefit from this position, as heritage centres 'rich with time' (Urry, 1994). As Buzard (1993) puts it, these sites are 'saturated with culture', and 'as long as European travel – or "travel" in the value-laden sense – commanded a price in the cultural markets of Britain and America, tourists would remain strongly motivated to press claims of having witnessed *essential, symbolic* qualities of the places they visited' (p. 212, emphasis in the original).

There are signs that this pattern persists, in spite of the efforts of the heritage industry to create new centres of cultural consumption elsewhere. In the UK, for example, even though there has been a significant increase in heritage attraction supply outside London, the bulk of heritage-related investment has been concentrated in the capital. Figures from the English Tourist Board (1991) indicate that a doubling in the value of heritage attraction investment between 1986 and 1991 was accompanied by a growing concentration of investment in London and South East England, from 69% of all reported heritage investment in 1986 to 75% in 1991. These two regions also accounted for over half the visits to cultural tourism attractions in England in 1992 (English Tourist Board, 1993). Further evidence is provided by the Policy Studies Institute (1993) analysis of UK museums, which showed that the larger national museums in the UK, located predominantly in London, increased their visits considerably, whereas smaller museums in provincial locations fared less well. Similar patterns are found in other European countries. In The Netherlands, for example, Amsterdam has about 5% of the Dutch population, but houses 26% of all designated historic monuments, and accounts for 24% of all museum visits.

Part of the explanation for the spatial concentration of cultural tourism lies in its reliance on the built heritage. Heritage resources are usually place-dependent, whereas art production and consumption is relatively place-independent. For example, it is only possible to visit the Notre Dame in Paris, or the Vatican in Rome. The increasing importance of notions of authenticity (Urry, 1990) make it difficult to reproduce these sights in other places, except as theme-park pastiche. Drama or musical performances or art displays, on the other hand, are far more mobile. The musical CATS, for example, has been staged in 130 cities worldwide (see also Roth and Langemeyer, Chapter 9 this volume). The increasing pressure for galleries and museums to stage 'blockbuster' exhibitions means that more and more art works are travelling the globe in search of an audience. This distinction between place-dependent heritage and place-independent arts is far from fixed, however. The staging of major events often depends on the financial security of a large audience, which can often be best guaranteed in the existing 'cultural capitals'.

As the number of events multiplies, there is a growing need for supposedly footloose events to use the uniqueness of location to differentiate themselves. Britton (1991:455) argues that many cultural events have lost their uniqueness: 'having been persuaded to buy a commodity package, tourists are by and large conditioned to look for the qualities associated with a cultural model, staged performance, or lifestyle representation, rather than its authenticity'. What emerges is therefore a range of depthless, superficial cultural products specifically created for tourism. As Britton points out, this creates a contradiction in a market in which the sensory threshold of novelty is constantly being raised. The 'shelf-life' of these products is therefore constantly shortening, and consumers must become more discerning and sensitive to authenticity in tourism products. Walsh (1991) has suggested that a similar process can be recognized in the commodification of museums.

In the spiralling competition for the attention of potential consumers, the established cultural capitals still seem to have a marked advantage. The continuing popularity of established centres of high culture is underlined by Townsend's (1992) study of attendance at cultural attractions in the UK, which shows that 'the growth of new kinds of urban tourism and museums has been relatively unsuccessful . . . the most successful urban sites are the pre-industrial ones' (p. 32). In spite of promotion of industrial heritage at national level in the UK and efforts by provincial centres such as Bradford to use tourism as an engine for economic development and image enhancement, this has not resulted in a significant geographic shift in the pattern of cultural tourism consumption.

The cause of the geographic inertia of European cultural tourism lies also in the strong influence exerted by consumption on cultural production. This relationship is examined in the following section.

The social production of cultural tourism

As consumption becomes a more central feature of modern life, so consumption patterns come increasingly to influence patterns of production. Zukin argues that 'much of the experience of consumption today is highly *mediated* by new producers' (1991:45, emphasis in original). The search for authenticity, for example, relies on a constant flow of reliable, authoritative information (e.g. alternative travel guides, TV programmes, etc). As the complexity of products and services on offer increases, furthermore, so the amount of knowledge, or self-investment required also grows. These 'new producers' identified by Zukin belong to the same group as the 'new cultural intermediaries' of Bourdieu. This group seeks to maintain its high level of cultural capital, and to compensate for low levels of economic capital through the pursuit of authenticity in tourism.

Just as cultural capital is unequally distributed among individuals, so 'real cultural capital' is unequally distributed in space. The important advantage that the 'preindustrial' sites have is the presence of sedimented real cultural capital. It is this cultural capital which is unlocked and exploited by the 'new producers' (Zukin, 1991) or the 'new cultural intermediaries' (Bourdieu, 1984). This key group of cultural producers and consumers is strongly represented in the centres of old cities, close to the sites of cultural consumption and real cultural capital production (Verhoeff, 1994). The ATLAS cultural tourism research also indicates that those involved in cultural production are likely to have an important role in cultural consumption. In the case of cultural tourism, it seems that the relatively small group of 'specific cultural tourists', also has a strong link with the cultural industries, and tends to be concentrated in the major cultural capitals of Europe. The characteristics of this group of 'specific cultural tourists' comes closest to the class faction identified as the 'new cultural intermediaries' by Bourdieu (Richards, 1996).

In order to capitalize on their productive activities, the new cultural intermediaries must have a sufficiently large pool of consumers. Munt (1994:107) suggests that Bourdieu's 'new bourgeoisie' fulfils the main consumer function in tourism, being 'firmly located in the service sector with finance, marketing and purchasing as occupational exemplars, a class faction high on both economic capital (finance) and cultural capital. It is with the new bourgeoisie that taste and travel unite and are celebrated'. These are the tourists who would seem to conform most closely to the traditional image of the cultural tourist as older, wealthier and well educated (Berroll, 1981), and who fit the profile of the 'general cultural tourist' identified in the survey research (Richards, 1994). In contrast the 'specific cultural tourists' are more likely to be young, self-employed and with an occupation related to culture, a profile closer to that of the 'new cultural intermediaries' (Bourdieu, 1984). The indications are that this relatively small group of specific cultural tourists, or 'culturally motivated tourists' (Bywater, 1993) have a disproportionate influence not only on the consumption of cultural tourism, but also on its production, particularly in the major cultural capitals of Europe.

In spite of the powerful arguments advanced by Zukin and others for a concentration of cultural power in the major metropolitan centres, however, there is also evidence that this globalization of culture is being accompanied by a concurrent trend towards localization and regionalization, which O'Connor and Wynne (1993) characterize as the resistance of the vernacular to the extension of 'landscapes of power' under globalization (Zukin, 1991).

Globalization and localization

The democratization of culture in the early twentieth century was based on an unquestioning acceptance of the international nature of high culture. This view is epitomized by the remark of French composer Eric Satie that 'art has no country'. One of the original motives for state support of culture in Europe during the nineteenth and early twentieth centuries was the need the nation state had for a 'national culture' as a cement for nationhood. In the postwar era, national 'British' or 'French' or 'Italian' cultures became abstractions used to sell tourist destinations as well. One of the major reasons why Americans travel to the UK, for example, is to experience 'English' or 'British' culture, even though the identity and meaning of these cultures is hotly contested from within the cultures themselves (Long and Richards, 1995). Similar conflicts over the link between cultural identity and place are evident in Spain. The image of 'Spanish culture' promoted at national level often meets resistance in areas which do not identify with the predominantly Castilian cultural image of Spain promoted abroad. In Mallorca, for example, the message to British tourists (in English) comes from window stickers which proclaim 'Mallorca is not Spain', a clear statement of Mallorquin resistance to 'Spanish' cultural domination.

The globalization of culture represented by 'McDonaldization' (Ritzer, 1993) and 'Disneyfication' is seen by many as being a threat to national, regional, and local cultures everywhere. Walsh (1991) argues that the destruction of difference under modernity is reflected in the globalization of heritage, which as a superficial representation of history contributes to the process whereby places begin to lose their distinctive identities. Tourism contributes to this process through the creation of a series of mythical places (Cookson Country, Robin Hood Country) which are more 'real' for the tourist than the authentic regional identities that they replace (Prentice, 1993).

There is, however, evidence of growing local resistance to the pervasive forces of creative destruction under international capitalism. Internationally homogeneous high culture is now being countered by promotion of the vernacular, or through the appropriation of elements of the landscape of high culture into the vernacular (O'Connor and Wynne, 1993).

In Europe as a whole, it can be argued, a reaffirmation of difference is in progress, which has profound implications for cultural tourism. 'In the Europe of the regions, a continent that is undeniably becoming more fragmented, there is a particular attention being paid to the geographic origin of artists and their cultural identity. Differences are increasingly being emphasized' (Depondt, 1994:1). As Hannerz (1993) suggests, difference is what attracts tourists to a particular place. The cultural resources most attractive to tourists are therefore things which are not everywhere, the 'unique', the 'authentic'.

The place-bound nature of heritage attractions, such as monuments, museums and heritage centres are likely to be more attractive to tourists than the generalized high culture represented by art performance.

Appeals to the spatial uniqueness of cultural heritage manifestations abound in tourism marketing strategies. In an increasingly globalized and homogenized cultural landscape, the need to establish local difference through ownership of customs, rituals, art works, buildings, and even whole landscapes becomes even more acute. The need to own cultural artefacts as a tourism resource is sharply demonstrated by the cultural imperialism engaged in by some tourism marketeers. For example, the British city of Bradford effectively laid claim to a large swathe of the surrounding Yorkshire Dales in an attempt to claim such cultural gems as the Brontë sisters and the location of the television programme 'Emmerdale Farm'.

Although local or regional culture can provide a good basis for cultural tourism development, it is important that the degree of difference must not be too great that it alienates the tourist. Ashworth (1992) has pointed out that heritage tourists often demand a generalized, globalized tourism experience which contradicts with the localization of heritage resources.

THE IMPACT OF TOURISM ON CULTURE

Cultural provision has had an impact on tourism, but tourism is also beginning to have increasing impacts on the cultures which provide a basic motivation for tourism. A great deal has already been written on the general cultural impact of tourism (e.g. Mathieson and Wall, 1982; Smith, 1989). It would therefore be superfluous to try and review the full range of argument here. This section gives a brief overview of some key sources, and highlights issues of particular significance for cultural tourism.

Because cultural tourists are arguably motivated by local cultures in choosing to visit a particular location, they have been identified as both a blessing and a blight as far as their social and cultural impact is concerned. Some authors have suggested that culturally motivated tourists are desirable, because they tend to be relatively few in number, and they are also more sympathetic in their approach to the local population and their culture than other tourists (Smith, 1989). Cultural tourists also tend to spend more money than other types of visitor, and can therefore play an important role in providing financial support for local cultural manifestations. Others have suggested that it is precisely this cultural motivation which makes cultural tourists less desirable in some areas. Butler (1990) has suggested that 'alternative' tourists seeking authentic cultural experiences can open up culturally fragile areas, acting as a 'Trojan Horse', opening the way to potentially more damaging mass tourism. Wheeler (1991) has gone further, arguing that cultural tourists who seek authentic experiences of local culture can inflict severe damage on local communities in spite of (or perhaps because of) their low numbers. Those in search of active contact with the local population are likely to cause far more disturbance by seeking out 'local' places which may cause the friction between the local population and the tourists to increase rather than diminish.

One potential solution to the potentially damaging search by cultural tourists for 'authentic' cultural experiences is to create cultural artefacts and phenomena specifically for tourist consumption. Cohen (1992), for example has demonstrated the way in which arts production in many tourist centres has become adapted to the needs of tourists. Cohen (1988) asserts that even cultural products specifically designed for tourist consumption can come to be considered as 'authentic' to a certain degree, even by the local population. This form of 'emergent authenticity' can be observed in a wide range of products and rituals which we now accept as being traditional cultural products.

Many would argue that it is just this kind of commodification process which represents the worst effect of cultural tourism development. By turning cultural phenomena into commodities for tourist consumption it is argued, culture is stripped of its original meaning, and the 'product' sold to the tourist is divorced from the 'way of life' which produced it. Others might argue, however, that commodification is common to all areas of tourism (Watson and Kopachevsky, 1994) and to the capitalist system in general (Britton, 1991). Commodification is, therefore, to some extent unavoidable. The key question in cultural tourism is the extent to which communities retain control over their own culture and the products derived from it (Hall, 1994). Whose culture is being sold to whom, and why?

As the analysis of cultural tourism policy in Chapter 5 makes clear, cultural tourism is often promoted for political and economic reasons which have little connection to the 'way of life' of local residents. Examples of struggles over the meaning and exploitation of cultural tourism can be found in the European City of Culture event, already introduced in Chapter 2. In Glasgow in 1990, there was a bitter debate about the content and aims of the event, between organizers trying to maximize economic revenue from wealthy tourists coming to see cultural highlights such as Pavarotti, and local activists trying to promote a more 'Glaswegian' culture (Boyle and Hughes, 1991). Similar debates between 'cultural elitists' and promoters of local culture emerged in the 1993 event in Antwerp. Many criticized the lack of Flemish art and culture in the programme, but this criticism was rejected by one organizer who remarked that 'promotion of local art can never be an objective of the Cultural Capital programme' and that demands for local cultural representation were 'founded on an outmoded and false impression of how cultural value originates and how it is consecrated' (Corijn and van Praet, 1994:28). It is not just the process of commodification involved in cultural tourism which is at issue, therefore, but also the control of that commodity once it is produced. A further example of

struggles over the ownership of cultural heritage is provided by the development of the Baroque Cultural Itineraries in France (see Bauer, Chapter 8 this
volume).

Tourism can also have a direct physical impact on cultural goods. The
crush of tourists in historic European cities such as Venice and Bruges is producing a growing number of negative environmental and social impacts (see
van der Borg and Costa, Chapter 12 and Munsters, Chapter 6 this volume).
Because heritage tends to be place-bound, cultural tourists often congregate in
the same areas of historic city centres at the same times. Costa and van der Borg
(1993) have demonstrated that at peak tourist periods Venice is essentially
'full'. The crush of visitors in St Mark's Basilica means that the frescos are being
damaged by the condensation of the visitors, breath, and the stones underfoot
are worn away by the stream of visitors (Costa, 1988).

However, cultural tourism is also viewed as part of the solution to such
problems of tourism concentration. Because cultural tourism is based on
specific interests and motivations, it is argued, they can be persuaded to visit
less popular destinations or to go at less popular times of the year. This is
certainly one of the arguments underpinning the promotion of cultural tourism by the European Union (see Richards, Chapter 5 this volume).

It has also been argued that cultural tourism can play a role in helping to
preserve cultural traditions. Grahn's (1991) analysis of cultural tourism
development in Lapland indicates that cultural tourism can play a positive role
in enhancing traditional culture, providing control is retained locally. Cultural
tourism can also arguably enrich the quality of life, both in urban and rural
settings (Jafari, 1992).

The major problem in assessing the positive and negative impacts of cultural tourism, and particularly the impact of tourism on local cultures, is the
lack of longitudinal impact studies (Wilson, 1993). Many previous studies
have tended to ascribe all cultural change to the impact of tourism, without
placing tourism in the context of wider social and economic changes. As Smith
(1989) has pointed out, the intrusions of tourism into local culture can often
pale into insignificance alongside other agents of change, such as television.
The initial pessimism about the negative effects of tourism on culture have now
been replaced by more balanced appraisals, in which tourism is also recognized
as having the potential to strengthen local cultures. In many cases the funds
provided by tourism are being used to support local cultural traditions and
ways of life which in the absence of tourism would probably die out. As Greenwood (1989) has pointed out in his study of the *Alarde* festival in the Basque
region of northern Spain, living cultures inevitably change, and they have the
potential to make creative use of tourism, using it to develop 'interest in local
culture, pride in local traditions and an improved sense of cultural worth'
(p. 185).

CONCLUSION

Participation in cultural tourism has been stimulated by a wide range of social changes, including rising education levels and increasing leisure time. A number of studies have indicated, however, that the possession of cultural capital is a good predictor of cultural tourism consumption. This means that cultural tourism is concentrated particularly among the 'new middle class', for whom acquisition of high levels of cultural capital form an important source of distinction. The development of cultural capital through consumption is also concentrated spatially, because of the accumulation of 'real cultural capital' in specific locations. Cultural tourism consumption has therefore become socially and spatially concentrated. The effects of social concentration can create a great social and cultural distance between cultural tourists and their hosts. The effects of spatial concentration can include the physical destruction of the very artefacts and social structures that cultural tourists come to see. There are growing signs, however, that local cultures are also resilient enough to absorb and turn to creative use the changes wrought by tourism.

REFERENCES

Ashworth, G.J. (1992) Heritage and tourism: an argument, two problems and three solutions. In: Fleischer-van Rooijen, C.A.M. (ed.) *Spatial Implications of Tourism*. Geo Pers, Groningen, pp. 95–104.

Berroll, E. (1981) *Culture and the arts as motives for American travel*. Proceedings 12th Annual Travel and Tourism Research and Marketing Conference, Salt Lake City, pp. 199–200.

Bevers, T. (1993) *Georganiseerd Cultuur*. Dick Coutinho, Bussum.

Bianchini, F. and Parkinson, M. (1993) *Cultural Policy and Urban Regeneration: the West European Experience*. Manchester University Press, Manchester.

Bonink, C. (1992) *Cultural tourism development and government policy*. MA dissertation, Rijksuniversiteit Utrecht.

Bourdieu, P. (1984) *Distinction: a Social Critique of the Judgment of Taste*. Routledge & Kegan Paul, London.

Bourdieu, P. and Darbel, A. (1991) *The Love of Art: European Art Museums and Their Public*. Polity, Cambridge.

Boyle, M. and Hughes, G. (1991) The politics of 'the real': discourses from the Left on Glasgow's role as European City of Culture, 1990. *Area* 23, 217–228.

Britton, S. (1991) Tourism, capital and place: towards a critical geography of tourism. *Environment and Planning D: Society and Space* 9, 451–478.

Bruin, K. (1993) Rembrandt in Amsterdam, Berlijn en Londen. In: Bevers, T. (ed.) *De Kunstwereld: Produktie, Distributie en Receptie in de Wereld van Kunst en Cultuur*. Erasmus Universiteit Rotterdam, pp. 336–377.

Butler, R.W. (1990) Alternative tourism: pious hope or Trojan horse? *Journal of Travel Research* 19, 40–45.

Buzard, J. (1993) *The Beaten Track: European Tourism, Literature and the Ways to 'Culture' 1800–1918*. Oxford University Press, Oxford.

Bywater, M. (1993) The market for cultural tourism in Europe. *Travel and Tourism Analyst* 6, 30–46.

Claval, P. (1993) The cultural dimension in restructuring metropolises: the Amsterdam example. In: Deben, L., Heinemeijer, W. and van der Vaart, D. (eds) *Understanding Amsterdam*. Het Spinhuis, Amsterdam, pp. 111–139.

Cohen, E. (1988) Authenticity and commoditization in tourism. *Annals of Tourism Research* 15, 467–486.

Cohen, E. (1992) Tourist arts. *Progress in Tourism, Recreation and Hospitality Management* 4, 3–32.

Corijn, E. and van Praet, S. (1994) Antwerp 93 in the Context of European Cultural Capitals: Art Policy as Politics. Paper presented at the Conference on City Cultures, Lifestyles and Consumption Practices, Coimbra, 15–16 July 1994.

Costa, P. (1988) Measuring the carrying capacity of a major cultural tourism destination: the case of Venice. Paper presented at the Workshop on Cultural Tourism in Mediterranean Islands, University of Malta, Malta, October 1988.

Costa, P. and van der Borg, J. (1993) Tourism management in cities of art. *CISET Working Paper* 2/93, University of Venice, Venice.

Davies, L. (1995) *Mobility and Older People*. AIT/FIA, Brussels.

Depondt, P. (1994) Internationalisatie doodt de Kunst. *de Volkskrant* 24 March, p. 1.

Donat, O. and Cogneau, D. (1990) *Les Practiques Culturelles des Francais*. Documentation Français, Paris.

Dunford, M. and Perrons, D. (1983) *The Arena of Capital*. Macmillan, London.

English Tourist Board (1991) *Tourism Investment Report*. ETB, London.

English Tourist Board (1993) *Sightseeing in 1992*. ETB, London.

Errington, F. and Gewertz, D. (1989) Tourism and anthropology in a post-modern world. *Oceania* 60, 37–54.

European Travel Commission (1995) *Europe's Youth Travel Market*. ETC, Paris.

Faché, W. (1994) Short break holidays. In: Seaton, V., Jenkins, C.L., Wood, R.C., Dieke, P.U.C., Bennett, M.M., MacLellan, L.R. and Smith, R. (eds) *Tourism: the State of the Art*. Wiley, London, pp. 459–467.

Featherstone, M. (1991) *Consumer Culture and Postmodernism*. Sage, London.

Ganzeboom, H. (1989) *Cultuurdeelname in Nederland : een empirisch-theoretisch onderzoek naar determinanten van deelname aan culturele activiteiten*. Van Gorcum, Assen.

Grahn, P. (1991) Using tourism to protect existing culture: a project in Swedish Lapland. *Leisure Studies* 10, 33–47.

Gratton, C. (1992) A perspective on European leisure markets. Paper presented at LSA/VVS Internationalisation and Leisure Research Conference, Tilburg, The Netherlands.

Gratton, C. (1995) A cross-national/transnational approach to leisure research: The changing relationship between work and leisure in Europe. In: Richards, G. (ed.) *European Tourism and Leisure Education: Trends and Prospects*. Tilburg University Press, Tilburg, pp. 215–232.

Greenwood, D.J. (1989) Culture by the pound: an anthropological perspective on tourism as cultural commoditization. In: Smith, V.L. (ed.) *Hosts and Guests. The Anthropology of Tourism*, 2nd edn. Basil Blackwell, Oxford, pp. 171–185.

Hall, C.M. (1994) *Tourism and Politics: Policy, Power and Place*. Wiley, Chichester.

Hannerz, U. (1993) Cities as windows on the world. In: Deben, L., Heinemeijer, W. and van der Vaart, D. (eds) *Understanding Amsterdam*. Het Spinhuis, Amsterdam, pp. 157–172.

Harvey, D. (1989) *The Condition of Postmodernity*. Basil Blackwell, Oxford.

Heilbrun, J. and Gray, C. (1993) *The Economics of Art and Culture: an American Perspective*. Cambridge University Press, Cambridge.

Irish Tourist Board (1988) *Inventory of Cultural Tourism Resources in the Member States and Assessment of Methods Used to Promote Them*. DG VII, European Commission, Brussels.

Jafari, J. (1992) Cultural tourism and Regional Development. *Annals of Tourism Research* 19, 576–577.

Knulst, W. (1989) *Van Vaudeville tot Video*. Sociale en Cultureel Planbureau, Rijswijk.

Law, C.M. (1993) *Urban Tourism: Attracting Visitors to Large Cities*. Mansell Publishing, London.

Linder, S.B. (1970) *The Harried Leisure Class*. Columbia University Press, New York.

Long, J. and Richards, G. (1995) European tourism: changing economic and cultural dimensions of tourism in a unifying Europe. Paper presented at the European Leisure Studies Group Winter University, Bilbao, April.

Lynch, K. (1972) *What Time is this Place?* MIT, Cambridge, MA.

Mathieson, A. and Wall, G. (1982) *Tourism: Economic, Physical and Social Impacts*. Longman, Harlow.

Merriman, N. (1991) *Beyond the Glass Case: The Past, the Heritage and the Public in Britain*. Leicester University Press, Leicester.

Ministère de la Culture (1989) *Nouvelle enquete sur les practiques culturelles des Français en 1989*. La Documentation Français, Paris.

Munt, I. (1994) The 'other' postmodern tourism: culture, travel and the new middle classes. *Theory, Culture and Society* 11, 101–123.

Nederlands Bureau voor Toerisme (1988) *Waarom Komen Buitenlanders voor Vakantie naar Nederland?* NBT, Leidschendam.

O'Connor, J. and Wynne, D. (1993) *From the Margins to the Centre*. Manchester Institute for Popular Culture, Manchester.

Policy Studies Institute (1993) Museums and galleries. *Cultural Trends* 19, 1–44.

Prentice, R. (1993) *Tourism and Heritage Attractions*. Routledge, London.

Richards, G. (1994) Developments in European cultural tourism. In: Seaton, V., Jenkins, C.L., Wood, R.C., Dieke, P.U.C., Bennett, M.M., MacLellan, L.R. and Smith, R. (eds) *Tourism: the State of the Art*. Wiley, London, pp. 366–376.

Richards, G. (1996) Production and consumption of cultural tourism in Europe. *Annals of Tourism Research* 23, (in press).

Ritzer, G. (1993) *The McDonaldization of Society*. Pine Forge Press, Thousand Oaks.

Roetman, E.E. (1994) Motivatie in Retrospectief: een Onderzoek Naar Motivatie Voor Cultuuroerisme Tijdens de Mondriaantentoonstelling te Amsterdam. MA dissertation, Tilburg University.

Schor, J. (1991) *The Overworked American: the Unexpected Decline of Leisure*. BasicBooks, New York.

Schuster, J.M.D. (1993) The public interest in the art museum's public. In: Gubbels, T. and Hemel, A. (eds) *Art Museums and the Price of Success: an International Comparison*. Boekmanstichting, Amsterdam, pp. 45–60.

Scitovsky, T. (1976) *The Joyless Economy*. Oxford University Press, Oxford.

Shaw, G. (1991) Growth and employment in the UK's culture industry. *World Futures* 33, 165–180.

Smith, V.L. (1989) *Hosts and Guests. The Anthropology of Tourism*, 2nd edn. Basil Blackwell, Oxford.

Taylor, B. (1987) *Modernism, Post-modernism, Realism: a Critical Perspective for Art.* Winchester School of Art Press, Winchester.

Townsend, A.R. (1992) The attractions of urban areas. *Tourism Recreation Research* 17, 24–32.

Urry, J. (1990) *The Tourist Gaze: Leisure and Travel in Contemporary Societies.* Sage, London.

Urry, J. (1994) Cultural change and contemporary tourism. *Leisure Studies* 13, 233–238.

van der Borg, J. (1994) Demand for city tourism in Europe. *Annals of Tourism Research* 21, 832–833.

Verhoeff, R. (1994) High culture: the performing arts and its audience in the Netherlands. *Tijdschrift voor Economische en Sociale Geografie* 85, 79–83.

Walsh, K. (1991) *The Representation of the Past: Museums and Heritage in the Post-modern World.* Routledge, London.

Watson, G.L. and Kopachevsky, J.P. (1994) Interpretations of tourism as commodity. *Annals of Tourism Research* 21, 643–660.

Wheeller, B. (1991) Tourism's troubled times. *Tourism Management* 12, 91–96.

Williams, R. (1983) *Keywords.* Fontana, London.

Wilson, D. (1993) Time and tides in the anthropology of tourism. In: Hitchcock, M., King, V.T. and Parnwell, M.J.G. (eds) *Tourism in South-East Asia.* Routledge, London, pp. 32–47.

Zukin, S. (1991) *Landscapes of Power: from Detroit to Disney World.* University of California Press, Berkeley.

The Economic Context of Cultural Tourism

4

C. GRATTON[1] AND G. RICHARDS[2]

[1]School of Leisure and Food Management, Sheffield Hallam University, Pond Street, Sheffield S1 1WB, UK; [2]Department of Leisure Studies, Tilburg University, PO Box 90153, 5000 LE Tilburg, The Netherlands

INTRODUCTION

In most European countries, subsidies to the arts and culture have grown considerably in the postwar period so that government is a major provider of financial support for culture. The traditional arguments for such subsidies have been based on the educational role of the arts and the equity objective, to broaden the audience for cultural products and ensure equality of access to all social groups. Failure to show clear benefits from subsidies on either of these objectives, particularly the equity objective, together with increasing pressure to reduce public expenditure seriously threatened the level of government support for arts and culture in Europe in the 1980s.

At the same time, particularly at city level, a new argument for subsidies to arts and culture emerged: investment in the arts for purposes of economic development and industrial restructuring. Law (1992, 1993) has indicated that many European cities in the 1980s adopted an urban tourism strategy following the examples of such strategies in American cities such as Baltimore and Boston in the 1970s. Within such an urban tourism strategy, urban cultural policy has become increasingly important. In Britain, the link between arts and tourism became much more important after the publication of Myerscough's (1988) study of the economic importance of the arts. In many ways, the economic arguments in favour of government support for the arts and culture changed during the 1980s away from arguments concerned with education, cultural appreciation, and cultural integration, towards arguments concerned with the economic benefits generated by the arts through their attraction of tourists. This economic motivation for public investment in arts and culture has been a major focus of government policy in Europe in recent years.

This chapter focuses on the shifting patterns of cultural funding between state, market and voluntary sources, highlighting the approaches adopted in different countries, and the implications of these changes for cultural tourism in Europe. Attention is then given to the increasingly economic motives underlying the promotion of culture as a tourist attraction, and the economic impact of cultural tourists on European destinations.

THE STRUCTURE OF CULTURAL FUNDING IN EUROPE

Table 4.1 shows government expenditure on arts and culture at national and state level for ten European countries. Compared with all the other major European economies Britain stands out for the low level of government support for the arts. The Netherlands, with about one-quarter of the population of Britain, has higher government expenditure (in total) than Britain. When we compare expenditure per capita, only Ireland and Portugal from the countries in Table 4.1 have lower government expenditures on the arts, and in many countries cultural expenditure per capita is over three times greater than that in Britain. Table 4.1 does not include expenditure at the municipal, local, and regional level but Frey and Pommerehne (1989) suggest that for countries such as Germany over half the subsidies for the arts came from local government. This is not the case in the UK, again reinforcing the point of much lower subsidy levels in the UK.

Table 4.1. Government expenditures for culture: ten European countries, central and state levels 1985 (ECUs).

	Expenditures (millions)	Expenditure per capita (purchasing power parity)
Belgium	221	27.1
Denmark	181	31.9
France	1151	28.9
Germany (Fed. Republic, 1983)	1368	22.7
Great Britain	117	9.5
Ireland (1981)	22	8.0
Italy	1271	27.5
Netherlands	197	37.2
Portugal	50	7.6
Spain	564	22.0

Source: Frey and Pommerehne (1989).

A similar comparative study of arts expenditure by Schuster (1985) indicates that public support for the arts is generally much higher in Europe than in the United States. In the US, however, levels of additional funding through tax benefits, donations and sponsorship were much higher. When this additional spending was included, per capita arts spending in the US was actually higher than in the UK, which again is far behind most of its European neighbours. This position may change in future as funding from the National Lottery begins to be channelled to arts organizations in the UK (see Foley, Chapter 16 this volume).

More recent work by Feist and Hutchison (1990) showed that per capita expenditure in the United Kingdom on arts subsidies remains substantially below other European countries such as France, The Netherlands, former West Germany, and Sweden. A specific evaluation of public funding for cultural tourism in the UK and The Netherlands (Bonink, 1992) indicates that funding is about a third lower in the UK.

Towse (1994:143) identifies some fundamental differences in arts and heritage policy which underlie the distinctions between the UK and other 'English speaking' countries and the 'nationalized cultural industries of continental Europe'. In the UK, she argues, culture is freer of government control, and real or threatened reductions in subsidy have been used to put pressure on cultural organizations to increase commercial income. By 1990, therefore, theatres and orchestras in the UK earned over 50% of their income from commercial sources, about double the level achieved in other western European countries.

Over time, the balance between public, commercial and voluntary funding for culture has shifted considerably. In The Netherlands, Bevers (1993) demonstrates that many existing cultural institutions were established in the nineteenth century by a relatively small group of private individuals, who could be considered as a 'cultural elite'. It rapidly became clear that these private initiatives, including theatres, concert halls, etc., served too small a sector of the public to survive through audience receipts and private subscriptions and donations alone. Most of these cultural organizations therefore turned rapidly to the state for financial support. In most cases that support was forthcoming, not least because of the influence which the cultural elite was able to wield in political circles. These originally private institutions turned gradually into state-financed ones. The level of state subsidy in The Netherlands now represents over 82% of income for performing arts institutions, and 73% of museum income. This pattern of voluntary sector initiatives being appropriated by the state is repeated in many other European countries.

The predominance of state subsidy for cultural production is often contrasted with the situation in North America, where income from private sources, such as donations and sponsorship, is often four times the European level (Bevers, 1993). However, this system of arts funding is effectively supported by the state, through significant tax advantages offered to private and corporate donors.

There are now growing signs, however, that the high tide mark of public sector funding of culture may have been reached in Europe, and that declining public sector expenditure is having a growing impact on state and local government culture budgets. In the UK, for example, although cultural spending has risen over the last few years (Shaw, 1991), the increase in spending has not kept up with inflation. In Italy, there were real cuts in the national cultural budget in 1994, with a 15% reduction in spending in 1994–1996 compared with 1991–1993.

In addition to cuts in public funding, cultural organizations face the additional problem that costs inevitably rise faster than costs in the economy as a whole, since they have difficulty in substituting capital for labour in the production process (Heilbrun and Gray, 1993). As costs of cultural production grow, so the ability of the public sector to fund the arts is diminished.

Falling public expenditure also has a particularly serious impact in the area of cultural heritage, since the stock of heritage is still expanding rapidly. In order to avoid a seemingly open-ended commitment to maintaining a growing number of old buildings, national governments have begun to pass these responsibilities on to local government or to the commercial or voluntary sectors. Shifting responsibilities have been partly responsible for the growth in cultural expenditure by local and regional governments (Bianchini and Parkinson, 1993). The combined budgets of local authorities in the areas of both culture and tourism frequently exceed expenditure in these areas at national level (Bonink, 1992; Richards, 1992). In major cities, cultural funding has now become a major issue as cities compete to generate income and jobs, and to attract inward investment by raising their cultural profile.

A further sign of the declining public sector support for culture is the growth in voluntary sector activity, either indirectly through fund-raising or directly through the input of labour. The activities and membership of voluntary bodies concerned with heritage preservation, such as the National Trust in the UK, have grown significantly in recent years. Voluntary labour now represents a significant proportion of all human resources deployed in culture and heritage. In the Netherlands over 21,000 volunteers in the cultural heritage sector contribute 55% of all labour input, and in Denmark volunteers account for 75% of labour deployed in cultural projects (see Richards, Chapter 13 and Hjalager, Chapter 7 this volume).

Another popular European solution to the problem of expanding cultural funding needs and shrinking public expenditure is to raise funds from gambling or lotteries, as is the case in Greece and the UK (see Foley, Chapter 16 this volume). Even more popular have been moves to encourage cultural institutions to become more commercial, or even to privatize them.

Commercialization and privatization

As state funding for culture declines, so increasing emphasis is being laid on other sources of funding, particularly admissions revenue and sponsorship. The impact of reductions in state funding have been felt across the entire range of cultural activity, from the reduction of social security benefits for artists in The Netherlands to the reduction of *Grands Projets* expenditure in France (see Bauer, Chapter 8 this volume). The public debate surrounding the funding of culture usually centres on high profile, high culture institutions with large visitor numbers. Because the state subsidies for these institutions also tend to be large, they are often under the greatest pressure to reduce their dependence on the public purse.

In the UK, the impact of declining public funding has been most dramatically seen in the national museums. Falling subsidies during the late 1980s and in the 1990s have forced the national museums to look for other sources of income. The most obvious means of raising income was to charge for admission to the museums, which hitherto (apart from a brief period in the early 1970s) had been free. The first museum to introduce charges in the 1980s was the Victoria and Albert museum, and even though these charges were (and still are) 'voluntary', there was an immediate 40% drop in visitor numbers (Wood, 1990). Other museums which subsequently introduced charges experienced similar declines in attendance.

Pressures to earn more income and to reduce reliance on subsidies have been evident at many heritage attractions in recent years. In the UK, admission prices to major historic attractions have risen far faster than inflation (Middleton, 1989). English Heritage, the major body responsible for the built heritage in England, increased its income from visitor admissions from £1.9 million in 1986 to £4.9 million (ECU 6.2 million) in 1992, with admissions earnings per visitor rising from £0.59 to £0.96 over the same period (Policy Studies Institute, 1992). There have also been substantial increases in revenue earned from visitors through merchandizing and catering in heritage attractions. In Italy, for example, the photography charge in museums rose from L 50,000 to L 100,000 in 1993, one of the measures taken by Culture Minister Ronchey in his attempt to make Italian museums more market and visitor-orientated (see van der Borg and Costa, Chapter 12 this volume). There is some evidence to suggest that this policy is already having an effect. In 1994 the 1.2 million visitors to the Doge's Palace in Venice generated L 11 billion (ECU 6.13 million) in income from ticket sales and shop purchases. In France, the Musée d'Orsay had a turnover of FFr 65 million (ECU 10 million) from its shop alone in 1993.

A further step in making publicly funded museums more market-orientated is privatization. In The Netherlands the national museums are being privatized, with the aim of reducing public subsidy to 85% of current levels (see Richards, Chapter 13 this volume). Privatization has also been proposed for local authority museums in the Hague, although in this case with no loss of subsidy. Although moves in The Netherlands and the UK to give national museums more freedom from direct state control give more flexibility in most areas of management, this flexibility is accompanied by tighter financial controls and performance indicators in relation to the remaining subsidies. These performance indicators are often stated in terms of measures of efficiency, such as income per visitor, which places more emphasis on raising visitor numbers and expenditure.

Falling subsidies and the need to become more commercially minded and market-orientated have forced many cultural attractions to compete actively with other leisure attractions to attract more visitors. In many cases, this means attracting cultural tourists, who can not only supplement the local visitor market, but who in many cases also spend far more in the attractions themselves and in other sectors of the local economy. The income-generating potential of cultural tourism has also caused many policy-makers to change their view of culture from a drain on public spending to a potential source of local income and jobs. Many regional and local governments across Europe are now actively trying to stimulate the development of the cultural industries.

THE CULTURAL INDUSTRIES

The increasing emphasis on the commercialization and the economic value of the arts and culture coincided with the use of the term 'cultural industries' to define this sector. Cultural industries refers to a broader view of the arts as Wynne (1992:1) explains:

> We define the culture industry as including all forms of activity associated with what is traditionally understood as art and popular culture. This includes the live performance and singular artistic production, together with the recorded and reproduced productions in the audio and visual media. We have adopted this broadest of definitions because of the increasing 'crossovers' between forms of cultural activity, and because we believe that the culture industry and the benefits which flow from it, both economic and social, gain nothing from an artificial separation produced by distinguishing their form. Importantly we reject the distinctions which regard culture as limited to a definition of art as 'high culture'; which distinguishes between commercial and non-commercial consumption and production of cultural provision and products; and which define cultural policy simply as the provision of leisure and arts facilities. We believe that a wider definition is important in order to promote the conceptual leap necessary if the arts are to take their proper place in the new economy upon which successful regeneration strategies need to be based. A new economy which demands investment in the arts (culture industry), education and training, and a high technology infrastructure.

This broader view of the arts was adopted by Myerscough (1988), who split the economic activities associated with arts and culture into three constituent parts:

1. presentation of arts events and attractions (museums and galleries, theatres and concerts);
2. production and distribution of performances by mechanical means (through broadcasting and the cinema);
3. creation of cultural items for sale (books, pictures, discs and videos, craft items).

The activities under these headings make up the major economic contribution of cultural industries estimated at £7.3 billion (ECU 9.3 billion) in terms of turnover in 1985 (£0.85 billion for events and attractions; £2.8 billion for mechanical performance; and £3.67 billion for cultural products). It is interesting to see that the narrow view of arts referred to by Wynne as 'high culture' is the smallest of these sub-sectors in economic terms. In addition, the cultural industries generate other economic activity through expenditure on food, transport, accommodation, and other expenditure associated with attendance at arts events. Myerscough estimated this ancillary spending at £2.6 billion (turnover) in 1985 so that overall total turnover associated with cultural industries was around £10 billion (ECU 14 billion) in 1985.

In the UK, employment in the cultural industries grew from 153,000 employees in 1981 to 175,400 in 1993. The number of jobs in the cultural industries therefore increased by over 22%, and the proportion of all UK employment accounted for by the cultural industries grew from 0.72% in 1981 to 0.84% in 1993 (Policy Studies Institute, 1993). The concentration of cultural tourism and other cultural activities in London is also reflected in the distribution of employment, however. London accounted for 38% of all cultural industries employment in the UK in 1991, and the proportion of the workforce employed in culture was almost three times the national average. This again emphasizes the important economic impact of the accumulated 'real cultural capital' which is found in the capital cities of Europe (see Richards, Chapter 3 this volume).

The cultural industries approach to economic regeneration is currently spreading across Europe. In Germany, for example, the North Rhine–Westphalia region (Task Force 'NRW Culture Industries Report', 1991) has emphasized the increased importance of the arts for increasing the attractiveness of the region, stimulating a creative environment, building 'social competence' and flexibility, and contributing to economic growth and job creation.

PATTERNS OF CULTURAL EXPENDITURE

We have fairly good information on the pattern of expenditure by cultural tourists. Such information is necessary for the estimation of the economic impact of the arts and cultural events, which is discussed below, and given the increasing interest in such economic impact studies we have an increasing amount of data on the expenditure pattern of visitors to arts attractions. Most studies divide visitors into three categories, tourists (staying overnight for at least one night), day visitors, and residents. The expenditure measure adopted is normally average spending per head per day. In general, tourists spend more than day visitors, who in turn spend more than residents.

Myerscough (1988) reviewed the pattern of daily expenditure by different types of visitor. On average, tourists to art attractions spent 50% per day more than day visitors but this is almost totally explained by expenditure on accommodation which accounts for about one-third of a tourist's daily expenditure. For residents and day visitors to theatres and concerts the largest item of expenditure is expenditure within the venue on tickets, refreshments, etc. This accounts for about 55% of daily expenditure. Food and drink outside the venue accounts for a further 15% of daily expenditure with the other 30% going on travel, shopping, and other expenditure.

A study of arts-related expenditure in Amsterdam in 1984 (van Puffelen, 1987) indicated total arts visitor spending to be Fl 450 million (ECU 220 million) a year. Of this total, foreign tourists accounted for Fl 350 million, or 77% of the total. Domestic tourists spent Fl 75 million (17%), and spending by residents (excluding admission fees) accounted for only Fl 25 million (6%).

In Ireland, MacNulty and O'Carroll's (1992) study of visitors to heritage attractions in 1991 estimated that total expenditure by the 4.6 million visitors in 1991 was IR£ 11.45 million (ECU 14.4 million), or IR£ 2.49 per visit (Table 4.2). This study only covered spending inside the attractions themselves, however. In France, the Ministry of Culture has estimated that 10% of visitors to

Table 4.2. Expenditure at heritage attractions in Ireland, 1991.

Item	Total expenditure	
	IR£ million	%
Admissions	6.64	58
Food and drink	2.70	24
Crafts	0.41	3
Souvenirs	0.74	6
Literature	0.52	5
Other	0.45	4
Total	11.46	100

Source: MacNulty and O'Carroll (1992).

French heritage sites will spend an average of FFr 250 (ECU 38) per person per day on accommodation, food, transport, and shopping.

There is considerable variability in the level and pattern of tourist's expenditure with foreign tourists spending more than domestic tourists, and foreign tourists on short-break holidays having the highest levels of daily expenditure.

THE ECONOMIC IMPACT OF CULTURAL TOURISM

Tourists make an important contribution to the economic importance of the arts. Tourists make up a significant proportion of the audience for museums, galleries, theatres, and concerts, particularly in capital cities. Myerscough (1988) showed that in London 44% of attendances at museums and galleries were tourists, as were 40% of theatre and concert audiences, and 37% of theatre audiences in London's West End were from overseas in 1986. Such foreign visitors normally spend much more than day visitors or residents and therefore are a target market for policy-makers devising urban tourism strategies since the economic impact they generate is so much higher. The arts are increasingly an important part of such a tourism strategy.

It is at the level of the city that most interest has been generated in the economic importance of cultural tourism. Many European cities in the 1980s faced problems of decline in their existing industries and were forced to consider new economic development strategies based on service industries. Many cities developed tourism strategies hoping to attract a new type of visitor to the local economy.

Within such an urban tourism strategy, urban cultural policy has become increasingly important. Bianchini (1990:2) suggests that the aims of urban cultural policy go beyond simply the promotion of cultural tourism:

> In the course of the 1970s and 1980s many cities in Western Europe have become increasingly aware of the potential of cultural policy to implement a range of strategic goals: to reconstruct their internal and external images; to attract new investment and skilled personnel; to find new economic niches and functions; to trigger off a process of physical and environmental regeneration; to revitalize local public social life; to stimulate community organization and strengthen civic identity and pride; to establish links with other cities and networks of cities in Europe and beyond.

Despite these wide-ranging objectives for cultural policy, the tourism objective has become increasingly important for European cities over the 1980s and early 1990s.

Bianchini argues that there are two particular categories of European cities where cultural tourism is a primary objective of cultural policy. The first of these is 'declining cities'. These have used cultural policy to support strategies for the diversification of their economic base and the reconstruction of their image. These cities have suffered decline due to the disappearance of their old manufacturing base. New investment in inner city arts and cultural projects became the means for reconstructing the external image of many European cities. The aim was to attract new investment and to generate physical and environmental renewal through service industries expansion. Investment in the arts sector was a major catalyst for economic development. Within this category he includes Glasgow, Sheffield, Liverpool, Birmingham, Hamburg, Bochum, Rotterdam, Lille, and Genoa.

Glasgow made a major attempt in the mid-1980s to change its image, firstly with the promotional campaign 'Glasgow's Miles Better' together with the introduction of Mayfest, a major annual arts festival. In 1990, Glasgow became European Cultural Capital (see Richards, Chapter 2 this volume) and prior to this £2.5 billion (ECU 3.5 billion) was invested in infrastructure and in new cultural facilities. Glasgow is the only city to carry out a full assessment of the impact of the Cultural Capital event (Myerscough, 1991). The study indicated that the Cultural Capital event stimulated over £28 million (ECU 39 million) in visitor spending, against a total public sector investment of about £22 million (ECU 30 million). During 1990, 3 million visitors came to Glasgow, compared with 2.4 million the year before. However, much of this visitor flow was diverted from other parts of Scotland (including Edinburgh), and although the regional benefits may have been significant, the additional benefits to Scotland at national level may have been much smaller. In spite of the impressive evidence of job creation and image improvement during the year itself, doubts also remain about the long-term impact. Myerscough also provides evidence that the image benefit of the Year of Culture was already beginning to decline in January 1991. A study by Van den Berg et al. (1994) also indicates that tourism employment in Glasgow fell by 5% from April to September 1992, compared with a 10% growth in tourism employment in Scotland as a whole.

Bianchini's other major category of cities where cultural tourism is particularly important he refers to as 'cultural capitals'. These are cities which are recognized as major cultural centres but which have had to invest heavily in cultural infrastructure just the same because of competition from other European cities. They are investing to maintain their lead in the European league table. Included in this category are London, Edinburgh, Paris, Copenhagen, Amsterdam, Berlin, and Rome. Thus, in Paris in the 1980s we have seen prestigious projects such as the Musée d'Orsay, the Museum of Science and Technology, the Louvre Pyramid, and the Opera at La Bastille (see Bauer, Chapter 8 this volume). In fact, Bianchini argues that since the mid-1980s and abolition of the Greater London Council, London has lost out to other European cities in this competition (most notably to Paris) since there is no central authority to plan and coordinate cultural policy in London.

One of these cities, Edinburgh, is interesting in that an important part of its tourism and cultural policies is based on festivals. The Edinburgh festivals are unique in that two studies of their economic impact have been carried out, the first in 1976 (Vaughan, 1977) and the second in 1990/91 (Scottish Tourist Board, 1993) and we discuss the main results of these studies below. These studies are important since festivals have been used increasingly as an important element of urban cultural policy in the recent past. There has been a tremendous growth in the number of festivals in the United Kingdom in recent years. Out of 527 UK arts festivals reviewed by Rolfe (1992), 56% were established in the 1980s and 1990s.

The main Edinburgh festivals, the International Festival (opera, music, dance, and theatre), the Fringe Festival (theatre, mime, drama), and the Film Festival, spanning virtually the whole of August and the beginning of September, are now one of the longest running festival events held in the United Kingdom, having first been staged in 1947. In Rolfe's (1992) survey of festivals in the UK only 5% predate the Edinburgh festivals. Other festivals now take place over the same time, the Book Festival, the Jazz Festival, and the Military Tattoo, which is the largest of the three events. Taken together they have become the largest festival event in the United Kingdom. In 1990, as well as taking more on the box-office than virtually any other festival (at around £1.5 million), the festivals received support from Edinburgh District Council, the Scottish Arts Council, and commercial sponsors (each contributing around £0.6 million). In addition, three other Edinburgh festivals take place at different times of the year: the Folk Festival (March), the Science Festival (April), and the Children's Festival (June). Thus, Edinburgh can justly claim to be one of the main festival cities in Europe, justifying on this claim alone Bianchini's description of the city as a cultural capital.

Edinburgh is the capital of Scotland, is an attractive historical city, and is a major tourist destination in its own right irrespective of the festivals (see Foley, Chapter 16 this volume). Much of the rest of tourism outside the festival period could also be referred to as cultural tourism but has more to do with 'heritage tourism' than with 'arts tourism'. What has interested policy-makers most, however, is what economic benefits investment in such festival events generate.

The aim of economic impact analysis is to estimate the additional expenditure that is generated within a local economy and region from the staging of a particular event such as an arts festival. This additional expenditure provides *direct income* to the arts organizations involved, *indirect income* to the suppliers to these organizations, and *induced income* when the local income earned as a result of the direct and indirect income is respent in the local economy. The additional income continues to circulate around the economy but with each successive round of expenditure the flow of income is reduced as income leaks out of the local economy to firms and organizations based outside the region. The total of the direct, indirect, and induced income expressed as a proportion of the initial expenditure is referred to as the multiplier, and most economic impact studies of arts events and festivals involve estimating the level of additional expenditure due to the staging of the event primarily by surveying the visitors to the event and using a multiplier derived from previous studies to estimate the level of additional income and employment resulting from the event. This was the approach taken in the 1990/91 study of Edinburgh festivals. In the 1976 study, much more detailed investigations were carried out which allowed the calculation of different multipliers for different types of visitor.

Total additional expenditure due to the festivals in 1990/91 was estimated at £43.9 million (ECU 56 million), which generated an estimated 1319 full-time equivalent jobs in the local economy. This compares with an additional expenditure due to the festivals in 1976 of £3.7 million (at 1976 prices). After allowing for inflation, total real additional direct expenditure on the Edinburgh festivals in 1990/91 was 369% higher than in 1976, a substantial increase. The main reason for such an increase was a large rise in the number of festival visits and a large increase in the average daily expenditure of visitors, indicating the increasing economic importance of cultural tourism between 1976 and 1990.

Three festivals dominated the net addition to expenditure in Edinburgh due to the festivals: the Tattoo, International, and Fringe Festivals accounting together for 84% of additional spending due to the festivals. These three attract the highest number of visits, have the highest proportion of tourist visits (i.e. those staying at least one night in Edinburgh), and the highest average daily spend per visitor (Table 4.3).

Of the total additional expenditure 86% was incurred by tourists spending at least one night in Edinburgh. Most of the rest (11% of additional expenditure) was by day-visitors, non-residents who visited Edinburgh for the festivals but did not stay overnight. Less than 3% of additional expenditure was due to residents. The reasons for the low contribution to additional expenditure by residents was their low average daily expenditure and the small percentage of

Table 4.3.   Spending by Edinburgh Festival visitors (£ million).

	Resident	Day-visitor	Tourist	Total
Fringe Festival	0.625	0.686	9.050	10.361
International Festival	0.197	1.149	5.564	6.910
Military Tattoo	0.004	1.881	17.689	19.574
Jazz Festival	0.152	0.162	0.880	1.194
Film Festival	0.013	0.014	0.426	0.453
Folk Festival	0.016	0.004	0.158	0.178
Science Festival	0.000	0.536	0.155	0.691
Book Festival	0.130	0.092	1.620	1.842
Children's Festival	0.000	0.003	0.011	0.014
Multiple Visitor Festival	0.120	0.403	2.124	2.647
Total	1.257	4.930	37.677	43.864

Source: Gratton and Taylor (1992).

expenditure that was 'additional', in the sense that much of this expenditure would have taken place in Edinburgh anyway.

One important aspect of the 1990/91 study was the attempt to assess the importance of the Edinburgh festivals in generating tourism and the resultant economic impact in other parts of Scotland. Visitors that create a further economic impact in the rest of Scotland are those that spend further nights elsewhere in Scotland as part of their visit to the Edinburgh festivals. The most unexpected result of the study was the importance of this effect, with an estimated additional direct expenditure in the rest of Scotland of £28.19 million (ECU 36 million). This is equivalent to a further 1190 additional full-time equivalent jobs generated by the spending of festival visitors in Scotland as a whole. The important point about these results is that about 40% of the economic impact of the festivals in Scotland as a whole is due to expenditure outside Edinburgh.

The evidence from Edinburgh suggests that festival tourism can make a significant economic contribution to the local and regional economies of cities. Given the relatively small amount of public subsidy given to the festivals, it is a very efficient way of generating local income and employment as well as regional and national employment.

As pointed out earlier in this chapter, the expenditure generated by cultural tourists becomes increasingly important as state cultural spending falls, and cultural institutions become more dependent on admissions revenue both as a source of income and as a justification for continued state subsidy. Cultural tourists can also provide an important injection of expenditure into regional and national economies, helping to generate economic growth, investment and employment. Cultural tourists have long been identified as upmarket and high-spending, and therefore a prime market segment for generating economic benefit for a destination. The economic value of cultural institutions is now an important consideration in allocating scarce public sector funding, which is increasingly being targeted at basic economic development goals.

The effectiveness of using cultural tourism as a tool for economic development, however, depends on the context in which such a policy is pursued. The case studies of Edinburgh and Glasgow serve to illustrate this point. Edinburgh, with an established cultural base, and a large amount of 'real cultural capital' has managed to derive considerable economic benefit from its existing cultural facilities through developing cultural tourism. The economic benefits have also been cumulative over time, and spatially distributed. In Glasgow, the lack of an existing cultural base necessitated a strategy of investing in new cultural attractions and events. In spite of the spin-offs to other areas of the economy in Glasgow itself, there is little hard evidence to suggest that the events have generated a lasting tourism benefit to Glasgow, which needs to constantly stage new events to attract tourists. In the absence of 'real cultural capital' accumulated over a long period of time, as in Edinburgh, Glasgow finds itself currently on a cultural investment 'treadmill', with new investment

Table 4.4. Cultural expenditure in selected cities, 1990.

City	Total expenditure on arts/ culture/museums (MECU)	Expenditure per head (ECU)
Paris	860	46
London	431	64
Berlin	410	196
Frankfurt	214	340
Bonn	57	201

Source: Coopers and Lybrand Deloitte (1991).

continually being required to compete with other cities, notably Edinburgh. In the long run, of course, the investments currently being made by Glasgow will be converted into 'real cultural capital' which can then be exploited by the tourism and culture industries much more effectively. In the short term, however, there is little doubt that 'new' cultural destinations, such as Glasgow or Rotterdam, are at a distinct competitive disadvantage relative to the established cultural capitals of Europe, such as Edinburgh or Amsterdam. The latter have a critical mass of cultural attractions which stimulate a higher degree of overnight and foreign tourism, which significantly increases the economic benefits of cultural tourism. As Table 4.4 indicates, 'culturally deprived' (Bianchini and Parkinson, 1993) European cities trying to establish themselves as cultural destinations, such as Frankfurt, need to spend proportionately far more on culture than established 'cultural capitals' such as London or Paris.

CONCLUSIONS

This chapter has given a broad overview of the economic importance of the arts and cultural industries before focusing specifically on the economic impact of cultural tourism. Formerly, arts and culture were defined narrowly and received funding from government primarily because they were thought to provide a means of satisfying objectives related to education and cultural integration. In the 1990s, the economic argument for supporting cultural industries has become dominant. This argument relates to a broader definition of cultural industries that includes broadcasting, the cinema, and the production of cultural products such as books, videos, and crafts.

In spite of this shifting balance of economic power between the various sectors of cultural production, Bevers (1993) emphasizes the interdependent nature of actors involved in the cultural system. The state needs artists as advisers and judges of artistic production to determine subsidy policies, the artists are heavily dependent on state funding for their livelihoods, and both the state and the artists depend on the public to justify cultural production and cultural policy. The growing interdependence of policy-makers, cultural producers and consumers creates what Bevers calls a system of 'organized culture', in which cultural production increasingly takes on attributes of commercial organizations and public bureaucracies, such as policy, management, organizational structures and finance. Decisions about cultural production are therefore no longer simply cultural, but also economic and political in nature. The integration of economic and cultural policies in the field of cultural tourism provides the focus of the following chapter.

REFERENCES

Bevers, T. (1993) *Georganiseerd Cultuur*. Dick Coutinho, Bussum.

Bianchini, F. (1990) Cultural policy and urban development: the experience of West European cities. Paper delivered at the conference: Cultural Policy and Urban Regeneration: The West European Experience, Liverpool, 30–31 October 1990.

Bianchini, F. and Parkinson, M. (1993) *Cultural Policy and Urban Regeneration: the West European Experience*. Manchester University Press, Manchester.

Bonink, C. (1992) *Cultural tourism development and government policy*. MA Dissertation, Rijksuniversiteit Utrecht.

Coopers and Lybrand Deloitte (1991) London World City: Summary Report. Coopers and Lybrand Deloitte, London.

Feist, A. and Hutchison, R. (1990) Funding the arts in seven western countries. *Cultural Trends* 5, 1–74.

Frey, B.S. and Pommerehne, W. (1989) *Muses and Markets: Explorations in the Economics of the Arts*. Basil Blackwell, Oxford.

Gratton, C. and Taylor, P. (1992) Cultural tourism in European cities: a case-study of Edinburgh. *Vrijetijd en Samenleving* 10, 29–43.

Heilbrun, J. and Gray, C. (1993) *The Economics of Art and Culture: an American Perspective*. Cambridge University Press, Cambridge.

Law, C.M. (1992) Urban tourism and its contribution to economic regeneration. *Urban Studies* 29, 599–618.

Law, C.M. (1993) *Urban Tourism: Attracting Visitors to Large Cities*. Mansell Publishing Ltd, London.

MacNulty, P. and O'Carroll, C. (1992) *Visitors to Attractions in Ireland in 1991*. Tourism Development International, Dublin.

Myerscough, J. (1988) *The Economic Importance of the Arts in Britain*. Policy Studies Institute, London.

Myerscough, J. (1991) *Monitoring Glasgow*. Glasgow City Council.

Middleton, V. (1989) Marketing implications for attractions. *Tourism Management* 10, 229–234.

Policy Studies Institute (1992) The built heritage. *Cultural Trends* 15, 21–57.

Policy Studies Institute (1993) Employment in the cultural sector. *Cultural Trends* 20, 1–35.

Richards, G. (1992) The UK Local Authority Tourism Survey 1991. Centre for Leisure and Tourism Studies, University of North London.

Rolfe, H. (1992) *Arts Festivals in the UK*. Policy Studies Institute, London.

Schuster, J.M.D. (1985). *Supporting the Arts: An International Comparative study*. US Government Printing Office, Washington.

Schuster, J.M.D. (1993) The public interest in the art museum's public. In: Gubbels, T. and van Hemel, A. (eds) *Art Museums and the Price of Success: an International Comparison*. Boekmanstichting, Amsterdam, pp. 45–60.

Scottish Tourist Board (1993) Edinburgh Festivals study: visitor survey and economic impact. *Festival Management and Event Tourism* 1 (2), 71–78.

Shaw, G. (1991) Growth and employment in the UK's culture industry. *World Futures* 33, 165–180.

Task Force 'NRW Culture Industries Report' (1991) *Dynamic Culture Industries in North Rhine-Westphalia*. Archiv fur Kulturpolitik, Bonn.

Towse, R. (1994) Achieving public policy objectives in the arts and heritage. In: Peacock, A. and Rizzo, I. (eds) *Cultural Economics and Cultural Policies*. Kluwer Academic Press, Amsterdam, pp. 143–165.

Van den Berg, L., van der Borg, J. and van der Meer, J. (1994) *Urban Tourism*. Erasmus Universiteit, Rotterdam.

Van Puffelen, F. (1987) The economic importance of the arts in Amsterdam. In: Hillman-Chartrand, H., Hendon, W.S. and Horowitz, H. (eds) *Paying for the Arts*. Association for Cultural Economics, Ohio, pp. 231–242.

Vaughan, R. (1977) *The Economic Impact of the Edinburgh Festival*. Scottish Tourist Board, Edinburgh.

Wood, H. (1990) The Victoria and Albert Museum. In: Richards, G. (ed.) *Case Studies in Tourism Management*. Papers in Leisure and Tourism Studies, 2, University of North London, pp. 22–28.

Wynne, D. (1992) *The Culture Industry: The Arts in Urban Regeneration*. Avebury, Aldershot.

The Policy Context of Cultural Tourism   5

G. RICHARDS

Department of Leisure Studies, Tilburg University, PO Box 90153, 5000 LE Tilburg, The Netherlands

As we have seen in the preceding chapters, policies relating to cultural tourism have developed at a range of different scales in Europe. Local, regional, national, and transnational bodies have all helped to determine the shape of cultural tourism in all areas of Europe. This chapter examines the development and influence of policies at these different levels, and the relationships between them.

Richards (1995) has reviewed the development of tourism policy in the UK in relation to major political, economic, and social trends. The stages of tourism policy development broadly match those found in leisure and cultural policy in the UK (Henry, 1993), and parallel policy developments can also be found in other western European countries (Bramham *et al.*, 1993). In the immediate postwar phase of 'traditional pluralism', tourism and cultural policies were developed through voluntary sector initiatives, supported by the state where significant externalities, such as balance of payment benefits, could be identified. The growing importance of tourism and cultural consumption during the 1960s led to a new 'welfare reformism' policy style, which was marked by concerns for access to tourism and leisure consumption and the democratization of culture. Increased state intervention in tourism and culture at this time included the creation of national tourist boards, leisure and arts bodies. The broad political consensus supporting such intervention began to erode in the 1970s, as the oil crisis and economic restructuring forced many European governments to make significant cuts in public expenditure.

The following period of 'economic realism' in social policy in the UK (1976–1984) therefore signalled attempts to reduce welfare spending, and a focus in tourism, leisure and culture policies on attacking social problems such as unemployment and inner city decline (Coalter *et al.*, 1988). At the same time, tourism was identified as a potential job creator for the inner cities and, as unemployment soared, for the country as a whole. Growing economic and social uncertainty prompted increased interest in heritage, both as a means of regaining national pride and creating new jobs (Hewison, 1987). The National Heritage Act and the launch of major heritage tourism marketing initiatives date from this period. The shift towards 'disinvestment and the flexible state' (1984–1992) was marked by reductions in tourism and cultural spending, commercialization of state provision, and an economic development focus to tourism and cultural policy. In tourism, commercialization of local authority provision is also evident in the creation of visitor and convention bureaus (Richards, 1994), and tourism has also seen significant cuts in public sector spending (Richards, 1992). In culture and heritage there have been similar moves to reduce public sector funding and increase commercial revenues (see Gratton and Richards, Chapter 4 this volume).

Similar trends in policy development can be found in other western European countries. In Germany and The Netherlands, for example, state support for national tourism organizations has been reduced, and in Sweden the responsibility for tourism marketing has been completely given over to the private sector (Richards, 1995). In Italy, the Ministry of Tourism has been dismantled. In the cultural sector, public subsidies are increasingly being replaced by commercial sources (e.g. the National Lottery in the UK) or voluntary sector support (such as the creation of the Open Monument Association in the Netherlands, or proposals for a 'national trust' in France). Tourism and culture are increasingly viewed as productive activities which are able to support themselves through commercial activities, or through the direct or indirect support of participants.

The current policy climate for both tourism and culture in Europe therefore emphasizes the externalities to be gained from stimulating production, rather than subsidizing consumption. In such a climate it is not surprising that policies relating to tourism and culture exhibit a high degree of convergence, as both tourism and culture become primary elements of economic development strategies aimed at creating jobs and income, while the distribution of associated social and cultural benefits (such as social tourism or access to culture) is increasingly left to market forces.

The impact of changing economic and social conditions on cultural and tourism policy is perhaps most visible in European cities. Cities have been particularly hard hit by economic and social transitions which have devastated manufacturing industry and created structural unemployment problems. Culture and tourism have both become more central to the urban policy agenda as they are perceived as being important for the economic revitalization of cities, as tools for social integration and emancipation of multiethnic communities and the regeneration of the public functions of run-down inner city areas

(Corijn and Mommaas, 1995). Tourism and cultural policies have, therefore, become more integrated into economic development strategies, and the definitions of both 'culture' and 'tourism' have widened to facilitate the new economic role assigned to them.

The new economic focus of cultural and tourism development at local level is also reflected at national and European levels, as concerns about employment creation have pushed other issues further down the policy agenda. In spite of a shared wish to develop culture and cultural tourism, however, there is often a lack of coordination between the different policy levels, and frequent disagreement about how policies should be implemented. The following sections explore some of the major policy issues in cultural tourism at local, regional, national, and European levels. As numerous examples of the local and regional development of cultural tourism are covered in the national chapters in Part 2, the analysis here will concentrate on issues which illustrate wider European concerns.

REGIONAL AND LOCAL POLICIES

The development of policy relating to cultural tourism has perhaps been most evident at local level. Culture has been one of the main tools of economic restructuring in European cities in the past 20 years (Bianchini and Parkinson, 1993), as cities have struggled to replace lost productive capacity with consumption. In the increasingly competitive 'Europe of the Regions', culture has become a major tool for city marketing. Economic and social changes in rural areas, such as out-migration and the removal of land from agricultural production, have also stimulated cultural tourism development in the countryside, however. Programmes to develop 'agrotourism' are now a significant feature of local tourism development and marketing programmes, particularly in southern Europe (see Maiztegui-Oñate and Bertolín, Chapter 15 this volume, for example).

The new economic role of cultural development has been a major factor in persuading local authorities to develop cultural tourism. Expenditure on tourism development and marketing has often suffered from the perception that tourism facilities only benefit tourists, who by definition are not among the electorate for the local authority. By emphasizing the income and job creation benefits of tourism, and the fact that cultural facilities can benefit both residents and tourists, cultural tourism policies have succeeded in gaining more local support for tourism development than might otherwise have been the case. At the same time, however, the economic importance of tourism has created a competitive environment in which regions must compete for their share of the tourist market and the economic benefits that it can bring.

As competition between neighbouring cities and regions for tourist business increases, many cooperative ventures are being formed by local governments in different countries, who do not see each other as an immediate competitive threat. Transnational cooperation in the development of cultural tourism has also been promoted by a number of initiatives from the European Commission (see below). An example of such a development is the Art Cities in Europe network. A group of 30 cities in 11 European countries have joined together 'in the interest of culture, to make cultural activities and tourist services available to a wider public' (Art Cities in Europe, 1995). This is essentially a marketing initiative, which operates in conjunction with the German cultural tour operator IfB – *Institut für Bildungsreisen*. Through IfB the facilities offered by the various cities are bookable via the computer reservation systems START, AMADEUS and GALILEO. The brochure produced by the network gives details of cultural events and attractions in each city, as well as accommodation. The range of facilities offered in the brochure is heavily weighted towards 'high' culture, with a few notable exceptions, such as the promotion of comic books by Brussels, rugby in Cardiff and shopping in Manchester. The upmarket nature of the products is underlined by the selection of hotels, which are predominantly in the four or five star categories. The distribution of the cities participating in the network is also revealing. The majority of cities are located in north-west Europe, and a large number are also cities which have suffered from the decline of manufacturing in recent years, centres which Bianchini (1990) characterizes as 'declining cities'. In the UK, for example, the members are Glasgow, Manchester, Birmingham and Cardiff, all cities which have tried to use culture to stimulate economic regeneration in recent years. A similar picture emerges in France, where next to the established cultural capital, Paris, the brochure features Lyon, Dijon, and St Etienne. In southern Europe, the cities represented are largely established cultural centres, such as Madrid, Barcelona, and Lisbon.

In the struggle to attract more visitors, events and festivals are becoming a feature of local cultural tourism policies. Events serve to distinguish a city or region from its competitors, and can renew or animate an existing attraction-based tourist product (Richards, 1993). Although there is an enormous range of cultural events in Europe, from village festivals to the European City of Culture event (see Richards, Chapter 2 this volume), it is the large events which have attracted most attention. Harvey (1989) argues that the growth of 'blockbuster' events is a feature of the increasingly rapid turnover of consumption. Events, unlike material goods or fixed attractions, can generate new 'products' in a relatively short space of time, therefore generating repeat visits and higher spending.

Blockbuster events in themselves are not new. Major exhibitions and fairs have been regularly staged since the Great Exhibition of 1851, often attracting millions of visitors. Modern blockbusters are, however, quantitatively and qualitatively different from their predecessors. Before the Second World War, festivals were aimed largely at celebrating progress through production, but their modern equivalents are celebrations of consumption (Zukin, 1991).

Major exhibitions and festivals are also now more frequent, more geographi-cally widespread, and more specifically aimed at attracting tourists. In a survey of arts festivals in Britain, for example, Rolfe (1992) demonstrates that over 50% of existing arts festivals originated during the 1980s, and that this growth was at least partly aimed at increasing tourism to many towns and cities. In the USA, Janiske (1994) has demonstrated that the number of community festivals has grown exponentially over the past 40 years.

A comparison of visitors to the Rembrandt exhibitions in Amsterdam in 1969 and 1992 (Bruin, 1993) indicated that the proportion of international tourists visiting the exhibition in Amsterdam doubled between 1969 and 1992, to reach 45% of all visitors. The range of countries represented among the visitors was also much broader in 1992, which Bruin attributed to the globalization of the cultural tourism audience. The Rembrandt exhibition which toured Amsterdam, Berlin, and London in 1992 attracted 941,000 visitors in total, and illustrates that cultural tourists can now often choose the location where they want to see a particular exhibition. In the case of the Rembrandt exhibition, the proportion of international visitors was over 40% in Amsterdam and London, but only 20% in Berlin.

Numerous examples now exist of cities and regions combining event and attraction development to stimulate cultural tourism. The example of Glasgow, considered in Chapter 4, shows that new events can successfully attract tour-ists to new regions. Some doubts are now being expressed over the extent to which such 'marketing led' cultural policies produce long-term economic and social benefits. Henry (1994) describes the problems of the 'Right Post-Fordist' tourism strategy of Birmingham (UK) designed to create jobs and income through, among other things, the opening of a concert hall and the creation of a cultural industries quarter. This policy led to a diversion of funds from social and welfare purposes, with little apparent benefit to inner city residents, and has saddled the new facilities created with large debts.

The convergence of cultural tourism strategies adopted by cities across Europe, and the increasing cooperation evident between cities at European level reflects the fact that globalization has effectively decoupled urban identi-ties from national identities. Cities now increasingly position themselves cul-turally in a European, rather than a national context (Corijn and Mommaas, 1995). The diverging interests of national and local cultural tourism policies creates problems of coordination between different policy-making levels which are discussed in the next section.

NATIONAL POLICIES

As at local level, the development of tourism policy at national level in Europe usually has the twin goals of generating economic benefits and supporting culture, although at national level it is usually 'national culture' which is being promoted. Since the nineteenth century, culture has been used as a means of boosting feelings of national identity and cohesion. The democratization of culture was designed to support the national culture, and cultural policies aimed to promote access to high culture. The recent convergence of cultural and economic policies has therefore created challenges for administrations which were created on strict divisions between the cultural and economic spheres, and between high and popular culture. In the Netherlands, for example, the separate ministries of Culture and Economic Affairs have begun to work together to develop cultural tourism (albeit with different aims, see Richards, Chapter 13 this volume). In the UK the *de facto* convergence of culture, tourism and economy has been recognized in the creation of a separate ministry which combines these responsibilities (see Foley, Chapter 16 this volume).

In almost all cases, the identification of cultural tourism as a legitimate area of policy formation for national governments has come only recently. A review of cultural tourism policies in the European Union in 1992 undertaken for the ATLAS Cultural Tourism Project revealed that only two of the 12 member states then had a specific policy for cultural tourism. In some countries, such as Germany, the lack of a national policy stems from the fact that the government does not consider such central government intervention in tourism to be appropriate. In other cases, such as in the UK, cultural tourism is considered to be simply one part of a broader tourism product (Bonink, 1992).

A further barrier to cultural tourism policy development at national level has been the diverse range of interests involved. Both the 'tourism industry' and the 'cultural industries' are very fragmented, and as the national chapters in Part 2 of this volume illustrate, encouraging cooperation between cultural and tourism interests is not always easy. In Ireland, for example, responsibility for culture and tourism is spread over at least eight different public, commercial and voluntary sector bodies (see O Donnchadha and O Connor, Chapter 11 this volume), and Foley identifies a similar fragmentation of responsibility in the UK (Chapter 16 this volume). A major task of national bodies in developing cultural tourism is therefore to coordinate the work of tourism and cultural organizations to create a unified cultural tourism 'product'. In The Netherlands this has been achieved through the designation of specific themes by national government, which then delegated the coordination responsibility to specially created task forces (see Richards, Chapter 13 this volume). By moving cultural tourism development and promotion outside the direct control of the public sector, it is hoped to increase the speed and flexibility of decision-making, as well as overcoming conflicts of local and sectoral interests which often hinder the implementation of cultural tourism policy.

As at local level, the national cultural tourism policies which do exist tend to emphasize the economic aspects of cultural tourism development. This reflects not only the policy priorities of most national governments, but also the way in which policies have evolved. As Bonink (1992) has demonstrated in the UK and The Netherlands, the initiative for developing cultural tourism has usually come initially from those involved in tourism. Cultural organizations, formerly more concerned with attracting public subsidy, have only become actively involved as financial pressures have forced them to try and attract more visitors and generate more income. The common interest of the diverse range of bodies involved in creating the cultural tourism product is therefore inevitably an economic interest. In general, arts bodies have been more resistant than heritage organizations to commercialism and the development of cultural tourism, with the result that many national cultural tourism policies still focus mainly on heritage, rather than the arts. This is slowly changing as more arts organizations look to cultural tourism as a way of generating much-needed income (Arts Council of Great Britain, 1991).

In addition to stimulating economic development, cultural tourism is also perceived to have other advantages relating to the national development and management of tourism. Because every region has a culture to offer for tourist consumption, cultural tourism is considered to be a good means of combatting the regional imbalance of tourism evident in many countries. Cultural tourists, it is argued, are less likely to congregate in overcrowded coastal resorts, and are more likely to travel further afield to seek out cultural features of specific interest to them. This idea has been central to the development of many cultural attractions in peripheral areas, which are often over-dependent on natural resources for their tourist flows (e.g. Friesland in The Netherlands). The concept of using culture to spread tourists geographically is also behind the creation of national and European 'Cultural Itineraries' (see below). As a form of 'special interest tourism' (Weiler and Hall, 1992) cultural tourism is also used as a means of tackling seasonality in many local and national tourism policies. The development of heritage tourism was a cornerstone of the attempt by the British Tourist Authority to attract off-peak tourists in the 'Britain for All Seasons' marketing campaign.

A glance at the range of different national approaches to cultural tourism policy contained in the chapters in Part 2 of this book reveals a continuum of different approaches ranging from 'top-down' to 'bottom-up' policy development. In the Netherlands, the initial approach to policy development was firmly centralized and top-down. An initial review of the cultural tourism market and the supply of heritage attractions by national government resulted in a national tourism policy containing clear cultural tourism themes, and with clearly identified policy implementation mechanisms and budget allocations (see Richards, Chapter 13 this volume). In Denmark, on the other hand, the much slower development of cultural tourism policy can in part be attributed to the lack of centralized decision-making, and a cultural policy based on principles of public access and artistic autonomy (see Hjalager, Chapter 7 this volume). In most countries, the development of policy falls somewhere between these two models, with government initiatives attempting to coordinate the actions of a wide range of public, voluntary and commercial actors in developing cultural tourism.

A further important aspect of national cultural policy which concerns tourism is the protection of the 'national heritage' usually by preventing artworks going abroad, but occasionally through repatriation of works which have been acquired by foreign owners. Most countries have regulations governing the export of 'cultural property', which often means antiquities. In Greece and Egypt, for example, all antiquities are deemed to be the property of the state, and may not be exported. In Britain, the laws are somewhat more flexible, as recent arguments about the export of 'national treasures' such as the Three Graces statue illustrate. The struggle between the place-specific heritage and globalized market forces are therefore regulated by government policy. The need to retain important elements of the heritage has become even more important as cultural tourism has grown, and competition to attract cultural visitors has increased.

The Acropolis in Athens, for example, has attracted much attention as the focus of an international row over the ownership of cultural heritage. The Parthenon, constructed on the Acropolis in the fifth century BC, was decorated with superb marble sculptures. These survived almost intact until the occupation of Greece by the Turks in the seventeenth century. Lord Elgin, British Ambassador to the Ottoman Empire at the end of the eighteenth century, was appalled to find that the Parthenon was rapidly becoming a ruin. He obtained a permit from the Turkish authorities allowing him to remove the sculptures from the site, in order, as he believed, to save them from destruction. The 'Elgin Marbles', as they became known, including half of the original frieze, were later presented to the British Museum.

The Greeks themselves bitterly resented the removal of pieces of the greatest symbol of Ancient Greece, and the single most important national monument. There have been numerous attempts to secure the return of the Elgin Marbles to Greece, and there were even signs that in the early 1960s the British Foreign Office had some sympathy with the Greek position (Bailey, 1994). However, the position of the British Museum has always been that the Marbles were legally obtained, and that the museum has a legal obligation not to dispose of its acquisitions. It is also argued that the Marbles are currently enjoyed by millions of visitors to the British Museum, and many museum curators are worried by the precedent which might be set if the Marbles were returned.

The debate over the ownership of the Elgin Marbles flared again in the 1980s when Melina Mercouri became Greek Culture Minister. She pledged to make return of the Marbles a top priority. 'It's my life work to get the Marbles back to Greece. The Marbles are our soul'. Pressure on Britain to return the Marbles will increase with the construction of a $100 million (ECU 80 million) museum to house the existing Parthenon sculptures, which will leave space for the Elgin Marbles.

This debate over the ownership of cultural property is just one example of a growing problem in relation to 'movable cultural heritage', which is now developing at European level. Much controversy still surrounds cultural objects removed from various countries during the Second World War, for example. In the case of the Parthenon, however, the debate has taken on a much wider significance, because it concerns an element of the cultural heritage which is not just culturally significant as a symbol of European culture, but also a tourist icon for Greece itself. Not only would the return of the Marbles be a significant psychological boost for the Greek nation, but it would also provide a substantial economic boost by increasing the flow of cultural tourists to Athens.

The increasing globalization of cultural production and consumption also means that governments are increasingly working together to stimulate cultural developments of mutual benefit. A good example of this is the recent donation of Fl 2.3 million (ECU 1 million) to the UNESCO masterplan for the development of the Hermitage in St Petersburg, Russia. The money comes from funds allocated by the Dutch Government to development projects in Eastern Europe. The funding agreement was signed in December 1993 at the opening of the 'Kingdom of the Scythians' exhibition in Amsterdam, which was staged using some of the Hermitage's most prized exhibits. A proportion of the entrance fees from the exhibition was also donated to the Hermitage. The Hermitage also loaned objects for the Fine Art Fair in Maastricht in 1994, and the Dutch and Russian governments are currently negotiating over the return of the Koenig drawing collection to The Netherlands.

TRANSNATIONAL POLICIES

Policies which influence the development of cultural tourism at a transnational level come mainly from the European Union, but increasingly the work of the Council of Europe and UNESCO have begun to have an influence on areas inside and outside the EU.

The European Union

The original Treaty of Rome (1957) envisaged no specific cultural role for the European Union, which was then seen basically as an economic union. As culture became increasingly important as an economic sphere of activity during the 1960s and 1970s, however, it became increasingly difficult for the EU to refrain from intervening in cultural affairs. In fact, Jean Monnet is reputed to have said 'if we had to do it all again, I would start with culture'.

Calls for the EU to be actively involved in the field of culture first emerged in the late 1960s and early 1970s. In 1974, the European Parliament passed a resolution calling for Union action in the field of culture, and passing a resolution on measures to protect the European cultural heritage. Progress was slow until 1977, when the Commission decided to re-interpret the Treaty of Rome, which was henceforth considered to apply to the field of culture as well as other fields of social and economic activity. Culture was defined as 'the socio-economic whole formed by persons and undertakings dedicated to the production and distribution of cultural goods and services'. This was effectively an economic definition which allowed the EU to intervene in culture on economic grounds.

In 1982, the Commission outlined the nature of such intervention, leaving most cultural action to the member states, and limiting direct EU action to 'high profile initiatives' designed to boost the image of the Union. These measures included the formation of the EU youth orchestra, the restoration of the Parthenon, and the launch of the European City of Culture event (see Richards, Chapter 2 this volume). In spite of the recognition of the importance of culture, however, EU action 'amounted to no more than a disjointed, poorly structured and clearly inadequate response' (European Commission, 1992a).

More concerted action in the field of culture began in 1987, when a Committee on Cultural Affairs was established, and the EU set out its cultural role in the document *A Fresh Boost for Culture in the European Community* (European Commission, 1987). Growing EU interest in cultural affairs was finally consolidated in 1991 with the inclusion of article 128 in the Treaty of Maastricht, which explicitly defines a cultural role for the Union. Union action is envisaged in the following areas:

- improvement of the knowledge and dissemination of the culture and history of the European peoples;
- conservation and safeguarding of cultural heritage of European significance;
- non-commercial cultural exchanges;
- artistic and literary creation, including in the audio-visual sector.

In its review of *New Prospects for Community Cultural Action* (1992a), the Commission identified a twofold 'cultural challenge' facing the Union in its new role:

> Cultural action should contribute to the flowering of national and regional cultural identities and at the same time reinforce the feeling that, despite their cultural diversity, Europeans share a common cultural heritage and common values. (p. 1)

The basic aims of Union cultural action are therefore:

- to preserve Europe's past by helping to conserve and increase awareness of our common cultural heritage in all its forms;
- to generate an environment conducive to the development of culture in Europe;

- to help ensure that the influence of European culture is felt throughout the world by encouraging cooperation with non-member countries.

The role of cultural heritage in achieving these aims is seen as particularly important, and a special programme for cultural heritage, called 'Raphaël', was drawn up in 1995 to guide EU activities in this area. The main objectives of the Raphaël Programme are to:

- help to preserve and promote cultural heritage;
- encourage cooperation and the pooling of knowledge, expertise and practice in the field of heritage preservation at European level;
- improve public access to heritage and the supply of information on it for the public at large so as to contribute to the affirmation of a European citizenship through greater knowledge of heritage;
- provide support for enriching mutual understanding and practices and realize Europe's potential;
- foster cooperation with non-member countries and other international organizations, in particular the Council of Europe (European Commission, 1995).

In achieving these objectives, actions will be taken under the Raphaël Programme between 1996 and 2000 to develop and promote cultural heritage, stimulate networks and innovation and develop networks and partnerships. The proposed budget for the programme is ECU 70 million, 50% of which will be allocated to the development and promotion of heritage, including support for some 250 sites and 10 'memorable sites' projects.

Tourism therefore has an important role to play in the attainment of the cultural aims of the EU. Tourism can help to conserve and increase awareness of cultural heritage, and is important in transmitting European culture to other parts of the world. Equally, as the *Community Action Plan for Tourism* (European Commission, 1992b) recognizes, visitor management is required to ensure that the European cultural heritage survives the growth of tourism.

The development of tourism policy in the EU mirrors that of cultural policy. Tourism was not specifically mentioned in the Treaty of Rome, and so measures affecting tourism have developed largely in the context of wider economic or competition policy. Proposals for Union action in the field of tourism began to emerge in 1983, when the importance of coordinating tourism policy across all areas of EU activity became apparent. However, it was not until the Single European Act of 1986 that tourism was fully accepted as an area for Union intervention (Von Molkte, 1993). The first formal meeting of European Tourism Ministers took place in December 1988, and, following proposals from the Commission, 1990 was designated as European Tourism Year. A large number of the actions undertaken in 1990 were related to cultural tourism (Long and Richards, 1995). The EU now feels it is important to stimulate cultural tourism in Europe as a 'new tourist product', which can contribute to improving the competitive position of European tourism, providing employment, lessening pressure on the environment and developing a higher quality of tourism product. Cultural tourism is therefore regarded as playing an important role in developing sustainable tourism in Europe (Von Molkte, 1993).

In spite of the growing recognition of the importance of tourism within the Commission, EU policy on tourism is still constrained by the fact that tourism, like culture, is not specifically mentioned as an area of activity in the Treaty of Rome. This means that EU intervention in tourism, as in the area of culture, can only be justified if it stimulates economic activity. There is a possibility that this will change after ratification of the Treaty on European Union in 1996. DGXXIII is pushing for tourism to be included in the new treaty, and it is likely that culture will also form a specific area for Union action. After 1996, therefore, it is possible that the scope for actions to implement tourism policy at European Union level will be greatly enhanced, as will the funds available to do so (the current DGXXIII tourism budget is only ECU 6 million per year).

Even if tourism and culture are specified in the new Treaty, however, EU action will still be constrained by the important concept of 'subsidiarity'. Subsidiarity means that no actions should be taken at European level which could be taken at national or regional levels. This implies that EU action in the field of cultural tourism, as in all other policy areas, should be of a transnational nature, and should not duplicate activities which could be undertaken by national or regional bodies. This explains to some extent why EU-funded cultural tourism programmes have tended to concentrate on transnational cultural itineraries and marketing programmes in border regions, which clearly require transnational cooperation to succeed.

DGXXIII has supported over 50 projects linked to the development of cultural and rural tourism since 1991 (European Commission, 1994a). For example, the Phoenician Route Project aims to link areas around the Mediterranean settled by the Phoenicians through a series of guide books, cultural tours and the creation of tour operator packages. The Route to the Roots Project aims to market Europe to Americans whose ancestors emigrated from the Old World. The project will link the major ports used by emigrants, such as Rotterdam, Bremen, Hamburg, and Liverpool, with the major home regions of the emigrant communities, such as Saxony in Germany (Richards and Bonink, 1995). These projects are designed as pilot projects which spearhead the development of cultural tourism and act as a catalyst to developments in other countries and regions.

However, the EU can assist the development of cultural tourism in a particular country or region where this is deemed important for European tourism as a whole. This argument has been used to finance restoration work on monuments and sites 'that are particularly important to European culture' (European Commission, 1994b). In 1993, for example, ECU 4.25 million was given to 'symbolic' restoration projects in Greece (Mount Athos in Macedonia and the Acropolis in Athens) and Portugal (Chiado in Lisbon). The concept that certain elements of the cultural heritage belong to a wider, European culture has echoes of the modernist concept of a universal culture with its roots in Europe (see Richards, Chapter 1 this volume).

Most EU funding for tourism is, however, channelled through regional development funds, which are the responsibility of DGXVI. EU regional development aid to tourism projects amounted to ECU 1684 million between 1989 and 1993, or 5.6% of total aid from the structural funds (European Commission, 1994b), and much of this aid went to projects linked to cultural heritage. EU regional development funding has been particularly important in peripheral regions (see Chapters 11 and 14). In Portugal, for example, EU regional aid has accounted for about 60% of expenditure on national cultural tourism programmes.

DGX of the Commission has also been involved in funding cultural tourism development through funding for heritage preservation. A number of pilot projects designed to protect the European architectural heritage have been undertaken, with projects covering themes such as religious and civil monuments (1989), historic urban and rural buildings (1990), testimonies to agricultural and industrial production (1991), conservation in towns and villages (1992), gardens of historic interest (1993), historic buildings related to entertainment and the performing arts (1994), and religious monuments (1995). The total support provided for the 257 projects undertaken between 1989 and 1994 was ECU 15.9 million.

The Council of Europe

The Council of Europe was founded in 1949. Its aim is

> to achieve greater unity between its members to safeguard the European heritage and to facilitate their economic and social progress through discussion and common action in economic, social, cultural, educational, scientific, legal and administrative matters and in the maintenance of human rights and fundamental freedoms.

> (Darvill, 1994:64)

Unlike the transnational European Union, the Council of Europe is an international body, which relies on coordinated action by individual nation states. The Council of Europe therefore has no specific powers beyond those of its national members, and it has no independent source of funding.

The main concerns of the Council of Europe in the field of culture are the concept of cultural democracy, the role of the animateur, the impact of the cultural industries and the financing of culture (Fisher, 1990). The Council of Europe has been particularly active in the area of cultural heritage, and sees cultural tourism as a means of spreading awareness of European heritage. Tourism is also increasingly coming to be seen as a source of funding to support culture. The aims of the Council of Europe in relation to cultural tourism are primarily cultural, a feature which clearly distinguishes its policies from those of the European Union. Issues of interest to the Council of Europe itself in the broad field of culture include:

- human rights (including cultural rights);
- the intercultural, and the multicultural;
- cultural identity;
- recognition of minorities;
- cultural tolerance and solidarity;
- the new humanism (Ronconi, 1994).

As early as 1964, the Council of Europe began to consider the development of cultural routes as a means of increasing awareness of European culture through travel. These initial deliberations led in 1987 to a number of activities designed to establish 'European Cultural Routes', linked at a transnational level (Council of Europe, 1988). The Cultural Routes Project has three aims.

1. To make Europe's common cultural identity more apparent and better appreciated and to bring the European public face to face with its shared cultural identity;
2. To safeguard and enhance the European cultural heritage as a means of improving daily life and as a source of social, economic and cultural development;
3. To provide the public with a new scope for fulfilment in their leisure hours by according a special place to cultural tourism and related practices.

The cultural routes must cross more than one country or region, and be 'organized around themes whose historical, artistic or social interest is patently European' (Council of Europe, 1988). There are now ten such routes, including the Santiago de Compostella Route, the Baltic States, Mozart, the Baroque (see Bauer, Chapter 8 this volume for a description of the Baroque Route in France), the Silk Routes, and the Heinrich Schickhardt Route. The Schickhardt Route, for example, traces the travels of the seventeenth century German architect, linking German and French communities on either side of the Rhine. This route has brought together public and private sector partners in Germany and France, and has produced a range of publications, educational materials, media coverage, and package tour products (Voisin, 1992). Full descriptive itineraries for the routes have been produced (Hernando, 1991), and there are plans to create a number of new routes, including a Goethe Route, a Vivaldi Route, an Iron Route, and a Danube Route (Council of Europe, 1992). These developments are predominantly based on a notion of 'high culture' tourism resources, and there are some doubts as to the effectiveness of the routes in attracting large numbers of tourists (Richards and Bonink, 1995).

The distinction between the forms of consumption presented by the Council of Europe programme and 'ordinary' tourism is summed up by the emphasis on 'not sightseeing, but lifeseeing'. The role of the routes is viewed from a socio-pedagogical perspective – the basic idea being that the public for these routes consists of tourists plus communities.

The Council of Europe approach is now beginning to influence the development of cultural tourism beyond Europe as well. The Council of Europe model has, for example, been adopted by UNESCO for their Silk Road project, which aims 'to make people living in the present day aware of the need for a renewed dialogue among themselves, and to help them rediscover the historical record of human understanding and communication which provided a mutual enrichment for the different civilizations along these roads'.

The Council of Europe has also had a role in promoting the conservation of 'cultural landscapes'. The Council of Europe initially concentrated on individual buildings designated under the Convention for the Protection of the Architectural Heritage of Europe, signed in Granada in 1985. In recent years, however, attention has also been paid to the wider issue of whole 'cultural landscapes' including both natural and built heritage features. The Council of Europe is therefore in the process of drawing up a European Recommendation on the conservation and management of Cultural Landscape Areas (Darvill, 1994).

UNESCO programmes

The United Nations Educational, Scientific and Cultural Organization (UNESCO) is an intergovernmental agency of the United Nations which has an important role in cultural development. UNESCO facilitates international exchange of knowledge through seminars, meetings, publications, and information campaigns. One of its major campaigns has been the preservation of cultural heritage, which began with the adoption of the World Heritage Convention in 1974. A World Heritage Committee appointed by UNESCO decides which monuments, sites or even whole cities are eligible for inclusion on the World Heritage List (see Richards, Chapter 1 this volume). The Committee also recommends the allocation of assistance from the World Heritage Fund for the protection of these sites. As in the case of most national inventories of heritage sites, the World Heritage List has grown rapidly in recent years, from 288 sites in 1988, to 322 in 1991, and 441 in 1994. In spite of the worldwide coverage of the list, European sites still dominate, with 12 EU states accounting for a quarter of all listings in 1991.

The impact of listing by UNESCO can be significant. For example, Melegati (1994:15) reports that '(t)he first time international opinion began really to be moved by the war in former Yugoslavia was when ancient Ragusa – modern Dubrovnik – . . . designated by UNESCO a monument of world importance, was shelled by Serbian forces'. In spite of the UNESCO listing, however, some 68% of the buildings within the city walls sustained damage. After the shelling,

UNESCO organized a census of affected buildings, and set up a system of adoption, where money can be donated to restore specific buildings.

The European Travel Commission

The European Travel Commission (ETC), the body responsible for the worldwide promotion of Europe as a tourism destination, has recognized that 'Europe's culture is the foremost motivation for travel from overseas'. The ETC sees culture not only as an essential binding force for a 'European tourism product', but also as a source of essential differences that can make Europe appear 'exotic' to visitors from other world regions. 'Conserving this exoticism is the best way of ensuring "sustainable tourism"' according to the ETC (European Travel Commission, 1994:33).

Policy tensions in Europe

The differing context, goals, and application of cultural tourism policies at different levels inevitably leads to tensions between policies implemented at different administrative levels. As Ashworth (1992) has pointed out, the success of heritage tourism depends on its ability to appeal to tourists. A unified 'European Culture' may therefore seem an appropriate product for the EU to market to Americans or Japanese tourists, but this is likely to be fiercely resisted by national tourism administrations jealously guarding their own national identity. Homogeneous national heritage products are in turn likely to be resisted by regional and local bodies, with a vested interest in preserving and promoting their own culture. As Europe increasingly becomes a 'Europe of the Regions', this problem is likely to increase.

Growing competition in cultural tourism supply is likely to be exacerbated by the fact that the base market for cultural tourism is not expanding as fast in the 1990s as it did in previous decades (see Richards, Chapter 2 this volume). The future development of cultural tourism in Europe is therefore likely to see a growing number of cultural tourism products chasing a stable and relatively small group of up-market tourists. At all levels of policy-making there also remains a crucially important and largely unresolved issue: that of effectiveness. Cultural tourism is promoted by public sector bodies across Europe, and yet the extent to which cultural tourism fulfils the basic goals assigned to it, primarily the creation of income and the support and dissemination of culture, is largely unknown. Isolated economic impact studies have indicated the amount of money spent by cultural tourists in different locations (see Gratton and Richards, Chapter 4 this volume), but their has been far less consideration of the extent to which this expenditure is additional, or directly related to culture, or being fed back into cultural provision. Unless the longer-term benefits of cultural tourism development become more evident, the current enthusiasm for such development among policy-makers could well decline.

In assessing the benefits of cultural tourism development, the crucial question will remain: whose culture is being developed, and for whom? This issue is highlighted by the political struggles surrounding the European City of Culture Event (Boyle and Hughes, 1991; Corijn and Van Praet, 1994). The growing economic focus of the event has led to accusations that local culture is being ignored in favour of a more globalized, and therefore more accessible international culture, and that the interests of visitors are being served above those of local residents. Many authors have also argued that we should not lose sight of the fact that there are basic cultural values at stake as well as economic ones. For example, the report of the English conference on Silk Routes in 1992 (Thomas, 1992:13) notes:

> The Council of Europe is one of the few European institutions which can use cultural cooperation programmes to help get Europe, the whole of Europe, out of the absurd conflict between unity and diversity in which it is perversely locked. In other words, at a time when nationalist wars are being waged on European soil, it cannot be the Council of Europe's job to promote the 'economic product' aspect of cultural tourism. Quite the contrary, its role is in the vanguard, and on the side of moral values.

Although the commodification of culture implied by cultural tourism development may be distasteful to some, the increasing convergence of economic and cultural policies at all administrative levels in Europe make it increasingly difficult to ignore. From a theoretical perspective, the growth of interest in local cultures may well be linked to the alienation and uncertainty caused by globalization and time–space compression (Harvey, 1989), but at a practical level, culture is one of the few resources that policy-makers can use to create competitive advantage for their countries or regions in an increasingly competitive European and global tourism market. The national chapters in Part 2 of this volume contain numerous examples of the use of culture to develop and promote tourism across Europe.

REFERENCES

Art Cities in Europe (1995) Cities Brochure. Art Cities in Europe, Constance.

Arts Council of Great Britain (1991) Today's Arts Tomorrow's Tourists. ACGB, London.

Ashworth, G.J. (1992) Heritage and tourism: an argument, two problems and three solutions. In: Fleischer-van Rooijen, C.A.M. (ed.) Spatial Implications of Tourism. Geo Pers, Groningen, pp. 95–104.

Bailey, M. (1994) Britain's Foreign Office would have returned the Elgin Marbles. The Art Newspaper 34, 17.

Bianchini, F. (1990) Cultural policy and urban development: the experience of West European cities. Paper delivered at the conference: Cultural Policy and Urban Regeneration: The West European Experience, Liverpool, 30–31 October 1990.

Bianchini, F. and Parkinson, M. (1993) *Cultural Policy and Urban Regeneration: the West European Experience*. Manchester University Press, Manchester.

Bonink, C. (1992) Cultural tourism development and government policy. MA dissertation, Rijksunivesiteit Utrecht.

Boyle, M. and Hughes, G. (1991) The politics of 'the real': discourses from the Left on Glasgow's role as European City of Culture, 1990. *Area* 23, 217–228.

Bramham, P., Henry, I.P., van der Poel, H. and Mommaas, H. (1993) *Leisure Policies in Europe*. CAB International, Wallingford.

Bruin, K. (1993) Rembrandt in Amsterdam, Berlijn en Londen. In: Bevers, T. (ed.) *De Kunstwereld: Produktie, Distributie en Receptie in de Wereld van Kunst en Cultuur*. Erasmus Universiteit Rotterdam, pp. 336–377.

Coalter, F., Long, J. and Duffield, B. (1988) *Recreational Welfare: the Rationale for Public Leisure Policy*. Avebury, Aldershot.

Corijn, E. and Mommaas, H. (1995) *Urban Cultural Policy Developments in Europe*. Council of Europe, Strasbourg.

Corijn, E. and Van Praet, S. (1994) Antwerp 93 in the context of European cultural capitals: art policy as politics. Paper presented at the Conference on City Cultures, Lifestyles and Consumption Practices, Coimbra, 15–16 July 1994.

Council of Europe (1988) European Cultural Routes. *ICCE (88) 9*, Council of Europe, Strasbourg.

Council of Europe (1992) Cultural Routes of the Council of Europe. *ICCE (92)* 21, 11pp.

Darvill, T. (1994) Planning, tourism, and cultural landscapes. *Tourism Recreation Research* 19, 59–64.

European Commission (1987) *A Fresh Boost for Culture in the European Community*. EC, Brussels.

European Commission (1992a) *New Prospects for Community Cultural Action*. EC, Brussels.

European Commission (1992b) *Community Action Plan to Assist Tourism*. DGXXIII, EC, Brussels.

European Commission (1994a) *Eurotourism: Countryside and Culture*. DGXXIII, EC, Brussels.

European Commission (1994b) *Report from the Commission to the European Parliament and the Economic and Social Committee on Community Measures Affecting Tourism*. Com(94) 74, Brussels.

European Commission (1995) *European Community Action in Support of Culture: Raphaël*. COM(95) 110, Brussels.

European Travel Commission (1994) *Annual Report*. ETC, Paris.

Fisher, R. (1990) *Who Does What in Europe?* Arts Council, London.

Harvey, D. (1989) *The Condition of Postmodernity*. Oxford, Basil Blackwell.

Henry, I.P. (1993) *The Politics of Leisure Policy*. Macmillan, Basingstoke.

Henry, I.P. (1994) Leisure research and politics: the British tradition. *Vrijetijd en Samenleving* 12 (4), 19–31.

Hernando, F.L. (1991) *Guide of the Cultural Itineraries of the European Regions*. ARE Permanent Delegation for Tourism, Madrid.

Hewison, R. (1987) *The Heritage Industry: Britain in a Climate of Decline.* Methuen, London.

Janiske, R.L. (1994) Some macroscale growth trends in America's community festival industry. *Festival Management and Event Tourism* 2, 10–14.

Long, J. and Richards, G. (1995) European tourism: changing economic and cultural dimensions of tourism in a unifying Europe. Paper presented at the European Leisure Studies Group Winter University, Bilbao, April.

Melegati, L. (1994) Unesco coordinating the effort to restore Dubrovnik. *The Art Newspaper* 35, 15.

Richards, G. (1992) *The UK Local Authority Tourism Survey 1991.* Centre for Leisure and Tourism Studies, University of North London.

Richards, G. (1994) *The Operation of Visitor and Convention Bureaux in the United States: Implications for Europe.* British Travel Education Trust, London.

Richards, G. (1995) The politics of national tourism policy in Britain. *Leisure Studies* 14, 153–173.

Richards, G. and Bonink, C. (1995) Marketing European cultural tourism. *Journal of Vacation Marketing* 1, 173–180.

Richards, W.S. (1993) *How to Market Tourist Attractions, Festivals and Events.* Longman, London.

Rolfe, H. (1992) *Arts Festivals in the UK.* Policy Studies Institute, London.

Ronconi, D. (1994) Les Réseaux Culturels et Leurs Rapports avec les Institutions Culturelles et les Opérateurs Culturels et Touristiques. Paper presented at the conference Eurotourism: Culture and Countryside, Athens, May.

Thomas, M. (1992) The Silk Routes: launch of the English project. *ICEE SOIE* (92) 19, Council of Europe, Strasbourg.

Voisin, J-C. (1992) A European cultural itinerary, Heinrich Schickhardt: evaluation. *COE ICCE* (92), 17, Council of Europe, Strasbourg.

Von Molkte, H. (1993) *Quality Tourism on a European Scale.* Forum dello Sviluppo, Turin.

Weiler, B. and Hall, C.M. (1992) *Special Interest Tourism.* Belhaven Press, London.

Zukin, S. (1991) *Landscapes of Power: from Detroit to Disney World.* University of California Press, Berkeley.

NATIONAL ANALYSES 2

Cultural Tourism in Belgium   6

W. MUNSTERS

Faculty of Hospitality Management, Hogeschool Maastricht, PO Box 3900, 6202 NX Maastricht, The Netherlands and *Centre for Postgraduate Studies of the University of Limburg, Diepenbeek, Belgium*

INTRODUCTION

As in all the countries in north-western Europe where beach holidays are very dependent on the weather, culture is for Belgium a substantial element of the tourism product, and represents one of the most important attractions in the framework of tourism marketing policy. An essential asset for developing cultural tourism in this country is the historical consciousness of the Belgian people. Their remarkable interest in and knowledge of the country's heritage is to be attributed to the age-long struggle their ancestors had to wage against foreign occupying powers, including the Spanish, the French, and the Dutch. The preservation of cultural identity offered a reliable beacon during times of political and military oppression that lasted until 1830, the year in which the Belgians gained their independence. The importance of cultural and historical knowledge is reflected in the programmes of the institutes for tourism education which traditionally pay much attention to the history of art and civilization. Thus, it may safely be said that cultural tourism finds receptive ground in Belgium.

SUPPLY AND FUNDING OF CULTURAL ATTRACTIONS

One of the strengths of Belgium as a tourism product is the diversity and the concentration of the cultural–historic as well as the artistic heritage. All categories of cultural attractions and events covered by the typology of Munsters

Table 6.1.   General typology of cultural tourism resources.

1. Attractions
  (a) Monuments
      Religious buildings
      Public buildings
      Historic houses
      Castles and palaces
      Parks and gardens
      Defences
      Archaeological sites
      Industrial–archaeological buildings
  (b) Museums
      Folklore museums
      Art museums
  (c) Routes
      Cultural–historic routes
      Art routes
  (d) Theme parks
      Cultural–historic parks
      Archaeological parks
      Architecture parks

2. Events
  (a) Cultural–historic events
      Religious festivals
      Secular festivals
      Folk festivals
  (b) Art events
      Art exhibitions
      Art festivals

Source: Adapted after Munsters (1994).

(1994) (Table 6.1) can be found in Belgium, within a radius of 100 km from the centrally situated capital Brussels. With regard to the distribution of cultural tourism resources in Belgium as a whole, Flanders (northern Belgium) can – generally speaking – be considered as a region characterized by an extensive medieval heritage resulting from a long period of economic prosperity, whereas the Walloon provinces of southern Belgium possess a richer supply of industrial archaeology dating from the Industrial Revolution.

Attractions

Monuments

The most important cultural–historic and artistic monuments include:

- religious buildings: the Gothic Cathedral of Our Lady in Antwerp; the norbertine abbey of Floreffe;
- public buildings: the Gothic Town Hall on the Grand-Place of Brussels;
- historic houses: the *beguinages* (almshouses) of Bruges, Louvain and Diest; the medieval merchant houses in Ghent;
- castles and palaces: the medieval complex of Alden-Biesen;
- parks and gardens: the French and English gardens of Beloeil and of Annevoie;
- defences: the Roman Walls round Tongeren;
- industrial buildings and machinery: the industrial–archaeological site of Grand-Hornu in the former mining area Borinage.

Museums

Folklore museums

This category covers a large number of indoor museums with a general character, such as the Museum of the Living in the Walloon provinces in Liège. These museums give an impression of the various aspects of the folk culture: furniture, agricultural tools, old crafts, traditional customs and art forms.

A separate category is composed of the thematic museums which have specialized in a particular element of the cultural–historic heritage, for example:

- artistic crafts: the Museum of Lacework in Marche-en-Famenne;
- festivals: the International Museum of the Carnival and the Mask in Binche;
- industrial archaeology: the Mine-museum in Beringen.

Also worth mentioning is Bokrijk, an open air-museum for the Flemish folk culture offering a collection of reconstructed farms, mills, barns and other buildings from the countryside.

Art museums

The Royal Museums for Fine Arts of Belgium in Brussels present the rich history of Belgian painting from the Middle Ages to the twentieth century. The park of Middelheim in Antwerp is an open-air art museum containing a collection of nineteenth and twentieth century sculptures.

The policy of the art museums is aimed at improving accessibility for the public. To this end they develop interactive events, such as the action *Musée en famille* of 30 Walloon museums which takes place every year during the first weekend of June and which encourages families to a surprising and amusing museum visit by means of rallies, searches, and voyages of discovery (Hut, 1992).

Routes

Cultural–historic and art routes are often inspired by a theme making it possible to link places of interest.

Built heritage

In this case a particular type of monument serves as guideline, for example the *beguinages* in the cities and characteristic regional farms in the countryside.

Gastronomy

Regional products of farming and fishing provide the themes for routes such as the hop route round Poperinge and the gin route in the province East Flanders.

Theme parks

Mini-Europe in Brussels is an architecture park presenting miniatures of the landmarks of the EU countries, including the Acropolis, the Arc de Triomphe and Big Ben.

Events

Cultural–historic events

Religious festivals

Tourist attractions with a religious background include the processions that are held each year in cities such as Bruges, Veurne, and Tournai. Saint Hubert is known for the pilgrimage that is organized yearly at the beginning of November. The high mass in the basilica dedicated to Saint Hubert, the patron saint of hunting, is followed by the consecration of the dogs and a hunt in the wooded hills of the Ardennes.

Secular festivals

This category includes the feasts that bring to life aspects of the folk culture during a particular historical period, for example the five-yearly parade of Louvain which in 1993 represented the Burgundian age. The parades of giants also belong to these celebrations. These processions, such as the Gouyasse Vespers-parade of Ath, are inspired by the medieval popular belief in the protecting power of superhuman beings.

Besides the parades, one should mention the celebrations that go back to folk traditions which marked the main moments of professional life in early times, especially in farming and fishing:

- the harvest festivals of Aalst, offering parades of ancient agricultural machinery and demonstrations of old crafts, such as threshing;
- the shrimp feasts and parade of Oost-Duinkerke where the prawning is done in the old-fashioned way by fishermen on horses.

Folk festivals

The vivacious folk music, folk songs and folk dances are the breeding ground for a flourishing folk festival tourism. Some festivals have specialized in folk dance (the international dance festivals of Jambes and Schoten) and some in folk music (the folk festival of Dranouter).

Art events

Art exhibitions

Belgium offers a broad range of visual and performing arts events. Measured by their impact on domestic and incoming tourism the most important kinds of art exhibitions are exhibitions about civilized peoples, such as 'The Gold of the Scythians' (Brussels, 1991) and 'Precolumbian Art' (Brussels, 1992) and masterpiece exhibitions presenting a survey of the oeuvre of a painter such as 'Hans Memling, Five Centuries of Reality and Fiction' (Bruges, 1994).

Art festivals

The biennial Europalia is a total festival that encompasses the various facets of the art and the culture of one particular country: music, opera, ballet, dance, theatre, film, literature. The organizers invite not only European countries to present themselves, such as Italy (1969), France (1975) or Greece (1982), but also – in spite of the festival's name – Asian (Japan, 1989) and American (Mexico, 1993) countries.

Events and attractions

Various events can be connected with cultural attractions: performances (theatre, music, dance), demonstrations, exhibitions, markets, and (guided) tours. Thanks to their motivating power, these events are an excellent way to revive heritage and to attract the less culturally minded tourist towards monuments and museums. Major crowd-pullers are events in which the built heritage plays the key role. A good example is provided by the annual Open Monument Days that since 1989 have given a broad public free access to monuments (many of which are not usually open to the public) in order to stimulate interest in historical buildings. Each year a different theme is chosen, such as the relationship between architecture and light in Flanders in 1993 and industrial heritage in the Walloon provinces in 1994.

Classical music is on the programme of the yearly Festival of Flanders and its counterpart the Festival of the Walloon provinces. What makes these festivals very special, is the fact that the concerts are given in the historical surroundings of cathedrals, abbeys and castles.

Other, more local events include the medieval fair in the castle of Bouillon, where the visitor can attend duels, jousts, competitions of archery and historical meals, and the gin feasts in Hasselt where the National Gin Museum is the centre of activities. The Gin Museum gives demonstrations of distilling, and serves as the starting point of a gin route leading the public to other industrial–archaeological sites in the town.

CULTURAL TOURISM PRODUCT DEVELOPMENT

The tourism industry and tourism organizations – often together with national, regional and local authorities, and cultural institutions – create tourism products out of the cultural attractions and events by integrating them into packages of facilities and services the modern tourist desires. We can distinguish three main kinds of cultural tourism products: historical establishments, cultural packages, and cultural tours.

Historical establishments

The growing interest in heritage stimulates the demand for hotels and restaurants offering a historical ambience for a dinner, an overnight stay or a conference. In some cases the historical building has fulfilled a hotel or restaurant function from the beginning, for example Hotel Sint-Joris Hof in Ghent, one of the oldest inns in Europe (1228). However, most historical establishments have to be converted for a tourist function into fashionable, fully modernized accommodations. After renovation or restoration, castles function as restaurants or hotels and old regional farms become holiday cottages.

If no historical building is available for transformation, imitation provides a solution. Several hotels and holiday villages have been built which are obviously inspired by traditional architecture. The step-gabled front of the new Novotel hotel constructed in the centre of Brussels is in harmony with the medieval built environment. Likewise the style of modern cottages in the holiday village Ysermonde borrows strongly from the ancient Flemish farms (De Groote and Molderez, 1993).

Cultural packages

Special cultural packages have been developed mainly for two target groups: Belgian tourists who are interested in culture and want to take a short break in their own country, and foreign tourists who are very interested in culture and want to take a short hotel-based holiday in an historic city. These packages can be based on all kinds of cultural events or attractions, such as monuments and museums in the package composed by the Tourist Office of Mechlin and the local hotels, including a conducted tour through the historical centre and a visit to the municipal museum.

Cultural tours

The incoming tourist is the target group of these organized tours, which aim at broadening the knowledge of the culture of the country to be visited. The Belgian art cities offer a rich heritage and various cultural events which lend themselves to thematic tours, for example art styles such as art nouveau in Brussels, and mega-events such as Antwerp 93, Cultural Capital of Europe.

CULTURAL TOURISM DEMAND

In Belgium cultural tourism demand has grown tremendously. A significant indicator of this trend is the growing number of visitors to recurring cultural events, such as the annual Open Monument Days (Table 6.2) and the biennial Europalia (Table 6.3).

The growth of cultural tourism in Belgium has been stimulated by the increasing interest of a broader public in art, culture and history. Furthermore, cultural tourism profits from the increase in leisure time enabling tourists to make one or more short breaks out of season. Between 1982 and 1991 the number of short breaks in Belgium rose from 1.7 million to 3.4 million (Vanhove, 1993). This type of holiday is mostly spent in Belgium or a neighbouring country during a long weekend. Short breaks stimulate visits to monuments, museums and events in cities, because this kind of leisure activity is less dependent on weather conditions.

This development is occurring not only in Belgium and its neighbouring countries, such as The Netherlands, but also in Italy and Spain. Consequently, a growing number of tourists coming from western and southern Europe make a short stay in Belgium (Table 6.4). Their main motive is visiting old cities. Generally speaking, they travel by car or coach, make stops in historic towns, like Bruges, and stay for a longer period in the capital Brussels, which is among the most visited European culture cities (van der Borg, 1994).

The segment 'Others' in Table 6.4 comprises for the most part non-European tourists, mainly Americans, Canadians, and Japanese. Many of these

Table 6.2.   Number of visitors to Open Monument Days in Belgium.

1990	725,000
1991	800,000
1992	860,000
1993	930,000

Sources: Secretariats of the Open Monument Days in Flanders and in the Walloon provinces.

Table 6.3.   Numbers of visitors to Europalia, 1969–1993.

Year	Theme	Visitors
1969	Italy	180,000
1975	France	500,000
1982	Greece	750,000
1989	Japan	1,800,000
1993	Mexico	1,200,000

Table 6.4.   Market segments of the Belgian art cities (1990).

Country	% visitors
Netherlands	14
France	14
UK	12
Germany	11
Italy	5
Spain	5
Others	39
Total	100

Source: VCGT (1994).

Table 6.5. Origin of foreign tourists staying in Bruges (1990).

Country	% tourists
Belgium	10.8
Netherlands	13.8
France	14.1
UK	21.8
Germany	12.0
Italy	2.6
Spain	2.2
USA and Canada	11.5

Source: Boerjan *et al.* (1992).

long-haul tourists visit the Belgian art cities during a so-called 'Grand European (Tour)', a sightseeing by coach of the highlights of European culture with short stays in different countries.

These observations are supported by the 1990 national overnight stay statistics, which reveal that: (i) the art cities make up 40% of foreign tourism demand, and (ii) tourist demand in the art cities is almost exclusively (92%) composed of foreign tourists (Vanhove, 1993), as is also evident from the overnight tourist statistics for Bruges (Table 6.5).

CULTURAL TOURISM POLICY

Two National Tourist Offices (NTO) are responsible for the promotion of the Belgian tourism product: the *Vlaams Commissariaat-Generaal voor Toerisme* (VCGT) for the promotion of tourism in Flanders and the *Office de Promotion du Tourisme de la Communauté Française* (OPT) for the promotion of tourism in the Walloon provinces. The cultural patrimony is a major component in the marketing strategy of both NTOs. It is therefore used as an instrument of tourist promotion in brochures and other advertising material. Culture and heritage are efficient means to visually distinguish tourist destinations from their competitors and to influence tourist destination choice. That is why the Belgian heritage (folklore, art, cities, gastronomy) is often used as a subject or background in promotional photos. A great advantage when promoting Belgium is that this country possesses a recognizable landmark: the Atomium in Brussels, a steel and aluminium construction with a height of 100 metres and consisting of nine spheres that represent an iron atom. The Atomium was built in 1958 as part of the World Fair held in Brussels in that year. As with all such landmarks, a visit to the Atomium is almost a 'must' for every foreign tourist.

Being above all a part of the tourism product and a motive to visit Belgium, heritage is, however, principally used as a raw material for tourist promotion.

The promotion of art cities and of cultural theme years provide clear illustrations of this marketing philosophy.

Art cities

Given the present demand for cultural holidays, it is not surprising that in the strategic marketing policy of the Belgian NTOs, heritage has been chosen as one of the promotion themes for both domestic and incoming tourism. The art cities especially play a key role in tourist image building (Claeys, 1992). This is the background of the recommendations formulated by the study group 'Image Building and Promotion' within the framework of the congress *Tourism Flanders 2002*, which was established by the VCGT:

> One should strive to build an image on solid values such as the precious cultural and artistic heritage of the Flemish art cities and the Flemish art of living [...]. The cultural–historic patrimony constitutes the basis of our image. On all levels the re-valuation and the valorization of the Flemish heritage have to be continuously guaranteed.

> (Daman, 1993: 98)

Measured in terms of the number of overnight stays, Antwerp, Bruges, Brussels, and Ghent are the most attractive art cities (Vanhove, 1993). Second-tier cities include Tournai, Louvain, Liège, Mechlin, and Tongeren. The art cities are promoted in a separate brochure by the Belgian NTOs, that gives information about museums, events, accommodation and access. In the VCGT promotion plan of 1993 city trips are considered the principal product for all markets. Prioritized markets in order of visitor potential are Germany, the United Kingdom, The Netherlands, France, Italy, and Spain.

In order to keep up with the competition from neighbouring countries which offer a similar product, a strength–weakness analysis of the art cities has been carried out as tool for the improvement of supply (Table 6.6).

For the art cities the principal objectives in the field of tourism are:

- quality improvement;
- better exploitation of supply;
- lengthening of stays;
- stimulating tourist expenditure.

Table 6.6. Strengths and weaknesses of Belgian art cities.

Strengths	Weaknesses
Rich cultural heritage	Lack of organized entertainment
Geographic concentration	Lack of accommodation in the smaller cities
Human scale	Lack of structured products

Experiencing art serves as a guiding development theme for the regional Flemish and Walloon art cities. Further markets should be added to the traditional target groups composed by the neighbouring countries. In this connection, the sense of hospitality is the strength that should be exploited in particular. The positioning of art cities in relation to the competitors will be founded on the following concept:

> A cluster of enjoyable cities, full of atmosphere and on a human scale, with a concentrated and a rich historical, artistic and cultural heritage.

(VCGT, 1994)

Cultural theme years

Theme years make it possible to cluster attractions and to focus attention on them in the destination promotion. Usually they are inspired by an event facilitating product renewal or renewed presentation of the existing product. Theme years generate repeat visits so that they offer the opportunity to work at 'customer relations'.

Between 1971 and 1976 the Belgian NTO launched promotion campaigns on cultural themes like castles, abbeys, *beguinages*, urban monuments, folklore and gardens. In 1977 the Rubens year was held to commemorate the fourth centenary of the painter's birth. Whereas the cultural promotion campaigns of the 1970s were focused mainly on permanent attractions and especially on selected elements of the built heritage, in the 1990s the cultural theme years are based more on specific events:

- Feast in Belgium (1991): processions, parades, markets, folk events and festivals illustrated the great variety and the large quantity of cultural events in Belgium;
- Attractions (1992): the numerous cultural attractions (monuments, museums, historic cities) in Belgium were promoted together with other forms of attractions;
- Antwerp 93, Cultural Capital of Europe (1993).

The honorary title of Cultural Capital of Europe offers a unique chance for the marketing of the elected city. Antwerp did not miss this opportunity. The local authorities, the tourism industry, the tourist organizations and the cultural institutions cooperated intensively in order to create an attractive programme of exhibitions, concerts, performances and festivals, such as:

- 'Antwerp, the history of a metropolis', an exhibition on the economic and cultural power of the city in the sixteenth and seventeenth century;
- Concerts of ancient music held in historic monuments in the city;

- 'New sculptures for the Middelheim', a project set up to enlarge the collection of the open air-museum, illustrating how a cultural event can contribute to a renewal of the existing supply.

The decision of the VCGT to select Antwerp 93 as its year theme gave supplementary support for the promotion of the event. The main objective of the NTO was to turn the image of Antwerp as a port and industrial town into that of an historic town offering everything the city tripper is looking for: monuments, museums, cultural events, shops, gastronomic restaurants and a pleasant ambience. One of the reasons why this publicity campaign worked out very well is that Antwerp 93 fitted the VCGT definition of the 'ideal' cultural event:

> An important event with supra-regional and preferably international impact, taking place in a historic city with sufficient tourist infrastructure and facilities, at a well chosen moment and lasting a long time.
>
> (Brouwers, 1993)

Judging by the number of visitors, Antwerp 93 was a success story from beginning to end. At the opening of the mega-event there were already more visitors than expected. At the close the official figures spoke volumes: more than 2.2 million people had attended the cultural programme and the city had received 10 million visitors, four times as much as the annual average.

MANAGEMENT AND MARKETING OF CULTURAL TOURISM: THE CASE OF BRUGES

The attractiveness of Bruges is to be found in the medieval centre, which was radically restored after the Second World War. At the same time the city has developed its tourist infrastructure by constructing parking space for cars and coaches and by extending the supply of large-scale hotel accommodation. In summary, the strengths of the tourism product of Bruges are:

- the townscape: an intact and small-scale historic centre, which due to its many canals and bridges has earned the appellation 'Venice of the North';
- cultural attractions (monuments, museums) and events;
- facilities: a rich supply of restaurants, hotels, and shops;
- central location in western Europe and good accessibility (Boerjan *et al.*, 1992; De Lannoy and de Buck, 1992).

All this explains why Bruges is overflowing with a growing number of visitors. In 1990, 540,000 tourists stayed overnight in the town, over twice as many as in 1975. In the period October 1990–September 1991, 2,176,000 day-trippers came to Bruges, flows in the high season reaching almost 12,000 a day. The number of day-trippers in 1991 was 3.7 times the 1975 total (Boerjan *et al.*, 1992).

The case of Bruges shows the various effects that cultural tourism can have on a vulnerable historic city with respect to its physical capacity and its social functions. It also indicates what kind of solutions can be developed in order to manage visitor streams.

The pattern of visits

Recreational sightseeing

Most tourists and almost all day-trippers come to Bruges for a brief sightseeing tour of the city centre on foot, by carriage or by canal touring boat. They spend most of their money in cafés, restaurants, and shops (Boerjan *et al.*, 1992). The built heritage serves merely as an attractive background for these leisure activities. This behaviour explains why the number of museum visits does not keep pace with the yearly growth in the number of tourists visiting the city. Just 14% of day-trippers visit one of the museums, compared with 43% of overnight tourists. The only historic buildings that day-trippers enter frequently are churches, because these lend themselves to a quick visit (Boerjan *et al.*, 1992).

Short stays

Bruges is mainly a high-season destination for day-trippers, who in 1990–1991 were predominantly Belgians (45%), French (16%) and Dutch (10%). Coming mostly by car or by coach, the majority arrive at about 10 a.m. and stay an average of 4.5 hours. With regard to the overnight tourists, the average stay is 1.66 nights (Boerjan *et al.*, 1992).

Spatial concentration

The tourist visit pattern is focused on a limited part (20%) of the historic centre. Within this area 90% of the tourists follow two principal walk routes with a length of 3 km which conduct them around the 'must-see' sights.

Tourist capacity

The social climate in the historic city suffers from the overcrowding, congestion, parking problems, and environmental pollution (dirt, odour, and noise nuisance) that the tourist mass causes in the small streets. The curiosity of the visitors bothers many inhabitants in their daily routine. Moreover, the town centre is losing its function as a residential area. Private houses and small shops have been replaced by restaurants, hotels and souvenir shops or have been chosen as a location by non-tourist companies looking for distinguished business premises. On the one hand this transformation process has led to a rise in the cost of living and housing costs, which have become prohibitive for the local population. On the other hand it also has an adverse effect on the authenticity of the built heritage since it results in so-called 'façade architecture', the front of buildings being the only historical element that remains after renovation. In the worst cases, historic houses have simply been demolished by property developers to make way for international chain hotels, whose dimensions and modern functional architecture stick out like a sore thumb against the small medieval houses (Winkelman and Van Hesse, 1990; Jansen-Verbeke, 1992; De Lannoy and de Buck, 1992; Van den Abeele, 1993).

All this explains why worried inhabitants have united in the action group 'SOS for a livable Bruges', founded in 1990. This group blames the problems produced by the tourist streams and the traffic jams on the lack of visitor management by the local authorities. It also criticizes the construction of large-scale hotels, the power of the property developers and the inadequate heritage policy which has led to the demolition of historic buildings. The SOS group pleads for a policy which puts first the livability of the city centre for the permanent inhabitants (De Lannoy and de Buck, 1992).

Tourism policy measures

The local government of Bruges has been neither blind to the problems nor deaf to the critics. In 1990 it responded to the action of the group 'SOS for a livable Bruges' by distributing a white paper that stresses the economic blessings of tourism as well as the attention paid by the authorities to the quality of life, the preservation of cultural heritage and the traffic problems in the town centre (De Lannoy and de Buck, 1992). Measures have been proposed and taken in order to find a middle course between attracting tourists and protecting both the heritage and the social environment.

Heritage protection

Now that the hotel capacity targets set up by the local government in the 1970s have been attained, building rules have been promulgated to regulate the construction of hotels. It is no longer permitted to construct new hotels in the historic centre of Bruges.

Staggering of tourist visits

In comparison with monuments and museums, visitor management in historic cities is much more difficult because the freedom of movement is laid down in the constitution of every democratic country. Every tourist who wants to has the right to visit Bruges. As the closing off of the centre would be both undesirable and physically impossible, other measures have been worked out in order to regulate the visitor stream in space and in time.

Traffic and zoning plans

Staggering tourism in space by means of efficient traffic and town planning is one of the methods chosen to reduce the concentration of tourism in the city centre. In order to relieve the congestion problems a traffic plan was drawn up in 1992 which gives priority to public transport. It discourages the use of individual cars and allows coaches to enter the centre only for dropping off and collecting passengers (De Lannoy and de Buck, 1992). Within the scope of the town planning strategy one of the options for the future is the staggering of tourism in zones on the basis of a scheme indicating the purpose of each city district: tourist, residential or other (Jansen-Verbeke, 1992).

Routes

Tourist routes are very efficient steering mechanisms. In order to diminish tourist pressure and to make a better use of the visiting capacity, routes have been plotted across the whole city centre of Bruges. This policy cannot succeed without the cooperation of the tourism industry. Therefore coach companies which currently drop their passengers at a limited number of places are being asked to spread the tourists across the starting points of the alternative routes.

Product differentiation

Another way to stagger tourism in time is diversification of the supply in order to stimulate overnight tourism which, in comparison with day tourism, offers more advantages: higher expenditure, less use of cars, more cultural tourists travelling individually and causing less pressure. So Bruges is trying to reduce its current dependence on day tourism through diversification, and, as a result, the city is actually cutting its promotion of day-trips. The present tourism policy is more directed at the development of products that stimulate short-stay tourism across the whole year, such as cultural weekend packages, seminars, and conferences (Boerjan *et al.*, 1992). The infrastructure has already been adapted in so far that the required capacity and quality of accommodation is offered by the new international hotels in the city centre.

TRENDS AND ISSUES IN CULTURAL TOURISM

Trends such as the growth of cultural holidays and city breaks, the demand for small-scale tourism products and the search for authenticity offer favourable opportunities for the future development of cultural tourism in Belgium. The point is to take advantage of this evolution in tourism demand by exploiting the strengths of the supply, especially in the art cities. In this regard, the traditional hospitality and language skills of the Belgians are invaluable when attracting the international tourist, who has become more widely travelled and demanding.

The sound development of cultural tourism must be based on the preservation of cultural heritage. For without culture as an attraction, there is simply no cultural tourism. This awareness is growing in Belgium as the following examples demonstrate.

The success of the Open Monument Days has led to a tripling of the budget for the preservation of monuments and historic buildings. By putting more financial means at the disposal of the King Baudouin Foundation (the Belgian National Organization for the Preservation of Monuments), the Belgian government has underlined the importance it attaches to the built heritage as tourist attraction and to cultural tourism as source of income (Knops, 1993).

The cultural event Antwerp 93 was the reason for the renovation of historic buildings such as the Bourla Theatre, the Central Station and the Cathedral of Our Lady. The *Fédération Internationale des Journalistes et Ecrivains de Tourisme* (FIJET) granted the 'Pomme d'Or' Award 1993 to the city for the way its preservation policy stimulates cultural tourism.

In the countryside the development of cultural tourism and rural tourism goes hand in hand. Remains of the folk culture are restored in order to increase the attractiveness for tourists. In the context of the Open Monument Day in 1992, the Tourist Board of Limburg charted a chapel route. The sanctuaries were renovated and a local guide informed visitors about their origin. In response to the tourist demand for authentic, small-scale residences, farmhouses have been transformed into accommodation after the model of the French *gîte rural* and *chambre d'hôte*. Thanks to this rural tourism, old regional houses have survived both in Flanders and in Wallonia.

In tourist promotion quality has priority over quantity. Increases in visitor volume should only be attained by staggering tourism in time and in space. Only quality tourism guarantees sustainable development, especially in the art cities (Daman, 1993). In this respect, the plans for improvement of the visitor management during the Open Monument Days are worth mentioning. The problems due to the overcrowding of some monuments will be solved by limiting the number of visitors per hour, spreading visitors across several rooms or places and the strategic positioning of information points (Knops, 1993).

CONCLUSION

Belgium has much to offer the cultural tourist, but it should take care not to rest on its laurels because the competition is keen. It will have to develop a well-thought-out product development strategy if it wants to compete with the neighbouring countries that offer a comparable supply of cultural attractions. The Netherlands is a particularly formidable competitor since The Netherlands Tourist Board also uses culture and cities as promotional themes in its campaigns (see Richards, Chapter 13 this volume). Furthermore, The Netherlands is well advanced in the organization of supply and in the development of cultural tourism projects.

Fortunately there are clear indications that the Belgian tourism industry, public sector administration and cultural organizations are becoming more convinced of the necessity of adopting a well-structured approach to cultural tourism, based on goal-oriented research and sound organization in order to develop quality tourism. The international marketing plan of the Belgian NTOs, the tourism policy of Bruges and the visitor management during the Open Monument Days are good examples of this approach. Another opinion which is gaining ground is that the management of cultural tourism is a task of both the tourism sector and the cultural sector. The will to cooperate is shared by the VCGT and the King Baudouin Foundation who commissioned a study entitled *Built Heritage and Tourism in Cultural Perspective* (Yzewyn, 1995). The results of this study were presented at a symposium held in Ghent in February 1995. They will serve as a framework for new projects combining the opening up of monuments with the interpretation of their cultural–historic value for visitors. Approved projects qualify for advice and financial assistance from the King Baudouin Foundation. All things considered, the future development of cultural tourism in Belgium looks very promising.

REFERENCES

Boerjan, P., de Wandel, E. and Monballyu, M. (1992) *De ekonomische betekenis van het toerisme te Brugge.* Facetten van West-Vlaanderen 37. Westvlaams Ekonomisch Studiebureau, Assebroek.

Brouwers, F. (1993) Culturele Evenementen als Toeristisch Produkt. Paper presented at the congress *Evenementen en Toerisme*, University of Limburg, Diepenbeek.

Claeys, U. (1992) *Beleidsnota Toerisme in Vlaanderen.* Vlaams Commissariaat-Generaal voor Toerisme, Brussels.

Daman, F.J. (1993) Imagovorming en promotie. In: Claeys, U. (ed.) *Toerisme Vlaanderen. Fundamenten voor de Toekomst.* Acco, Louvain-Amersfoort, pp.89–101.

De Groote, P. and Molderez, I. (1993) *Ronde van België, een Toeristisch-Geografische Verkenning.* Volume 1, Kempen en Ardennen. Volume 2, Kust en Achterland. Garant, Louvain-Apeldoorn.

De Lannoy, W. and de Buck, K. (1992) Toerisme en leefbaarheid in Brugge. *Vrijetijd en Samenleving* 2(3), 59–67.

Hut, A. (1992) Tourisme et musées: complémentarités interactives! *Téoros* 11(2), 42–44.

Jansen-Verbeke, M. (1992) Toerisme en de draagkracht van de historische binnenstad. *Geografie* June 1992, 22–26.

Knops, G. (1993) Het Bouwkundig Erfgoed, een Pijler van het Cultuurtoerisme. Paper presented at the congress *Evenementen en Toerisme*, University of Limburg, Diepenbeek.

Munsters, W. (1994) *Cultuurtoerisme*. Garant, Louvain-Apeldoorn.

Van den Abeele, A. (1993) Toerisme en monumentenzorg, bondgenoten of vijanden? In: *Cultuurhistorisch Toerisme: Kip Met de Gouden Eieren of Paard van Troje?* Report of the National Study Day on Monuments (Deventer, 2 April 1993), Stichting Nationaal Contact Monumenten, Amsterdam, pp. 9–15.

van der Borg, J. (1994) Demand for city tourism in Europe. *Annals of Tourism Research* 21, 832–833.

Vanhove, N. (1993) Sociaal-economische betekenis van het toerisme in Vlaanderen. In: Claeys, U. (ed.) *Toerisme Vlaanderen: Fundamenten voor de Toekomst*. Acco, Louvain-Amersfoort, pp. 19–76.

VCGT (1994) *Marketingplan voor het toerisme uit Nederland, Duitsland, Verenigd Koninkrijk, Frankrijk, Italië en Spanje 1995–1998–2000*. Vlaams Commissariaat-Generaal voor Toerisme, Brussels.

Winkelman en van Hesse (1990) *Masterplan cultuurhistorisch toerisme*. Winkelman en van Hesse, The Hague.

Yzewyn, D. (1995) *Bouwkundig Erfgoed en Toerisme in Cultureel Perspectief*. King Baudouin Foundation, Brussels.

Cultural Tourism in Denmark   7

A.-M. HJALAGER

Advance/1, Science Park, Gustav Wieds Vej 10, 8000 Aarhus C, Denmark

INTRODUCTION

A newly published comparative study of arts policies in Europe has found evidence of the existence of a distinct Nordic cultural policy model. In 1961 a historic political compromise led to the Danish implementation of a cultural policy ensuring artists and art institutions the best material circumstances in Europe, but not necessarily the most conducive conditions in which to achieve a flowering of artistic creativity (Duelund 1994).

Over the last three decades three main elements can be identified in Danish cultural policy.

1. A broad and liberal perception of culture, which was introduced by clergyman, philosopher and political activist N.F.S. Grundtvig in the mid-nineteenth century. Since then, the theory and practice of his philosophy has had a marked influence on cultural enlightenment traditions favouring a 'bottom-up' perspective and stressing participation and the freedom of the individual in combination with a popular, egalitarian cooperative movement. In the nineteenth century, the economic modernization of agriculture and industry also took place much in accordance with his philosophies. In spite of the major economic and political changes which have taken place since then, it is a fact that the Danes are still extremely faithful to 'Grundtviganism'.
2. The social democratic principle of equal access to cultural assets. As a consequence of this principle, a distribution in space of cultural institutions of nearly all kinds has taken place. The introduction of popular and fine arts into

school curricula and the participation model (Langsted, 1990) was enforced during the last three decades, and was only recently challenged by liberal political representatives.

3. The culturally radical demand for the autonomy of artists, and the right of publicly supported artists to criticize and provoke without ideological interference. The organization of intellectual property rights, which focus on the artists and not the funders, directly reflects this cultural policy choice.

This trinity of elements is of major importance in understanding cultural tourism in Denmark, and they must not be ignored when evaluating the performance and the future of cultural tourism.

This chapter concerns itself with the present and the future situation of cultural tourism in Denmark. The present state of affairs is illustrated by recent data on the supply and demand for cultural tourism.

In connection with the analysis of future opportunities and the future situation, the newly devised cultural tourism policy is presented. The preparations for 'Copenhagen Cultural Capital 1996' will be presented as a case study, demonstrating the management and marketing of the opportunities provided by cultural tourism.

The principles of Nordic cultural policies developed in the past will not necessarily continue unchanged in the future. Some shortcomings of the Nordic liberal welfare model have already become apparent. In particular, the fact that this type of welfare policy tends to be expensive is beginning to influence the attitudes of some politicians. Cultural budgets are increasing, but in the future cost constraints could nevertheless turn out to be a forceful modifying factor in cultural politics, and consequently perhaps in cultural tourism.

The impact of culture on innovation in the tourism industry is often assumed to be substantial, and this assumption leads to the conclusion that if only the conditions for cultural activities are improved, higher quality products will result, and thus demand will flourish. This hypothesis is also discussed within a Danish framework.

CULTURAL TOURISM POLICY

Elements of cultural tourism promotion have been developed at regional and local levels for a number of years. However, the marketing of cultural attractions tends to be subsumed as one element in general destination promotion, and the development and subsequent marketing of specific cultural tourism products is rare. There has also been little regional or inter-regional coordination of cultural tourism initiatives, and a national cultural tourism policy was not initiated until 1993. In this respect Denmark may be regarded as a very late starter.

The development of a national cultural tourism policy was linked with the creation of the first ministry with a clear-cut responsibility for tourism in 1993. In the same year, the Ministry of Communication and Tourism launched into a cooperative effort with the Ministry of Culture in order to encourage the mutual exchange of ideas and cooperation between tourism and the arts.

To motivate the development of cultural tourism activities, which would attract both Danes and foreigners, the two ministries created a joint financial incentive programme costing ECU 2 million. This money was intended to co-finance (i) the improvement of the services and information available at cultural institutions, (ii) the coordination of the activities of individual cultural institutions and (iii) the development of themes or events in Danish cities. The funds may also be used for launching pilot projects involving the integration of cultural marketing and tourism marketing (Paulsen, 1993, 1994).

The immediate result of this joint initiative was the co-financing of 15 projects. The largest project is a festival: 'Golden Days in Copenhagen'. Some of the titles of other projects still in the preparatory phase are: 'Traces of the Vikings in the Danish Landscape', 'Chamber Music in Denmark', 'Coordinated Marketing of 20 Art Museums', 'Information and Signposting', 'Multi Sculpture Festival', 'Medieval Exhibition at Christiansborg' (the Parliament building) and 'Hans Christian Andersen Festival'.

On its own initiative, the Ministry of Communication and Tourism is motivating a more intensive use of cultural resources for urban tourism and themed marketing. The four largest Danish cities are now developing tourism strategies in cooperation with the Ministry of Tourism, and culture is definitely going to play a major role in these strategies.

In the spring of 1994, the Minister of Tourism published the national outline for a tourism policy. It may be observed that this policy is mostly concerned with organizational issues, and it is very general in nature. Cultural tourism initiatives could be emphasized, but they may find themselves in competition with other approaches to tourism development.

Within the fields of responsibility of the Ministry of Culture, the orientation towards the needs of the tourist is marginal. The legislative framework applying to the arts does not mention any obligation to service tourists specifically; however, the appropriate way of presenting a subject to an audience can always be found as one among other objectives of the cultural institutions. On its own initiative, the Ministry of Culture has published a museum guide in order to compensate for the lack of comprehensive information on Danish museums.

From this outline of the policy framework underlying the cultural tourism phenomenon in Denmark it may be concluded that the authorities only very recently identified cultural tourism as a political issue. It occupies a limited role in national tourism policy as such, and an even more marginalized role in cultural policy.

Specific cultural tourism policies are more visible when they form part of local and regional strategies.

The national authorities' reluctance to impose the cultural tourism imperative on cultural institutions and other agents is very understandable considering the Nordic cultural model as described in the introduction. The 'Grundtviganistic' tradition often leads to congenial presentations of art and history affording Danish visitors an easier access than foreign tourists. The egalitarian principle does include tourists as users along with locals, but tourists are not given priority. The freedom of the arts, which manifests itself through very decentralized organizational structures, limits intervention possibilities at the national level. Instead opportunities and incentives are offered, e.g. the cultural tourism programme.

This lack of national priority does not, however, mean that cultural tourism does not exist *de facto*, as will be shown in the next section.

CULTURAL TOURISM SUPPLY

As pointed out by Bonink and Richards (1992) the definition of cultural tourism is not an easy one, and the choice of definition is often determined by the data available. This is also the case in Denmark, where no specific research on cultural tourism has been conducted. The approach in this chapter must therefore be pragmatic. Particular use is made of data on fine arts, which are more readily obtainable than data on other areas of cultural consumption. There is unfortunately less scope for international comparison.

To analyse supply it is convenient to distinguish between the ' infrastructure' and the 'superstructure' for cultural tourism. The infrastructure for cultural tourism may consist of both popular and fine arts, and other resources such as attractive urban environments, heritage sites and rural environments brought into existence by means of human activities. These are basic cultural resources which do not necessarily perform a direct function for the visitor.

The superstructure consists of enterprises (public and private) and other facilities delivering the actual experience or service to the cultural tourist – or any other visitor. The superstructure facilitates the identification of cultural tourism products by the tourists and/or organizations assisting in the actual packaging or sales services.

For the purpose of this analysis it will be of interest to gain acquaintance with the actual size and composition of the infrastructure and the superstructure, respectively. In addition, developments which have taken place over the last decade will be used to illustrate the priority which Danish society has been giving to culture in general and thus the changes in available cultural tourism supply.

The infrastructure of cultural institutions

The number of fine arts organizations grew considerably between 1980 and
1985. From 1985 to 1990, however, growth was relatively slow (Table 7.1).

The database of the National Tourist Council provides an overview of other
products available to cultural tourists in 1994 (Table 7.2). Unfortunately,
comparative data are not available for previous years to illustrate the development in supply of these products. Because the database relies on reports from
the local tourist boards, it is also not necessarily complete.

Table 7.1.   Number and development of enterprises/institutions within the fine arts,
1980–1990.

	1980	1985	1990	% growth 1980–1990
Museums[a]	303	364	361	19.1
Performing arts[b]	693	879	886	27.8
Galleries and artists	162	178	179	10.5
Total	1158	1391	1416	22.3

[a] The number of museums estimated.
[b] Including intermediaries for the performing arts.
Source: Framke (1993).

Table 7.2.   The provision of cultural tourist resources in Denmark, 1994.

	Number of entries in the database
Museums and collections (including private collections and archives)	502
Castles and manor-houses	226
open to the public	83
offering accommodation	16
Relics of antiquity	315
Monuments, statues, landart, etc.	937
Churches	1114
Specialized parks and gardens	119
Classical music events	395
Rock music events	151
Jazz music events	198
Folk music events	63
Theatre events	384
Festivals	259
Markets	149
Enterprises, workshops, etc. open to visitors	532

Source: Dandata (1994), registered by reports from local tourist boards.

Not all types of supply of importance in connection with cultural tourism are registered on the database. For instance, more than 100 folk high schools are located in Denmark. Most offer short summer courses dealing with (inter)cultural, social and educational issues. The number of courses increased every year until recently, as capacity limits have now been reached.

Though not fully documented in every detail it is safe to say that there is a considerable supply of cultural tourism resources, and that this 'cultural tourism capital' increases each year.

The superstructure of cultural tourism

There is no systematic information on foreign tour operators or travel agencies operating as intermediaries for Danish cultural tourism products. In respect of the number of enterprises and the scope of activities, the incoming sector of the Danish travel trade is limited. Only 43 tour operators and travel agencies had incoming activities in 1993 (Hjalager, 1993). Some of these do, however, cooperate with cultural institutions to create package products, as do some local tourist offices.

In 1994, ARTE, a semi-public ticket and arrangement bureau covering most cultural facilities in Denmark, launched a new decentralized reservation system. Customers for cultural events can buy tickets and obtain information about events at up to 1 300 post offices. This innovation in the organization of the distribution of cultural tourism products takes advantage of a reorganization of the postal services in Denmark.

The sparse evidence available enables us to say that there is a considerable supply of 'infrastructure' resources for cultural tourism, and that the developments which took place during the 1980s enhanced this supply. However, 'superstructure' resources – particularly services for foreign tourists – still tend to be more limited in scope and coordination. In addition, the use by infrastructural bodies of modern technology for distribution is only at a very early stage.

This means that in order to experience the Danish cultural product, tourists will have to rely very much on their own intuition and their explorative abilities.

Political priorities and dependence on public funding

In the past, state financing of cultural institutions has been generous. Table 7.3 shows that funds made available to the fine arts rose by nearly 50% in real terms between 1980 and 1992. Theatres received especially large allocations of funds, although their funding has remained static in real terms since 1980. Museums and music, on the other hand, received large budget increases during this period.

Table 7.3. Public funds (state and local government) for fine arts, ECU per inhabitant, 1980 and 1992 (1992 prices).

	ECU per inhabitant 1980	ECU per inhabitant 1992
Support for artists and writers	0.65	1.60
Music	6.43	10.00
Theatre	18.27	18.08
Museums	10.85	14.35
International relations and general purposes	0.51	10.82
Total	36.71	54.85

Source: Calculations based on statistics from Kulturministeriet (1993) and Framke (1993).

Increasing sums were earmarked for 'general purposes' and international relations. In relation to cultural tourism it may be seen as an advantage that to an increasing extent budgets make room for experiments and projects outside the traditional breakdown of fine arts categories and outside the well-established organizations.

It is widely accepted that the museums and fine arts institutions cannot be made financially viable. In many cases public subsidies per visitor considerably exceed the entrance fee. For instance the Royal Theatre in Copenhagen receives subsidies of nearly ECU 100 per visitor. On average, however, subsidies are lower. For example, the average subsidy per visitor for museums is ECU 6.80, for theatres ECU 36.53 and for zoos ECU 2.53 (Framke, 1993). In particular the performing arts seem to be in need of substantial public funding. As noted by Frey and Pommerehne (1989) this is the case all over Europe, a situation which is completely different from the situation in the US for instance.

Turning to the Danish 'infrastructural' sector, the incoming travel services are nearly all privately owned, whereas the destination services are usually subsidized by local, regional, or national authorities. These subsidies are estimated at 60–70% of expenses, or about ECU 10 million per year (Kommunernes Landsforening, 1992). It is not possible to give any indication of the sum allocated for cultural tourism purposes.

In addition to growing state expenditure, development of other sources of funding contributed to the growth in cultural supply during the 1980s and 1990s. These sources of funding include:

1. An extensive and increasing use of professional and semi-professional labour made available via job training schemes and unemployment activities. On average, museums in Aarhus employed 0.7 job training scheme person for each permanently employed person. Many institutions and cultural projects rely on this financing mode to an even higher degree. No comprehensive statistics exist concerning the utilization of job training staff.

2. The cultural sector as such (including popular culture) is assisted in its operations by numerous volunteers. An increase in the willingness to perform voluntary work is presently coinciding with the general increase in unemployment rates. Though in some cases against the law, the general unemployment benefits 'pay the salaries' of the cultural sector, and this has been tacitly accepted by the authorities. Two analyses stress the importance of unemployment benefits as a platform leading to professionalism (Thomsen, 1989; Schneidermann, 1991). An evaluation study performed by the Cultural Foundation, the purpose of which is to stimulate the interaction of popular and professional culture, noted that amateurs participated in 774 projects and invested 1.9 million unpaid working hours in them. Professionals spent 670,000 paid working hours in the same projects (Andreasen *et al.*, 1992). The public investments made to reach this level of activity amounted to ECU 12 million.

3. Evidence of the importance of sponsoring activities is extremely scarce, although these activities are claimed to be increasing (Karsholt, 1990). The large foundations of the Danish breweries Carlsberg and Tuborg have been allocating funds to the arts, to culture and science for decades. A substantial increase in sponsored activities has taken place because the funds accumulated in the state football and games pools have in part been redirected into cultural activities.

4. Admission fees and incomes from retail sales, membership, etc. The cultural institutions and enterprises usually derive a very limited financial input from these funds. Investigations of how this source of income has developed over the years do not exist for the cultural sector (Kulturministeriet, 1993).

Based on this analysis it seems evident that the Danish cultural sector is extremely dependent on public funds and subsidies, either directly or indirectly through labour market schemes or sponsorship funds and programmes. In comparison to this financial composition, entrance fees and other 'business' incomes obtainable from cultural tourism seem quite unimportant. This is the most obvious explanation for the lack of motivation shown in regard to giving specific attention to the opportunities afforded by cultural tourism. Only a very few 'pioneers' among museums and other cultural attractions find it worthwhile to break the umbilical cord and to rely more on a 'business model'.

Only very recently, the (still insignificant) changes in the financing systems – moving away from 'automatic' subsidies towards a system of support depending on the quality and creativity of the projects – have introduced a more competitive environment into the cultural sector than has ever been seen before. If this trend is continued it might in the long run result in a change of attitudes towards cultural tourism.

Table 7.4.   Attendance in thousands at certain fine arts attractions.

	1980	1985	1991
Theatres	2856	2818	2575
Concerts	235[a]	263[a]	325
Opera	157	146	148
Museums	8220	8731	9336

[a] Estimates based on information on the number of concerts.
Source: Danmarks Statistik *et al.* (1993).

CULTURAL TOURISM DEMAND

The demand for cultural tourism is only dimly illuminated by statistics. We shall thus have to rely on indicators which give at least a partial view of the situation in Denmark. Table 7.4 shows the attendance at some fine arts events and attractions.

Between 1980 and 1991, museums experienced a considerable growth in the number of visitors. Classical concerts are also becoming increasingly popular, whereas drama and opera attendances have fallen. This may explain why subsidies for theatre have not increased whereas support for music performance has grown (Table 7.3).

Culture is in increasing demand among the Danes themselves. In 1987, 45% claimed to have visited cultural or historical attractions during their holidays. In 1990, 51% had made such visits. Those aged between 20 and 50 are more frequent visitors than other age groups. Social class 1 is overrepresented in relation to other social classes (Danmarks Statistik *et al.*, 1993). Another study of visitors at art museums shows that 61% of the visitors are female (Hørup, 1993).

Table 7.5 shows that foreign tourists made almost 3.5 million visits, or 35% of the total number of visits to Danish museums in 1992. It is not surprising that the Germans contribute generously to this total: Germany is the most important market for Danish tourism products as such. It is striking that tourists obviously try to bridge cultural and language gaps. As already noted above, they have to demonstrate a considerable explorative ability in order to obtain information of existing opportunities in the first place, and secondly to interpret the contents and the context of the various exhibitions.

Swedish tourists tend to visit more art museums than other visitors, and German tourists prefer history museums, while the special-subject history museums and other museums seem particularly attractive to tourists from the rest of Europe (Danmarks Statistik *et al.*, 1993).

Unfortunately, there is no systematic evidence concerning foreigners attending other cultural institutions and events. In this connection it may be worth mentioning that in order to attract a tourist audience, the Royal Theatre

Table 7.5.   Visits to museums by foreign tourists, 1992.

Nationality	Number of visitors, total (1000)	Number of visits per tourist
Swedish	461	1.69
Norwegian	164	1.91
German	2083	2.31
Dutch	218	2.73
British	65	2.24
Other Europeans	258	2.63
American	65	2.10
Japanese	23	1.92
Others	85	2.18
Total	3422	2.21

Source: Danmarks Statistik *et al.* (1993).

has for the first time started its season in August. The Jutland Opera claims to have attracted a substantial number of German short-trip tourists to its ambitious Wagner performances. As one of the few cultural events, the Wagner programme was marketed as part of a tour package.

Over the years, the Danish Tourist Council has performed a number of market analyses in the most important markets for Danish tourism. If they had been comparable in regard to methodology, over time and from country to country, these analyses could have been of great value to this analysis. Unfortunately, no such consistency exists, and only a few tentative conclusions can be drawn.

The opportunity of gaining cultural experiences/learning experiences motivates 16% of the German tourists to travel to Denmark, while this motive to travel is important to 31% of Germans choosing other holiday destinations (Danmarks Turistråd, 1988). From this it may be concluded that the reputation of Denmark as a cultural tourism destination has not manifested itself in the most important source market.

About 60% of the Swedes prefer cultural experiences over other activities during their vacations. But nevertheless, they do not expect to find this need well catered for when visiting Denmark (Danmarks Turistråd, 1989).

Norwegians on their second or third trip to Denmark reported fewer visits to cultural sights than Norwegians on their first visit (Danmarks Turistråd, 1990). There is no research evidence of the same pattern occurring with other nationalities. As many Germans visit Denmark every year, however, this may explain to some extent their lower than average level of cultural participation.

A study referred to in GEATTE (1993) also concludes that the reputation of Denmark as a cultural tourism destination has not been clearly established. The country is much more well-known and appreciated for its rural attractions and unspoiled landscapes. Support for this contention comes from the fact that very few tourists (1–3%) asked for information on cultural issues before entering the country (Danmarks Turistråd, 1991).

In conclusion, it may be said that an apparently contradictory pattern may be observed in the demand for cultural tourism in Denmark. The country is visited by a large number of tourists, who do not expect to have their needs for cultural experiences fulfilled. Nevertheless, first-time visitors to the country do generate considerable demand for cultural attractions. It may be, that as in Ireland (see O Donnchadha and O Connor, Chapter 11 this volume) the basic cultural attractions of the country have more to do with the 'way of life' and the natural landscape than with built attractions. On their first visit to Denmark, however, visitors may feel obliged to visit museums, to find out more about the history and culture of the country. A 'marketing gap' may therefore exist between first-time visitors and repeat visitors.

COPENHAGEN CULTURAL CAPITAL 1996: MANAGEMENT AND MARKETING

There is currently no comprehensive management and marketing of cultural tourism in Denmark, also the national tourism policy is not particularly precise about the matter. Instead, a sprawling patchwork of local initiatives of limited scope and scale have been and are being launched. This patchwork structure is an expression of the decentralized and autonomous structure of the tourism and cultural sectors, and it is in no way the result of political priorities, or a systematically planned, coordinated and managed transregional marketing effort.

Cases drawing on experience gained over a long period of time are impossible to find. For this reason the preparations for the Copenhagen Cultural Capital 1996 initiative were chosen to illustrate some of the issues raised in the management and marketing of Danish cultural tourism (for a discussion of the Cultural Capital programme as a whole, see Richards, Chapter 2 this volume). Though far more ambitious than any other cultural (tourism) initiative, the Copenhagen project is indebted to the fundamental traditions of Danish cultural policy.

The objectives of Copenhagen 1996

> The ideological basis for the Action Plan is not a uniform one. In it is represented a social democratic principle of everyone's equal access to the world of the arts, and the importance of imparting this world to a larger public. It also encompasses a liberal conception of culture in the broad sense – the way we live, the way we organize our lives, our language and cuisine, our festivals and our work, as well as our artistic expressions . . . The Plan expresses a cultural policy which posits the

human dimension centrally and gives room to advanced forms of artistic expression alongside tradition and folk culture.

(96 Magazine: 9)

Copenhagen is the last in the original cycle of 12 European Cultural Capitals, and is also one of the most ambitious. The strategy includes the improvement of the image of the city and the launching of a long-term framework for the development as a Cultural Capital. The planning horizon is 1996 and beyond. The involvement of the population and the business community is crucial, and simultaneous stimulation of educational resources is inevitable resulting in new networks and cooperative constellations. The Cultural Capital concept involves the whole of the metropolitan region, not just the city. A separate environmental strategy is also being launched. Physical infrastructure is to be upgraded and organizational infrastructure will be created in order to ensure the progress of national and international cooperation after 1996. The total budget (DKK 750 million, ECU 100 million) is higher than in Glasgow (1990), but is composed of funds from many sources.

The objectives of the Copenhagen Cultural Capital initiative are as follows:

- *To ensure a broad, long-term commitment to art and culture.* (To launch innovative cultural expressions to new audiences. To make experiments bridging popular, industrial, educational and avant-garde artistic forms. To improve the geographic spread of cultural resources).
- *To create better conditions for art and culture.* (Physical facilities, networks and immaterial conditions, financial support).
- *To make visible the diversity and quality of art and culture.* (The launching of a poly-centric cultural view).
- *To integrate Danish art and cultural life into international fora.* (To make manifest the features of Nordic democracy internationally, to bring in new impulses, and to link up with artistic environments and cities abroad).
- *To draw attention to international trends in contemporary creative art.* (Focus on artistic trends in order to provide an art programme of a very high standard).
- *To highlight the capital's distinctive geographical, physical and historical features.* (Copenhagen must become attractive to local inhabitants, visitors and tourists alike).
- *To reinforce Copenhagen as a unified geographical area and the nation's capital.* (To cooperate across organizational, sectoral and geographical barriers).
- *To emphasize Copenhagen's position as a regional centre in Europe.* (Copenhagen as the centre of North–South and East–West axes. Copenhagen as a centre for cultural tourism and international congresses).
- *To promote individual growth and creativity.* (To excite all the senses and to appeal to reflection and imagination).
- *To focus on particular social groups.* (Children, youths, elderly, disabled, refugees and immigrants). (Kulturby 96, 1993).

Within this framework of objectives, a whole range of projects will be feasible. Cultural tourism does not have a specific objective of its own, but could be developed as part of other projects. To a large extent this is consistent with the general ideology of also allowing visitors access to the full scope of cultural resources in Denmark.

Organization and management in the preparatory phase

The preparations were initiated in 1992 and began with the creation of the '96 Foundation' with board and committees. A general secretariat was formed (i) to administer the use of the available funds; (ii) to coordinate; (iii) to give advice; (iv) to act as partner; (v) to initiate; (vi) to be an organizer; and (vii) to create networks.

During 1992 and 1993 a dialogue was opened which was intended to create commitment and to stimulate ideas from all driving forces in the Copenhagen region. The discussion phase was used as a basis for information dissemination and to gather ideas for projects from a wide range of sources.

The financial coordination of the event is particularly important, as funding will come from many sources. One of the main concerns of the secretariat is the potential for obtaining sponsorship. But as sponsorship is a relatively new phenomenon in Danish cultural life, coordination will be necessary in order not to exhaust sponsors and in order to provide them with the most relevant opportunities and services.

In the period running up to 1996, a large number of projects will have been supported by the Foundation and by other funding sources. As many as four programme rounds will be held, and the first rounds in February and August 1994 resulted in the approval of 179 projects. The estimated number of approved projects will grow during the next rounds as the goal to be achieved before 1996 is fixed at 500 projects.

Tourism interests have been represented on the board and in the committees of the Copenhagen Cultural Capital initiative, and the tourist organizations will play a role on many occasions during the process leading up to 1996 and during the year itself.

The role of tourism in the approved projects

The final status of tourism in the Copenhagen Cultural Capital initiative is still not clear. Examples from the list of approved projects may, however, give a hint of the creativity and innovative supply of resources:

- *The Dandelion Route* through urban ecology 'power centres' and demonstration projects.

- *Sustainable Youth Hostel.* The establishment of a new urban hostel based on 'ecotourism' principles.
- *Historical markets* of four periods combined with a regatta.
- *Viking Action Centre.* Workshops inviting visitors to participate in Viking culture and technology.
- *Convent of Esrom.* Establishment of accommodation facilities and a cultural centre for foreign artists and researchers.
- *The Cascades.* Renovation of baroque water cascades.
- *Copenhagen Water Festival.* Music, entertainment, art, sailing sports.
- *'Update'.* Bienale for young artists.
- *Copenhagen Experience.* Multimedia show concerning foreign influences on Danish life modes.
- *European Radio Symphony Orchestras.* Visiting concert programme.
- *International Boys Choir Festival.*
- *Children's Fantasy City.* Children's requirements in relation to a human city demonstrated on a full-scale model.
- *The Global Holiday Resort.* Design of a new holiday resort using inspiration from foreign residents in Denmark.
- *'Don't fight parties'.* Street parties agitating against city violence.

The projects will result in the provision of new tourism facilities, some of them based on concepts differing very much from the traditions of the tourism industry. One of the most conventional proposals, the water festival, was suggested by tourist organizations. In comparison the more experimental projects have their roots in the cultural sector.

Information and marketing

The secretariat of the 96 Foundation administers a communication budget of ECU 10 million. Tourist information and international marketing efforts were integrated into the total communication strategy launched in 1994.

The Cultural Capital initiative will perform the marketing and information tasks by means of traditional channels and media on the one hand. On the other hand, the Cultural Capital initiative will want to stress the links with culture and the arts by way of extraordinary events and remedies. For instance, the 'Kronborg' ferry, which is at the disposal of the Cultural Capital initiative, will be sent on tours in Denmark and abroad up to and during 1996. For a short period in 1994 it was moored alongside the quays of Lisbon, the Cultural Capital of 1994. The ferry has been refurbished and is now equipped for exhibitions and events.

Another example of a communication project already initiated is the development and launching of an advanced electronic destination service system. Terminals in all parts of the city and of the region will keep visitors informed of specific events and sights near the place where he/she is at any one time. General information will also be made available. The system will be more comprehensive than other known systems, include information retrieval on many levels, cover subjects by means of key words and indexes, and it will also operate in several languages.

Conclusions

In comparison to other Cultural Capital projects the Copenhagen Cultural Capital initiative introduces several innovations in comparison to the traditions of Danish cultural and tourism policies.

- The project will assist the launching of a wide range of new cultural resources. Many of these will benefit tourism as well as local cultural life.
- It insists on sustaining the strategy and the impacts of 1996 far beyond that year. In this respect the 1996 project represents a platform for further expansion.
- It creates new organizational networks and modes of operation and cooperation. It will bring culture and tourism closer together.
- It involves the utilization of new and more experimental marketing techniques and the establishment of high-tech destination services and information systems.

Experience from the preparatory stage shows that the fulfilling of the ambitions will not be without complications and battles. The organizational barriers and the traditional prejudices between cultural and tourism sectors are difficult to overcome completely within a short span of time.

TRENDS AND ISSUES IN CULTURAL TOURISM

In an increasingly competitive European tourism market, it is vital for countries such as Denmark to be innovative in the creation of new tourism products. In this concluding section the dimensions inherent in the innovation of the tourism product will be discussed in relation to cultural supply and demand. This discussion will be based on the conceptual framework for the study of innovation in tourism as presented in Hjalager (1994).

Which types of innovations and whose innovations?

In their analysis of tourism in historic cities Ashworth and Voogd (1990) argue that although places (i.e. cities or destinations) are sold to tourists, the actual commodity does not necessarily have to be well defined. Each tourist will find his or her own unique product or combination of products within the same geographical space. The producers, for instance of package tours, lack control of 'their' product, as it is managed by other organizations, perhaps involving a set of objectives which does not include the concept of tourism.

The same may be said to apply to the cultural resources which are available to the tourists. These facilities are never or only very rarely controlled by the traditional suppliers of tourist commodities, e.g. the accommodation or the travel sectors. Nevertheless, these types of organizations draw heavily on the cultural sector for their marketing purposes and as parts of packages, etc. In Denmark this issue stands out even more distinctly as inclusive tours into the country account for only a very small share of incoming tourism.

The absence of large incoming groups limits the scope of 'staged' (semi)-authentic cultural events and artefacts, and the established cultural sector must provide the events – mostly on its own terms. In this sense Danish tourism is very much taking the lead within the international trend of a 'new and flexible tourism' in contrast to mass tourism (Poon, 1993).

In the absence of well-developed mass tourism products or tourist industry distribution, the innovation of cultural tourism products must be initiated by the cultural sector itself. Innovations will thus follow the trends and currents of the cultural industries. The cultural institutions and organizations (whether involved in popular culture or fine arts) define their products on the basis of a cultural *raison d'etre* and are influenced by the evaluations of cultural critics and colleagues. Naturally, tourism aspects of cultural products will be given second priority.

The financial autonomy of individual cultural institutions also prevents the efficient coordination of activities involving the participation of several cultural institutions, e.g. in connection with a themed event. This type of innovation, which often has significant tourist appeal, must overcome greater obstacles in Denmark than in many other countries.

It has often been claimed that the cultural sector is afraid of being connected with tourism and that this hampers the speed with which innovation of the cultural tourism product takes place (Almegaard, 1994). The tourist industry most often refers to the fact that a Miro exhibition staged in Denmark attracts more (foreign) visitors than an unknown Danish artist, and that a Pavarotti concert has the same effect. Though debateable in terms of the detailed allocation of resources, it is by now, however, an established policy that the scope of cultural manifestations should include the elitist, experimental, and avant-garde along with the popular.

The innovation of the core product is therefore protected from the influence of the most populist dreams of the tourist industry. This is not entirely the case when it comes to the peripheral product. The role, for instance, of museum shops, membership facilities, restaurant services, etc., has been acknowledged as important to the total experience of the cultural sight or event. But the professionalization of the merchandising functions is not implemented in the same way as for instance in the UK or the US.

Innovations of the production process of the cultural institutions and events to suit the needs of the tourists have been carried out. The modes of presentation are to an increasing extent, though not entirely, reflecting the levels of knowledge and the command of languages possessed by the audience. The need to excite and entertain by being more spectacular, or by providing 'hands-on' experiences, is also affecting the practice of nearly all cultural institutions and events. Cultural tourism policies do, however, indicate that this development could be expanded in order to create better value cultural tourism products.

In principle, the willingness to gratify culture observers/participants with experiences of still greater quantity and higher quality is in harmony with the intentions of Danish cultural policy. But increases in cultural provision are currently inhibited by the operating environment of cultural institutions. The high cost of labour inhibits the expansion of permanent staff, and increases reliance on volunteers and trainees. This is the reason why the introduction of technology for servicing the audience and the provision of 'self-service' facilities are especially crucial to Danish cultural institutions. The need to combine this financial imperative with cultural preferences for human interaction between the staff and the audience represents a major challenge to the cultural sector in Denmark.

In recent years, a wider perspective in the field of process innovations has revealed itself in the world of museums. The implementation of multimedia equipment facilitates the reintegration of research, public display and the processing of information for administrative and marketing purposes. Though technically feasible, these possibilities have only been marginally applied in Denmark. A small gallery/art exhibition (Kunstnernes Hus) has pioneered efforts in this field.

One effect of the use of multimedia is that exhibitions will tend to become more 'foot-loose' in a spatial sense. It will be easier and less costly to let exhibitions go 'on tour', as did a very popular Italian-produced exhibition on the excavations at Pompeii. The need of tourists to travel in order to experience or 'dream' (Horne, 1984) will be less pronounced and demands for authenticity will decrease (Urry, 1990). However, the Danish cultural sector has also been very reserved in this expansive/export-oriented area.

The arena where culture and tourism may meet and innovate more easily is distribution. Distributive innovations consist of integrated and coordinated measures, the development and demonstration of which we have been witnessing in connection with the Copenhagen 1996 project.

The leading agents of change in the innovation of cultural tourism

As discussed above, substantial innovations in cultural tourism arise out of changes of demand and changes in technology. But other driving forces also modify the innovation process. The autonomy and the more or less automatic lump sum subsidization of cultural institutions and organizations ensure a certain product stability and remove the drive to innovate. No dramatic changes in the organization of cultural policy have been seen in recent years, but a parallel system of subsidizing projects rather than institutions or organizations is beginning catch on. The organizational set-up of the Copenhagen 1996 initiative embodies such a philosophy.

If new systems of funding are developed, and if qualitative and quantitative performance requirements as a result become more explicit, more rapid structural changes may take place in the cultural sector. This may for instance lead to non-competitive institutions being closed down, to horizontal and vertical integration and diversification.

Reductions in the availability of free or cheap labour as a consequence of a general economic recovery, will have the same effect on the cultural sector.

The tourist industry is presently suggesting improvements in cultural tourism products and their marketing, but the role of the tourist sector as an agent of change in the cultural sector is limited. There is no immediate financial incentive to become more deeply engaged in the development of the cultural sector's contributions to tourism.

Seen in a wider perspective and compared, for instance, to the agro-industrial sector or the medico-industrial sector, no 'national innovation system' (Lundwall, 1992) exists within the (cultural) tourist industry in Denmark. It remains to be seen, however, how long the current conservatism of the Danish cultural sector can resist calls for change and innovation from funders and users alike.

REFERENCES

Almegaard, J. (1994) Større samspil mellem kultur og turisme. *Berlingske Tidende*, 8 February.

Andreasen, L.B., Dyekjaer, T.M. and Nielsen, E.G. (1992) *Kulturfonden trekvartvejs. Tværgående analyse af 774 initiativer støttet af Kulturfonden.* Udviklingscentret for Folkeoplysning og Voksenundervisning, Copenhagen.

Ashworth, G. and Voogd, H. (1990) Can places be sold for tourism? In: Ashworth, G. and Goodall, B. (eds) *Marketing Tourism Places.* Belhaven, London, pp. 1–16.

Bonink, C. and Richards, G. (1992) *Cultural Tourism in Europe. A Transnational Research Initiative of the Atlas Consortium.* ATLAS, University of North London, October.

DANDATA *Tourism Statistics Database.* Danish Tourist Board, Copenhagen.

Danmarks Statistik, Kirkeministeriet, Kulturministeriet, Ministeriet for Kommunikation and Turisme (1993) *Dansk kultur- og mediestatistik 1980–1992*. Copenhagen.

Danmarks Turistråd (1988) *Analyse af det tyske marked*. Copenhagen.

Danmarks Turistråd (1989) *Analyse af det svenske marked for rejser til Danmark*. Copenhagen.

Danmarks Turistråd (1990) *Norgesanalyse*. Copenhagen.

Danmarks Turistråd (1991) *Udenlandske turisters informationsbehov*. Copenhagen.

Duelund, P. (1994) *Kunstens vilkår*. Akademisk Forlag, Copenhagen.

Framke, W. (1993) *Kulturområdet*. Arbejdsnotat 5 til ressourceområdeanalysen Turisme/Fritid. Erhvervsfremmestyrelsen, Copenhagen.

Frey, B.S. and Pommerehne, W.W. (1989) *Muses and Markets. Explorations in the Economics of the Arts*. Basil Blackwell, Cambridge, MA.

GEATTE (1993) *Le Tourisme Culturel en Europe*. DGXXIII, European Commission, Brussels.

Hjalager, A.-M. (1993) *Rejsebureauer/rejsearrangører*. Arbejdsnotat 1 til ressourceområdeanalyse Turisme/Fritid. Erhvervsfremmestyrelsen, Copenhagen.

Hjalager, A.-M. (1994) Dynamic innovation in the tourist industry. *Progress in Tourism, Recreation and Hospitality Management* 6, 197–224.

Horne, D. (1984) *The Great Museum: The Re-presentation of History*. Pluto Press, London.

Hrup, I. (1993) *Kunstmuseets publikum, en analyse*. Århus amt, Århus.

Karsholt, E. (1990) Kultursponsering. In: Nielsen, O. (ed.) *Sponsering i virksomhedens markedsføring*. Handelshøjskolen, Copenhagen, pp. 213–237.

Kommunernes Landsforening (1992) *Kommunerne og turistpolitikken*. Kommuneinformation, Copenhagen.

Kulturby 96 (May 1993) *Handlingsplan*. Copenhagen.

Kulturministeriet (1993) *Kulturens penge*. Copenhagen.

Langsted, J. (1990) Strategies in cultural policy. In: Langsted, J. (ed.) *Strategies: Studies in Modern Cultural Policy*. Aarhus University Press, Aarhus, pp. 11–24.

Lundwall, B.-Å. (1992) *National Systems of Innovation*. Pinter, London.

96 Magazine (1993) *Magazine for Copenhagen Cultural Capital*. No. 1, Copenhagen Cultural Capital, Copenhagen.

Paulsen, E. (1993) Skal museerne synliggøre sig i turistbilledet og hvordan? *Danske Museer* 5, 8–10.

Paulsen, E. (1994) Turisterhvervet og kulturen samarbejder. *Kulturkontakten* 1, 18–19.

Poon, A. (1993) *Tourism, Technology and Competitive Strategies*. CAB International, Wallingford.

Schneidermann, H. (1991) *Kulturelt vækstlag undersøgelse*. Aarhus.

Thomsen, K. (1989) *Kunstnere i vækst*. Københavns kommune, Magistratens 1. afdeling, Copenhagen.

Urry, J. (1990) *The Tourist Gaze. Leisure and Travel in Comtemporary Societies*. Sage, London.

Cultural Tourism in France   8

M. BAUER

LTA, Université de Savoie, PO Box 1104, 73011 Chambéry Cedex, France

INTRODUCTION

Cultural tourism is important in France not just because of the rich physical cultural heritage of the country, but also because of the breadth of the French concept of culture. For the French, the cultural heritage (*patrimoine*) covers not just the built heritage, but also includes elements of the natural heritage, individual cultural performers, gastronomy and even the sex tourism attractions of the Moulin-Rouge. The French understanding of cultural tourism contains two major elements: culture as heritage, and culture as ethnography.

In the minds of the French, culture and travel are closely associated with the concept of heritage. The role of heritage is particularly strongly reflected in the built heritage in France. As the French philosopher Lyotard (1988) has observed, the disappearance of the ideas of progress and rationality under postmodernism means that heritage is being re-created in the present, through the use of quotations and components taken from the past. This constant development of the built heritage has been reflected in recent years by the *Grands Projets*, designed to create new national monuments, which take much of their meaning and power from the use of references to the past. The personal and political monuments created through the *Grands Projets* have taken on the role of tourist attractions, as is the case with the Pompidou Centre (Beaubourg) in Paris. Built 20 years ago by President Pompidou as a national cultural and arts centre, it is now one of the most visited buildings in France, attracting over 7 million visitors a year. More recently, the extension of the Louvre, commissioned by President Mitterrand, doubled the number of visitors to this already popular attraction. Other projects which have stimulated cultural tourism in the capital include the new museums for Picasso and at Orsay.

There are signs, however, that the era of the *Grands Projets* may be coming to an end. The culture budget for 1995 of FFr 13.4 billion (ECU 2 billion) is 2.5% lower in real terms than in 1994. Spending on the *Grands Projets* will drop from 20% to 17% of the total arts budget. These cuts must, however, be seen in the light of the massive increases in cultural funding made by the incoming socialist government in 1981. Even with the current cuts, culture will still represent 0.91% of government spending, compared with 0.48% before 1981. The new culture budget gives an even more prominent role to the built heritage, with a 1.6% increase in spending, compared with a slight budget cut for museums (Fessy, 1994).

In addition to the built heritage, cultural tourism for the French is also a search for culture as a 'way of life', in customs, habits and traditions. This approach in cultural tourism is relatively new, although research into cultural roots is currently in vogue in a country in which the peasantry was until recently very important. In spite of the importance of the arts in French social life, the ethnographic approach is still less significant than the *patrimoine*. The makers of this living tradition (musicians, dancers, potters) are not however designated as national monuments, in contrast with the situation in Japan, for example.

CULTURE AND TOURISM

It was in 1837 that Stendhal first used the English term 'tourist' in place of the French *voyageur* in his book *Mémoires d'un Touriste en Dauphiné* (Stendhal, 1989). In Stendhal's time, tourism was concerned with the active involvement of the visitor with the inhabitants, landscapes, and economic activities, customs and heritage of the regions visited. The cultured traveller travelled alone or with a small group of friends, directly paying his hosts for board and lodging, and being in close contact with the daily lives of the local community, even if considered an outsider by them. This is no different from the way a cultured individual travels today. But is a cultured person a cultural tourist? There are increasing signs that the market for cultural tourism in France is now expanding beyond the cultural elite.

In the last ten years there has been a growth in new forms of tourism connected with culture, but marketed as mass tourism products. The context of cultural tourism has therefore changed. Today, there is 'a latent opposition between the supporter of economic development, which always risks modifying or destroying the heritage, and those who only wish to protect it' (Pation, 1987).

The French wish to protect their heritage is exemplified by the resistance to 'Disneyfication', and moves to protect the French film industry from foreign imports. The arrival of Disneyland in Paris, for example, was referred to by the then Minister of Culture, Jack Laing, as 'a cultural time-bomb'. Similarly, a proposal by the local authorities to fund the restoration of the 2000-year-old Pont du Gard by building a Gallo-Roman theme park was abandoned because it was thought 'wise to avoid the "Disneyfication" which is more and more a threat to the French heritage' (De Roux, 1994).

CULTURAL POLICY

Until relatively recently, there was no specific cultural tourism policy in France. The supply of potential cultural tourism attractions, however, has been strongly influenced by the general cultural policies of the French government over the past 35 years. A national Ministry of Culture was first established in 1959, under the direction of Andre Malraux. Under Malraux, a national cultural policy was developed, and a long-term approach to cultural investment was established. Under his directorship, which lasted until 1969, measures were taken to preserve national heritage, support the visual and performing arts and to democratize cultural consumption. The concern for national heritage, or *patrimoine*, continued after Malraux, and gained impetus from the involvement of successive French Presidents in the promotion of the *Grands Projets*.

The scope of cultural policy has broadened considerably since 1959, partly through an extension of the powers of the Ministry itself (for example into audio-visual production and publishing) and partly because of the broadening scope of the definition of 'culture'.

> The policy of conserving the national cultural heritage now encompasses most human and social activities and has begun to deal with works from the latter half of the 19th century and the beginning of the twentieth century. The furtherance of artistic creation now covers the popular arts and crafts and what were considered, in the past, to be minor forms of expression. More recently the emphasis has been put on the role the Ministry can play in developing scientific and technological knowledge.

(Council of Europe 1991:240)

This broadening scope of cultural intervention is today reflected in the wide range of facilities which are used for cultural tourism, as will be seen later in this chapter.

As well as broadening the supply of cultural tourism attractions, cultural policy has also aimed to broaden the cultural audience in France. Cultural life in France has traditionally been quite elitist, but in recent years a number of measures have been taken to democratize cultural participation. Decentralization measures taken in 1982, for example, stimulated each region, department and town to think about cultural provision, and many of them have used cultural tourism as a means of improving their image. In museums, measures have been taken to improve the quality and accessibility of museums, through increasing guided tours and audiovisual presentation. Between 1961 and 1990, the number of visitors to the national museums rose from 3 million to over 9 million, and it is estimated that a high proportion of these visitors are tourists. The number of monuments open to the public has been increased, and information campaigns have been launched to stimulate visits to monuments, particularly during holiday periods (Council of Europe, 1991).

Extra funding was allocated to maintenance of existing national monuments in 1994, with FFr 590 million (ECU 90 million) being spent on work at the cathedrals of Rouen, Bourges, and Notre Dame, the standing stones at Carnac and the Palais Garnier (the old Paris Opera).

To date, the preservation of the French heritage has been largely the responsibility of the state. As the scale of the task increases more rapidly than the available budget, however, there are suggestions that France needs to have a voluntary body to play a similar role to the National Trust in Britain, or the Open Monuments Association in The Netherlands (Hugot and De Nicolay, 1994).

CULTURAL TOURISM SUPPLY

The estimation of the supply of cultural tourism attractions in France is complicated by the administrative organization of the country. France has 36,000 *communes* or administrative divisions, as many as the other EU member states combined, largely because the government has preserved the feudal parish system. The provision of cultural facilities therefore tends to be polarized between large-scale facilities, concentrated in Paris and other major cities, and small, local facilities provided by the communes.

The heritage attractions recognized by the Ministry of Culture are dominated by religious buildings. Almost 12,000 buildings and structures were listed in 1991, of which over 45% were religious structures (Table 8.1). The expanding supply of the officially recognized heritage is emphasized by the 6% increase in listed structures between 1988 and 1991. In contrast, elements of popular or folk culture are conspicuously absent from the list. The largest concentration of national heritage is found in the Ile de France Region (around Paris), which has 80 *patrimoine classé* (officially recognized heritage structures) per square kilometre. In contrast, Brittany and Normandy have only 40 monuments per square kilometre, and Corsica less than 10 per square kilometre. The geographic concentration of cultural supply in the French capital is further underlined by the fact that 60% of national expenditure on culture was accounted for by Paris alone in 1986 (Council of Europe, 1991).

This distribution underlines the centralized nature of the French system, and the immense cultural power and accumulated cultural capital of Paris.

Table 8.1.   Classified historic monuments by category, 1988 and 1991.

Category	Number		
	1988	1991	% change
Prehistoric antiquities	1297	1319	1.6
Historic antiquities	489	525	7.3
Chateaux	1315	1476	12.2
Military architecture	476	501	5.2
Cathedrals	89	87	−2.2
Places of worship	4259	4427	3.9
Chapels	600	639	6.5
Monasteries	500	598	19.6
Public buildings	538	550	2.2
Private buildings	1119	1231	10.0
Others	1318	1387	5.2
Total	12,000	12,740	6.1

Source: Ministry of Culture.

The strong link between important national monuments and the development of the national culture is also seen in the designation of *sites protégés* (sites protected by the government) which include 'natural' landscapes of national significance. Even these apparently natural features are culturally interpreted, however. The sites are often protected because of their connections with literature (Falaise d'Etretat), the arts (Forêt de Fontainbleau) or paintings (Collines de Provence). The sociologist Andre Micoud has argued that a visit to a *site protégé* is not just a walk in the park, but to identify yourself as being French (Micoud, 1991). In their totality, the *sites protégés* are supposed to form an image of France, as in the novel by Bruno, *Le Tour de France par Deux Enfants*, in which two children learn about French history and culture by touring the *sites protégés* (Gruno, 1976). This strong bond between the national heritage and national identity presents problems in developing cultural tourism. What do these cultural monuments mean to foreign tourists, and how should they be interpreted, both for French people, and for other tourists?

At the other end of the spectrum, the growing interest in local culture is reflected in the increasing number of communes with their own museum. One guide to French Museums (SEAT, 1994) describes over 6000 museums or permanent collections, located in 3900 communes. One problem with such estimates, however, is the fact that the word 'museum' is not legally protected, and has therefore come to be applied to a very wide range of facilities (a similar problem exists in The Netherlands – see Richards, Chapter 13 this volume). Figures from the Ministry of Culture, for example, record almost 4000 museums, whereas another survey lists only 1600 (Ministère de la Culture, 1991). Whatever the total number of museums and other cultural attractions, however, there is no doubt that the supply has grown rapidly in recent years.

Table 8.2. Cultural supply in French Communes, 1980-1990.

Communes with at least one	1980	1990
Museum	1437	2009
Public library	7371	9418
Theatre	2331	2732
Cultural centre	1346	1848
Music school	4202	5985
Fine art school	498	1173

Source: *Developpement culturel*, no. 92, January 1992.

Table 8.2 indicates that the number of communes with a museum grew from over 1400 in 1980 to over 2000 in 1990, an increase of over 40%.

CULTURAL TOURISM DEMAND

Bourdieu's study of art museum visitors made a major contribution to his understanding of the relationship between lifestyles and cultural consumption (Bourdieu, 1969). He found a strong correlation between museum visiting, educational attainment and social position. Museum visits were an almost compulsory part of the lifestyle of bourgeois families. Initiation into the arts through the family (the *habitus*) became an important determinant of cultural consumption in later life. The expansion of the middle class in the last 30 years has therefore made a major contribution to increasing the size of the cultural audience. With the development of a large critical public, the nature of cultural production has also changed. As Bourdieu has remarked, cultural 'works are created twice, by the actors and the audience and by the culture in which the audience lives' (Bourdieu, 1979).

The growth in the educated audience for cultural manifestations can be judged by the fact that the number of students in France grew from 200,000 in 1958 to 2.5 million in 1993. As education levels have increased, so the number and range of cultural attractions and events has also grown. Culture became a much larger concept than purely 'high' culture, with, for example, the expansion of Jack Lang's Ministère de la Culture in the 1980s, when culture ranged from gastronomy to rap music. In tourism, these trends are reflected in the emergence of the 'cultured traveller' who wishes to be distinguished from the common tourist. The modern cultured traveller is a member of the elite who, 'deprived of his monopoly through social progress and the right to travel . . . sees in tourism only commercial degradation' (Urbain, 1991).

The search for distinction has contributed to a considerable growth in cultural tourism demand in France in recent years, measured in terms of visits to cultural attractions. A study of tourist attractions with over 20,000 visitors

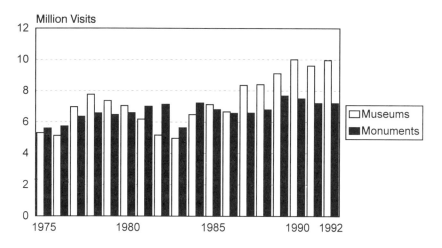

Fig. 8.1.   Museum and monument attendance in France (source: ATLAS database).

in 1991 indicated that cultural sites account for about 46% of attraction visits in France, with religious buildings (135 million visits) by far the biggest category (Monferrand, 1994).

The number of paying visits to major national monuments grew by over 37% between 1975 and 1990, and visits to national museums rose by 78% over the same period (Fig. 8.1). This growth has been far from even, however, as visits decreased during the early 1980s before recovering strongly in the latter half of the decade. Visits to the Louvre in Paris alone more than doubled, rising from 2.7 million in 1988 to over 6 million in 1994. Over 57% of visitors to the Louvre came from abroad in 1994, emphasizing the important role of tourists in cultural visits. The official figures do not, however, include visits to 'free' monuments and sites, which the Ministry of Culture has estimated to be about 100 million per year (Council of Europe, 1991). The proportion of the French population visiting historic monuments rose from 30% in 1981 to 37% in 1987 and to 57% in 1993 (Faucheur, 1994).

There is also evidence to suggest that cultural consumption during holiday trips by the French is significant. In the summer of 1991, 42% of French tourists visited a historic monument, and 34% visited a museum (Bywater, 1993). Culture is also an important motivation for foreign visitors to France. A survey in 1989 indicated that culture was important in the destination choice of 85% of American visitors, 78% of Japanese, 73% of Austrians 71% of Swiss, 66% of Spanish and 62% of English and German visitors (Chazaud, 1994). These relatively high levels of cultural tourism consumption were also reflected in the ATLAS cultural tourism research conducted in 1992.

Visitor surveys were conducted at the Pompidou Centre in Paris, the Chateau de Blois in the Loire valley and L'abbaye de Cluny, near the Saone valley. These attractions played an important role in stimulating tourism, with over 50% of visitors indicating that the attractions were important in making the decision to travel. In the case of the Pompidou Centre, however, the attraction itself tended to be less important, since it is just one of the many cultural features which stimulate visits to the capital. A third of the visitors came from abroad, with the neighbouring countries of Germany, Belgium and Italy being the major source markets. Most cultural tourists stayed a relatively short time in France, with almost 80% of respondents spending less than a week in the country.

In comparison with ATLAS surveys in other countries, the foreign tourists interviewed in France tended to be older. In the European surveys as a whole, over 40% of foreign tourists were aged under 30, compared with only a third of those interviewed in France. The proportion of students among French respondents (15%) was also notably lower than in other surveys (about 30%). This pattern was reflected across all three French survey sites, with no significant difference observed in age distribution by site.

Monuments were particularly important elements of cultural consumption, with 74% of visitors indicating that they had visited a monument during their stay, compared with less than 60% who had visited a museum. The frequency of monument visits in France was therefore much higher than in other survey countries (average 58%). Art galleries were only visited by 23% of respondents, and only 6% had visited a festival. The attendance at visual and performing arts attractions was therefore lower than in other countries. The relative importance of historic monuments in French cultural tourism also extends to outbound tourism from France. Over 60% of French visitors interviewed abroad had visited a monument during their trip, compared with just over 40% of Italian and British tourists, and 55% of American tourists in Europe.

The concentration of the supply of cultural attractions around Paris also has a big influence on the geographical distribution of demand. Of the top ten most visited monuments and attractions in France, only Mont Saint Michel (in Normandy) is located outside Paris (Table 8.3).

One problem with estimating the demand for cultural tourism attractions is that a large number of these are free. The banks of the river Seine in Paris, for example, are designated as a world heritage monument by UNESCO, and are enjoyed by uncounted millions every year. The cathedral of Notre Dame in Paris has an estimated 13 million visitors a year, but again access is free, whereas St Paul's Cathedral in London, which charges an entry fee, only had 1.4 million visitors in 1992. The problem of estimating the total number of cultural visits to 'free' attractions is again highlighted by Table 8.3. Although paid visits to the Abbey at Mont Saint Michel number less than one million, free visits to the attraction as a whole are estimated to be about 7 million.

Table 8.3. Most visited monuments and museums, 1992.

Attraction	Visits (millions)	Location
Beaubourg (Pompidou Centre)	7.7	Paris
Tour Eiffel	5.7	Paris
Cité des Sciences	5.7	Paris
Musée du Louvre	4.8	Paris
Chateau de Versailles	4.2	Paris (Banlieue)
Musée d'Orsay	2.6	Paris
Musée Beaubourg	1.1	Paris
Musée Invalides	0.9	Paris
Mont Saint Michel	0.8	Normandy
Arc de Triomphe	0.7	Paris

Tour operators and travel agents

The role of the 'travel industry' in the distribution of cultural tourism products is relatively small. In part this stems from the limited use of packages by the French themselves, as 93% of French tourists organize their own holidays. There are a number of specialist cultural tourism tour operators, the largest of which, CLIO, has about 12,000 clients a year. The role of tour operators is, however, made more difficult by the prevalent attitude that the national heritage was not created for tourists. The major national museums in particular try and limit tourist groups. At the Louvre, for example, groups must pay between Ffr 100 and Ffr 500 for a compulsory reservation, and at the Orsay museum, groups are excluded from temporary exhibitions.

THE MANAGEMENT OF CULTURAL TOURISM PRODUCTS

Cultural tourism, in common with other forms of tourism services, forms part of a *servuction* (Eiglier and Langeard, 1987), which unites facilities, staff, and customers in creating a product. In cultural tourism, however, the management of the product is complicated by the fact that it occurs in an open system, in which many of the product elements are facets of the 'way of life' or of non-tourism functions. Cultural tourism may include, for example, church services, streetlife, the view of a castle, museums whose function is the protection of heritage, and other 'free' public goods. The tour operator, however, must endeavour to sell these elements of the cultural tourism experience in the same way as commercial products, such as transportation, accommodation, food, or even staged folk dances.

The management of such an open system is much more difficult than a self-contained attraction, such as a Club Med or a Disney theme park. The cultural tourism manager must coordinate the actions of both voluntary and involuntary actors, without revealing the coordination involved. The management of cultural tourism also has to combine the management of people with the marketing of tourism products, as the following example demonstrates.

The world-famous caves of Lascaux, in south-western France, were opened as a museum in 1948. However, the breathing of visitors progressively increased the humidity and carbon dioxide in the caves, and by the beginning of the 1960s, microscopic vegetation began to grow and damage the cave paintings. In 1963 scientists persuaded the authorities to close the caves, robbing a relatively poor region of a major tourist attraction. The local tourism industry sought alternatives in other prehistoric caves, but it was not until a replica of the Lascaux caves was opened next to the original in 1983 that visitors began to return in large numbers. This goes to show that cultural tourists are attracted by 'authenticity', no matter how tenuous.

By 1987, however, scientists had discovered that the development of the new caves ('Lascaux 2') was creating a new risk to the original site. Parking spaces had been built next to the old site, and visitors were going into the woods above the old caves to walk or picnic, compressing the soil, and altering the air and water circulation in the caves. New solutions to the problem of visitor management include moves to limit the number of visitors to the site, and also the length of time spent by visitors at the caves. This is not very popular with the local tourist industry, however.

Another solution to the visitor pressure created at sites such as Lascaux is to try and spread visitors geographically. A report written for the Fourth National Tourism Plan in 1970 had already suggested shifting the emphasis away from mass tourism by encouraging cultural tourism in inland areas. 'A stay in a Breton seaside resort does not have to be "the back against the wall". Means have to be provided to break into the hinterland to get to know the real life of Brittany' (Parent, 1970).

The perceived advantage of cultural tourists is that they are more willing to go 'off the beaten track' than most other tourists. As Croizé (1984) has observed:

> There is an explorer in the cultural tourist. He has to take the deserted roads and find the hidden country (such as the route to Santiago de Compostella). Contrary to the tourist fixed in one place (a beach, or ski resort) he has to wander without stress. He will discover without too much trouble under the superficial bark of contemporary life, the diversity of local traditions.

Cultural tourism managers have to ensure that the tourist rediscovers 'itinerancy', and leaves the idleness of 'the customs and habits of the beaches' behind (Urbain, 1994). One contribution towards this is the creation of various cultural itineraries, which are becoming increasingly common in France (see the case study below).

The idea of managing the tourist experience is not new in France. After the creation of holidays with pay in the 1930s, the trade unions were concerned that workers should take advantage of their holidays not only for a *vacance*, or rest, but also to develop their minds (culture) and bodies (sport) (Ouvry-Vial *et al.*, 1990). As a consequence, social tourism facilities began to provide *animation*, a concept derived from the latin word *anima*, meaning soul. In other words, a way of giving meaning to a holiday, in place of simply resting.

Over the years, however, *animation* began to take on a broader meaning. Commercial providers, such as Club Med, began to add *animation* as part of their products, by employing *animateurs* to entertain their guests, but *animation* can also be found in a wide range of activities, such as lively street scenes, festivals, guided tours and *son et lumières*. Today, physical cultural resources, such as an old abbey, a museum or local food are not considered sufficient to form a cultural tourism product. These products have to be created as a *servuction* of facilities, information, interpretation, *animation* and activities. Good examples of the way in which *animation* is now applied in cultural tourism are provided by events, exhibitions and festivals.

Exhibitions

Major exhibitions form the boundary between urban cultural leisure activities and cultural tourism, attracting local residents and foreign tourists alike. They are also used as an important element of attraction and destination marketing. Malraux, the first Minister of Culture (1959–1969), launched this development on a national scale with the Tutankhamen exhibition in Paris, which attracted 1.25 million visitors in 1967. Large exhibitions have now become a feature of the French cultural calendar (Table 8.4).

Festivals

The marketing manager of *Maison de la France* (the body which promotes France abroad), has stated that France is the 'first country for festivals in number and diversity', with 500 festivals annually attracting more than 5 million visitors (Anonymous, 1994). Festivals were not considered as tourist events until recently, but festivals are slowly turning into tourist products organized and sold to specific market segments. Some 15–20% of visitors to major festivals are now foreign tourists. The *son et lumières* concept in particular has turned into a cultural tourist product which has spread around the world. *Son et lumières* events with floodlighting of historic buildings, fireworks and often hundreds of actors, are designed to portray a particular version of

Table 8.4.   Major exhibitions in the National Museums.

Exhibition	Date	Visits
Tutankhamen	1967	1,240,975
Renoir	1985	793,544
Manet	1983	735,197
Gauguin	1989	623,739
Toulouse-Lautrec	1992	653,853
Cézanne	1996	630,000
Turner	1983	548,496

history to their audience. Launched by a conservative politician, *Le Puy du Fou*
re-enacts the story of the French Revolution in front of 10,000 spectators, and
attracted a total of 340,000 visitors in 1993.

Feasts (La Fête)

Feasts are similar to festivals, but they have a much longer history. Formerly,
every commune had its own feast, usually linked to the rhythm of the seasons,
such as harvest feasts. Today, the National Federation of Feast Committees has
115,000 affiliated associations (Fédération Nationale des Comités des Fêtes,
1994). Many of these traditional feasts have become part of the tourist product
in France. One problem for the staging of these traditional events is that the
advent of the automobile has eroded the availability of open spaces for staging
such events. One solution is to ban cars temporarily from the centre of small
villages or towns. Another possibility is to enclose the feast in a privatized space
as a paying attraction, although this option has not proved very successful.
More recently, feasts have been developed in large buildings, such as museums,
schools and factories.

Educational tourism

Travelling has long been a means of broadening human knowledge. The Grand
Tour was an early form of *Bildungsreisen* (educational travel) for the upper
classes, keen to find the roots of European culture. The concern with education
is carried on in modern travel brochures, which often emphasize the educational benefits to be gained from a particular destination: a chance to learn
about history, anthropology, foreign languages and culture in general. Many
new opportunities are now being offered to link tourism and education. In
1992 the Ministry of Education and Science launched *Sciences en fêtes*, a series
of events designed to give people the opportunity to find out what was happen-
ing in research and technology in schools and factories. Over 1.5 million

visitors were attracted to 600 *Sciences en fêtes* events in 1993 (Guides Hachette, 1994).

Industrial tourism is also being developed through the scientific and industrial cultural centres (*Centres Culturel Scientifique et Industriel*), which are opening hydroelectric or atomic power stations, saltmines and aircraft factories to visitors, and supporting the development of automobile and railway museums. These facilities require special *animation* to engage and entertain the tourist, and to explain the evolution and application of technology. The presentation of industrial heritage is particularly problematic in France, where until recently heritage was considered to end in the nineteenth century, or even before the French Revolution. The objective of presenting these more modern aspects of heritage to the French people, however, is 'to preserve heritage in order to better understand changes in the present' (Centres Culturel Scientifique et Industriel, 1986).

A specific attempt to link past and present is the creation of Ecomuseums (*écomusée*), which are open-air anthropological museums, presenting a picture of the life or technologies of a specific region. The Ecomuseum of Alsace, near Mulhouse, for example, provides a picture of Alsatian culture through a collection of buildings typical of the region, workshops demonstrating old crafts and daily cultural events.

Religious heritage

French culture is deeply catholic, in spite of increasing secularization. The catholic heritage attracts a lot of foreign tourists from other catholic countries, such as Ireland or Poland. The popularity of pilgrimages to Lourdes, for example, means that this small provincial town has one of the largest airports in France. A number of other shrines, such as Ars, Lisieux, Paray-le-Monial, and Pontmain attract large numbers of pilgrims, and have little to offer secular tourists. In some areas, such as Brittany, however, there have been distinct attempts to secularize religious events, in order to prevent them being overrun by tourists (Nolan and Nolan, 1992).

A good example of the interweaving of the different strands of cultural tourism in France is provided by the following case study of the Savoie region in eastern France.

BAROQUE ART IN SAVOIE

The small Savoie region in the French Alps has only 350,000 inhabitants, but is very important as a tourist destination for both winter sports (19 million tourist nights in 1993) as well as summer tourists (6.4 million nights in 1993). Winter tourism is based on the ski slopes of the Tarentaise valley, whereas summer tourists congregate around the lakes at the foot of the mountains. The image of Savoie is thus connected more strongly with sport and leisure than with its historic heritage of churches, castles and monasteries.

In 1988, a number of factors combined to cause Savoie to reassess its image. The selection of Albertville in Savoie as the site for the 1992 Winter Olympics raised concerns about the role of local culture. The Olympics themselves were controlled by politicians, top civil servants, and marketeers. Local leaders in Savoie felt that there was a need to inject an element of local culture into the games, rather than simply being a reflection of national prestige. At the same time, the Ministry of Culture was promoting the development of ethnographic or archaeological routes, and the Council of Europe was launching a European Baroque Route as part of its European Cultural Routes Programme (see Chapter 5). This combination of factors convinced the Savoie region that they should create a new cultural tourism product: Baroque Art in Savoie (*les chemins du Baroque*).

The basis of cultural tourism in Savoie

Until recently, the link between modernization and progress was a central idea for most Savoyards. The past of the region was linked with poverty and out-migration. As a result, the physical heritage of the area was not well protected. Savoie developed huge hydro-electric power stations, aluminium plants or purpose-built ski resorts (e.g. Tignes, Val Thorens).

In the process of modernization, the turbulent history of Savoie as a border region, and a meeting place for different languages, religions and cultures was forgotten. In the seventeenth century, however, Savoie was at the centre of a power struggle between the catholic and protestant churches. Geneva, once part of Savoie, was a protestant stronghold, and so the catholic authorities constructed a large number of magnificent churches in the surrounding mountain villages to provide a defence against the further spread of protestantism. The construction and decoration of the churches was strictly controlled by the archbishop, Charles Borromée (Borromée, 1643). 'Artists don't work independently, but follow the orders of priests or bishops . . . the numerous rosary reredos are a testimony of the struggles against the protestants' (Cerclet, 1994). However, the style of these decorations was adapted to local taste, rather than that of the bishops, producing a unique style.

Today, the small mountain villages of Savoie have a rich heritage of churches, chapels and oratories. As the population of the villages has been reduced through out-migration, and social life has become increasingly secularized, however, services are increasingly poorly attended. The buildings have survived in part because of the support of the regional authorities, which receive state aid to maintain these religious buildings. Until recently, however, this rich Baroque heritage was largely neglected in France, where its peripheral location caused the term 'baroque' to become a synonym for the absurd, odd or strange. In the 1971 Michelin guide to the Alps, for example, much attention is paid to Roman or Renaissance heritage in the region, but the Baroque features are not mentioned at all.

It was against this background of past neglect that the Baroque Art in Savoie Programme was launched in an attempt to rekindle local pride and to act as a draw for tourists (Bauer, 1993).

The initiators

The Savoie Museum, one of the driving forces behind the Baroque Art in Savoie Programme, emphasized from the beginning that heritage is a living system, rather than simply a collection of buildings (Gachet and Richard, 1987). The original plan therefore called for the linking together of communities, attractions and tourists through the construction of ethnographic routes, which would meet the requirements of the Council of Europe for designation as a European Cultural Itinerary (see Richards, Chapter 5 this volume).

The first step in constructing the route was a survey of ethnology, culture and tourism in the region, carried out for the regional authorities (Seve, 1990). The study found that the users of such routes were likely to be families with an interest in heritage, and fond of walking, village atmosphere and *animation*. For foreign tourists, the important aspect of the Savoie product was found to be mountain culture, rather than specific religious heritage.

In 1992 the regional authority launched the '1992 Heritage Programme' with FFr 65 million (ECU 10 million) funding from the national Ministry of Culture. The management of the project was vested in the *Foundation pour l'action culturelle en Montagne* (FACIM), a cultural organization funded by the regional government. This semi-public body set out to develop a unique and coherent image of the heritage of Savoie in the tourist market.

Marketing and management

The different elements of the cultural tourism product are designed to provide easy access for the independent tourist, even if the interpretation of the product is strictly controlled. Churches and chapels are signposted along major roads to promote access. Guide books are available for the route, and two interpretation centres have been created along it. Guides and 'heritage volunteers' are being trained to provide *animation*. The emphasis is placed as far as possible on the local volunteers, who not only provide interpretation of the built heritage, but can also inform visitors about daily life in the villages.

This has caused some quarrels between the volunteers and existing commercial guides, who fear that their income will be threatened by the newcomers. The local priests have also become involved in the interpretation of the religious heritage, which is beginning to undermine the original aim of FACIM to provide a coherent interpretation for the heritage of the region. Although the built heritage belongs to the commune, or local authorities, the local priests control to a large extent what happens inside the churches themselves. Not all priests are happy to let the guides into their churches, and there have also been conflicts about the opening times of those churches which are accessible. The local authorities have also refused to manage or to make a financial contribution to facilities provided by FACIM. Without the cooperation of the church and the local authorities, it is very difficult for FACIM to implement a coherent heritage management plan for the region.

The heritage of Savoie is therefore open to a variety of different interpretations, which depend on the origins of the cultural visitors, and the role of the cultural intermediaries both within and outside the region. The following three examples illustrate very different views of the Savoie heritage:

Die Zeit (German newspaper)

with naïve images from the gospel, and multicoloured images of the stations of the cross, respect for the Eucharist was instilled in the 'readers' of these alpine villages. Peasants sometimes had to kill their last pig to celebrate the foundation of these pompous monuments. As well as these strip cartoons without speech balloons, sixteenth century frescos shine in the chapels at Lanslebourg and Bessans. Horrible scenes of martyrdom can be enjoyed here . . .

(Von Kieffer, 1992)

Havas (Major French tour operator)

Baroque art in the Savoie mountains, with its gorgeous scenes, shows us the vitality of the inhabitants and, at the same time demonstrates the huge effort of the (catholic) church to preserve its authority.

(Brochure text between photos of Baroque churches, Havas, 1992)

FACIM

The catholic church determined to bring God back to earth and displayed along the alpine arc the beautiful ribbon of its reredos of lights, in order to halt the calvinist advance

(FACIM, 1992)

These conflicting versions of the same 'reality' illustrate the problems of educating through cultural heritage. Is cultural tourism actually a means of education, or is it a confirmation of existing prejudices? Do the cultural tourists in Savoie involve themselves in the realities of local culture any more than the tourists lounging on the Mediterranean beaches? The educational effect of the Baroque Arts in Savoie Programme is called into question by the number and type of tourists it attracts.

Results

The project has not been too successful if the results are viewed purely in terms of tourist numbers. About 60,000 people visited the Baroque attractions in 1993, although only about 10,000 visits were made to attractions which charged an entrance fee. Most of the visitors are family groups on walking tours in the region, and most visits are concentrated in the summer period. There is little evidence so far that specific 'arts tourists' are being attracted to the region. There are also very few Baroque Arts package tours being sold.

Rather than being a cultural tourism product in its own right, it seems that the Baroque in Savoie is being used as an additional attraction for the existing tourist products in the region. For example, Havas, a major French tour operator, sell their ski holidays in Savoie using pictures and descriptions of the Baroque churches. This does indicate that the aim of building a more cultural image for the region has been successful, even if it is not generating large numbers of specific cultural tourists at present.

CONCLUSIONS

This chapter has illustrated the growth in cultural tourism supply and demand in France in recent years. This expansion is in some respects due to the extension of the French concept of culture to include many aspects of living culture alongside traditional sites and monuments. New initiatives, such as the development of cultural itineraries, are redefining the boundaries of cultural tourism consumption. In a highly centralized country like France, however, the commanding heights of the cultural tourism landscape remain clustered around Paris and other traditional centres. In particular, the *Grands Projets* in Paris, such as the Pompidou Centre and the extension to the Louvre, have set the scene for a new form of mass cultural tourism, in which the centres of traditional culture are reinvented and rediscovered by a wider audience.

REFERENCES

Anonymous (1994) Les festivals montent en force sur la scene touristique. *L'Echo Touristique* no. 2240, 13 May.

Bauer, M. (1993) Tourisme religieux ou tourisme en milieu religieux. *Cahiers Espaces* March, 24–28.

Borromée, C. (1643) *Instructionum Fabricae Ecclesiasticae et Supellectilis Ecclesiasticae* (de la Construction et de l'Ameublement des Eglises).

Bourdieu, P. (1969) *Les Musées d'art Européen et Leur Public.* Les Editions de Minuit, Paris.

Bourdieu, P. (1979) *La Distinction, Critique Sociale du Jugement.* Les Editions de Minuit, Paris.

Bruno, G. (1976) *Le Tour de France par Deux Enfants.* Belin, Paris.

Bywater, M. (1993) The market for cultural tourism in Europe. *Travel and Tourism Analyst* 6, 30–46.

Centres Culturel Scientifique et Industriel (1986) *Actes du Colloque pour un Tourisme Industriel Transfrontalier.* CCSTI, Thionville.

Cerclet, D. (1994) *Approche Anthropologique de l'Art Religieux des Vallées de Savoie.* La Fontaine de Siloe, Chambéry.

Chazaud, P. (1994) Sociologie du tourisme culturel et strategie marketing. *Cahier Espaces* 37, 99–110.

Council of Europe (1991) *Cultural Policy in France.* Council of Europe, Strasbourg.

Croizé, J.C. (1984) Signification culturelle et valorisation touristique du patrimonie Bali. *AIEST*, 25, Saint Gall.

De Roux, E. (1994) Eviter la Disneylandisation. *Le Monde*, 23 May.

Eiglier, P. and Langeard, E. (1987) *La Servuction.* MacGraw Hill, Paris.

FACIM (1992) *Les Chemins du Baroque*, no.1, FACIM, Chambéry.

Faucheur, P. (1994) Mise en valeur du patrimoine et amenagement du territoire. *Cahiers Espaces* 37, 174–177.

Fédération Nationale des Comités des Fêtes (1994) Faîtes la fêtes. *Marketing et Communication* 68, July.

Fessy, E. (1994) The end of the Grands Projets. *The Art Newspaper* 41, 1.

Gachet, L.J. and Richard, D. (1987) *Proposition au Conseil Général de la Savoie d'un Plan de Valorisation Patrimoniale des Vallées de Savoie.* Musée Savoisien, January.

Guides Hachette (1994) *Le Guide de la Science en France.* Guides Hachette, Paris.

Havas (1992) *Brochure Nieges 92/93.* Havas, Paris.

Hugot, J.P. and De Nicolay, R. (1994) Pour une Fondation du Patrimoine français. *Cahiers Espaces* 37, 74–82.

Lyotard, J.F. (1988) *Le Postmoderne Expliqué aux Enfants.* Editions Galilée, Paris.

Micoud, A. (1991) *Tourisme et Environnement: Colloque de La Rochelle.* La Documentation Française, Paris.

Ministère de la Culture (1991) *Développement Culturel*, no. 90, March.

Monferrand, A. (1994) Le patrimoine culturel. *Cahiers Espaces* 37, 39–45.

Nolan, M.L. and Nolan, S. (1992) Religious sites as tourism attractions in Europe. *Annals of Tourism Research* 19, 68–78.

Ouvry-Vial, B., Louis, R. and Pouy, J.B. (1990) *Les Vacances.* Editions Autrement, no. 111.

Parent, M. (1970) *Exploitation et Promotion du Patrimoine Culturel.* Rapport Pour la Commission du Tourisme du IVeme Plan. Paris.

Pation, V. (1987) *l'Image du Patrimonie et le Consommation Touristique.* Recontres Internationales pour la Protection du Patrimoine Culturel, 3ème Colloque, Avignon, pp. 19–25.

SEAT (1994) *6,000 Musées et Collections en France. Guide SEAT 1994.* Le Cherche Midi Editeur, Paris.

Seve, N. (1990) *Itinéraires Ethnologiques en Savoie, du Produit Culturel au Produit Touristique.* Unpublished Report, Conseil Général, Chambéry.

Stendhal, H. (1989) *Mémoires d'un Touriste en Dauphiné.* Glénat, Grenoble.

Urbain, J.D. (1991) *l'Idiot du Voyage Histoires de Touristes.* Librarie Plon, Paris.

Urbain, J.D. (1994) *Sur la Plage – Moeurs et Coutumes Balnéaires.* Payot, Paris.

Von Kieffer, R. (1992) Baroque Routes. *Die Zeit*, 17 January.

Cultural Tourism in Germany   9

P. ROTH AND A. LANGEMEYER

Fachhochschule München, Am. Stadtpark 20, 81243 München, Germany

INTRODUCTION

Germany has long been one of the major engines of the tourism boom, providing an essential support for the tourism industry in the beach destinations of the Mediterranean. Nowadays, however, the people of *Dichter und Denker* have also rediscovered culture as part of their holiday experience. Sun, sea, and sand are no longer the main reasons for a holiday trip. A new type of German traveller sets out to discover European culture – with German thoroughness, an Italian flair for art and French *savoir-vivre*.

This change is not just important for the destinations outside Germany which benefit from the international *wanderlust* of the Germans, but it is also having an increasingly important impact at home. Cultural events as promotional tools are now important elements in the economic policies of cities and tourist regions. Cultural activities are an indicator of the quality of life and indicate a modern, innovative direction and intellectual vitality of people and regions.

The dual role of culture both as a binding force and as a celebration of diversity is clearly seen in Germany. The federal structure of the country has promoted a high degree of regional independence in both political and cultural terms, with the individual *Länder* (regions) having a large degree of autonomy. Physical and political division of Germany between a Capitalist West and a Communist East were only removed by the fall of the Berlin Wall, which has paved the way for the reunification of the country. The process of reunification has also created a role for culture as a source of unity, and in defining a new identity for a unified country. The export of major cultural events through Europe supports a new internationalism and is an effective antidote to complacent self-satisfaction and provincialism.

THE ADMINISTRATION OF CULTURAL TOURISM IN GERMANY

Presenting Germany as a land of culture is the job of many organizations, with different approaches. The *Goethe-Institut* and the *Deutsche Zentrale für Tourismus* (DZT) are responsible for culture and tourism. The *Goethe-Institut* promotes the German language and culture worldwide, whereas the DZT promotes Germany as a holiday destination. Promoting Germany abroad is a job with as many facets as there are organizations. One has to be aware that the cultural and historic development of Germany over the centuries makes it impossible to present a single, unified image. 'Thus, the image of Germany and the Germans, in the past and present, is a mosaic of small fragments which, depending on the position of the observer, may be as attractively light as they can be frighteningly dark' (Hillman, 1988).

This applies especially to the presentation of the German Federal Republic as a land of culture. The complexity of historic and cultural developments in this century alone cannot be summarized in short slogans. Extreme changes as in art between primitivism and *Neuer Sachlichkeit* present a distorted picture. Similarly the attempt to paint Germany as a romantic travel destination with castles and forts, long favoured by the DZT, has now been replaced by contemporary presentations from different views.

Local and regional festivals fulfil a similar function. 'In the '80s ambitious municipal authorities and generous sponsors organized ever more new open-air festivals'. However, the festival boom has reached the end. 'State funds are being cut due to the worrying state of the treasury. Industry has also changed its attitude with the recession. Sponsorship for cultural activities is often withdrawn. It is now carefully assessed whether promoting culture is compatible with the marketing objectives of a company' (Anonymous, 1994).

Because of the federal structure of the country, cultural funding in Germany takes place at three levels: state, regional, and local. The federal state (the *Bund*) is responsible for cultural events and attractions of national and international importance. However, it is the largely autonomous regions (the *Länder*), which are in principle responsible for all cultural policy. At local level the local authorities (*Gemeinden*) deal with cultural matters delegated to them by the *Länder*. In 1988 total cultural funding was almost DM 9 billion (ECU 4.8 billion), of which the *Bund* contributed 15%, the *Länder* 39% and the *Gemeinden* the remaining 46%. This system is complicated by a transfer system, in which funds can be shifted vertically, for example from national to regional level, and also horizontally, from richer to poor regions (Angioni, 1994). This transfer system has caused major problems for cultural funding in West Germany since unification.

About DM 3.4 billion (ECU 1.8 billion) has been spent in new *Länder* on culture since reunification. This high level of investment has helped to avoid the collapse of cultural infrastructure seen in other former Communist states in Eastern Europe (Jung, 1994). At the same time, the high cost of reunification has had a negative impact on cultural expenditure in West Germany, as *Länder* in the West have received less funding from central government. Some DM 700 million (ECU 370 million) was cut from the federal cultural budget in 1994.

The decentralized nature of the German political system also means that there is no effective national policy for cultural tourism. The development of cultural tourism is left effectively to the individual *Länder*. This explains why the level of cultural tourism development and promotion varies considerably from one part of Germany to another.

CULTURAL TOURISTS

The unifying characteristic of travellers interested in culture and art is that they want to learn about other cultures. As Richards (Chapter 2 this volume) has pointed out, identifying 'cultural tourists' poses problems of definition. In this chapter we follow the ATLAS definition of cultural tourists, by analysing tourists for whom cultural experiences are an important motivation for travel, and who are primarily interested in the educational aspects of tourism. In Germany, 'cultural tourists' broadly correspond to those participating in study and educational trips provided by tour organizers, educational bodies and adult education organizations.

On the basis of the results of the travel analyses undertaken over many years by the Studienkreis für Tourismus (1988) German cultural tourists can be described as follows:

1. Gender: More women than men participate in study and educational trips. However, this is also partly due to the higher proportion of women in all age groups born after 1930. When the classification is refined it is found that men in the age group 30–49, in the 'highly educated' group (equivalent to those with A-level and degree-level qualifications) are relatively highly represented.
2. Age: The age structure of cultural tourists is relatively equally divided over the groups 'under 30', '30 to 50' and 'over 50'. Increased education levels have boosted the proportion of younger people participating in study tours, while it appears that older travellers feel more secure in organized groups than alone.
3. Education: Compared to other forms of travel, the 'highly educated' group is most highly represented among cultural tourists. This is also due to the general increase in the number of graduates in the past 20 years.

4. Net household income: About half the cultural tourists are 'higher earners' (net household income over DM 3500), although one has to bear in mind that organized study trips are relatively expensive.

5. Destinations: Countries outside Europe attract approximately 25% of cultural tourists. These are followed by Great Britain and Ireland, France, Italy and East European countries. Domestic travel within Germany accounts for 30% of trips, and it is likely that many of these domestic trips are second holidays.

6. Motivation: Clear reasons are given for choosing these holiday destinations, e.g. 'broadening your horizons, doing something cultural and educational', 'experiencing other countries, seeing something of the world, meeting local people' and 'new experiences, learning about something different'. About two-thirds of study tour participants cite such motives, a much higher level than for other tourists.

7. Holiday activities: The list of the activities of 'cultural and educational tourists' is headed by 'sights, buildings, museums' (over 90%). Excursions to and driving through the surrounding area and talking with other people follow, each with about 80%.

It seems that German cultural tourists are wealthier and better educated that the average German tourist, although cultural tourism participation is not as dominated by older travellers as is often assumed.

This picture of German cultural tourists was to a large extent confirmed by surveys carried out as part of the ATLAS Cultural Tourism Project in 1992. A total of 601 surveys were conducted at the Neue Pinakothek in Munich, the Porta Negra in Trier and the Altes Museum in Berlin. Almost 23% of those interviewed indicated that the cultural site visited was 'very important' in their decision to travel, and this proportion was slightly higher for the Porta Negra (28%) than the other locations. Respondents interviewed in Germany tended to be slightly older, with almost 16% of respondents aged between 50 and 59, compared with 12% of respondents overall (Figure 9.1). Older visitors were particularly well represented in Berlin, where almost 80% of visitors were aged over 30, compared with less than 60% of visitors in Munich and Trier. German respondents were particularly likely to have visited historic monuments (64%), but relatively few indicated that they had visited a museum (48%). German cultural visitors were particularly likely to take multiple holidays during the year, with almost 70% having taken a short-break holiday in the last 12 months, two-thirds of whom had taken more than one short break in this period. Visitors to Munich (41%) and Berlin (41%) were particularly likely to be on a short-break holiday (three nights or less) compared with 25% of visitors interviewed in the ATLAS survey overall.

The location of the different sites in Germany had a great influence on the origin of cultural visitors. Foreign visitors were far more common in Munich (37%) and Trier (28%) than in Berlin (5%). Munich is clearly the most globalized of the three cultural destinations, with 53% of foreign visitors coming from

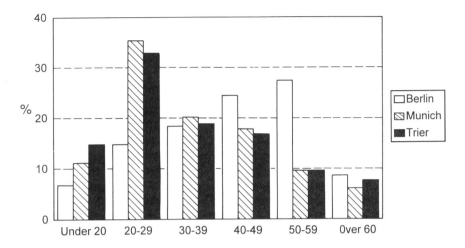

Fig. 9.1.   Age profile (%) of visitors in Munich, Trier and Berlin.

Table 9.1.   Culture as a motive for tourism, 1983–1991.

	% of tourists stating culture as main motive for travel
1983	7.5
1985	7.0
1987	7.1
1989	8.0
1991	7.7

Source: Reiseanalyse, Studienkreis für Tourismus (1983–1991).

outside western Europe, compared with 17.5% in Trier. Munich is firmly established as part of the modern 'Grand Tour' of western Europe, whereas Berlin is still striving to re-establish its touristic centrality following unification.

CULTURAL TOURISM DEMAND

Successive surveys by the Studienkreis für Tourismus (1983–1991) indicated that the proportion of German tourists whose main motive for travel was cultural remained at around 7–8% of all tourists between 1983 and 1991 (Table 9.1). Separate surveys carried out on forms of holidays between 1991 and 1993 also indicated that the level of participation in cultural trips remained at similar levels to previous years (Lettl-Schröder, 1994). Cultural tourism has not therefore grown as a proportion of all German tourism in recent years, but the overall growth in tourist numbers means that the estimated number of German cultural tourists has grown from 3 million in 1983 to 4.6 million in 1991, a growth of over 50%.

Apart from these general data on cultural tourism demand, it is difficult to trace the growth of cultural tourism through demand for cultural attractions, as is the case in many other countries. The Federal system in Germany prohibits the collection of comparative statistics at national level. There are, however, a number of organizations which try and compile figures on the use of cultural facilities, such as theatres and museums. In this section we will use these sectoral statistics to highlight major trends in cultural tourism demand in Germany.

Theatre in Germany

German culture is characterized by a broad spectrum of cultural events. The comprehensive data used in this contribution is based on the annual *Theaterstatistik* (Theatre Statistics) of the *Deutsche Bühnenverein* (German Theatre Association) in Cologne. Data about theatre in general do not provide information about the development of individual theatres, which may or may not follow the general trends.

Trends in attendance

The number of theatre visits in West Germany has been fairly constant at about 25 million a year for several decades. The stagnation in overall attendance seems astonishing as West German society underwent major changes during this period, for example increased mobility, more leisure time, greater interest in environmental issues and the much discussed changes in values. The lack of growth in 'high culture' performances does, however, mirror trends in other western European countries during the same period.

There have been shifts in attendance over the years between the various forms of theatre. During the 1980s, occupancy levels at opera and ballet performances in West German theatres fell, whereas attendance at musicals grew. Commercial theatres, which specialize in more popular forms of culture, therefore saw their audiences grow by about 60% between 1974 and 1992, while public sector theatres saw their audiences shrink by 15% between 1977 and 1991.

Attendance at private sector theatres is greatly affected by the incredible success of the commercial musicals such as 'Cats', 'Phantom of the Opera', and 'Starlight Express', which have been fully booked since the start of their runs (Table 9.2).

Table 9.2.   Attendances at the three major musicals: Cats, Starlight Express and Phantom of the Opera.

	85/86	86/87	87/88	88/89	89/90	90/91	91/92
Cats	123,650	450,842	457,754	440,874	451,041	471,464	452,000
Starlight Express			75,000	559,447	696,446	650,000	715,000
Phantom of the Opera					126,397	748,862	730,000

The demands made of this form of theatre are completely different from those made of the public sector theatres which, with their subsidies from the federal and state authorities, also have a cultural–political task. Public sector theatres enhance the diversity and the range of theatre available in Germany and create a cultural climate from which the private sector theatres also benefit.

In 1992 theatre subsidies from the federal, state and municipal authorities, public bodies and private organizations amounted to DM 3.3 billion (ECU 1.74 billion). The discussion about the need for and level of cultural funding is something we will leave to others. However, it should be noted that since 1982 the annual rise in public sector funding has lagged behind earned income. Slower growth of public funding has begun to place increasing importance on the generation of admission revenue and other sources of income.

Tourism and theatre visits

The major increase in attendance at theatre performances is also very interesting from the tourism perspective. In Hamburg, for example, 700,000 people come to see the 'Phantom of the Opera' every year, and many of them come from outside the city. The musicals have become an important element in the tourist attractions of this city. They may either be the primary purpose of a trip or tourists may consider them as an additional element of their holidays.

According to a press release from the Hamburg Tourist Authority

> . . . about one-third of musical visitors . . . spend at least one night in Hamburg. The musicals will result in some three-quarters of a million overnight stays (on average these visitors stay for two nights) . . . Apart from the ticket revenue musical-tourists spend between 150 and 200 million DM annually in Hamburg.

One of the most marked developments in recent years has been the booming attendance at festivals, with an overall growth of 106% since 1977. This growth has been largely attributable to increased tourism activity (see the Schleswig-Holstein Music Festival case study below).

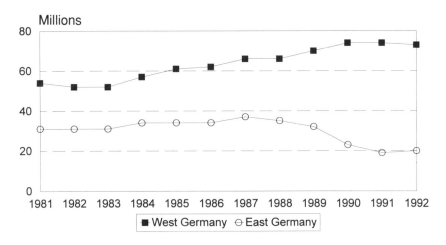

Fig. 9.2. Museum visits (millions per year) in Germany, 1981–1992.

Museums in Germany

Divergent trends in museum visits are evident in West and East Germany, particularly after reunification. In the early 1980s, there were steady increases in museum visits in both East and West Germany, with the total number of visits in Germany increasing from 85 million in 1981 to 103 million in 1987 (Fig. 9.2). The political, social and economic upheaval associated with reunification caused museum visits in East Germany to fall by 27% in 1990 and by a further 19% in 1991. This decline in cultural visits in East Germany mirrors the pattern found in other former Communist states during this period (Jung, 1994).

This trend was reversed in 1992 when the museums in the new federal states reported an increase of 3%, while the number of visitors to West German museums, which had previously been stable, fell by almost 1.2 million (relative to the museums included in the surveys in 1991). The slight increase in the number of visitors in 1992 is probably due to special events organized by the museums, which are increasingly using special exhibitions and themes to attract visitors.

If the museums are classified by visitor numbers, we find that 50% of the museums which provided data in 1992 were small museums with fewer than 5000 visitors per year. These are mostly museums with folkloristic and local history collections. Only 5% of museums had 100,001 to 500,000 visitors per year. Much of the recorded growth in museum attendance has therefore resulted from an expansion of the number of smaller museums. As a result, the

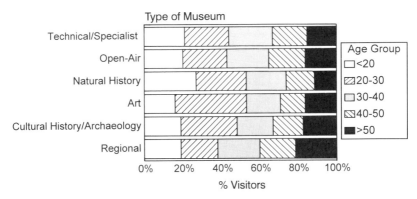

Fig. 9.3.   Age profile of visitors by museum type (source: Klein, 1990).

average number of visitors per museum has fallen from 40,000 in 1982 to 26,000 in 1992.

Museum visitors

In the absence of national statistics for Germany, analyses of museum visitors have to be drawn from local or regional studies. The following explanation is based on studies of 33 museums in the Westphalia-Lippe region and four museums in West Berlin, during a period of three years (Klein, 1990).

This study indicated that more than 55% of museum visitors were men. Male visitors were particularly well represented at technology and specialized museums (64%), but the gender balance was more even at natural history (53% male) and art museums (52%). As far as the age of museum visitors is concerned the different types of collections attract different age ranges (Fig. 9.3). The natural history museums and culture history museums which are not regionally limited are most attractive to young people whereas those in their twenties amount to almost 40% of visitors to art museums. Open-air and technology museums are more popular with the over-thirties.

Museum catchment areas

The proportion of local visitors and tourists clearly depends greatly on the size of the town and the population density in the surrounding area. Among the museums at similar locations we can distinguish between those which are only known locally and those which attract visitors over longer distances due to the nature of their collections and reputation (Fig. 9.4). Smaller museums in the

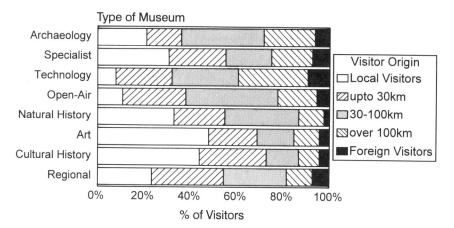

Fig. 9.4.   Visitor origin by museum type (source: Klein, 1990).

country, particularly when connected with historical buildings, tend to attract many non-local visitors as they are tourist attractions. In the area studied about half the visitors were from the local area (within 30 km radius). At museums in the Ruhr area this proportion rose to two-thirds, whereas the reverse situation applied in West Berlin, where two-thirds of museum visitors were from outside the area. This underlines the greater importance of cultural tourism in major cultural capitals such as Berlin.

CULTURAL TOURISM SUPPLY

Cultural tourism supply in Germany can be divided into three main elements: cultural attractions (e.g. museums, historic buildings), cultural events (e.g. the performing arts, festivals), and cultural tourism packages supplied by commercial tour operators and educational organizations. This section presents an overview of the supply of cultural events and attractions in Germany, as well as case studies of a commercial cultural tourism supplier, Studiosus Reisen, and the development of a music festival in the Schleswig-Holstein region of Germany.

The growth in the supply of cultural attractions can be judged from increase in museums and theatres in both East and West Germany in the last decade. Between 1982 and 1992 the number of museums in Germany reporting visitor numbers grew from 2096 to 3615, a growth of over 70%. The bulk of this growth occurred in West Germany, where the supply grew by almost 100%, compared with a 15% growth in the East.

Theatres

In the past 20 years, the number of towns with theatres has remained constant at 74. However, the number of venues has risen from 279 (1974/75) to 385 (1984/85) and to 462 (1991/92). The number of seats has risen from 146,858 to 184,523 and 204,328, respectively.

CITY TRIPS AND CULTURAL TOURISM

On the supply side cultural tourism can be classified as study trips (see also the Studiosus case study below), educational trips, opera and musical trips, theatre trips, experience-oriented cultural trips, and thematic cultural trips. City trips are a special case of cultural tourism as they are often involve visits to several cultural attractions and/or events.

The range of city trips on offer is more and more determined by major cultural events which are another reason to visit the city, in addition to its permanent attractions such as an historical town centre or buildings. The options for cultural tourism available in cities are manifold, ranging from museums and art exhibitions to concerts and festivals and to cultural history and culinary weekends.

These cultural attractions are often specially marketed. Advertisements and stands at fairs as well as promotional brochures and posters published by the city's tourist information office are most commonly used to promote the attractions to a broad audience. Depending on the size of the town and the available advertising budget, the town may also be promoted abroad, for example in cooperation with the DZT. Another possibility is to cooperate with travel agents or representatives and local hotels. This is mainly limited to large cities such as Berlin (and Potsdam), Dresden (and Meissen), Munich or Hamburg.

Educational trips are generally limited to those organized by *Volkshochschulen* (adult education centres) and similar non-profit or private educational organizations. In accordance with their education briefs these organizations are also active in organizing cultural trips.

Cultural trips aimed at undergoing specific experiences or thematic cultural trips are often offered by specialist tour organizers or coach trip organizers. These cover an extremely broad range, from the Fireworks Festival (*Rhein in Flammen* – Rhine Alight) to regional tours (*Romantische Strasse* – Romantic Road).

Studiosus: market leader in cultural tourism

Studiosus Reisen Munchen GmbH is the leading European tour operator in 'study tours', or cultural package tours. Established in 1954, the company started by organizing trips to classical destinations such as Italy and Greece, conducted by Dr Werner Kubsch, the company's founder. In the first season there were only 500 clients, but today Studiosus carries over 80,000 tourists to over 300 destinations. Studiosus has grown rapidly by adapting to changing customer needs. The original classical bus tours have been supplemented over the years by walking tours, cruises, city tours, language tours, and incentives. It is, however, the maintenance of a clear company policy over the years which is at the core of its success. This case study is based partly on work by Vetter (1992).

Company policy

The basic objective of Studiosus is to organize study tours in their broadest sense, with a tour leader to provide a broad-based introduction to the countries visited and their culture. Rather than the destination being the focal point of the tour, however, the emphasis is on the process of learning, or as the French say *voir et connaitre*, to see and understand. The Studiosus traveller is led to new experiences, acquires knowledge and understanding, and gains an informative *studium generale* of the countries visited.

Studiosus wishes to maintain its position as market leader in Germany by providing a high quality travel product which is compatible with the social and physical environment of the destinations visited. The key to achieving this is the use of expert tour guides, who are able to interpret local cultures and environments, adding value to the product and the tourist experience.

The study tour market

Study tours are a special form of package tour which are only important in German-speaking countries. In other countries, culture is often offered as a part of a tour, but it lacks the educational focus of the German variety. The concept of the study tour is characterized by the following features:

- a tour with a number of locations for overnight stops and sightseeing;
- a fixed programme, which is listed in the brochure as an obligatory part of the tour;
- a tour leader who is responsible for the educational and organizational aspects of the tour.

Study tours are offered by a number of suppliers in Germany, including specialist cultural tour operators, adult education institutes and associations. The main competitors of Studiosus are the TUI study programme 'Culture and Experience', Meiers Weltreisen, Klingenstein, Ikarus Reisen, and Marco Polo Reisen. The market for package tours offered by commercial operators was estimated to be 150,000 in 1990, and this had grown to 250,000 by 1994. Studiosus remains the clear market leader, with a 30% market share in 1990, rising to 32% in 1994, with total capacity of 88,600 clients and a turnover of DM 301 million (ECU 160 million).

The study tour participants tend to be single, over 45, well-educated, and experienced travellers. These people take study tours mainly to broaden their horizons, to get to know other countries and cultures, and to experience travelling in a group. The market has traditionally been rather conservative, with operators offering tried and trusted destinations, with a clear focus on humanistic educational ideals. This began to change in the 1980s, as competition increased, and new products, such as hiking tours and cruises were introduced. Such product innovations still form the basis of growth in the study tour sector. In addition, however, the number of senior citizens is expanding, producing an overall growth in the target market for these products.

Marketing cultural holidays

Studiosus has established itself as the market leader in cultural holidays in Germany through a consistent marketing strategy of market and product development, supported by a strong brand image and quality control. The marketing aims of Studiosus are:

- to maintain market share through continuous growth;
- consolidation of a quality image;
- extension into new market segments.

In order to achieve these aims, Studiosus tries to maintain a clear product range structure and quality standards for existing products, while identifying new markets for future expansion. The basic elements of the study tour product (transport, accommodation, food, programming and guiding) are common to all operators, and competitive advantage must therefore be created through creative use of these elements and the quality of the overall experience.

Commitment to quality is therefore a vital part of company philosophy. Tour groups are kept small, with an average of 20 participants, accommodation is usually in four or five star hotels and additional services, such as obtaining visas, are also a basic part of the product. The most important element of the product, however, is the tour guide. The tour guide must have the following wide range of skills and knowledge:

- expert knowledge and a good general education;
- the ability to convey information clearly and vividly;

- a knowledge of the host country, its people and their customs, ecology, economy, culture, history, religion and tradition;
- the ability to entertain and involve clients in tour activities;
- the ability to make the experience come alive for the participants;
- be a good organizer and logician;
- have a love of 'their' country.

The 650 tour guides used by Studiosus receive continuous training, and meet regularly to exchange ideas and experiences.

Quality control is exercised through questionnaires distributed to every tour participant, 68% of which were returned in 1994. The questionnaires are machine-read to give instant feedback on the satisfaction level of clients. In 1994, over 90% of clients rated the guide services as 'very good' or 'good', and only 2.5% as 'not satisfactory'. Studiosus also runs a Clients Advisory Board, which meets twice a year to discuss product quality issues.

In recent years Studiosus has launched a number of new products to expand its sales. In 1989 a special city tour programme was launched to meet the growing demand for short-break holidays. By 1994 sales of this programme had reached 7180 packages, or 8% of total packages sold. In 1995 a special product for people aged between 25 and 35 was launched under the 'Young Line' brand name. The Young Line packages concentrate on less traditional cultural destinations such as Andalusia, Portugal, and Morocco, and are led by younger guides who are versed in the popular culture of the destination as well as the traditional high culture attractions. These packages are modestly priced in comparison with the main study tour products, with European tours costing between DM 1540 and DM 2550, compared with an average Studiosus package turnover of DM 3400 (ECU 1800). This product is expected to attract 1500 clients in its first year of operation.

As well as paying attention to product quality for individual clients, Studiosus is also concerned to develop good relationships with suppliers and distributors. Sales of Studiosus packages through 5900 travel agency outlets in Germany, Austria, Switzerland, Luxembourg and The Netherlands account for 96% of all business. Studiosus carefully selects the agents it uses, and tries to develop a personal relationship with them. Every travel agent receives a bunch of flowers for every tenth reservation.

Careful attention to product quality and identification of niche markets has made Studiosus a highly successful cultural tourism operator. At present, Germany and Austria are the only markets in which such cultural packages are sold in large volumes. It remains to be seen whether the Studiosus formula can be extended into a Single European Market.

The Schleswig-Holstein Music Festival

At the beginning there was, as so often, just a vague idea of a few people involved with the arts, government, and commerce. The idea was to present music performed by world-class artistes to a broad audience, in their home town. Thus, a consumer-oriented approach replaced the traditional attitude of the culture industry.

No longer does the customer have to go to the music, the music comes to the customer. The informal nature and almost homely atmosphere of the concerts appealed to new audiences. The festival is for the people. A greater identification of the people with their *Land* (federal state) as a result of the festival is a beneficial side-effect of the performances and a promotional tool for the whole region whose value should not be underestimated.

The festival improved the image of Schleswig-Holstein, a popular holiday destination. Holidays in this, the most northerly *Bundesland*, are no longer only associated with the beach and coastal landscapes. Enriching the range of cultural events with 'top quality music in the north' meant that another group of potential tourists was addressed, in addition to nature and beach lovers.

The Schleswig-Holstein Music Festival is a non-profit organization which takes the form of a registered charitable association. There is a manager who is responsible for the organizational aspects and marketing and the artistic side is handled by director Justus Franz.

In 1986, the first year the festival was held, there were 96 concerts with a total audience of 100,000, at 15 venues. The number of concerts and venues was increased the next year. The audience doubled and has stabilized at this high level.

The programme consists of several 'product lines'. Besides major events with well-known orchestras and conductors such as Yehudi Menuhin and Leonard Bernstein, the festival also features talented young artistes. Solo performances, chamber music, and master classes enhance the programme. Unusual venues such as barns and castles lend a special atmosphere to the concerts which is reinforced by the northern landscape. Special annual themes such as 'Music of the Baltic countries' or 'Jewish Music' are further attractions.

The consistent application of a mature marketing mix was one of the keys to the success of the Schleswig-Holstein Music Festival. A clear corporate identity consisting of a combination of music and the countryside (lakes, open land, the sea) means that the festival is multifaceted. Individual performances and the festival itself are promoted through advertisements, brochures, posters, etc. Promotional items such as T-shirts and stickers are not neglected. In addition to the advertising activities the professional public relations are also a key to the success of the festival. Regional radio stations provide daily information about the concerts. Director Justus Franz gives innumerable interviews and participates in performances with large audiences. The members of the festival association include many prominent artists and politicians – clear 'opinion leaders'.

The financial outlay for the festival is high, some DM 15.4 million (ECU 8.2 million) in 1993, and the festival would not be feasible without the financial support of the government of the *Land* and private sponsors. The private sponsors, for example, contribute over DM 3 million (ECU 1.6 million).

As the objective of the festival, to make art accessible to a wide audience, requires ticket prices which are lower than normal for classical music, the aim is not to make a profit, but rather to minimize losses. The average ticket price of DM 35 (ECU 18), ranging from DM 15 to DM 100, is relatively low. The loss of DM 6 per seat incurred in this situation is also extremely low compared to subsidies to normal concert halls and opera houses.

After nine years the Schleswig-Holstein Music Festival has now established itself as a clear cultural event. Despite many copycat attempts those responsible have managed to develop the festival into an independent and valuable contribution to the whole region. Its unique flair and the way in which it contributes to the quality of life means that both local residents and audiences strongly identify with the festival. The range of performances offered to a broad audience has an effect beyond the boundaries of Schleswig-Holstein in terms of understanding and advertising.

CULTURAL TOURISM IN EUROPE: OPPORTUNITIES AND THREATS

> One cannot, as Adorno once stressed, understand a period in history when one only knows its painting but not its music. Similarly one cannot understand a region, or should we say: a group of people, if one visits its castles but ignores how today's people live.
>
> (Maraite, 1993)

A comprehensive understanding of a culture forms a valuable contribution to cultural tourism and is the key to the mutual understanding of people and cultures. In our experience-oriented society a modern development of the 'supply' is a necessity. However, it would be wrong to limit oneself to just the 'big names'. Culture and cultural appreciation starts at a small scale.

The basic premise in all this is *vive la différence*. Nowadays, if you look at any large city, it becomes more and more difficult to decide where you are. The uniformity imposed by advertising and increasing similarity in lifestyles leads to cultural impoverishment. A reconsideration of their own culture and preservation of their identity would benefit many cities and regions. This is particularly true of German cities and regions whose characteristics have largely been lost, with a few exceptions.

We are not referring to a narrow-minded regional approach, but rather to a description of one's own culture together with an invitation to examine it. This interest in 'foreigners' and a reflection on one's own environment is what modern cultural tourism is about, across all borders.

Cultural tourism can provide opportunities for many in society to obtain a new perspective on other cultures. On a large scale this applies to Europe as a whole, just as it applies to East and West Germany on a smaller scale. The process of European integration is highly dependent on understanding other cultures in a dialogue, an exchange of experiences and values. Cultural tourism should be the motor of this process. 'Only those who experience culture as the whole of everything in life will be able to judge, when in doubt, what it means to live where they do. And this ability to judge is the basic condition for the peaceful coexistence of the peoples in Europe' (Maraite, 1993).

REFERENCES

Angioni, M. (1994) Cuts of DM700 million to the federal budget. *The Art Newspaper* 34, 4.

Anonymous (1994) *Frankfurter Allgemeine Zeitung*, 30 July.

Hillman, H. (1988) Deutschland als Kulturland – Zeitgemässe Darstellung des Deutschlandbildes im Ausland. In: *Kultur und Tourismus*, seminar documentation, German seminar for international tourism. Berlin.

Jung, B. (1994) For what leisure? The role of culture and recreation in post-Communist Poland. *Leisure Studies* 13, 262–276.

Klein, H.-J. (1990) *Der Glaeserne Besucher: Publikumsstrukturen einer Museumslandschaft*. Berliner Schriften zur Museumskunde. Bd. 8, 404 pp.

Lettl-Schröder, M. (1994) Further reconciliation of preferences in East and West. *FVW International* 7/94, 5–6.

Maraite, J. (1993) Kulturtourismus – Eine Perspektive für Europa. In: *Kulturtourismus in Europa: Wachstum ohne Grenzen*. Trier.

Studienkreis für Tourismus (various years) *Reiseanalyse*. Studienkreis für Tourismus, Starnburg.

Vetter, K. (1992) The quality concept of Studiosus Reisen, the market leader for cultural study tours in Germany (in German). In: Roth, P. and Schrand, A. (eds) *Touristik-Marketing*. Verlag Franz Vahlen, Munich, pp. 297–307.

Cultural Tourism in Greece 10

H. KALOGEROPOULOU

TEI Larissa, 41110 Larissa, Greece

INTRODUCTION

Culture has long played an important role in the development of tourism in Greece. The archaeological sites of Greece and their associated museums have always been a major draw for foreign visitors, and these same resources have played an important role in the national self-image of Greece. More recently, however, attention has shifted towards broadening the range of cultural attractions to include aspects of modern Greek culture as well.

In the past, culture has been viewed as an integral part of the Greek tourism product, rather than a specific form of tourism in its own right. Cultural tourism is now seen as being particularly important in a country whose tourism product has been largely based on beach holidays – a market which is coming under increasing pressure from competing destinations in the Mediterranean and elsewhere. Tourism demand is also highly seasonal and spatially concentrated. Cultural tourism is therefore seen as one potential vehicle for diversifying the basic beach holiday product, for spreading the tourism season, and persuading tourists to discover hitherto unknown areas of Greece. This may explain why the potential for cultural tourism development is perceived as being greater in Greece than in any other EU country (Irish Tourist Board, 1988).

At the same time, there is an increasing realization of the potential negative effects of visitor pressure on some of Greece's major cultural attractions, most notably the Acropolis.

THE SUPPLY OF CULTURAL ATTRACTIONS

Classical sites act as a major attraction for incoming tourism to Greece. The EU Inventory of Cultural Tourism Resources (Irish Tourist Board, 1988), lists 173 attractions in Greece, the majority of which are based on classical sites or artefacts. Greece has 38 sites of international significance listed in the inventory, two-thirds of which are classified as either 'archaeological' or 'historical' resources.

The distribution of major sites reflects their predominantly classical origins. Only 16 cultural sites are located in Athens, or 9% of inventoried sites. In comparison, Rome accounts for almost 18% of Italy's listed sites. Many of the Greek sites are located in rural areas, away from major towns and cities. This has tended to inhibit the growth of urban-based cultural tourism in Greece. As Fatourou (1995) notes, most foreign tourists in Greece stay outside the major cities, and only make day trips to museums or archaeological sites. This underlines the relatively early origin of most of Greece's cultural tourism resources. Even so, the centralized nature of Greek administration and funding, coupled with the strong feeling for national identity, have tended to place much emphasis on a few major sites of international significance. Those archaeological sites which have been developed for tourism therefore tend to be close to major urban centres, such as the Acropolis (Athens) and Knossos (Heraklion).

Financial constraints have also tended to limit the development of the thousands of sites of potential historical and cultural interest which exist throughout Greece. As economic development has proceeded, however, pressure from local inhabitants has led to the opening of sites in rural areas, where tourism can provide a substantial boost to the local economy. Examples of such developments are to be found in the archaeological sites at Dion, Dodoni, Pylos, Phaistos, Sparti and Mystras. It should be recognized, however, that for the Greek population antiquities represent far more than simple tourist attractions – they form a basic element of Greek identity and tradition. The former Greek culture minister Melina Mercouri emphasized that in the development of cultural resources the maintenance of Greek identity should take precedence over economic or tourism development.

The Greek interest in traditional culture is reflected in the number of museums. The 240 national and regional museums listed by UNESCO in 1979 had increased to 267 in 1990 (UNESCO, 1994). It is at local level that most supply growth has taken place. There are now 365 folklore museums, of which 62 are located in Athens, founded mainly by cultural societies and local authorities, with encouragement from the Ministry of Culture.

As in Italy, there are a large number of unused or underutilized cultural resources. Only a small number of the archaeological collections in Greece are open to the public, because in many cases safety measures are not adequate to allow public access. There are, however, a number of new developments being planned which will help to upgrade the cultural tourism resources of Greece. EU funding is helping to restore the Acropolis, and the monastic buildings at Mount Athos in Macedonia. The Goulandris Foundation Museum of Modern Art is to be built in the centre of Athens, and is due to open in 1997. The $14 million (ECU 17.5 million) construction costs and all running costs are to be met by the foundation established by a Greek shipping family.

As with other Mediterranean destinations with a heavy reliance on a basic sun, sea and sand tourism product (see Maiztegui-Oñate and Bertolín, Chapter 15 this volume, for example), Greece is busy trying to diversify its tourism offer. Cultural tourism is seen as one important means of achieving diversification. In Chios, a small, relatively undeveloped island, for example, they are trying to avoid the pitfalls of mass tourism development with the help of a development policy based around cultural tourism (ECTARC, 1989; Munsters, 1994). The policy, developed with the help of Austrian advisers, was based on a number of measures designed to stimulate local cultural production to help maximize the tourism income accruing to local residents. Measures proposed included a programme of cultural events, promotion of medieval heritage and traditional architecture, and the development of products typical of the island for sale to tourists. Measures were also proposed which would ensure the continuation and enrichment of local traditions, including the establishment of workshops for artists, which could be used by artists from other regions of Greece, and the staging of an international architectural symposium, based on the built heritage of the island (Munsters, 1994).

DEMAND FOR CULTURAL TOURISM

Tourism demand in Greece is dominated by the inbound tourist market. Foreign tourists generate 75% of overnight stays, and represent the major market for cultural attractions. Tourism is highly concentrated, both seasonally and spatially (Donatos and Zairis, 1990). About 60% of foreign tourists arrive between June and September, and four regions (Crete, Rhodes, Corfu and Athens) accounted for 62% of overnight stays in 1990. This creates considerable pressure on sites located in these areas during the high season.

The importance of classical archaeology in the cultural tourism product of Greece is underlined by the fact that archaeological sites attracted over 7 million visitors in 1990, over twice as many as visited Greek museums. Most museum visits are also connected with classical archaeology, since almost half the museums in Greece are archaeological museums. Greece in fact has the highest proportion of archaeological sites of international importance in the EU (Irish Tourist Board, 1988).

Visitor figures for museums and archaeological sites only cover paid admissions, and are therefore likely to be a significant underestimate of total

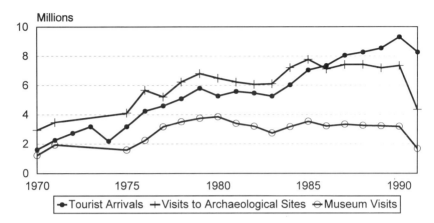

Fig. 10.1. Visits to Greek archaeological sites and museums compared with total tourist flows (source: ATLAS database).

attendances, since public cultural attractions do not charge for admission on Sundays, which is the most popular day for Greek visitors. Attendances at both archaeological sites (+150%) and museums (+159%) grew significantly between 1970 and 1990. The most dramatic expansion in visitor numbers took place in the 1970s, however. In contrast with most other EU countries, paid museum visits in Greece stagnated during the 1980s.

From a comparison of the pattern of paid visits to archaeological sites and museums and the level of tourist arrivals in Greece (Fig. 10.1), it is clear that there is a relationship between tourist arrivals and cultural visits. Tourist arrivals are particularly strongly correlated with the number of visits to archaeological sites during the period 1975–1991 ($r = 0.76$), but less strongly correlated with the level of museum visits ($r = 0.57$). The fact that tourist arrivals seem to be more strongly related to archaeological site admissions may explain to some extent the relative lack of growth in museum visits during the 1980s. A potentially worrying trend which emerges from Fig. 10.1 is the relative decoupling of archaeological sites admissions and tourist arrivals in the late 1980s. This may suggest that incoming tourists are relatively less interested in culture than tourists in previous years. This is perhaps understandable in view of the fact that much of the market expansion in Greece during the 1980s was accounted for by cheap package holidays, which might tend to attract relatively fewer culturally motivated tourists.

The importance of culture in attracting foreign tourists was also underlined by research undertaken by the Greek National Tourist Office (GNTO) in the mid-1980s (Buckley and Papadopoulos, 1986). Greek antiquities were cited as a reason for visiting by 9% of all tourists, and the combination of climate and antiquities was cited by a further 18% of tourists. Table 10.1

Table 10.1. Reasons for choosing Greece as a holiday destination, 1984–85.

Origin country	% respondents	
	Antiquities	Antiquities and climate
Australia	15	13
Austria	4	21
France	12	32
Italy	25	21
Japan	35	9
Netherlands	7	23
Spain	41	18
Sweden	1	14
UK	3	10
USA	24	13
West Germany	6	29

Source: Buckley and Papadopoulos (1986).

indicates that antiquities were a particularly strong attraction for visitors from Spain, Japan, the USA, and Italy. It is clear that for most northern Europeans cultural attractions in Greece take second place to climate, but culture is for many visitors a strong subsidiary factor which may give Greece an advantage relative to some competing sun, sea, and sand destinations.

The classical origin of much of the cultural attraction supply in Greece means that Athens is not as dominant in terms of cultural visits as some European capitals. The Athens region accounted for just over a quarter of all archaeological site visits in 1992, for example, the vast majority of which were accounted for by visitors to the Acropolis. The tendency to centralize collections of artefacts in museums in the capital, however, means that Athens accounted for about 40% of all museum admissions in 1992.

An important element of cultural tourism product development in Greece has been the creation of a large number of festivals and *son et lumière* performances in recent years. The GNTO lists over 300 festivals and cultural events in Greece, the most important of which in tourism terms are the Athens Festival (which celebrated its 40th anniversary in 1995) and the Epidaurus Festival. Both of these GNTO-organized events are located in ancient open-air theatres, making them particularly attractive for foreign tourists. These two events attracted over 100,000 visitors to 41 performances in 1993. The GNTO is also responsible for organizing *son et lumière* performances during the summer months in Athens, Rhodes, and Corfu. These events are aimed mainly at foreign tourists, with over half of the performances being in English. In 1993, the 383 *son et lumière* performances attracted over 88,000 visitors, generating over Dr 82 million (ECU 310,000) in ticket sales.

Surveys of visitors to cultural sites in Greece were conducted in the summer of 1992 as part of the ATLAS cultural tourism research project. Almost

Table 10.2. Origin of visitors interviewed at three cultural sites, summer 1992.

Visitor origin	% of respondents
Greece	40.3
UK	13.6
Germany	13.3
USA	10.9
France	2.7
Italy	2.7
Other Europe	12.6
Rest of the world	3.9

Source: ATLAS Survey (1992).

Table 10.3. Cultural attractions visited in Greece.

	% respondents visiting
Museums	73
Heritage centres	35
Historic monuments	41
Art galleries	34
Performing arts	31
Festivals	20

Source: ATLAS Survey (1992).

600 visitors were interviewed, equally distributed between three survey sites: the National Art Gallery in Athens, the archaeological site of Dion in Macedonia and the archaeological museum in Thessaloniki. Almost 60% of the visitors interviewed were foreign tourists, mainly from the UK, Germany, and the United States (Table 10.2). The proportion of American tourists was highest in Athens, whereas English and German tourists were more numerous at the two regional sites. Many of the foreign tourists were visiting Greece on package holidays, staying in hotels and spending two or three weeks in the country.

The majority of foreign tourists visited at least one other cultural attraction during their stay in Greece. Museums were the most frequently visited type of cultural attraction (these include archaeological museums attached to archaeological sites), and the visual and performing arts were far less important elements of tourism consumption (Table 10.3).

The motivating power of Greek archaeology is clear from a comparison of the three sites. Relatively few foreign tourists had travelled specifically to visit the art museum in Athens, whereas at the archaeological attractions almost half the visitors questioned indicated that the attraction was important in their decision to visit the location (Table 10.4). Those visiting the art museum in

Table 10.4.   Importance of cultural attraction in decision by foreign tourists to visit location.

Importance	% foreign tourists		
	National Art Gallery, Athens	Archaeological Site, Dion	Archaeological Museum, Thessaloniki
Very important	5.2	26.1	33.3
Quite important	16.7	22.5	21.7
Important	27.1	29.7	28.3
Unimportant	36.5	10.9	8.3
Very unimportant	14.6	10.9	8.3
	($n = 96$)	($n = 138$)	($n = 120$)

Source: ATLAS Survey (1992).

Table 10.5.   Occupations connected with culture – foreign tourists.

Occupation connected with	% foreign tourists		
	National Art Gallery, Athens	Archaeological Site, Dion	Archaeological Museum, Thessaloniki
Heritage/museums	16.3	17.0	20.8
Performing arts	13.3	14.9	16.7
Visual arts	23.5	5.7	13.3
	($n = 98$)	($n = 141$)	($n = 120$)

Source: ATLAS Survey (1992).

Athens were significantly more likely to have an occupation connected with the visual arts than visitors to the other two sites (Table 10.5).

One notable feature of the Greek surveys was the relatively high proportion of respondents who had visited festivals while on holiday. Over 20% of those interviewed at Greek cultural sites had visited a festival in Greece, compared with 11% for the ATLAS survey as a whole.

When compared with the results of ATLAS surveys in other countries, it appears that Greece tends to have fewer specific cultural tourists. However, as was suggested by earlier research, the presence of cultural attractions, and particularly archaeological sites, is an important secondary motive for visiting Greece.

CULTURAL TOURISM POLICY

Although cultural tourism was identified as an area of national importance as early as 1946, initiatives to plan for and develop cultural tourism have tended to proceed in a piecemeal fashion. Culture still tends to be seen as part of the generic Greek tourism product, rather than a specific market segment to be developed. In the 1950s and 1960s, the emphasis of tourism policy was placed on the development of the hotel supply and tourism infrastructure. During this period a number of hotels (*Xenia*) were constructed in locations connected with cultural tourism attractions, such as Delphi and Olympia.

In the 1970s, however, an attempt was made to diversify the tourism market for Greece, and to develop culture as one of the main elements of the Greek tourism product. Since 1975, the GNTO has been engaged in a programme of restoration and development of traditional buildings in a number of locations throughout Greece (Greek National Tourist Office, 1992). The aim of the programme is to preserve buildings and townscapes representative of Greek culture, and to develop these resources for tourist use, thereby creating income to support employment and further conservation. The programme concentrates on preserving and developing heritage in areas removed from the main tourist regions, particularly on the mainland. Many of these settlements are declining as a result of rural depopulation, so the development of tourism helps to generate economic activity which helps to stem out-migration. Basic principles applied to all these developments include the preservation of original architectural features and the aesthetic qualities of the local area, adaption to new uses (usually tourism) and strict control of new building to ensure compatibility with original buildings. By 1991, a total of 119 buildings in 16 villages had been restored, providing almost 700 tourist beds in regions with low levels of tourism development. The cost of the programme (Dr 727 million, ECU 2.75 million) was met by the Greek government, with support from the Mediterranean Integration Programme of the EU. A publication giving architectural details of all the projects completed was produced as part of the Greek contribution to the European Year of Tourism in 1990.

The development of Vathia in the Peloponnese provides an example of how the programme has worked. In 1975, the village of Vathia was almost abandoned, and had only 11 inhabitants. In 1978, the GNTO began to redevelop the settlement, with the aim of attracting tourists to the renovated traditional buildings, and persuading emigrants to return to the village. The GNTO building programme included nine hostels with a total of 50 beds, a restaurant, a coffee house and a folklore museum. The redevelopment also included infrastructure improvements, such as drainage and road widening. The original Dr 110 million (ECU 416,000) investment by the GNTO stimulated further private investment, which by 1991 had supported the renovation of a further 175 buildings, and the provision of a further 400 beds. Similar programmes are also being carried out in a number of other areas, including Santorini, Chios, and Cefalonia.

The protection of the natural and cultural environment has become an increasingly pressing policy issue in Greek tourism in recent years. The realization that previous developments had often damaged the basic natural and cultural resources on which tourism is based, has led to an increasing policy emphasis on alternative tourism and spreading tourism away from over-crowded resort areas. The current policy priorities for the GNTO, for example, are:

- Tourism, culture and friendship;
- Tourism, environment and health;
- Tourism all year round;
- Regional development of tourism.

Culture is also seen as an important expression of Greek national identity, and much government policy on culture is directed at strengthening the image of Greece both internally and externally. For example, the European Cultural Capital event (see Richards, Chapter 2 this volume) was the brainchild of Greek Minister of Culture, Melina Mercouri. Athens became the first Cultural Capital in 1985, and the event was heavily subsidized by the Greek government. Over 100 exhibitions were organized, which attracted over 700,000 visitors. The staging of the first Cultural Capital event in Athens was a recognition of the contribution of Greek culture to the shaping of a wider European cultural identity.

Responsibility for funding cultural tourism development is spread across several ministries, including the Ministry of Culture, the Ministry of Tourism, the Ministry of the Interior and the Ministry of Environment. Funding for cultural tourism, and for culture in general is fairly centralized, although there have been efforts in recent years to decentralize responsibilities and activities in culture (Fisher, 1990). There is an interministerial body which tries to coordinate the work of the Ministry of Culture and the Ministry of Tourism, although cultural tourism is not the *raison d'etre* of this body (Irish Tourist Board, 1988).

The Ministry of Culture devotes a large share of its budget to the preservation of heritage, and one of its main policy aims is to 'excavate, elevate and conserve' archaeological sites and monuments. Government funding for culture amounted to Dr 180 billion (ECU 681 million) in 1993, of which over 75% was spent on national heritage (mainly archaeological sites). Cultural expenditure accounts for 7% of the state budget, which is supplemented with 15% of the funds generated by state lotteries.

Greece has also made active use of European programmes aimed at promoting and protecting cultural heritage. As well as hosting the first European Cultural Capital event in 1985, in 1997 Greece will be the first country to host the event twice, this time in Thessaloniki. Greece has also been an active participant in the programme of DGX of the European Commission aimed at the Preservation of European Architectural Heritage. Under this programme conservation work has been undertaken at the Ancient Theatre of Filippi, in Macedonia, the Theatre of Lakki in Leros, the Ancient Conservatory in Kos and at the Aigli Open Air Cinema in Thessaloniki (European Commission, 1994). The importance of cultural heritage in the Greek economy is further underlined by the fact that a whole regional aid programme by DGXVI in Greece has been used for cultural heritage development.

THE IMPACT OF CULTURAL TOURISM

One area in which extensive research has been undertaken on tourism in Greece is the assessment of the social and cultural impacts of tourism (Briassoulis, 1993). Studies have tended to concentrate on the Greek islands, where the impact of tourism is often most pronounced. The development of tourism often leads to the commodification of local culture for consumption by the tourists. This includes the adaption of traditional feasts as tourist events, the proliferation of cultural stereotypes, such as bouzouki music, and the ubiquitous sale of 'Greek art' souvenirs. According to Briassoulis, this leads to the creation of a 'fake authenticity' in tourist destinations, in which traditional artefacts lose their original purpose, and serve merely as decorative objects.

Research on the islands of Ios and Serifos by Tartas (1992:527) indicates that the cultural changes initiated by tourism can have significant impacts on the cohesion and cultural identity of the islanders:

> People no longer attend the traditional feasts, either because these take place in the summer and they do not 'want' to leave their jobs, or because there has been a change in their lifestyle. The change on Ios is crucial – because the local feasts were always an opportunity to bring the inhabitants of all social and economic strata together, and helped islanders express themselves with the symbols of their common cultural identity (songs, dances, etc.).

Local culture is therefore not just an attraction for cultural tourists, but is also the source of resource struggles between local inhabitants and tourists, and among the local inhabitants themselves.

CASE STUDY: THE NATIONAL ART GALLERY, ATHENS

The National Art Gallery is situated close to the cultural heart of Greece, in the centre of Athens. Originally founded as a home for the art collections of the University and the Polytechnic of Athens in 1834, the Gallery has gradually become the home of the national collections of modern Greek and West European art.

During the nineteenth century, the original collection was augmented primarily through private donations, and the collection was used extensively for theoretical teaching in the Faculty of Arts in the Polytechnic. Interest from central government only emerged towards the end of the nineteenth century, when Alexander Soutsos, a major fine art collector, bequeathed his considerable collection for the establishment of 'a museum of paintings'. A commission was established in 1892 to study the feasibility of founding a National Art Gallery, and in 1900 the required legislation was passed by the Greek government. The transfer of the collections into public ownership brought significant changes in the management of the gallery, most importantly in the broadening of public access to the collections.

Today the National Gallery is managed by a Board of Directors which includes the president of the National Bank of Greece and a member of the Soutsos family (as stipulated in the will of Alexander Soutsos), and six members appointed directly by the Ministry of Culture. The Gallery has a traditional management structure, divided into three departments: Art History, Art Maintenance, and Administration and Finance. One sign of increasing flexibility in staffing, however, is the fact that one-third of the Gallery staff of 60 are on renewable short-term contracts.

Finance comes direct from the Ministry of Culture, which provides a budget for running costs and staff costs. Other income is derived from the National Lotto, entrance fees (although admission is free at weekends), merchandizing, donations, and sponsorship.

As a government institution, the basic function of the Gallery is educational. The collections of the Gallery present the evolution of modern Greek art, and illustrate its links with previous art traditions. Extensive provision has therefore been made for educational groups. An education centre is provided for lectures on the collections, and audio-visual facilities are also being planned.

Visitors

As a result of the primarily educational orientation of the National Gallery, relatively few tourists considered the Gallery to be an important motivation to visit Athens (22%). This also explains why the proportion of foreign tourists interviewed at the Gallery (49%) was lower than at the other two Greek survey sites (71% at Dion and 60% in Thessaloniki).

Visitor figures for the National Art Gallery are only available on the basis of ticket sales. As admission is free at weekends, ticket sales give only a rough indication of total visitor numbers. The wide variations in ticket sales from one year to the next (Fig. 10.2) illustrate the significant influence of individual exhibitions on ticket sales. Foreign visitors make an important contribution to boosting visitor numbers during such events. The National Gallery also stages a number of international exhibitions, and has, in recent years, featured major American, German, and Italian artists.

The general pattern of visitor numbers to the National Gallery seems to follow a similar trend to other Greek museums (Fig. 10.1). Although the peaks and troughs are clearly exaggerated by individual exhibitions, the overall trend in visitor numbers seems to be related to the strength of the economy and the

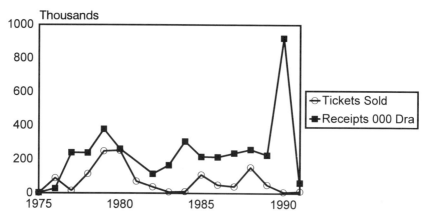

Fig. 10.2.   Tickets sold and receipts at the National Art Gallery, Athens (source: Statistical Yearbook of Greece, 1976–1993).

level of inbound tourism. At present, there is relatively little incentive for this government-run institution to actively market itself for cultural tourism to try and build a significant visitor base.

CONCLUSIONS

Although the rich cultural heritage of Greece is a major draw for tourists, and an important source of competitive advantage in the battle for tourism market share in the Mediterranean, cultural tourism as a distinct market segment is still poorly developed. Most tourists coming to Greece view culture as one part of the total tourism product, rather than a primary motivation for visiting the country. Cultural tourism is viewed in much the same way by policy-makers in Greece itself, and there has been little effort to develop specific cultural tourism products. There is no doubt, however, that Greece is keenly aware of the importance of preserving her cultural heritage as a source of national identity and not just as a basic resource for tourism.

ACKNOWLEDGEMENTS

The author wishes to thank the following individuals who were helpful in supplying information and assistance with the research for this chapter: Lazaros Georgakopoulos, S. Stavrou, A. Hatzidakis, M. Mitropoulos, Mrs Ragou (GNTO), K. Katsigianis (Vice Minister of Environment), Professor Dora N. Konsula (University of Athens), Professor Lambraki-Plaka (Director of the National Gallery), D. Pantermanlis (Professor of Classical Archaeology,

University of Thessaloniki), Mrs Vokotopoulou (archaeologist), Mrs Ignatiadou (archaeologist, Museum of Thessaloniki), A. Vassilopoulos (Ministry of Culture), Mrs Zafiraki (Statistics Service of the Ministry of Culture), Professor N. Methodiou (University of Athens), Professor T. Tsaliki (University of Athens).

REFERENCES

Briassoulis, H. (1993) Tourism in Greece. In: Pompl, W. and Lavery, P. (eds) *Tourism in Europe: Structures and Developments*. CAB International, Wallingford, pp. 285–301.

Buckley, P.J. and Papadopoulos, S.I. (1986) Marketing Greek tourism – the planning process. *Tourism Management* 7, 86–100.

Donatos, G. and Zairis, P. (1990) Seasonality of foreign tourism in the Greek island of Crete. *Annals of Tourism Research* 17, 515–519.

ECTARC (1989) *Contribution to the Drafting of a Charter for Cultural Tourism*. European Centre for Traditional and Regional Cultures, Llangollen, Wales.

European Commission (1994) *Preservation of the European Cultural Heritage*. DGX, European Commission, Brussels.

Fatourou, K. (1995) Erfolg uberdeckt die probleme. *FVW International* 5/95, 195–196.

Fisher, R. (1990) *Briefing Notes on the Organisation of Culture in EEC Countries*. Arts Council, London.

Greek National Tourist Office (1992) *Preservation and Development of Traditional Settlements in Greece*. GNTO, Athens.

Irish Tourist Board (1988) *Inventory of Cultural Tourism Resources in the Member States and Assessment of Methods Used to Promote Them*. European Commission DG VII, Brussels.

Munsters, W. (1994) *Cultuurtoerisme*. Garant, Louvain-Apeldoorn.

Tartas, P. (1992) Socioeconomic impacts of tourism on two Greek isles. *Annals of Tourism Research* 19, 516–533.

UNESCO (1994) *Statistical Yearbook*. UNESCO, Paris.

Cultural Tourism in Ireland   11

G. O Donnchadha and B. O Connor

School of Business and Social Studies, Tralee Regional Technical College, Clash, Tralee, County Kerry, Ireland

INTRODUCTION

Cultural tourism has assumed an ever-increasing economic and cultural significance in Ireland in recent years. The Irish Government and Bord Failte, the National Tourism Organization, have identified cultural tourism as one of their principal areas of investment for economic development. In addition, the Irish people in general and tourism entrepreneurs in particular have come to realize that in the Irish Culture in all its manifestations there survives something unique in the Western world, namely the last vestiges of the Celtic culture that was one of the parents of modern European culture. More than other Celtic regions, such as Brittany, Cornwall, Wales, the Isle of Man, and Scotland, Ireland has preserved for the modern tourist a culture that was almost lost and yet one that has helped mould the world and the values we know today.

In this chapter, we define 'culture' as the logical and mythological base that underlies and legitimates the everyday activities of a given people. These activities are cognitive, conative, and cathectic; they comprise conscious and unconscious thoughts, actions, and emotions. We may, then, define cultural tourism as travel in search of a particular logic of thought, action and emotion. The logic sought may be connected with the tourist as an emigrant or descendant of an emigrant; this is sometimes called the search for roots and may be seen as sentimental or nostalgic, or, it may be an effort to understand hidden or subconscious elements in oneself. On the other hand, the search may be for an alternate culture or logic which may be experienced and enjoyed in itself, recreationally as it were. The experience may also be educational, helping the

	Inner-worldly	World-fleeing
Rational	Protestantism World-dominating (Yang) Zweckrational	Catholicism Wertrational
Non-rational	Confucianism World-accepting (Yin) Traditional	Hinduism

Fig. 11.1.   Weber's typology of major world cultures.

tourist to understand better the taken-for-granted elements in their own culture and appreciating different values from other cultures.

According to Weber (1964, 1978), for five thousand years Europe and the Middle East have been divided between two archetypal cultures, 'Inner-worldly' and 'World-fleeing'. Weber argued further that different forms of these two basic cultures could be identified according to their degree of 'rationality'. Weber's typology, shown in Fig. 11.1, therefore comprises four major world cultures, related to protestantism, catholicism, confucianism, and hinduism.

However, in identifying the categories with different religions Weber was not talking about theology but of culture, of the spirit that informs a certain world-view or *Weltanschauung*. This point is underlined in the title of one of Max Weber's most influential writings, *The Protestant Ethic and the Spirit of Capitalism* (Weber 1952). It is not the place where one worships that determines one's cultural orientation but rather it is the spirit (*Geist*) that is already informed and enlivened by the culture one lives in, and by, that determines both our consciousness and world-view.

A mathematical rationality initially emerged in the Middle East and came to fruition in Ancient Greece. This rationality moulded the early Christian Church and its later rediscovery gave rise to the Renaissance and to Protestantism, particularly to Calvinism, about which Weber introduced the term 'the Protestant Ethic'. This protestant type of rational spirit is characterized by efficiency, individualism, and self-control. A second type of rationality developed in the ancient world, this time in Rome. This is the rationality of bureaucracy, law and logistics that were the basis of the strength of the Roman Empire and which continue today in the capitalist world and in the Roman Catholic Church. This rationality places more emphasis on authority and on the group. In all classical culture there is tight control. To take one example only, classical art is tightly representational and its architecture follows strict mathematical models like the golden ratio. Finally, because of its use of writing, classical rational culture has had an overpowering influence on the Western world.

Yet when this classical culture was at its height it was but one of two great western cultures. The other was the Celtic culture that is so much less available to us because the Celts did not use writing. The difference between these two cultures is emphasized by Nietzsche in his typology of Apollonian and Dionysian cultures (Nietzsche, 1917). The former is the classical – controlled, rational, analytical, individualistic – whereas the Dionysian is expressive, non-rational (or even irrational), synthetic, symbolic and group-oriented, all qualities found in Celtic culture. The best example of Celtic non-rationality must be Celtic art, the symbolic, tortuous, sometimes playful expressionism that decorates weapons, utensils, sacred vessels, and manuscripts.

Celtic culture once held sway from the Himalayas to the Blasket Islands; only recently has the world at large begun to understand its significance. We know of it at second hand from classical sources, from excavations at Hallstatt and La Tene, from the artefacts in the world's museums and, above all, from the surviving culture in Gaelic Scotland, Wales, and Ireland. Particularly in Ireland is there a vibrant expression of Celtic culture in the customs and everyday lives of ordinary people. The hospitality, the friendliness, the expressiveness described by Strabo (Delaney,1989) have become hallmarks of cultural tourism in Ireland; the two most important sources of enjoyment for tourists visiting Ireland are the beauty of the scenery and the friendliness of the people.

Irish culture is not merely Celtic. Just as the thunderous Atlantic is turned back upon itself from the mighty cliffs of the west coast of Ireland, so successive civilizations reached the Western Seaboard from landward and were thrown back upon themselves and on those that were there before them. Elsewhere in Europe prior civilizations were driven out or dispersed by those who succeeded them. Not so in Ireland. The farthest neolithic people live on in our genes and in our folklore as the 'little people', inhabitants of the underground and keepers of the old traditions. To this original culture were added the influences of successive newcomers, such as bronze-age traders, the iron-bearing Celts, the Norsemen, the Normans, and English and Scottish settlers.

All of these influences remain in the melting-pot that is Irish culture, a culture that is fascinating, enthralling, exasperating and unique in the Western world, combining as no other does, Weber's four types of culture. Modernization is providing a springboard for rational world-dominance which yet must contend with a deep traditional world-acceptance and a rigorous Hindu-like world-rejection that was so characteristic of the early Irish Christian monks and which has been reinforced by more recent Jansenism; it must also contend with a *Gemeinschaft* value-rationality of tribe and family that has always characterized Irish society. This rich cultural mixture provides the basic resource on which modern cultural tourism is founded.

CULTURAL TOURISM POLICY

Broadly speaking, the culture of Ireland has been and continues to be preserved and cherished by the Government and by its Office of Public Works, who act in consort with local groups to preserve sites and to set up heritage and inter-pretative centres. The National Museum, which is responsible for artefacts of Irish and Celtic culture and civilization, also has an important role to play. In terms of cultural tourism, however, it is Bord Failte which plays a key role in establishing policies and trying to coordinate the diverse strands of Irish cul-ture. In 1990 Bord Failte published an *Action Plan for Heritage Attractions*, which was an initial attempt to unify a very diverse and dispersed cultural tourism offer. A continued emphasis on heritage and cultural tourism is clear from subsequent policy documents published by Bord Failte (Page, 1994). Current national government policy on cultural tourism is set out in a com-munication from the Department of Tourism and Trade.

Heritage tourism

Ireland's unique cultural heritage fascinates foreign visitors. It is generally recog-nized that these visitors come to Ireland to discover just what it is that is so distinc-tive about our natural and man-made heritage as well as our vibrant cultural tradition. Last year alone over five and a half million visits were made by domestic and overseas visitors to heritage attractions subject to an entry charge in Ireland. A further two million visited National Cultural Institutions (e.g. Killarney National Park) which are not subject to an entry charge.

Generally tourists want heritage attractions to be old and different. Ireland has a vivid and colourful history with the added advantage that many of her at-tractions are a direct link with an age of myth and legend. Such distinguished at-tractions as Newgrange and Knowth, the Hill of Tara and the Ceide Fields date to the very dawn of human civilisation and allow great scope for imagination.

In addition to these ancient remains Ireland has castles, houses and gardens belonging to an age of aristocratic ease and political intrigue. King John's Castle and its surrounding medieval quarter, for example, is a Heritage Precinct of inter-national tourism significance. The thirteen acre Precinct contains several out-standing man-made and natural elements, including the 12th Century St Mary's Cathedral, the 13th Century King John's Castle, a scenic stretch of Shannon River frontage as well as many other medieval and post medieval buildings of historical significance. Similarly, the 14,000 acre demesne of Powerscourt with its magnifi-cent waterfall and gardens, rare shrubberies and deer park and great houses such as Castletown, Russborough and Westport house and gardens provide the tourist with a window through which they can catch a glimpse of our sometimes forgot-ten past. These attractions are a match for anything to be found anywhere in Europe.

Ireland also has a unique heritage with lyrical and literary qualities that influence Irish life to this day. The exalted position of the Bard in ancient Celtic society is reflected in the high regard afforded musicians and story-tellers in modern Irish Society. Irish music, both modern and traditional, is spreading throughout the world with the able assistance of performers such as U2, the Cranberries, Hot House Flowers, The Chieftains, Clannad, Enya and many more. Many people's first exposure to Irish culture is through such musicians which in turn inspires them to visit Ireland.

The success of Ireland's story-tellers has been immense. The list of Irish writers of international stature extends from Swift through Yeats, Joyce, Beckett and Behan to Roddy Doyle, a recent example of the international recognition afforded our story-tellers.

We also tell, with increasing success, our stories through the medium of film. Jim Sheridan and Neil Jordan excite the curiosity of many about Ireland, with their entertaining and thought-provoking films. Many such films are shot on location in Ireland and give their world-wide audiences a glimpse of the natural scenic beauty that is here in abundance.

A major part of the strategy for tourism growth in this country is based on the development and promotion of Ireland's heritage. Over the period of the last Operational Programme for Tourism 1989–1993 it is estimated that over IR£112 million has been invested in historic houses, castles and monuments, national parks, literary museums, interpretative centres and theme parks. A product marketing group, Heritage Island Ltd. was recently established to facilitate the group marketing of the heritage product. This group has over 60 members ranging from medieval castles to 18th century mansions to underground caves, and has recently published an illustrated guide.

These trends in investment and promotion are set to continue. The Government, in the National Development Plan, has proposed major investment in the areas of culture and heritage and marketing. It recognizes that culture and heritage products are emerging as one of the most popular forms of all-weather tourist facility in the Irish product range, with a crucial role to play in extending the tourism season.

(Department of Tourism and Trade, 1994)

The Government's concept of culture certainly casts a wide net! It will be shown later that significant further investment in cultural tourism is envisaged.

SUPPLY AND FUNDING OF CULTURAL ATTRACTIONS

Ireland has a rich supply of cultural and heritage attractions. An audit of the Irish national heritage in 1985 indicated the existence of 200,000 known archaeological sites and monuments, and 60,000 buildings of architectural or historic interest (Page, 1994). Until relatively recently, however, the

development of these potential attractions for cultural tourism was hampered by lack of coordination and funding.

Ireland has, however, made extensive use of European funding in recent years to improve cultural attractions and their accessibility. Tourism funding for Ireland under the European Regional Development Fund (ERDF) increased significantly in the late 1980s, helped by its status as a peripheral country. Grants totalling IR£ 147 million (ECU 185 million) were made from ERDF and European Social Fund sources between 1989 and 1993, and 40% of the ERDF funding was allocated to historical and cultural tourism products (Page, 1994).

The Government acts through its Department of Tourism and Trade and through Bord Failte to establish and implement tourism policy and development guidelines. The implementation of cultural tourism policy is largely the responsibility of a wide range of agencies and representative bodies. Some of the main bodies which play a role in cultural tourism are described in this section.

The most significant government body is The Office of Public Works (OPW), which is responsible for conserving and promoting Ireland's natural and built resources through the National Parks and Monuments, Waterways and Wildlife Services. The OPW has, to date, established interpretive and visitor facilities at over thirty sites, with guided tours, publications, exhibitions and audio-visual presentations. The National Heritage Council was established by *An Taoiseach* (the Prime Minister) to formulate policies and priorities to identify, protect, preserve, enhance and increase awareness of heritage. The Council has National Lottery funds available to assist heritage projects within its specific terms of reference (architecture, archaeology, flora, fauna, landscape, heritage gardens, and certain inland waterways) and will also consider educational and promotional projects in these areas. The Genealogical Office, which incorporates the office of the Chief Herald, is the State authority for Ireland in matters of heraldry, genealogy and family history. The authority was constituted in 1552 and has operated without a break since then. Important government-funded cultural institutions also include the National Museum of Ireland, the National Gallery and the National Library of Ireland.

In the voluntary sector, *An Taisce*, The National Trust for Ireland, is concerned with the conservation of the best of Ireland's heritage and with development which accords well with the environment and enhances it. It is recognized internationally as the most influential voluntary and independent environmental organization in Ireland, and is designated a prescribed body by the Planning Acts. Its members act through local associations throughout the country. Irish Heritage Properties is an association of most of the important houses, castles and gardens open to the public throughout Ireland. It was founded under the auspices of Bord Failte in 1971 and has 58 member properties including five properties of the National Trust for Northern Ireland.

The important human resource issues raised by cultural tourism development are also recognized by the Council for Education Recruitment and Training (CERT), the national institution with responsibility for recruitment, education and training standards in all areas of the tourism and catering trade in Ireland. Similarly, the Irish Heritage Education Network promotes heritage education in Ireland in the activities of museums, galleries, contemporary arts centres and other appropriate organizations.

A recent development in the commercial sphere is the establishment of Heritage Island Ltd, a heritage marketing organization, which works in conjunction with Bord Failte, the Northern Ireland Tourist Board, the OPW and the National Trust. Heritage Island offers tour operators and travel organizers a comprehensive sales and marketing support service including a central database with detailed information on every Heritage Island attraction, advice on itinerary planning and a library of brochures and fact sheets for individual attractions. Heritage Island markets 61 major cultural tourism attractions, including Dublin Castle, the Ulster-American Folk Park, the Irish National Heritage Park, the Connemara National Park, Dunmore Cave, Foxford Woollen Mills, Great Blasket Island, and other important heritage sites.

Two further areas of activity must be mentioned. First, literary and musical weeks (and longer) dedicated to the study of individual writers and musicians and, most recently, the Kerry International Summer School dedicated to living Irish authors. These schools study and celebrate Joyce, Beckett, Merriman, Kate O'Brien, Goldsmith, Willie Clancy, the piper, O'Carolan, the harpist, Padraig O'Caoimh, the Sliabh Luachra fiddler, Yeats, Magill, Parnell, Allingham, and Listowel Writers among others. There are festivals of opera, jazz, rock, film and all forms of Irish and Celtic song and dance. There are Oyster and Gourmet festivals and the like; Irish festivals may not be as spectacular as some internationally renowned ones but they are intense and fulfilling.

Secondly, the Government actively promotes Ireland as a place to study English as a foreign language for secondary school pupils and as a destination for academic exchange students. The National Council for Educational Awards (NCEA) actively encourages exchange of third level students within the EU and further afield. The growing awareness of this type of cultural exchange is evidenced by the exponential growth of participation by students and institutions in the many academic exchange programmes (Richards, 1995).

The Government continues to inject funding into Cultural Tourism. At the end of July 1994 a press release from Charlie McGreevy, Minister for Tourism and Trade, welcomed the announcement of Bruce Millan, European Commissioner for Regional Affairs, that the Commission had approved the new Government Programme for Tourism, 1994–1999 which provides for a total investment in Irish tourism of IR£ 652 million (ECU 820 million) including EU contributions of IR£ 369 million. This compares with an investment of IR£ 380 million (ECU 478 million) in the previous five years. This Programme was launched in September 1994 and has four primary objectives:

1. Increase overseas tourism revenue to IR£ 2250 million (ECU 2830 million) per year by 1999, compared with IR£ 1229 million (ECU 1546 million) in 1992;
2. Create up to 35,000 full-time jobs;
3. Substantially increase shoulder and off-season business;
4. Enhance the quality of service in Irish Tourism by the provision of high quality training programmes.

The main areas targeted for assistance under the programme are Product Development, Natural–Cultural Tourism, Marketing and Training.

A total of IR£ 125 million in assistance will be provided to public and other bodies to support the development of Ireland's unique cultural tourism attractions. Investment is planned in three specific areas:

1. Improving the facilities available at the National Cultural Institutions as well as promoting regional cultural activities;
2. Enhancing the quality of presentation to overseas tourists of significant National Monuments and historic properties;
3. Improving accessibility for visitors to the Country's waterways, nature reserves and national parks.

CULTURAL TOURISM DEMAND

The principal source of information on cultural tourism demand is the Central Marketing Department of Bord Failte who yearly publish statistical analyses of tourism trends in Ireland and elsewhere (Bord Failte, 1992, 1993).

In 1992 a total of 3,666,000 overseas tourists (excluding visitors from Northern Ireland) generated a revenue of IR£ 1229 million. Domestic tourists (including visitors from Northern Ireland) numbered 6,499,999, with revenues of IR£ 511.6 million. Due to a revision of methodology in 1991, the figures for domestic tourism are not comparable with previous years. Table 11.1 shows that overseas tourist numbers grew by 22% and overseas spending by 46% between 1988 and 1992.

Table 11.1. Overseas tourists and expenditure in Ireland, 1988–1992.

	Tourists	Revenue (IR£000s)
1988	3,007,000	841
1989	3,484,000	991
1990	3,666,000	1139
1991	3,535,000	1213
1992	3,666,000	1229

Source: Bord Failte (1993).

Table 11.2.   Overseas tourists and expenditure in Ireland by origin.

| | 1992 | | 1986 |
	Tourists (%)	Revenue (%)	Tourists (%)
Britain	55	36	60
France	7	8	5
Germany	7	9	5
Italy	3	4	1
Other Europe	10	13	7
N.America	13	17	18
Other areas	4	5	4

Source: Bord Failte (1993).

An analysis of the origin of overseas tourists (Table 11.2) shows that Britain's share of the market is declining while other European countries are becoming more important. The North American market is recovering after almost halving between 1985 and 1991. Almost half of all overseas tourists (1,762,000) came on 'specialist' holidays in 1992, and heritage visits featured in the itineraries of over a third of all visitors. For an estimated 150,000 overseas visitors, heritage attractions are the main reason for visiting Ireland. Thus, about 4% of all overseas visitors might be regarded as 'specific cultural tourists'. Table 11.3 illustrates the large number of North Americans who come on inclusive holidays and the huge popularity of cultural visits compared to everything else. The British are by far the least interested in cultural items.

Tourism Development International Ltd is the leading independent tourism research consultancy in Ireland, and has conducted extensive specialist research into tourism and cultural tourism on behalf of Bord Failte and others. Figures from their research on cultural tourism visits conducted in 1991 and 1993 (MacNulty and O'Carroll, 1992; MacNulty, 1994) show a growth of more that 50% in cultural attraction visits over this period (Table 11.4). In 1991 32% of all visitors to Irish attractions were Irish.

In 1993, 74% of visits to cultural attractions were made in the four months from June to September but only 50% of all tourists arrive during that time. One explanation for this imbalance may be the large proportion of students who visit these attractions during the summer vacation.

Dublin has a 27% share of visits to fee-paying attractions, with Cork/Kerry and Shannon regions each having 17%. Leading attractions are Dublin Zoo with 670,000, Bunratty Castle and Folk Park with 344,000, Trinity College with 320,000, Muckross House with 211,000 and Fota Wildlife Park with 200,000. The surveys indicated that visitor satisfaction was very high. The majority of European visitors and domestic tourists expressed a preference for visiting attractions without a guide. In contrast, 59% of North American visitors wished to have a guided tour.

Table 11.3. Overseas tourists: trip characteristics 1992.

	Total overseas	Britain	Other Europe	North America	Other areas
Total holiday-makers					
(000s)	1762	812	566	302	82
	(%)	(%)	(%)	(%)	(%)
Inclusive	26	17	31	43	24
Independent	74	83	69	57	76
Participated in					
Fishing	10	13	10	2	4
Golf	8	8	6	8	8
Equestrian	4	4	5	4	4
Cycling	9	4	19	5	9
Hiking/hill walking	15	11	22	12	15
Historic/cultural visits	48	31	62	62	61
Visits to houses/castles	30	16	43	41	43
Visits to monuments	22	10	33	27	37
Visits to gardens	17	9	26	17	25

Source: Bord Failte (1993).

Table 11.4. Visitors to Irish cultural attractions, 1991 and 1993.

	1993	1991
Historic houses/castles	2,350,000	1,300,000
Interpretive centres/museums	1,800,000	1,100,000
Nature/wildlife parks	590,000	935,000
Historic monuments	500,000	736,000
Heritage gardens	340,000	110,000
Other attractions	1,300,000	420,000
Total	6,880,000	4,600,000

Source: MacNulty (1994).

The level of multiple attraction visits is high, as 68% of tourists visiting Irish attractions visit more than one attraction during their stay in Ireland. Over 30% have visited five or more attractions. About 60% of visitors stay more than two hours at the attraction.

There is evidence in these figures of the depth and breadth of cultural tourism all over Ireland. Since 1991 many new cultural and heritage attractions have been opened to cater for increased demand. In County Kerry alone cultural attractions such as the Tarbert Bridewell, the Skellig Experience, Kerry the Kingdom, the Blasket Centre, Ardfert Cathedral and the Fenit Sea-World, have opened in the last three years.

In order to analyse cultural tourism demand in more depth, research was conducted in 1992 at Muckross House (County Kerry) and at the Rock of

Cashel (County Tipperary). A brief analysis of this research, conducted in the framework of the ATLAS Cultural Tourism Project, helps to illustrate the current nature of cultural tourism demand in Ireland. The cultural tourism survey covered 936 visitors, 828 at Muckross and 108 at Cashel. Because of the relatively sparsely populated nature of these locations, less than 4% of visitors surveyed came from the local area. Of the respondents, 40% were Irish and 60% were from overseas. A higher proportion of respondents in Cashel (31%) were American, compared with 10% of Muckross respondents, doubtless showing that Cashel is on the inclusive tour route more often than Muckross House. On the other hand, Muckross House had 13% respondents from the UK compared with 6.5% Cashel respondents. Just over a third of visitors to both locations were Irish, very close to the average of 32% for cultural attractions nationally (MacNulty and O'Carroll, 1992). The high proportion of overseas visitors explains the low level of repeat visits, with only 25% of respondents indicating they had visited the attraction before.

The average stay in the locality was 4.5 nights, although the mean length of stay at Muckross was 4.96 nights compared to 1.08 nights for Cashel. Again the influence of the inclusive bus tour shows as does the fact that Cashel tends to be a staging point between Dublin and the South and West of Ireland.

Visitors tended to be relatively young, with 18.7% being under 20; 54.9% under 30 and only 5.6% of respondents over 60 years of age. Cashel's visitors were significantly older than were those of Muckross (Chi-square = 40.8, df = 6, P = 0.0000). Here again the influence of the US visitor may be seen as 14.3% of American visitors were over 60, two and a half times the average. The high proportion of students (26%) also contributed to the low average age of visitors to Muckross, whereas only 7% of Cashel visitors were students. The highest proportion of students was from Germany (55.1%) and Austria (54.5%) whereas only 15.6% of UK visitors were students. This indicates a considerable youth cultural tourism market from continental Europe.

Over 10% of respondents had employment connected with heritage or museums or the visual arts, and 8.5% were employed in the performing arts. The level of cultural employment among Irish respondents was generally lower than among respondents from other EU states surveyed. This may reflect the relative lack of major cultural attractions in Ireland.

Most visitors did not seem to be out and out culture buffs. About 36% said the presence of the attraction was important in their coming to the area, and 35% said it was unimportant. Strangely, the presence of the Rock at Cashel was less important to visitors' decision to visit than was the presence of Muckross in Kerry. Perhaps this again relates to the package tour basis of many visits to Cashel, which may be regarded as just one element of the overall package, and may not have an important influence on a tourist's decision to travel. The attractions were regarded as significantly more important for younger people (Chi-square = 46.6, df = 24, P = 0.004) and the more highly educated held

Table 11.5. Visits to cultural attractions at home, on previous holiday and current holiday.

| Attraction | Cultural attractions visited | | |
	At home (%)	Last holiday (%)	This stay (%)
Museum	48.5	31.6	36.3
Heritage centre	30.1	22.1	35.1
Historic house	38.8	27.9	44.4
Art gallery	35.7	17.3	18.1
Performing arts	50.3	18.4	20.1
Festivals	43.9	18.8	20.1
National Park	46.5	32.1	56.7
Other	7.6	23.8	20.9

Source: ATLAS Survey (1992).

the attraction significantly more important than did the less well educated (Chi-square = 37.8, df = 12, $P = 0.0002$).

Respondents were asked about their attendance at cultural events at home, during their last holiday and during their current holiday. The overall level of cultural consumption both on holiday and at home tended to be lower for visitors to these Irish attractions than for visitors surveyed in other countries (Table 11.5). This may suggest that the motives of cultural tourists visiting Ireland may be less focused on specific cultural attractions than in other countries. This may be because cultural tourism in Ireland relies more heavily on intangible, 'way of life' factors than on specific attractions.

CASE STUDY: MUCKROSS HOUSE

The style of cultural tourism development in Ireland can be illustrated from the case of Muckross House. Muckross House is situated in Killarney National Park, 6 km south-east of Killarney Town, a premier tourist destination in Ireland. The house is set in world-renowned gardens and is adjacent to beautiful Muckross Abbey and since 1993 shares management with the newly developed Muckross Traditional Farms (known as the Kerry Country Life Experience, or *Ionad Saol Tire Chiarrai*). Adjoining the house is a working farm which supports a pedigree herd of some 100 Kerry Cattle. This case study has been largely based on a report by Breda O'Dwyer and Mary McKenna (O'Dwyer and McKenna, 1993).

Muckross House was built in 1843 for the Herbert family. It was designed by the Scottish architect, William Burn, in the Elizabethan Revival style with large mullioned windows, stepped gables and tall chimneys. The house is faced with cut Portland stone and overlooks the Muckross Lake. The first owner of the house was Henry Arthur Herbert, Member of Westminster Parliament for County Kerry from 1847 to 1866. It remained the residence of the Herbert family until the end of the nineteenth century when financial problems forced its sale. It was bought by Lord Ardilaun, a member of the Guinness brewing family who sold it to Mr and Mrs Bowers Bourne in 1910. They bought it as a wedding present for their daughter Maud when she married Arthur Vincent in that year. After her death in 1929 Vincent and the Bowers Bournes presented the house and 11,000 acre Muckross estate to the Nation as a memorial to Maud Bourne-Vincent.

Muckross House remained closed for the next 30 years, during which time much of its furniture was dispersed through State offices and Irish embassies throughout the world. In 1963 local doctor Frank Hilliard convened a public meeting and proposed that the house be leased from the Government and operated as a folk museum. Trustees nominated at the meeting got a lease of the house for four months in 1964, which was renewed for ten years in 1965 on condition that the trustees incorporate as a limited company.

Many of the original furnishings have survived or been recovered, many pieces dating from the visit of Queen Victoria in 1861. Most of the house is devoted to folk-life displays, including displays of the lifestyle of the landed gentry, and to operating craft workshops. The house and outbuildings also contain an audio-visual room with park information and displays, the park headquarters, offices and visitor facilities including restaurant, shop and toilets.

A joint management agreement between the OPW and the trustees was drawn up in 1976 and formally ratified in 1980. Under this agreement the Trustees of Muckross House remained in charge of, and responsible for, the development of the folk museum, craft workshops, retail shop, restaurant and reference library, while the house and park are owned by the State and managed by the OPW. The manager of Muckross House has responsibility for 24 full-time and 39 part-time staff. Some of the staff working in the house are park employees whereas others, including the craftworkers, are employed directly by the trustees. The agreement involves an unusual level of cooperation between a government body and a voluntary body and also facilitates local involvement with the park. At the same time it requires careful implementation to ensure that the needs of the park and of the folk museum both continue to be met.

Within the terms of its articles of association the Trustees of Muckross House (Killarney) Ltd outlined its objectives as follows:

- to establish a museum which would represent all aspects of Co. Kerry, but with a particular emphasis on its folk life; where Kerry People would learn more about their county; where visitors to the county could learn about its past and present; where research and educational programmes would be carried out;

- to provide working displays of local trades and crafts;
- to provide amenities for visitors along commercial lines;
- for the completion of the folk museum, to reconstruct in the open air house-types, craft workshops etc. which would be typical of Kerry.

The trustees have successfully achieved these objectives. The museum has developed in size and in the quality of its exhibitions; a research and reference library has been staffed for the past 12 years; an educational programme for touring school groups has been available since 1972.

The blacksmith's forge has been staffed since 1970, a harness maker's since 1972, a bookbindery since 1982 and a basketmaker from 1980 to 1985. In this time 11 apprentices have qualified or will do so soon. The retail shop and restaurant date from 1971. In 1981, the audio-visual centre was established and, in 1991, the laundry and forge wing of the basement was reconstructed to become the new audio-visual and visitor centre.

The overall mission of this folk museum is to 'preserve the past for the future'. This is in line with the vision of Arthur Hazelius (1833–1901) who in 1891 established the Nordic Museum and Skansen (open-air folk exhibit) in Stockholm, Sweden, the prototype of all folk museums. Hazelius realized that in an era of revolutionary change a collection had to be started at once if future generations were to know anything about the fast-disappearing past. As well as the crafts mentioned above, seasonal farming activities along traditional lines take place and are part of the 'working display'. The Muckross Traditional Farms provide an important addition to this, giving an interactive display of farm life in the 1930s before the introduction of modern, 'efficient' farming methods. Also included in this development are a labourer's cottage, a carpenter's cottage and a blacksmith's shop. A total of IR£ 1.25 million (ECU 1.6 million) was set aside for this project, of which IR£ 610,000 (ECU 800,000) was made available through European Regional Development Fund grant aid. It is expected that six permanent jobs will be generated by the project, and that this number should increase over the years.

In the last 25 years over 2 million people have visited the house and absorbed the representations and re-enactments of another age. OPW figures for paid entrance to Muckross House show a steady increase in visitor numbers, which almost doubled between 1987 and 1993 (Table 11.6).

Finance

All income generated by the visitor facilities and activities is reinvested in Muckross. Muckross also has access to public sources of finance which include Bord Failte, OPW and Government/EU funding.

Over the years Muckross House has received donations of more than 3000 items connected with folk life and tradition in Kerry. Organizations like *Muintir*

Table 11.6.   Visits to Muckross House, County Kerry.

Year	Visits
1987	118,400
1988	120,734
1989	151,989
1990	163,949
1991	166,755
1992	184,000
1993	211,000

Source: Muckross House.

Table 11.7.   Entrance charges for Muckross House, 1994.

	Entry charge (IR£)		
	House	Farms	Both
Adults	3	3	4
Group and OAPs	2	2	3
Children	1.25	1.25	2
Family	7.50	7.50	10

Source: Muckross House.

na Tire, Macra na Feirme and the County Committee of Agriculture have also helped towards the development of Muckross House. The Friends of Muckross House, an informal organization set up in 1968 with members representative of the whole county, gives invaluable advice and assistance to the directors. Money is also received from shop and restaurant leases, fees for groups visiting the grounds and teacher training courses. The major source of finance, however, is derived from entrance fees (Table 11.7).

Current markets

The ATLAS survey carried out in 1992 has already given an indication of the profile of visitors to Muckross House (see above). A study of 488 visitors conducted by Bord Failte in 1991 provides some additional market information. In the Bord Failte study, almost a third of visitors were Irish. The best represented overseas markets were the UK (18%), the USA (13%) and Germany (10%). Most visitors came in parties (61%) or family groups (23%).

The management at Muckross intends to expand existing markets, mainly in Europe and the US. They will continue to promote the tourist attraction in relevant magazines and trade journals and in other tourism centres both at home and abroad. A budget of some IR£ 15,000 to IR£ 20,000 (ECU

19,000–25,000) per annum is allocated to marketing. Consumer promotion includes direct mail, promotional flyers and posters which are placed in hotels and guest houses throughout Ireland. Trade promotion targets the trade press, tourist industry handbooks and Bord Failte travel trade workshops.

Future development plans and issues

Muckross House, its gardens and its immediate environs, including the farm complexes, are the focal point for visitors to Killarney National Park, which is open to the public free of charge. Muckross House can most effectively portray the lifestyles of the big Estate House, both 'upstairs' and 'downstairs'. Muckross House will continue to be presented primarily as a nineteenth century mansion fitted out with all the furnishings and artefacts of that period. In recognition of the generosity of the Bowers Bourne and Vincent families, however, one of the principal reception rooms will be presented in the style of their period of ownership between 1910 and 1932.

The restoration and furnishing of more rooms in period style will entail the relocation of some exhibitions, displays and craft workshops. This long-term aim will be achieved over a number of years. Upgrading of visitor facilities will include car parks, toilets, picnic areas, restaurant facilities and interpretative facilities for both park and house. Eventually, Muckross House will become a regional heritage centre and it will be necessary to retain some National Park interpretation at the house. To this end the laundry wing will be adapted for park interpretation with its own entrance.

Muckross Traditional Farms will be developed further and when completed will be one of the best such outdoor museums in Europe. This is a natural progression from the present displays at Muckross and will provide a valuable focus and forum for the authentic preservation and interpretation of the folklife and history of Kerry, which is the primary objective of the management at Muckross.

Among the issues which face management over the coming years are pressures to develop facilities like golf courses that would have a negative environmental impact. Management must give serious attention to the organization and control of the increasing number of diverse segments in the House and in its environs. Finally, seasonality is a major issue for Muckross as it is for the tourist industry in general.

TRENDS AND ISSUES IN CULTURAL TOURISM

Cultural tourism is clearly in vogue in Ireland; it has a growing clientele from the historical and archaeological aficionados to the consumers of upstairs–downstairs and classic gardens to the lovers of folklife, legend and musical, literary and artistic expression; it also has a government which realizes the potential of the market and cultivates and protects it through Bord Failte, the OPW and CERT. Added to the efforts of the Government, many individual entrepreneurs and local communities are aware of the profit potential either in money or in jobs that will entice the young to stay at home, rather than emigrating abroad to find employment.

There has been a veritable explosion of attractions, heritage and interpretive centres. The cynical might remark that soon we will need an interpretive centre to interpret and adjudicate between interpretive centres. So far, however, all seems well. The control of standards by the OPW and by CERT is very good, though in the past three years the OPW has been embroiled in controversy over the opening of interpretive centres in places like the Burren in Co. Clare, an area of exquisite natural beauty that many feel is threatened by the activities of the OPW.

The most important issue is the preservation of the three things that make Ireland unique: the scenery, the people, and the Irish culture. Each in its own way is under threat. The scenery is threatened by development in the most scenic and vulnerable areas, the people and the culture by modernization which can lead to a homogenization with the dominant Western culture; this is something that has been resisted successfully for 7000 years and the odds surely must be that Irish people and culture will not succumb now. Preserving this unique resource for cultural tourists requires hard work from all those involved in tourism and cultural development.

CONCLUSION

We have endeavoured to identify the unique place that cultural tourism plays in Irish life and the place that Irish cultural tourism plays in Europe and the world at large. Significant growth has taken place over the past decade in the number of tourists, particularly those interested in cultural tourism. The Government, through its own resources and through EU funding, is injecting development capital into cultural tourism and many are ready to rise to the challenge.

The major issue is to control the growth of cultural tourism, to direct it properly and to ensure that it always gives value, value for money and, much more importantly, value in the cultural sense of making people aware of the value of difference. That, after all, is the essence of Cultural Tourism.

REFERENCES

Bord Failte (1990) *Action Plan for Heritage Attractions*. Bord Failte, Dublin.
Bord Failte (1992) *Tourism Trends, 1983–1991*. Bord Failte, Dublin.

Bord Failte (1993) *Tourism Facts, 1992.* Bord Failte, Dublin.

Delaney, F. (1989) *The Celts.* Grafton Books, London.

Department of Tourism and Trade (1994) *Heritage Tourism.* DOTT, Dublin.

MacNulty, P. (1994) 1993 Visitor attractions survey. Paper presented at 'Heritage and Visitor Attractions' Conference, Dublin Castle, January.

MacNulty, P. and O'Carroll, C. (1992) *Visitors to Attractions in Ireland in 1991.* Tourism Development International, Dublin.

Nietzsche, F. (1917) *Die Geburt der Tragodie.* Kroener, Leipzig.

O'Dwyer, B. and McKenna, M. (1993) *Muckross House, A Case Study.* Tralee RTC, Tralee.

Page, S.J. (1994) Developing heritage tourism in Ireland in the 1990s. *Tourism Recreation Research* 19, 79–89.

Richards, G. (1995) *European Tourism and Leisure Education: Trends and Prospects.* Tilburg University Press, Tilburg.

Weber, M. (1952) *The Protestant Ethic and the Spirit of Capitalism.* Allen and Unwin, London.

Weber, M. (1964) *Theory of Social and Economic Organization.* Free Press, New York.

Weber, M. (1978) *Economy and Society.* University of California Press, Berkeley.

Cultural Tourism in Italy   12

J. van der Borg and P. Costa

CISET, University of Venice, Riviera San Pietro 83, 30030 Oriago di Mira
(VE), Italy

INTRODUCTION

According to a much cited, but never officially published, study by UNESCO,
more than 50% of the global cultural and historical heritage is concentrated in
Italy. Even if doubts may arise about the exactness of this figure, Italy surely is,
at least as far as cultural and historical heritage is concerned, one of the (if not
the) richest countries in the world. It has been touched by many ancient
civilizations, as much as by more recent artistic and cultural influences.

Art, culture and history are important motives for at least some of the
many people visiting Italy each year. Furthermore, they form a strong promotional vehicle for the destinations, even towards market segments which
are less sensitive to culture. This is despite the fact that until recently little has
been done by the authorities and the tourism industry to render the impressive
stock of cultural and historic resources accessible. Even less has been done to
increase the accessibility of the contemporary Italian culture and traditions.
This then explains why this chapter focuses on 'traditional' artistic and cultural goods and their use by national and international tourists. The lack of
reliable statistical information on other areas of cultural consumption reinforces this choice.

There is evidence that the somewhat nonchalant attitude of policy-makers
with respect to heritage is changing for the better. Since Italy's competitiveness
as a tourist destination is under pressure, ways to use cultural heritage more
efficiently as a tourism resource are being considered, mainly in order to win
back some of the ground lost to 'sun, sea and sand' destinations. The reform of

the museum system of Italy, that will be discussed later in this chapter, is but one example of this tendency.

This chapter on cultural tourism in Italy will focus on the paradoxical situation that, even if the presence of heritage is massive, the supply of accessible cultural and historic tourism products is marginal. According to the authors, cultural tourism policies ought in the first place to remove the barriers to using cultural resources properly.

The chapter first of all briefly sketches the main characteristics of the Italian stock of cultural and historic resources. Special attention is paid to territorial differences in supply, and to the accessibility of art and culture. Subsequent sections describe the demand side of the market for cultural tourism and give an analysis of the past, present, and future cultural tourism policies. Finally, a specific study of the Italian museum system illustrates some very recent changes in the attitude regarding cultural tourism policy.

THE SUPPLY OF CULTURAL GOODS IN ITALY

Italy: the cradle of European culture

It is beyond doubt that Italy is one of the cradles of European culture. It was through the Phoenician and Greek trade routes in the Mediterranean that culture and art were imported into what today is the south of Italy. The Etruscans left traces mostly in the central part of the country. It was during the most prosperous ages of the Roman Empire that large parts of Europe were confronted for the first time with what now is known as 'Made in Italy'. The Romans not only exported their culture, they spread much of it over the Italian territory as well.

After a relatively quiet second half of the first millennium, in which influences of the Byzantine empire indirectly touched various parts of the country, Italy became one of the focal points of the Renaissance. In cities as such as Venice and Florence, but also in many 'minor' cities of art in Italy, evidence of this period is still overwhelming.

The second half of the second millennium was again a relatively quiet period for Italian culture and art. There were city states which demonstrated particular dynamism during this period, as much as there were city states that lost their vitality. The country gradually lost its dominating grip on European culture and art. However, as in Flanders (Belgium), economic decline helped to preserve a wealth of built heritage which forms the basis of the Italian cultural tourism product (see also Richards, Chapter 3 this volume). Today, this physical basis is augmented by the imagination and creativity of the Italian population, known throughout the world. Many gifted actors, architects, cooks, dancers, designers, film directors, painters, musicians, sculptors, singers, and writers have either Italian nationality or are of Italian origin.

The supply of art and culture in Italy: a geography

A study by Preiti and Tanganelli, published in the Fourth Report on Tourism in Italy of the (former) Ministry for Tourism and Culture (Ministero del Turismo, 1991), confirms the high degree of diffusion of Italy's heritage. Since official statistics regarding artistic and cultural goods only deal with those possessed by the national, regional or local authorities, an alternative source of information had to be found. The authors therefore reconstructed the supply of cultural goods on the basis of the analytical tourist guides produced by the Touring Club Italiano. In these guides, for each municipality the monuments, museums, churches, excavations and so on, that are worth a visit, are carefully described. Museums on the one hand, and other types of heritage on the other, were treated separately by the authors.

According to the guide books, of the 8097 municipalities in Italy, 752 (9.1%) host cultural and historical goods of some interest. Obviously, merely counting the objects ignores the differences in value that there may be between them. Nevertheless, it clearly demonstrates that heritage is not only concentrated in Florence, Naples, Rome, and Venice, but that much of it is to be found elsewhere.

As far as the territorial distribution of heritage is concerned, the earlier mentioned study reveals that there are four clusters of provinces for which the density of heritage is far above average. The by far the largest of these clusters consists of the provinces of Parma, Reggio Emilia, Modena, La Spezia, Massa, Lucca, Pistoia, Ravenna, Forlì, Firenze, Livorno, Grosseto, Siena, Arezzo, Pesaro, Ancona, Macerata, Perugia, Terni, Viterbo, Roma, Latina, Termoli, and Pescara (or central Italy). In the north, the provinces of Bolzano and Belluno form a cluster. Two clusters can be found in the south: one on Sicily (Trapani, Enna, Ragusa, and Siracusa) and the other on the East Coast (Bari, Matera, Taranto and Brindisi). It is remarkable that the provinces situated in the 'Pianura Padana', including Turin and Milan, register a very low density of heritage. Figure 12.1 shows where the clusters of provinces are situated.

Some of the reasons for this distribution have already been mentioned above. A more complete explanation goes, of course, beyond the scope of this chapter and book.

Another interesting fact that emerges from the work of Preiti and Tanganelli is that the ten highest ranking provinces as far as the density of heritage is concerned, are not the ones in which the 'classic' Italian cities of art – Florence, Naples, Rome, Venice – are located. Table 12.1 shows this ranking.

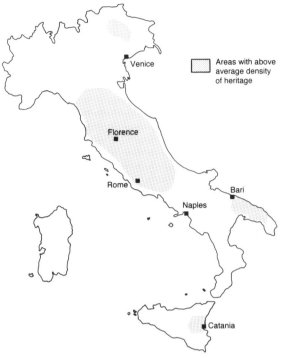

Fig. 12.1. Concentrations of heritage in Italy (source: based on Ministero del Turismo, 1991).

Table 12.1. Density of heritage structures in Italian provinces.

Rank	Province	Density/km²
1	Siena	50.0
2	Grosseto	46.2
3	Latina	42.4
4	Trapani	41.6
5	Ragusa	41.5
6	Arezzo	41.0
7	Livorno	40.0
8	Brindisi	40.0
9	Bologna	38.3
10	Bari	35.7

Source: Ministero del Turismo (1991).

As can be seen from the table, the provinces of Siena and Grosseto, both situated in Toscana (just as Arezzo, number six in the classification), register the highest density of cultural heritage. The presence of southern Italian provinces (Trapani (4), Ragusa (5), Brindisi (8) and Bari (10)) is just as striking.

Table 12.2. Publicly owned heritage by region and government level.

	State	City	Province	Region	Total
Piemonte	29	88	1	2	120
Valle d'Aosta				7	7
Lombardia	20	109	3		132
Trentino Alto Adige	9	11	5		25
Veneto	21	62	2		85
Friuli	23	29	4		56
Liguria	15	36			51
Emilia Romagna	50	137	2		189
Toscana	158	93	3		254
Umbria	30	32			62
Marche	25	73			98
Lazio	131	50			181
Abruzzo	20	15			35
Campania	61	12	5	3	81
Puglia	37	34	5	1	77
Molise	11	3			14
Basilicata	23	1	1		25
Calabria	21	10	1		32
Sicilia		36		30	66
Sardegna	26	18			44
Total	710	849	32	43	1634

Source: ENIT (1992).

The analysis of the density of Italy's supply of museums is slightly different from that of heritage in general. The presence of museums is less diffused in this country than that of heritage. Most museums are located in provincial capitals; the smaller municipalities usually do not possess museums. Two provinces are exceptionally rich in less important, but nevertheless interesting museums: Perugia and Bari.

Less rich, but still richer than the average province, are the provinces of Gorizia, Modena, Massa, Ravenna, Pistoia, Firenze, Forlì, Arezzo, Siena, Livorno, Pesaro, Macerata, Latina, Trapani, Enna, Ragusa, and Siracusa. These are to some extent the provinces that were mentioned for their high density of heritage.

Statistical material on the cultural goods possessed by the public sector, a consistent part of the total supply of traditional cultural goods, may be used to complete the picture given above. The material is occasionally gathered by the Italian National Tourist Board (ENIT). Table 12.2 presents the regional distribution of museums, art galleries, monuments, and excavations owned by the various levels of administration in 1991.

In 1991, there were, according to ENIT, 1634 public cultural structures. Almost half of them (710) were owned by the state. The other 924 belonged to local authorities, that is regions, provinces or municipalities. Of these, more than 90% were in the hands of the latter. In addition to these, Italy has somewhat more than 700 private institutions. Five regions host more than 100 public cultural structures: Toscana (254), Emilia Romagna (189), Lazio (181), Lombardia (132), and Piemonte (120). The proportion of national cultural structures is remarkably high in Toscana and Lazio (respectively 62.2% and 72.4% against the national average of 43.5%). In many other regions, particularly in the north of Italy, locally owned structures predominate.

The supply of cultural goods has been growing steadily from the beginning of the 1980s onwards. This is one of the consequences of the increasing interest in conservation activities of all levels of authority with regard to art and culture (ENIT, 1992). The total number of national cultural institutions grew from 229 in 1985 to 710 in 1991 (210%); most of this increase is registered in the category monuments and excavations.

The accessibility of art and culture

Although the number of cultural institutions has increased considerably, there has not been a corresponding growth in the supply of heritage for tourism uses. Having heritage is one thing, using it another. It is the accessibility of heritage which makes the difference. Italy is one of the countries where the stock of heritage attractions is infinitely large, but their accessibility amazingly low.

A study by ENIT has pointed out that, of the 710 institutions in national hands, only 274 (or 39%) are open all year. Of the structures possessed by local and regional administrations or private citizens, 58% open every day for the public. Of the institutions not open the whole year, a large proportion are closed all year, or open only on special request.

A further reduction to the accessibility of heritage is caused by the choice of the opening hours of the structures. Many are only open in the morning, some also in the afternoon, and only a few also in the evening. Shortage of personnel is often given as explanation for the user-unfriendly visiting hours.

As will be shown in the next section, the relatively low accessibility hinders the better utilization of Italy's heritage for, among others, tourism purposes. The fact that Italy does not seem to have experienced the expected – given the growing interest in art and culture – increases in the number of visitors of museums, galleries and monuments, can be attributed partly to the problems the country has to render heritage accessible.

CULTURAL TOURISM DEMAND

This section sets out to discuss the different dimensions of the demand for cultural tourism in Italy. Thereafter, the principal trends that have characterized the demand for cultural heritage in Italy are described, and attention is paid to the development of tourism in Italy's cities of art. Finally, a profile of the average consumer of an Italian cultural good is presented. It presents the characteristics as well as the behaviour of the user of Italy's heritage. This particular section is mainly based on the results of the survey organized and performed by the Italian research team for the ATLAS 'Cultural Tourism in Europe' project.

The use of heritage in Italy: some figures

To speak of cultural consumption in Italy means first of all to speak about the number of visitors to the three different types of cultural goods that are possessed by the national government: museums, galleries, and monuments and excavations. Additional information on heritage is either not reliable or absent. It has been shown previously that 40% of publicly owned heritage falls under the responsibility of the state. This 40% counts for more than 50% of the total number of visitors in museums, galleries, and monuments and excavations. The popularity of national heritage with respect to locally and regionally owned resources, not only stems from the relative importance of national heritage, but also from the fact that 7 out of 10 national institutes do not charge an entrance fee, whereas only 5 out of 10 locally and regionally owned structures are free.

Table 12.3 illustrates the development of the demand for national heritage in the 1984–1993 period. It is clear that the national heritage system is facing a severe crisis. The total number of visitors decreased by 17.6% between 1984 and 1993.

A study of the changes in demand in more detail, shows that within the time span of these 10 years, periods of decline are followed by renewed growth. In the years 1984, 1985, 1986, 1990, and 1991 the performance of the state-owned cultural goods was particularly worrying. In 1987, 1988, and 1989, however, the number of visitors increased. The most striking changes in the visitor numbers can be observed for 1990 (−4.3 million visitors) and 1987 (plus 3.8 million visitors). There are some signs of recovery in visitor numbers in 1993, with admissions to museums and galleries growing, although admissions to monuments, the largest category of cultural attractions, fell again in 1993.

It must be emphasized that the number of cultural institutions in the corresponding period rose notably (ENIT, 1991). The number of museums, for example, increased by 32% between 1984 and 1993. The decreasing visitor numbers, in combination with an increasing supply, have led to an even poorer performance by individual institutions in terms of visitor numbers.

What is furthermore remarkable is that the number of free admissions has declined more drastically than the number of paying visitors between 1984 and 1991: 2,869,659 fewer free admissions (−15.8%) compared with a drop of

Table 12.3.   Demand for national heritage between 1984 and 1993.

	Museums	Galleries	Monuments	Total
		Visits (× 1000)		
1984	3740	3428	18,803	25,971
1985	3529	3254	18,749	25,533
1986	2991	2919	17,501	23,411
1987	3156	3252	20,879	27,286
1988	3416	3488	20,803	27,707
1989	3488	3354	23,210	30,052
1990	3413	3093	19,231	25,737
1991	2806	2721	16,908	22,436
1992	2408	3146	15,947	21,502
1993	2637	3363	15,397	21,398
		% change		
1985	−5.6	−5.1	−0.3	−1.7
1986	−15.3	−10.3	−6.7	−8.3
1987	+5.5	+22.7	+19.3	+16.6
1988	+8.2	−0.6	+1.0	+1.5
1989	+2.1	+15.5	+13.0	+8.5
1990	−2.2	−19.4	−16.8	−14.4
1991	−17.8	−9.5	−9.6	−12.8
1992	−14.1	+15.6	−5.7	−4.1
1993	+9.5	+6.9	−3.4	−0.5
84/93	−29.5	−1.9	−18.1	−17.6

Source: ENIT (1992); Italian Statistical Yearbook (1994).

665,481 in paid admissions (−8.5%). This coincided with the doubling of the average entrance fee that took place in October 1990. The average entrance fee went from L 4000 (ECU 2) to L 8000 (ECU 4). On average, only one in three visitors pays an entrance fee, as shown in Table 12.4

The proportion of paying visitors is highest for galleries (70% of all visitors pay), and lowest for monuments and excavations (only 24% pay). The museums find themselves in between these two extremes, with 46% of their public paying to enter. The problem of accessibility, presented earlier as a crucial explanation for the crisis in which the Italian culture sector finds itself, does not seem, therefore, to be a matter of pricing policy. Not only do the majority of the visitors not pay, but cultural tourists are also assumed to be rather insensitive to changes in price.

The augmented entrance fee and the limited sensibility of paying visitors to price changes has led to an increase in income. However, under the current fiscal regime in which cultural institutions are operating, this increase goes straight to the Ministry of Finance.

Table 12.4. Paid and free admission to Italian heritage attractions.

	% of admissions							
	Museums		Galleries		Monuments		Total	
	Free	Paid	Free	Paid	Free	Paid	Free	Paid
1984	59	41	34	66	78	22	70	30
1985	59	41	26	74	75	25	55	34
1986	53	47	21	79	72	28	63	37
1987	52	48	21	79	74	26	65	35
1988	51	49	24	76	74	26	65	35
1989	49	51	24	76	76	24	67	33
1990	52	48	26	74	74	26	66	35
1991	54	46	30	70	76	23	68	32

Source: ENIT (1992).

Tourism in art cities

Art and culture are presumed to be important motives for tourists to choose Italy as their holiday destination. Survey data on tourism motivation are, however, scarce. In the absence of such information, attempts have been made to measure cultural tourism demand indirectly. The Italian Bureau for Statistics, ISTAT, does this by clustering arrivals and stays in municipalities where such a form of tourism is assumed to be dominant. Cultural tourism thus equals all tourism registered in municipalities that are of historical, artistic or cultural interest. In terms of arrivals, cultural tourism counts for about 33% of Italy's tourism; in terms of overnight stays this share is much lower: somewhat more than 20%.

Table 12.5 largely confirms the trend observed in visitor numbers to heritage attractions. Cultural tourism in Italy is contracting. There is no segment of the market (Italian/Foreign; Hotel/Other accommodation) that experienced an increase in arrivals or overnight stays between 1987 and 1992. Occasionally, there have been temporary improvements (1990 for those staying in hotels, for example), but the trend is decisively negative.

The cultural tourist's principal characteristics

In the absence of a well-organized information system regarding heritage, surveys among users of art and culture are indispensable to complete the discussion on the demand for heritage in Italy. Such a survey was conducted in 1992 in the context of the ATLAS Cultural Tourism Project. The objective of the project, its methodology and a comparative analysis of the material

Table 12.5. Cultural tourism demand in Italy.

	Italian		Foreign	
	Arrivals	Nights	Arrivals	Nights
Hotels (× 1000)				
1987	11,238	27,299	7959	20,169
1988	11,533	26,482	8243	20,525
1989	11,973	27,640	8801	22,301
1990	11,813	28,002	9032	22,773
1991	11,784	27,291	8000	20,423
1992 (est)	10,484	24,341	7157	17,965
Other types of accommodation (× 1000)				
1987	630	6762	1118	5856
1988	600	6483	1115	5873
1989	585	5756	1022	4327
1990	588	5493	1011	4210
1991	640	6092	1118	5071
1992 (est)	584	5824	905	4576

(est) = estimate
Source: FAIAT (1993).

gathered have been presented extensively in Chapter 2 of this volume. This section briefly discusses the results of the Italian part of the research programme.

The survey was organized among visitors to one of Venice's principal attractions, Palazzo Ducale, that is situated in Piazza San Marco, the core of the historical centre and the city's tourism system. The questionnaire was handed out to those people that were willing to pay to enter the Palazzo Ducale. Tourists who were just wandering around in the courtyard were not interviewed.

Only 15% of the survey respondents lived in the Municipality of Venice. The remaining 85% lived elsewhere. A more recent survey among visitors of four Venetian museums confirmed the relatively low interest of the inhabitants in their museums. The share of locals in the total number of visitors remained well below 10%, confirming that the museums in the city centre are tourism products, rather than higher-order cultural facilities. As far as the age of the cultural tourists is concerned, the survey indicates that the average age is rather low. Almost 12% of visitors were under 20 years. More than 67% fall in the category 20–49 years. Only one-fifth of respondents were over 50 years old.

The educational level of respondents was high. About 28% had a higher education diploma, almost 30% had reached the undergraduate level, and 23% had completed a postgraduate study at a University; 22% of the interviewed tourists were still studying. Almost half of the sample were employed, but 8% were retired, and the remaining 20% were either unemployed or house-man or housewife. Of those employed, one-fifth worked in the culture sector.

As far as the behaviour of the cultural tourists is concerned, the question-naire contained a separate section regarding the visit to the specific attraction and a section on previous holiday behaviour.

The majority of visitors indicated that a visit to the Palazzo Ducale was an important motive for visiting Venice (73%). Only 26% said the visit to the museum did not influence their decision to come to Venice. A third of the visitors had visited the museum on a previous occasion. Only a minority of those interviewed are very interested in visiting other museums, heritage centres, monuments or performances. Of these cultural attractions, it is the museums for which the propensity to visit is the highest (only 9% of the tourists did not visit at least one other museum). The survey evidence seems to confirm the Palazzo Ducale as a 'must-see' sight in Venice, particularly for foreign visitors.

CULTURAL TOURISM POLICY IN ITALY

As mentioned earlier there is no such thing as an Italian cultural tourism policy. There are indications that this is slowly changing for the better. Tradi-tionally, cultural tourism policy has meant restoration and maintenance of heritage, of the primary cultural and historical tourism resources. Prompted by stagnating tourism demand, Italy's former Ministry of Tourism chose cultural tourism as one of the potential market segments that may help the country to stimulate renewed tourism growth.

However, it is far too early to see this change in strategy translated into a consistent and coherent package of measures relating to cultural tourism. A referendum concerning the abolition of the Ministry of Tourism and Culture was accepted by the Italians, which halted policy implementation in tourism. The transformation of the Ministry into a Tourism Department of the Presi-dency of the Council of Ministers has now been completed, and most of the suspended tasks have been taken up again.

Several individual initiatives to *valorizzare* (an Italian expression that may be translated with 'to give more value') the artistic and cultural heritage of the country are worth mentioning.

The former Ministry for Tourism has, with the financial help of DGXXIII of the European Commission, designed various cultural itineraries, of which that of the 'Smaller Islands' and the 'Routes of the Phoenicians' are of interest. The routes are supposed to promote cultural destinations which are less known to the average tourist, and flatten the seasonal fluctuations in demand (DGXXIII, 1994).

Another organization that is active in the promotion of cultural tourism is the Touring Club Italiano (TCI). Each year, special attention is paid to specific regions which are rich in heritage and traditions. Most of the actions are exclusively directed to the national market. What is also interesting is that the TCI not only advises suppliers of heritage how to become more competitive, but also informs the users how to experience the products.

In addition to the initiative taken by the Department of Tourism and the TCI, on a local scale municipalities are reorganizing their supply of cultural goods that may be used for tourism purposes. Walking routes are being created, special cultural packages (that are supposed to appeal to especially up-market residential tourists) are being promoted, neglected monuments are being restored. However, stimulating cultural tourism development in Italy is almost entirely a task of the public sector. The TCI is one of the exceptions to this rule.

THE ITALIAN MUSEUM SYSTEM

A quick glance at the Italian museum system

The Italian museum system is, according to recent studies (see for example ICARE, 1993; van der Borg and Zago, 1995), a perfect example of the Italian paradox: a very rich system of museums with, due to inadequate policies, limited accessibility. Although former Culture Minister Alberto Ronchey characterized museums as 'the General Motors of Italy' (Fanelli, 1993), a radical change in attitude is needed before this potential powerhouse can function effectively.

The reasons for the lack of accessibility of the heritage found in museums depends for a great deal on the context within which the average Italian museum has to operate. Over 80% of Italian museums are state-run, and public funds account for over 89% of Italian museum income (Di Battista, 1993). Museums have been constrained by inflexible legislation and political neglect, which has produced problems in three major areas.

First, museums have to deal with the eternal conflict between conservation and utilization. The contrast between conservation and utilization has always been considerable in Italy. This can partly be explained by the fact that the legal context in which museums operate is just as limiting as the one for monuments and excavations, for which the accent on conservation may be more easily justified.

A second explanation for the poor performance of the museums is the absence of financial incentives to do better. The budget of the museum is more or less fixed; income goes straight to the Ministry of Finance, and cannot be reinvested in the museum itself. The absence of fiscal autonomy means that there is no relation between efforts and (financial) performance.

Finally, many museums, particularly those owned by regional and local authorities, are totally dependent on what are called the *Soprintendenza*, or decentralized departments of the Ministry of Culture. Public museums are not entitled to have a director, and control of staffing and finance is maintained by the *Soprintendenza*. This again means that the link between individual museum performance and the availability of resources has been very weak.

The following case study of a museum in Venice helps to illustrate some of these issues.

Case study: The National Museum Accademia, Venice

The National Museum Accademia in Venice is situated next to the Academy of Arts of Venice, very close to the Accademia bridge. The museum falls under the direct responsibility of the Ministry of Culture by which the museum is financed. Sponsors may co-finance specific exhibitions. The income produced from the sale of entrance tickets goes directly to the Ministry of Finance.

The museum is directed by a technical director and a conservator. The Accademia gives employment to several specialized restorers and about 30 attendants. The number of attendants is slightly higher during the summer months when the number of visitors reaches its peak. Training courses are organized to enlarge or renew the practical knowledge of the existing employees.

The museum offers the visitors frequently changing temporary exhibitions. The visitors are guided through the museum by means of plastic cards which contain information about the works exposed. A more sophisticated, electronic guidance and information system is considered to be undesirable, not only because of its cost but also because of the constant changes in the works exposed which require the system to be updated constantly.

Table 12.6 shows the numbers of people that visited the museum between 1975 and 1991. The 26% decline in visitor numbers between 1984 and 1991 is similar to the trend for Italian museums in general (Table 12.3).

The maximum number of visitors that the museum can contain has never been determined accurately. In theory, the museum's carrying capacity should depend on the physical integrity of the works exposed and of the building itself, and on the quality of the visitor's experience. In practice, a maximum of 180 visitors is allowed to enter the museum at one time due to anti-fire regulations.

As far as the timing of the museum's exhibitions is concerned, the museum is supposed to coordinate all its initiatives with the other Venetian museums and art galleries, not least to control the overall number of visitors to the city (for those interested in visitor management strategies in cities of art in general, and Venice in particular, see Costa and van der Borg, 1993). In practice,

Table 12.6.   Visitors to the National Museum Accademia, Venice.

Year	Visitors
1975	61,121
. . .	. . .
1982	197,503
1983	210,768
1984	225,727
1985	217,603
1986	211,140
1987	212,770
1988	227,187
1989	206,235
1990	183,475
1991	166,490

Source: ICARE (1993).

coordination is scarce. More than once exhibitions in different Venetian museums have competed with each other; the events being organized in the same periods and even handling similar themes.

National museums such as the Accademia do not have financial autonomy. The money that is earned from ticket and catalogue sales goes straight to the Ministry of Finance. It is therefore the Ministry that decides the price of the tickets. In 1990, the entry price was doubled, a decision based on the growing public interest in cultural goods. A recent survey among the museum's visitors revealed that 35.4% of visitors find the admission price too expensive. Almost all the museum's visitors are foreign tourists; the number of national tourists is low, but somewhat higher than that of the residents coming to visit the Accademia.

The museum's promotion policy is assumed to be of increasing importance, especially because the share of paying visitors is steadily decreasing. The Municipality of Venice has proposed promoting less-known cultural attractions together with more popular ones, introducing and promoting what in Italy are called *itinerari* (routes or itineraries). More than 56% of the visitors to the Accademia came to know about the museum by means of brochures and tourist guides. Being listed in these guides is thus of the utmost importance for a museum.

The Accademia has a well-organized laboratory for the restoration and conservation of paintings. Plans have been made to sell these services to third parties, in order to become more independent from a financial point of view. Other initiatives that will soon become regular practice for the Italian museums are discussed in the following section.

Museum management in the future

Recently some revolutionary changes to the Italian museum system (mainly the national ones) have been proposed. In 1992 the then Minister of Culture, Alberto Ronchey, proposed measures to reform the museum system. Before the proposal was officially approved by Parliament in 1993, several important museums were already following the suggestions formulated by the Ronchey Act. It is, however, too early to discuss the working of the law; we therefore limit ourselves to evaluating the intentions of the Ronchey Act against the background of heritage management in the past.

The principal objective of this legislation was to make the management of museums more business-oriented, offering them more flexibility and incentives to perform better. Furthermore, some changes were proposed to improve the accessibility of the museums.

As far as the first point is concerned, the Ronchey Act foresees for the national museums a proper director and an individual balance sheet. The relationship between efforts and performance is in this way guaranteed, as well as making the responsibilities clearly identified. It furthermore allows for increased mobility of museum employees, thus solving the problems of over- or under-employment in specific institutions. Currently, museums in the south of Italy tend to have more staff than strictly necessary, while those in the north do not have enough personnel to open the museum entirely. More flexibility in the management of human resources thus improves accessibility.

The new law foresees the 'privatization' of peripheral museum services, like shops, catering and audio-visual assistance. The management of a museum may offer space within the museum in which the latter may organize specific activities, compatible with the character of the museum. The museum receives a previously established compensation (in the form of rent or royalties, for example). Hence, it does not develop new activities itself, nor does it invest or take any risks.

Sponsorship by the private sector is already common. Intensification of the relationship between the museum sector and sponsors will be stimulated.

To improve museum accessibility, the Act deregulates the opening hours of the national museums. In Venice, an experiment with the opening of the museums during the evening hours was very successful. The additional hours worked by museum staff were paid for by an important multinational. The introduction of special museum cards, which give access to more than one museum or attraction, has been warmly welcomed. Ideas to create a pass that gives access to the national museums in Florence, Naples, Rome, and Venice have existed for years, but it has been necessary to render them truly operative. At a local level, combined museum tickets are being planned. That such an initiative is difficult to implement in such a bureaucratic country, is demonstrated by a plan by the City of Padova to bring several of its principal museums and monuments together in one admission ticket. It took 18 months to reach agreement and resolve administrative restrictions.

It is, of course, too early to say whether these changes will bring the Italian museum system much closer to those of other countries. It certainly seems to offer some valid incentives to make the public museums more aware of the costs and income their exploitation incurs, and makes a start in improving the accessibility of the heritage possessed by the museums.

CONCLUSIONS

Art, culture and history are important motives for some people visiting Italy. However, until recently not much has been done by the authorities and the industry to make the impressive stock of cultural and historic resources accessible. There is evidence that the somewhat nonchalant attitude of policymakers with respect to heritage is changing for the better, as has been shown throughout this chapter, in response to the pressure on Italy's competitiveness as a tourist destination.

This chapter on cultural tourism in Italy has dealt with the central assumption that, given the massive presence of heritage, the supply of accessible cultural and historic tourism products is marginal. Cultural tourism policies ought in the first place to remove the barriers to using the resources properly.

Heritage is concentrated in the central and southern part of Italy. Surprisingly, much of the country's heritage is to be found outside the traditional city trip destinations, such as Venice, Florence, and Rome. Although the number of cultural institutions has increased considerably, this has not led to a corresponding growth in the supply of heritage for tourism uses. The focus still lies on conservation, and tourism and conservation are seen as each other's eternal enemies. It is the accessibility of heritage which is compromised. In fact, Italy is one of the countries where the stock of heritage is infinitely large, but its accessibility amazingly low. Opening times and periods for cultural attractions are limited, and many are open only by special request.

This problem is compounded by the fact that cultural tourism demand is contracting. There is not one single segment of the cultural tourism market that has seen an increase in arrivals or overnight stays between 1987 and 1992. This is even more worrying when one realizes that interest in culture and its consumption is rapidly growing. Years of mismanagement, at national and local level, and at the level of the individual institution, is responsible for the current crisis.

There is currently no such thing as an 'Italian cultural tourism policy'. There are indications that this is slowly changing for the better. Initiatives have recently been developed by the Department of Tourism and the TCI to use heritage more efficiently. On a local scale, municipalities are reorganizing their supply of cultural goods that may be used for tourism purposes. Walking routes are being created, special cultural packages – that are supposed to appeal to especially up-market residential tourists – are being promoted, neglected monuments are being restored. As may have become clear, though, stimulating cultural tourism development in Italy is almost entirely a task of the public sector.

Resolving the contradiction between the richness of cultural tourism resources, and their limited accessibility means tackling some of the basic problems facing cultural institutions in Italy. The current rigid legislative frameworks, lack of financial control and inadequate management have to be addressed if Italy is to fully capitalize on its rich heritage. Whether new policy measures currently being introduced in the cultural sector will solve these problems, remains to be seen.

ACKNOWLEDGEMENT

The authors are indebted to Miss Silvia Begelle, who gathered most of the statistical information on which the chapter is based.

REFERENCES

Costa, P. and van der Borg, J. (1993) *Management of Tourism in Cities of Art*. CISET Working Paper 93/4, CISET, Venice.
DGXXIII (1994) *Eurotourism: Culture and Countryside*. European Commission, Brussels.
Di Battista, M. (1993) Art museums as enterprises? The case of Italian museums. Paper presented at the 2nd International Conference on Arts Management, Paris, June.
ENIT (various years) *Istituti d'Arte, Musei e di Antichità'*. ENIT, Rome.
FAIAT (1993) *Turismo Culturale in Italia*. FAIAT, Rome.
Fanelli, F. (1993) Our museums are Italy's General Motors. *The Art Newspaper* 33, 6–7.
ICARE (1993) *I Musei Veneziani*. ICARE, Venezia.
Ministero del Turismo (1991) *Quarto Rapporto sul Turismo* .Rome.
van der Borg, J. and Zago, M. (1995) *Museum Management*. CISET Working Paper 10/95, CISET, Venice.

Cultural Tourism in The Netherlands   13

G. RICHARDS

Department of Leisure Studies, Tilburg University, PO Box 90153, 5000 LE Tilburg, The Netherlands

INTRODUCTION

The Netherlands has traditionally regarded culture as a means of improving the quality of life of its citizens, rather than as a commodity to be sold to tourists. This attitude is slowly changing, however, as national, regional and local governments have begun to see the economic development potential of culture in general, and cultural tourism in particular. Cultural tourism has now become a major thrust of national tourism policy, and attracting tourists is now an acceptable goal for many cultural institutions.

Cultural tourism is seen as a potential solution to a diverse range of problems, including the funding of cultural institutions and the maintenance of the cultural heritage, spreading tourism seasonally and regionally, spreading cultural consumption geographically and socially, and building both national and regional identities. Achieving these ends also means addressing the current weaknesses of cultural tourism in The Netherlands. A lack of major 'must-see' attractions has, for example, been identified as a weakness of the Dutch tourism product. For many cultural attractions, there are also concerns about their accessibility for the general public, and tourists in particular.

Many argue that strengthening the cultural tourism product of The Netherlands can best be achieved by making cultural attractions more responsive to the visitor market. As government funding for culture comes under pressure, and subsidies give way to income generation, many cultural institutions are being forced to join the competitive hunt for the cultural tourist. This new climate is epitomized by the privatization of the national museums, which is the focus of the case study in this chapter.

CULTURAL TOURISM POLICY

As Bonink (1992) has noted, tourism and culture have only recently been considered as compatible by Dutch policy-makers: 'Traditionally, there has always been a certain tension between the monument policy and tourism policy. Monuments were there to be conserved, instead of being utilized' (p. 44).

The growing financial cost of heritage conservation combined with a recognition of the important role of cultural heritage in the Dutch tourism product have subsequently stimulated the promotion and development of cultural tourism by cultural and tourism policy-makers alike.

The origin of a specific cultural tourism policy dates back to 1983, when a report on the development of heritage for tourism was produced for the Ministries of Economic Affairs and Welfare, Housing and Culture (NRIT, 1983). This report concluded that The Netherlands possessed a significant supply of heritage attractions, but that these were poorly integrated with other tourism products, and there was little communication between cultural organizations and tourism suppliers. Those responsible for museums and monuments tended to see their job as conservation of heritage, rather than presenting heritage to a wider market (Munsters, 1994). The report recommended making heritage attractions more user-friendly, through animation, and for integration of the different attractions through themeing and regional collaboration.

The 1983 report led eventually to the development of a Masterplan for Cultural–Historic Tourism (Winkleman en van Hesse, 1989) in 1988. The Masterplan was designed to tackle the major problems identified in earlier studies, in particular the poor accessibility of cultural attractions. The Masterplan also attributed the low attendance at cultural attractions to the low awareness of the rich cultural heritage of The Netherlands among the Dutch themselves. By solving these problems, it was hoped to broaden the audience base for cultural tourism. More visitors would generate increased income and employment, meeting the objectives of the Ministry of Economic Affairs, and overall cultural participation would also grow, meeting the goals of the Ministry for Welfare, Housing and Culture (Munsters, 1994).

The recommendations of the Masterplan were quickly taken up in the new national plan for tourism in the 1990s 'Enterprise in Tourism' *(Ondernemen in Toerisme)*, which was introduced in 1990 (Ministerie van Economische Zaken, 1990). As the title suggests, this plan was based largely on increasing the economic potential of tourism, by building on the strengths of the Dutch tourist product and attempting to minimize its weaknesses. The plan was based on the identification of four themes which were considered to have considerable potential for tourism development: Netherlands-Waterland, Cultural–historic Heritage, Cities, and the Coast. Cultural heritage played a crucial role in integrating these themes, since it was recognized that the cultural resources concentrated in major cities and linked to the use of water (and the defences raised against the water) represented major weapons in the competitive struggle for international tourist business.

These four themes were subsequently incorporated as major pillars of the promotion strategy of The Netherlands Tourist Board (NBT). Cultural tourism was seen as being particularly significant in attracting international visitors to The Netherlands, and the most fertile source markets were identified as the UK, Spain, Italy, Switzerland, Austria, the United States, and Japan and the Far East (NBT, 1990).

The integration of culture with other themes was exemplified in the two major pilot projects launched in 1992 to try and give shape to the new policy. The first pilot project, 'Living Between the Waters' was established in North Holland, and concentrated on the centuries of struggle against the water from the sea and from the rivers. The second pilot project concentrated on the Dutch East-Indies Company (VOC), and its seventeenth century heritage in shipping, trade and industry. Finance for the first four years of these projects came from the Ministries for Economic Affairs and Welfare, Housing and Culture, after which regional organizations must bear the cost of continuing the projects.

The identification of cultural heritage as a specific theme in national tourism policy gave an immediate boost to cultural tourism development and promotion, not only at national level, but also regionally and locally. In the Province of Friesland, for example, cultural tourism has been adopted as a means of attracting more tourists to the region. The Province hoped to capitalize on 'the general trend towards growing interest in culture' through the integrated development and marketing of Friesland's rich, but previously uncoordinated heritage (Joustra, 1994:18). A regional development and action plan for cultural tourism launched in 1992 (Provincie Friesland, 1992), combined existing cultural tourism activities with new developments. Existing strengths, for example, included the designation since 1987 of a 'monument of the month' in different locations in the province. New elements included the creation of cultural tourism holiday packages and the publication of a magazine covering the cultural tourism products available in the region.

In the Province of Zuid Holland, regional and local authorities have joined together to develop a 'Cultural City' event. Each city will give a presentation of local art and culture, supplemented with events of national interest. Gouda was the first Cultural City in 1994, to be followed in subsequent years by Dordrecht, Delft, and Leiden. The first Cultural City event had somewhat mixed results. The total investment of over Fl 1 million (ECU 500,000) was covered mainly by regional and local government, with 8% coming from sponsorship. Arguments arose between the Provincial government and the city, because the Province wanted to promote professional culture to ensure the quality of this pioneer event, whereas the city wanted to place more emphasis on local, amateur culture. The events staged over the year attracted a total of 26,000 visitors, 6000 of whom came for a pop festival. In terms of broadening cultural participation the year was not successful, although it has arguably pushed culture higher up the political agenda in the city (Van der Wees, 1995).

In some of the larger Dutch cities, cultural tourism has taken on a much greater significance. In Rotterdam, for example, culture has been adopted as a major theme of tourism marketing. The strategic marketing plan for the Rotterdam city tourist office (VVV) for the period 1992–1994, for example, identifies the key elements of the tourist product as water, architecture, and culture. The weakness of Rotterdam is its relatively poor supply of traditional cultural facilities, particularly on an international level, compared with cities such as Amsterdam. Rotterdam has therefore decided to project an image of being a modern art city, using its futuristic architecture as a spearhead for the campaign. Product developments undertaken in relation to cultural tourism include the opening of the National Architecture Museum in 1993, staging architectural events and plans for a gallery of modern art (Bonink, 1992).

In Rotterdam, the general cultural policy has shifted away from the traditional Dutch model of decentralizing and subsidizing cultural resources (Bevers, 1993), towards lowering barriers to participation through marketing (Brouwer, 1993). By enriching the cultural life and profile of the city, the local authority hopes to be able to compete more effectively with other 'second cities' (such as Barcelona, Frankfurt, and Milan) in attracting tourists, investment and jobs. To achieve this, a development programme has been established with the aims of stimulating internationally orientated culture, building the image of Rotterdam as a cultural festival city, and supporting the applied arts, such as architecture, design, and photography. Brouwer argues that for Rotterdam, art is becoming increasingly interchangeable with sport and tourism, as another 'top attraction' that can be used to attract the 'new urban middle class', whose high incomes can stimulate the local economy.

SUPPLY AND FUNDING OF CULTURAL ATTRACTIONS

Supply

The challenge facing 'new' cultural tourism destinations such as Rotterdam is that the current distribution of cultural tourism resources is heavily weighted in favour of 'traditional' destinations, such as Amsterdam. In 1993, for example, Amsterdam housed 35 museums compared with only 17 in Rotterdam. A similar bias is found in the distribution of the 43,800 recognized monuments, 26% of which are located in Noord Holland, the province in which Amsterdam is located (Centraal Bureau voor de Statistiek, 1993a).

The uneven geographic distribution of cultural facilities in The Netherlands was a source of concern in the 1960s and 1970s, when government
policy was to increase subsidies for regional cultural venues (Bevers, 1993).
This approach tended to have relatively little impact on the distribution of
cultural consumption, however, as large cities continue to have higher proportions of cultural participation than smaller centres. Recent research has indicated that people with high levels of cultural capital and high propensity
towards cultural consumption tend to be concentrated in the central areas of
major Dutch cities (Roetman, 1994; Verhoeff, 1994). The realization that
cultural participation could not be spread geographically simply through subsidizing facilities helped to pave the way for a more market-orientated approach to cultural provision in the 1980s. A further boost to the supply of
cultural facilities came from the growing link between culture and tourism
over the past decade.

The combined efforts of state and market have helped to enrich the cultural
infrastructure of The Netherlands considerably in recent years. Figure 13.1
shows that the supply of museums has grown by 124% since 1970. Growth in
museum supply was particularly strong during the late 1980s. The number of
museums grew by 11% between 1980 and 1985, and then by 30% from 1985
to 1990 (Centraal Bureau voor de Statistiek, 1993b). The supply of monuments has shown a less spectacular growth (5% between 1980 and 1990),
albeit from a much higher base. The supply of theatres in The Netherlands
grew by 42% between 1970 and 1986, even though audiences for subsidized
theatre fell by 50% over the same period (Knulst, 1989).

More cultural attractions has also tended to mean smaller cultural attractions. The average size of museums opened before 1980 was 1175 m^2, compared with 381 m^2 for museums opened after 1980 (Centraal Bureau voor de

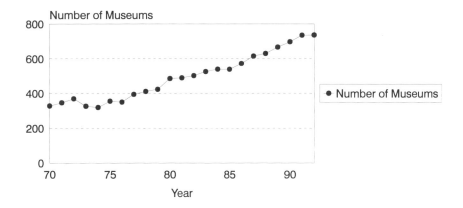

Fig. 13.1.   Museum supply in The Netherlands (source: CBS, 1993).

Statistiek, 1993b). The burgeoning number of small museums is a source of concern for many museum professionals, keen to protect the image and reputation of mainstream institutions. The Director of the Rijksmuseum in Amsterdam has remarked 'if someone has a couple of mediocre paintings at home, a special museum must be created for them. This also applies to matches or saltcellars. The Netherlands Museum Association (NVM) have rightly called for an end to this horrendous proliferation of museums' (Van Os, 1994:7).

One aspect of cultural supply which has received a great deal of attention in recent years is the staging of events. Events are seen as a means of attracting both international and domestic tourists, aiding the seasonal spread of tourism, animating the existing cultural attraction supply and renewing the tourist product. Major international events have come to form a crucial element of international tourism promotion, to the extent that 'blockbuster' events are almost considered essential to maintaining growth in incoming tourism, and generating repeat visits by foreign tourists (Bos, 1994). Many of these events have a cultural theme, such as the major exhibitions of works by Rembrandt (1991/92), van Gogh (1990) and Mondriaan (1995). An analysis of the impact of the Rembrandt exhibition is considered below in the case study of the Rijksmuseum in Amsterdam.

The supply of events has grown considerably, with a 43% increase in the number of events registered by the NBT between 1987 and 1992 (NRIT, 1994). Over this period there was a clear shift in the emphasis of cultural events, with a decline in arts events (−23%) and a growth in folklore events (+84%). It is the major arts events, however, which tend to attract large numbers of foreign tourists, and there is evidence to suggest that the number of tourists visiting arts events has increased over time. The Rembrandt exhibition held in 1969, for example, attracted about 100,000 foreign visitors, compared with almost 200,000 visiting the Rembrandt exhibition staged in 1992. The audience for such cultural events has also become more internationalized, with a smaller proportion of visitors from neighbouring countries (Bruin, 1993). The pulling power of major arts events is not totally guaranteed, however. The 1995 Mondriaan exhibition in The Hague, for example, attracted only 185,000 of the expected 300,000 visitors, and foreign tourist attendance was particularly disappointing. As Roetman (1994) found in her study of visitors to an earlier Mondriaan exhibition, the high level of cultural capital required to access the works of Mondriaan will limit the potential audience, and will be a much greater barrier to foreign tourists.

Funding

State funding of culture has historically been generous in The Netherlands, and accounted for almost 1% of Gross Domestic Product in the mid-1980s (Van der Wijk and Roukens, 1993). Economic pressures are now forcing a change towards less interventionist policies. In the cultural plan for 1993–1996 (Ministerie van WVC, 1992) the emphasis is on increasing self-reliance, through concentrating on quality and giving greater management flexibility to public cultural facilities. The emphasis on supporting quality has caused reorganization and mergers in the performing arts. Performances have also been spatially concentrated to reduce travel costs. The 49 museums funded directly by the national government are also being given more financial independence.

The total cost of public museums in 1991 was Fl 507 million (ECU 240 million), 75% of which was accounted for by subsidies. Museums managed by the public sector were subsidized for up to 80% of their costs. For all museums, self-generated income has grown substantially in recent years. Between 1985 and 1991 income from admissions and merchandising grew by 80%, while total subsidies grew by 30% over the same period. Increased self-generated income has come mainly from higher admission prices, which rose by almost 78% between 1980 and 1990. At the same time, the number of museums offering free admission fell from 27% to 22%. Admission revenue rose from 8% of museum revenue in 1980 to 13% in 1989 (Centraal Bureau voor de Statistiek, 1993b). This trend is likely to continue in the future, particularly as subsidy levels for the newly independent state museums continue to fall in real terms. The Open Air Museum in Arnhem, for example, forecast that admission charges would contribute 43% of its income in 1997, compared with 27% in 1994 (Nederlands Openluchtmuseum, 1994).

The system for funding monuments has changed in recent years. A centralized system based on a national list of monuments has been replaced by a localized system in which local authorities can draw up their own lists and provide partial grants to owners for restoration work.

Decreasing government intervention has created a greater role for the voluntary sector in cultural provision. A recent report on voluntary work in tourism and cultural heritage (Nederlands Centrum Voor Vrijetijdsvraagstukken, 1994) has indicated that over 21,000 volunteers are active in the area of cultural heritage. These volunteers contribute almost 3000 person-years of work per year, or about 55% of the total labour input in the field. In museums the total labour force has grown by 100% between 1980 and 1991, but volunteers account for a growing proportion, up from 23% in 1980 to 51% in 1991.

The Association for Open Monuments (*Vereniging Open Monumenten*, VOM) was established in The Netherlands in 1994. The VOM is modelled along the lines of the British National Trust (see Foley, Chapter 16 of this volume), and seeks to generate a contribution of around Fl 10 million (ECU 4.7 million) to the maintenance of Dutch monuments from its projected 350,000 members by the year 2000. It has recently begun opening a chain of 'heritage shops', designed to raise revenue for heritage preservation, thus making the 'unaffordable affordable' (VOM, 1994).

Commercial operators have also been playing an increasingly important role in cultural tourism, particularly in outbound markets. There are a growing number of small, specialist cultural tourism companies, although the market is not as well developed as in Germany. A feature of these tours, however, is the high price. Fully guided tours for groups of 20–25 participants can cost between Fl 4000 and Fl 8000 (ECU 1900–3800).

CULTURAL TOURISM DEMAND

Broadening support for the preservation of cultural heritage is also reflected in the growing numbers of visitors to cultural attractions in The Netherlands in recent years. The level of cultural participation in The Netherlands has grown strongly in recent years. In 1991, 72% of the Dutch population visited a cultural attraction of some kind, compared with 68% in 1979 (Centraal Bureau voor de Statistiek, 1993c). Most of this growth is attributable either to increased museum visiting (30% in 1979, 41% in 1991) or pop concerts (13% in 1979, 24% in 1991). In contrast, attendance at art galleries or theatres grew very little. In The Netherlands the broadening of the cultural audience which was evident until the early 1980s has now ceased, and the performing arts audience in particular has become more 'elite' in recent years (Knulst, 1989).

The engines of cultural tourism demand in The Netherlands have therefore been museums and monuments, both relatively accessible forms of cultural consumption. Museum attendance grew almost constantly from just under 8 million visits a year in 1970 to over 22 million visits in 1992 (Centraal Bureau voor de Statistiek, 1993a). Slight falls in attendance were recorded in the early 1980s and in the early 1990s, both periods with poor economic conditions. Between 1992 and 1994, museum attendances fell by over 6%.

Few historic monuments keep accurate visitor figures, and estimates of demand must therefore be derived from surveys. The annual Open Monument Day experienced a growth in visitor numbers from 350,000 in the first year (1987) to 700,000 in 1993 (Rietbergen, 1994). Surveys indicated that the event attracted predominantly older visitors (average age 45 years) and more highly educated individuals were over-represented. Most of the visitors lived locally (40%) or within 30 km of the site visited, so the proportion of tourists was quite low. Over three-quarters of the visitors indicated that they were interested in monuments, although this interest is often quite passive. Only 10% of survey respondents visited monuments frequently, 40% occasionally and 50% seldom or never. In contrast, 80% indicated that they watched 'cultural–historic' television programmes (Nelissen and van Hilst, 1992). The role of television in creating awareness of cultural heritage is also emphasized in the tourism strategy of the NBT (Bonink, 1992). This evidence suggests that cultural event attendance makes little contribution to broadening regular cultural participation. As with the performing arts, television seems to have been the greatest vehicle for spreading 'cultural consumption' to a wider audience (Knulst, 1989).

Table 13.1. Proportion of foreign tourists visiting The Netherlands for museums, old buildings or historic cities by nationality, 1988.

Nationality	% with cultural motivation
English	38
French	39
Belgian	19
Spanish/Portuguese	42
Italian	51
US/Canadian	57
Japanese	56

Source: NBT (1989).

There is evidence, however, to suggest that culture is becoming increasingly important as an element of Dutch tourism consumption. The NRIT report on heritage tourism (NRIT, 1983), produced survey evidence indicating that 80% of Dutch holiday-makers (or 56% of the population) visited a monument or museum on holiday. The level of cultural visits was higher for foreign holidays (60% of holiday-makers) than for domestic ones (40%). The greater importance of culture for foreign tourists is also reflected in incoming tourism to The Netherlands, as 30% of incoming tourists indicated that cultural heritage was an important motive for visiting the country in 1988 (NBT, 1989). Foreign visitors on the their first trip to The Netherlands were more likely to be motivated by cultural attractions (46%) than repeat visitors. The importance of cultural motives also varied considerably by visitor origin, with North American and Japanese visitors being particularly motivated by cultural attractions (Table 13.1). However, the proportion of visitors placing culture as the most important motive for visiting was much lower, only 8%.

A survey of day trips in 1990/91 indicated that cultural attractions accounted for 3% of total day trips (Centraal Bureau voor de Statistiek, 1992). Cultural attractions, particularly historic cities, tended to generate trips of relatively long duration (50% longer than eight hours) and tended to attract people from relatively long distances (65% more than 30 km). Another holiday survey indicated that 20% of the Dutch population visited a monument during a domestic holiday in 1991 (Zoest, 1994).

The ATLAS survey of cultural tourists in The Netherlands in 1992 covered two major attractions in Amsterdam, the Rijksmuseum (see the case study below) and the Van Gogh Museum. The 660 visitor interviews indicated that over 90% of visitors in summer 1992 were tourists, with the majority (80%) coming from abroad. The level of first-time visitation to both attractions was high, both for foreign tourists (79%) and Dutch residents (30%).

Youth tourists were well represented, with over 50% being aged under 30. Foreign tourists tended to be slightly older, and the average age of visitors to the

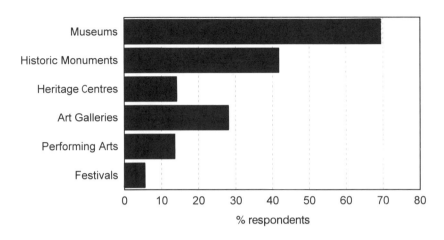

Fig. 13.2.   Cultural attractions visited in The Netherlands (source: ATLAS survey, 1992).

Rijksmuseum was higher than the Van Gogh Museum. Cultural tourists tend to visit a number of cultural attractions during their stay. Almost 70% visited more than one museum, almost 30% more than one art gallery, and over 40% visited at least one historic monument (Fig. 13.2). Multiple cultural visits were more common among foreign tourists, over 75% of whom had visited another museum, and 46% had visited a historic monument. Not surprisingly, the language barrier tended to minimize attendance at art performances, which attracted 11% of foreign visitors.

The average cultural tourist stayed about four nights in The Netherlands, and over three-quarters of foreign visitors stayed in hotels. The major origin countries for cultural tourists were the UK (28%), France (15%), USA (13%), Germany (12%), and Belgium (8%). A large proportion of cultural tourists are actually involved in the cultural industries, with over 23% connected with heritage or the arts. The link with the cultural industries was particularly strong for foreign tourists (26%) and for visitors to the more specialized Van Gogh Museum (27%).

Dutch tourists interviewed for the ATLAS survey during their trips abroad exhibited a high degree of cultural motivation. Over 36% indicated that cultural attractions were important in their choice of holiday destination. Half the Dutch tourists visited at least one museum during their trip, and over 55% visited at least one historic monument. The destinations with the highest proportion of Dutch cultural tourists interviewed were London, Berlin, Venice, and Athens.

CASE STUDY: THE RIJKSMUSEUM, AMSTERDAM

The Rijksmuseum is the national museum of The Netherlands, and houses the finest collection of Dutch paintings in the world. The Rijksmuseum was established in Amsterdam in 1808, originally as the Royal art museum, and later as the home of the national art collection. The museum is most famous for its collection of seventeenth century masters, including Rembrandt and Vermeer. The museum has in recent years undergone a significant restructuring, aimed at achieving a more even balance between the needs of conservation and the needs of the visitor (Van Os, 1994). In 1995 even more significant change is on the way, as the Rijksmuseum becomes independent, placed outside direct state control for the first time. This case study is based largely on work by Gratton and van Vugt (1993).

The Rijksmuseum attracts about one million visitors a year (Fig. 13.3), about two-thirds of whom are foreign tourists. The British are the largest group of foreign visitors, accounting for about 14% of all visits. The heavy reliance on foreign tourists means that visits tend to be concentrated in summer, particularly in July and August. As Fig. 13.3 suggests, visitor numbers can be radically influenced by special exhibitions. The Rembrandt exhibition held from December 1991 to February 1992 boosted attendances in the normally quiet months of January and February more than threefold, and helped to increase total museum attendance by over 20%.

The Rembrandt exhibition was staged as a deliberate attempt to attract cultural tourists. The Displays Director of the museum said later 'we decided to treat the exhibition as a touristic event'. Cooperation with the tourism industry had previously been difficult, because 'we considered them superficial with their tulips, windmills and Rembrandt's Nightwatch as the only painting. They

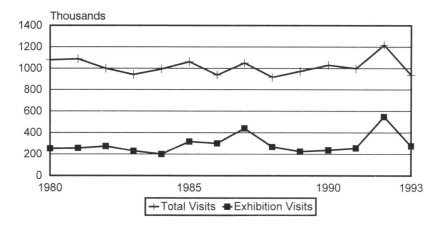

Fig. 13.3.   Visits to the Rijksmuseum, 1980–1993 (source: Rijksmuseum).

Table 13.2.   Origin of foreign visitors to the Rembrandt exhibition at the Rijksmuseum, 1991/92.

Origin	% visitors
France	26
Belgium	20
Germany	13
UK	6
Italy	6
Scandinavia	6
Rest of Europe	8
USA	8
Other countries	9

Source: Gratton and van Vugt (1993).
Figures add to more than 100% due to rounding.

considered us to be conceited and dull' (Bruin, 1993:338). Working with the NBT, the Amsterdam tourist office, American Express and KLM (the Dutch national airline), the Rijksmuseum hoped to attract a very broad public to the exhibition. It was estimated that some 430,000 visitors would generate an additional Fl 75 million (ECU 35 million) in tourist spending in Amsterdam.

In total, some 440,000 visitors attended the exhibition during its three-month run in Amsterdam. About 55% of the visitors came from The Netherlands, and 45% were foreign tourists. The foreign tourists came predominantly from nearby countries such as France, Belgium, and Germany (Table 13.2). The relatively low number of British tourists was attributable to the fact that the exhibition could also be seen in London. A large proportion of the foreign tourists (46%) had made an earlier visit to the Rijksmuseum, indicating the importance of such 'mega-events' in stimulating repeat visits. A study by the NBT indicated that the total tourist expenditure associated with the exhibition was Fl 150 million (ECU 71 million), of which foreign tourists accounted for Fl 30 million (ECU 14 million). The research also indicated that foreign visitors coming to The Netherlands especially to visit the Rembrandt exhibition spent Fl 46 million (ECU 22 million) (Bos, 1994). The contribution of the Rijksmuseum to the tourist economy of Amsterdam is therefore very significant.

In order to handle the extra demand generated by the exhibition, a special ticketing system was used to avoid serious queuing problems. About 90% of tickets were sold in advance, and each ticket specified a day and time of entry. Visiting times were arranged in one hour time slots, with a 750 visitor per hour capacity limit. This system was relatively successful, as 53% of visitors interviewed in Amsterdam indicated that they could see all the pictures well, compared with 46% of visitors to the same exhibition in London, and only 36% of visitors to the exhibition in Berlin (Bruin, 1993).

Because the Rijksmuseum effectively functions as a 'must-see' sight for foreign tourists, the museum is concentrating its promotional efforts on domestic tourists.

The total annual budget for the Rijksmuseum is around Fl 32 million (ECU 15 million), and has remained at this level for about the last ten years, failing to keep up with inflation. In an increasingly difficult financial climate, the government's solution to the financing problems of the national museums has been to make them 'independent', or effectively privatize them. From 1995 onwards, the Rijksmuseum will function as an autonomous organization, with its own board of trustees. Formerly, the government paid all the costs of the museum, and all revenue (about Fl 9 million, mainly from admission charges) went directly back to the government. In future, staff costs and some of the operating costs will be met by the government. The museum will retain all income, but will have to meet the remaining operating costs itself.

Making the Rijksmuseum and other state museums independent has two basic goals. The museums will have more freedom to control their own budget and determine staffing policy, and the government hopes to gain more control over the use of state subsidies. In place of a standard annual subsidy, the Rijksmuseum will now receive funding on the basis of a four-year plan. The plans are evaluated by the ministry, and good plans can be rewarded with extra funding, and poor ones with less (Kilian, 1994). The Rijksmuseum, along with the other newly independent museums, must therefore try and meet not only the needs of the market in order to earn more income, but must also be careful to meet the policy priorities of the government, to preserve its level of subsidy.

The need to attract more visitors and earn more income is reflected in the future priorities of the Rijksmuseum. A major aim is to increase visitor numbers, which have remained almost static for a decade, arguably because of competition from the growing number of museums and alternative attractions. By increasing visitor numbers, the museum hopes to raise more revenue, particularly from admission charges and merchandizing. Opening times will also be extended, with the museum open on Mondays and perhaps longer in the evenings. By becoming more visitor-orientated, the museum hopes that it can generate more income to support the basic functions of the museum: collection, stewardship, and scholarship.

CONCLUSIONS

The partnership between culture and tourism is of relatively recent origin in The Netherlands, which has drawn extensively on the British experience of developing heritage tourism during the 1980s. Most development has therefore taken place in the area of heritage (cultural–historical tourism), although arts tourism is increasingly being developed through 'blockbuster' exhibitions and events.

For many public cultural institutions, rising costs, tighter government funding and a need to prove their social value by increasing visitor numbers have led to a growing market-orientation. The established cultural attractions have been joined in recent years by a wide range of commercial and voluntary sector attractions, dramatically expanding the range of cultural opportunities for tourists and residents alike. The cultural tourism market has become increasingly competitive, especially as the growth in attraction supply has outstripped the rise in visitor numbers in recent years.

The cultural audience in The Netherlands expanded rapidly in the 1970s and early 1980s as a result of rising education levels. In recent years, however, this 'organic growth' of the domestic cultural audience appears to have levelled off. This means that any future growth in cultural audiences will be increasingly dependent on tourism, or in other words, capturing a share of the cultural market from other regions or countries. For this reason, the use of cultural tourism as an element of regional and national tourism development policies will continue to be important, and the current level of integration between cultural and tourism policies and between national and regional policies should prove an important advantage in future cultural tourism development.

REFERENCES

Bevers, T. (1993) *Georganiseerd Cultuur.* Dick Coutinho, Bussum.

Bonink, C.A.M. (1992) *Cultural tourism development and government policy.* MA Dissertation, Rijksuniversiteit Utrecht.

Bos, H. (1994) The importance of mega-events in the development of tourism demand. *Festival Management and Event Tourism* 2, 55–58.

Brouwer, R. (1993) Het nieuwe Rotterdam: de kunst, het belied, de zorg en de markt. *Vrijetijd en Samenleving* 11, 31–47.

Bruin, K. (1993) Rembrandt in Amsterdam, Berlijn en Londen. In Bevers, T., Van den Braembussche, A. and Langenberg, B.J. (eds) *De Kunstwereld: Produktie, Distributie en Receptie in de Wereld van Kunst en Cultuur.* Erasmus Universiteit, Rotterdam.

Centraal Bureau voor de Statistiek (1992) *Dagrecreatie 1990/91.* CBS, Den Haag.

Centraal Bureau voor de Statistiek (1993a) *Cultureel Jaarboek.* CBS, Den Haag.

Centraal Bureau voor de Statistiek (1993b) Musea: Kosten en Financering 1990–1991. *Sociaal-Culturele Berichten,* 1993–16.

Centraal Bureau voor de Statistiek (1993c) Cultuurparticipatie. *Sociaal-Culturele Berichten* 1993–14.

Gratton, C. and van Vugt, T. (1993) *The Rijksmuseum, Amsterdam.* Case study for ATLAS Cultural Tourism Project, Tilburg University, Tilburg.

Joustra, H.G. (1994) Kultuer en toerisme yn Fryslân. *Monumenten* 5/94, 18–21.

Kilian, K. (1994) Rijksmusea en WVC eens over subsidiering. *NRC Handelsblad* 22 February, 6.

Knulst, W. (1989) *Van Vaudeville tot Video.* Sociale en Cultureel Planbureau, Rijswijk.

Ministerie van Economische Zaken (1990) *Ondernemen in Toerisme.* SDU, Den Haag.

Ministerie van WVC (1992) *Investeren in cultuur: nota cultuurbeleid 1993–1996*. SDU, Den Haag.

Munsters, W. (1994) *Cultuurtoerisme*. Garant, Apeldoorn.

NBT (1989) *Grensonderzoek*. NBT, Leidsendam.

NBT (1990) *Keizen voor Kansen*. NBT, Leidsendam.

Nederlands Centrum Voor Vrijetijdsvraagstukken (1994) *Vrijwilligerswerk in Toerisme en Cultureel Erfgoed*. NCVV, Arnhem.

Nederlands Openluchtmuseum (1994) *Een Museum voor het leven. Ondernemingsplan-Nederlands Openluchtmuseum 1994–1997*. Nederlands Openluchtmuseum, Arnhem.

Nelissen, N.J.M. and van Hilst, P. (1992) Open Monumentendag: schoolvoorbeeld van cultuurhistorisch toerisme. *Recreatie en Toerisme* 2(11), 28–30.

NRIT (1983) *Erfgoed: Toeristisch Goed – een Onderzoek Naar de Toeristisch-economische Betekenis van Monumenten en Musea in Nederland*. Nederlands Research Instituut voor Recreatie en Toerisme, Breda.

NRIT (1994) *De Toeristische en Economische Betekenis van Evenementen in Nederland*. Nederlands Research Instituut voor Recreatie en Toerisme, Breda.

Provincie Friesland (1992) *Fries Cultuur-toeristisch Ontwikkelings- en Aktieplan*. Provincie Friesland, Leeuwarden.

Rietbergen, W.L.F. (1994) Cultuurtoerisme. *Handboek Recreatie en Toerisme*, 7020–1, Bohn Stafleu Van Loghum, Houten.

Roetman, E.E. 1994 *Motivatie in Retrospectief: een onderzoek naar motivatie voor cultuuroerisme tijdens de Mondriaantentoonstelling te Amsterdam*. Masters dissertation, Tilburg University.

Van der Wees, F. (1995) Succes Cultuurstad slechts van korte duur. *Delfsche Courant* 1 March, 19.

Van der Wijk, P. and Roukens, O. (1993) Openbare uitgeven voor cultuur, kunst en beheer. *Openbare Uitgeven* 1, 13–22.

Van Os, H.W. (1994) De kerk van de Helilige Conservator. *De Volkskrant* 10 October, 7.

Verhoeff, R. (1994) High culture: the performing arts and its audience in the Netherlands. *Tijdschrift voor Economische en Sociale Geografie* 85, 79–83.

VOM (1994) Erfgoedwinkels maken het onbetaalbare betaalbaar! *Open Monument* 1, 12.

Winkelman en van Hesse (1989) *Masterplan Cultuurhistorisch Toerisme*. Winkelman en van Hesse, Den Haag.

Zoest, J.G.A. (1994) Door emotionele en belevingsfactoren 'stoffig' cultuurtoerisme speels aan de man brengen. *Recreatie en Toerisme* 4(1), 26–27.

Cultural Tourism in Portugal   14

H. DE CARVALHO CURADO

SAGEI, University of Aveiro, Campo Universitário, 3800 Aveiro, Portugal

INTRODUCTION

Tourism, like many other social activities, depends on the cyclical whims of fashion. In the last few decades coastal resorts and mountain regions formed the natural basis of much of Europe's tourist flows, but recent trends are pointing to a growing interest in cultural and rural tourism, travelling for business purposes and conferences.

Portugal is a destination which has in the past largely capitalized on natural resources and its climate as the basis for its tourism development. The important question for the future development of Portuguese tourism is whether cultural tourism and other areas of 'new tourism' (Poon, 1993) can be developed to take advantage of these growth markets. This chapter examines the development of cultural tourism in Portugal, and its role in diversifying tourism demand. A critical assessment is made of the nature and availability of Portuguese cultural tourism resources, and the role that these have played in tourism marketing and promotion.

However, two specific problems arise in conducting such an analysis in Portugal. The first is the difficulty of defining cultural tourism in Portugal, and the second is the lack of systematic data on cultural tourism, which follows from the problem of definition. In addressing the problem of defining cultural tourism, this chapter adopts a broad approach to the subject, on the basis that

> nowadays there is a general agreement among experts who assume that cultural tourism should not only be the exploitation and valuation of cultural 'stone' heritage such as buildings, sites and historic monuments. It should also include the

conception and organization of products and services in this area, such as gastronomy, folklore, popular traditions, craftsmanship, etc.

(Palma, 1991)

The lack of statistical data on cultural tourism is harder to overcome, but an attempt is made here to link the scattered evidence which does exist to trends in Portuguese tourism in general.

THE DEVELOPMENT OF CULTURAL TOURISM

The geographic position of Portugal, isolated from the rest of Europe by Spain and the Pyrenees, has tended to slow the pace of industrialization and modernization, and with it the development of tourism. Tourism development only proceeded 'when cheap and comfortable logistic means were introduced. Obviously they came in fitting occasions: macadam roads (1815), steam engines (1815), trains (1825), telegraphs (1837), standard hotels (c.1930–1940) and finally the excellent operator of this huge machine – the modern travel agent (Thomas Cook, 1941)' (Pina, 1991:7). In the nineteenth and early twentieth centuries therefore, the development of tourism in Portugal lagged behind developments in northern Europe. Tourist guide books emphasized the landscape and the living culture of Portugal as major attractions. Tourism was seen as a useful means of earning foreign exchange, but also as a means of building national identity. Writers bemoaned the poor state of historic monuments, which led to the first moves to conserve the heritage, which was considered to show the uniqueness of Portuguese people.

Early voluntary sector efforts at promoting the country abroad, such as the *Sociedade de Propaganda de Portugal* (Secretariat for National Propaganda) were eventually subsumed by the state with the creation of the *Repartição de Turismo* (Department of Tourism) in the *Ministério do Fomento* (Ministry of Development) in 1911. This official recognition of tourism was linked to its growing economic and political significance. The State Budget for 1934–35 stated that 'tourism had developed so much that hundreds of thousands of pounds had been collected yearly' and in the opinion of the Central Bank, Tourism 'is the great new source of income to our economy' (Ministério do Comércio e Turismo, 1991:9).

It was recognized at an early stage that the relatively rural nature of the country and the lack of 'high culture' resources required a different approach in tourism promotion. In the 1930s the Secretariat for National Propaganda (SNP) proposed 'a touristic promotion of Portugal, based on popular features, instead of traditional cosmopolitan, learned activities with which the country wasn't at ease' (Ministério do Comércio e Turismo, 1991:9).

So, the director of SNP pointed out the typical characteristics of our villages as an alternative to the international magnificence of great artistic centres; the gaudy

colours of our craftsmanship were emphasized, instead of the excellent foreign
museums; the colour of our folklore, instead of great cosmopolitan amusement;
the generous simplicity of our hospitality, as alternative to the worldly man-
nerism of great social life; the simple, savory regional cooking, instead of the
cuisine of famous centres.

(Pina, 1988:97)

The development of transport and communications infrastructure, the
valorization of heritage resources and popular traditions and the creation of
specific legislation to support tourism, enabled Portugal by the 1960s to begin
competing with Mediterranean tourist destinations. Portuguese seaside resorts
were visited by 1 million foreigners in 1964 and this number doubled by 1968.
Tourism receipts grew so rapidly that by the end of the decade tourism was a
vital source of revenue to the national economy. In order to guide the development of tourism, in 1965 the government transformed the Department of
Tourism into the *Direcção-Geral de Turismo* (General Direction of Tourism) and
created the *Centro Nacional de Formação Turística e Hoteleira* (National Centre for
Training in Tourism and Hotel Management) to provide tourism staff with
suitable education. Tourism was recognized as an essential sector of economic
development, with a special chapter in the national development plans drawn
up for 1965–1967 and 1968–1973 (Ministério do Comércio e Turismo,
1991).

A break in the hitherto rapid development of tourism in Portugal came
with the April Revolution in 1974. The political and economic uncertainty
which resulted caused a significant drop in tourism demand, as well as a virtual
halt to tourism investment and development. The return to political stability at
the beginning of the 1980s led to the recovery of tourist demand. The Portuguese tourism industry which emerged again in the 1980s was very far
removed from its nineteenth century roots. The cultural values of the
nineteenth century emphasized the preservation of the cultural heritage and
the picturesque aspects of the Portuguese rural life. This traditional view of
culture was replaced in the twentieth century by popular culture values based
on the promotion of a 'sea and sun' product. However, some elements of the
original Portuguese approach to tourism and culture remain at the heart of
tourism policy today.

The rich cultural heritage of Portugal constitutes a strong unifying element for the Portuguese and a powerful attraction to foreigners. The early
policies aimed at developing popular cultural features were based on the assumption that this would help to strengthen national identity and the Portuguese character as well as extracting economic profits from foreign tourists.

As the country cannot boast a great number of monuments or museums as
the focal point to attract tourists, attention was focused on the preservation
and exploration of the valuable heritage resources which did exist. This concern for preserving and maximizing heritage resources has continued to the
present day.

The *Plano Nacional de Turismo* (Tourism National Plan) considers that 'integrated planning of tourism calls for the definition of priorities that consider the real tourist heritage of a country and the regions in which development is advisable' (Secretaria de Estado do Turismo, 1985:14). Although cultural heritage is not referred to as a priority, one of the aims set is the contribution to the development of cultural heritage and valorization of historical patrimony.

THE MARKET FOR CULTURAL TOURISM

As mentioned above, there is very little specific information on the market for cultural tourism in Portugal. This section therefore uses information from general studies of tourism to identify trends relevant to cultural tourism. The total number of foreign tourists entering Portugal has increased substantially in the last decade, from 2.88 million visitors in 1979 to 8.88 million in 1992 (Direcção-Geral de Turismo, 1994a). The countries that contributed most to this flow were Spain, United Kingdom, Germany, France, The Netherlands and the USA, Spain being responsible for half the total arrivals and the UK for 16%. Incoming tourism is highly concentrated, both seasonally and spatially. About 40% of all arrivals are recorded between July and September, and the Algarve region of southern Portugal accounts for almost 40% of all foreign tourism (Table 14.1). This concentration is the result of the increasing dominance of package tourism, which has been a source of growing concern to Portuguese policy-makers. The rise of package holiday business has been marked by a declining average length of stay, an increasing proportion of first-time visitors and a growth in the use of hotel accommodation. The problem of concentration is compounded by the fact that the Algarve is also the most popular destination for domestic tourists (Table 14.2), and that domestic tourism is even more seasonal than foreign tourism, with 50% taking their holidays in August.

Table 14.1.   Distribution of foreign tourists in Portugal by region 1979 and 1992.

	% foreign tourists	
Region	1979	1992
Costa Verde	16.8	9.7
Costa de Prata	15.3	12.1
Lisbon Coast	27.2	21.4
Mountains	3.5	5.9
Plains	4.9	8.0
Algarve	25.1	39.4
Madeira	6.2	2.6
Azores	1.0	0.9

Source: Direcção-Geral de Turismo (1994a).

Table 14.2.   Domestic tourism in Portugal by region, 1993.

Region	% domestic tourists
Costa Verde	19
Costa de Prata	21
Lisbon Coast	17
Lisbon	2
Mountains	19
Plains	11
Algarve	32
Madeira	16
Azores	–

Source: Direcção-Geral de Turismo (1994b).

Table 14.3.   Portuguese holiday motivations, 1989–90.

Motivation	% respondents
Rest and relaxation	71
Sea-related activities	26
Meeting people from other places	19
Sightseeing	19
Entertainment and shows	15
Sports	2
Social life	8
Family visits	4
Museums and historic monuments	4
Folklore, craftsmanship	–
Gastronomy	1

Source: Direcção-Geral de Turismo (undated b).

Ameliorating the problems of spatial and seasonal concentration of tourism is a major incentive to develop cultural tourism, which is considered to have a beneficial impact in terms of spreading tourism flows.

Motivations for travel

The analysis of the motivation of tourists in Portugal is complicated by the fact that national surveys use the basic motivation 'holidays' as a classification (Table 14.3). Foreign visitors to Portugal are predominantly holiday-makers (83.2% in 1979 and 91.5% in 1992). Other relatively important motivations identified for travel to Portugal are 'Business' (2.4% in 1992), 'Religion' (2.8%) and 'Visits to relatives or friends' (0.9%). 'Culture' seems at first glance to be relatively unimportant as a primary motivation for travel. However, many of those stating 'holiday' as their purpose of visiting Portugal may also have cultural motives, depending on the type of holiday they are taking. If one considers culture in its broadest sense, one should perhaps also include the category 'religion' together with cultural tourism. If these two items are taken together, the proportion of 'culturally motivated' tourists (3.4%) is not much lower than in Ireland, for example (see O Donnchadha and O Connor, Chapter 11 this volume). Surveys indicate that a higher proportion of cultural visitors arrive in the winter months. Tourists exhibiting the highest level of cultural motivation come from Italy (4.7%), Venezuela (2.1%), Spain (1.0%), Brazil (0.9%), and the Republic of South Africa (0.8%). This distribution indentifies two basic cultural tourism markets: those interested in comparing similar cultures (Italian and Spanish) and visits to their roots by Portuguese migrants (Venezuelan, Brazilian, and South African).

Surveys of the motives of domestic tourists indicate that the most important motives for travel are 'the need for a rest, physical and psychological recovery' (71%) and 'sea and sun activities' (26%). Popular culture, in the form of 'entertainment and shows' was also an important travel motivation (15%). More traditional forms of culture, such as visits to museums and historical monuments (4%) or gastronomy (1%) were less important, and folklore did not feature as a travel motivation (Table 14.3).

Some growth in cultural tourism is indicated by the increased attendance at Portuguese museums. Because of the negative impact of the Revolution on incoming tourism, museum attendances remained almost static between 1974 and 1982, at less than 3 million visitors a year. With the growth in tourism in the 1980s, however, museum attendances also rose significantly, from 2.8 million in 1982 to almost 6.8 million in 1988.

More recent data on cultural tourism in Portugal were gathered for the ATLAS Cultural Tourism Project, by Luisa Aires (Universidade Arberta) and Visi Pareda Herrero (Universidade de Porto). Almost 600 visitors were interviewed at the Museu de Arte Moderna, the church of São Francisco, and the historic monument Torre dos Clérigos in Porto. Almost two-thirds of those interviewed lived outside Porto, and 44% were foreign tourists. Over three-quarters of foreign tourists came from other European countries, although Brazil (6.8%) and the USA (5.7%) were also important source markets outside Europe. A large proportion of domestic tourists originated from Lisbon (56%). Over 55% of tourists indicated that the cultural attractions were 'very important' or 'quite important' in their decision to visit the city. Almost 60% of respondents had visited a museum or heritage centre during their stay, and 40% had visited an art gallery. The proportion of students (32%) was high, as in most other countries surveyed. Visitors under 30 years of age accounted for 53% of those interviewed, whereas only 9% were aged 60 or over.

The vast majority of tourists (80%) were staying less than one week in Portugal, and over half were staying three nights or less in the country. This short length of stay, combined with a high level of hotel usage among tourists (over 60%) indicates that many of those interviewed were on short touring holidays.

The growth of interest in cultural tourism is also underlined by the 5.7 million visitors who were attracted to the 41 exhibitions staged as part of the European Cultural Capital event in Lisbon in 1994. This is the best recorded visitor total for exhibitions in a Cultural Capital year, although total visitor numbers were below those achieved in Antwerp (1993). The evaluation of the Lisbon event by Myerscough (1995) indicated that it was hard for Lisbon to overcome a long history of low expenditure on the arts, but the event did succeed in raising expectations about cultural provision in the capital.

THE SUPPLY OF CULTURAL ATTRACTIONS

The *Plano Nacional de Turismo* (Secretaria de Estado do Turismo, 1985) recognized that integrated tourism planning required an assessment of tourism resources, and the role played by these resources at national and regional level. In order to address this need, the Plan incorporated the creation of a register of tourist resources. This inventory would facilitate tourist and regional planning, provide an assessment of tourist potential for each region, and could be used to develop promotional activities and guide tourism investment.

Tourist resources defined in the Plan include 'all natural elements, human activities or products able to attract tourists and occupy their free time'. They were classified according to their use by tourists and the nature of the resource. Tourist resources were considered to be used either for transient tourism or for permanent tourism, and as being either cultural, natural or recreation resources. Cultural resources were defined as consisting of 'all the elements created by man (sic) reflecting his history and being able to attract and motivate travel'.

The cultural heritage is deemed to provide a strong motivation for the flow of tourism, and determines to a large extent the tourist potential of the places that own such treasures. The National Tourism Plan stated that 'some specific Portuguese cultural events are fundamental tourist resources, not only as factors of attraction to native inhabitants but also as a tourist offer to foreigners' (Secretaria de Estado do Turismo, 1985:16).

It was also recognized, however, that cultural resources might also suffer from problems created by their own attractiveness. The Plan signalled 'the need to prevent some wearing down' of cultural resources and the serious problems arising from a lack of planning, such as destruction of open spaces, speculative building and the unplanned construction of tourist buildings. The valorization of cultural tourism resources was also proposed through the defence, protection and enhancement of rural and cultural tourism. Actions were taken in this area after the approval of a framework law concerning the defence and protection of cultural heritage and territorial planning. The Plan

Table 14.4.   General inventory of Portuguese tourist resources.

Primary resources			Secondary resources	
Heritage	Activities	Sectors	Activities	Sectors
Natural	Cultural	Cultural tourism	Gastronomy	Restaurants
Artificial	Sports	Sports tourism	Climate	Thermal baths and forests
	Entertaining	Entertainment tourism	Shopping	Shopping centres
	Business	Business tourism	Pilgrimages	Advertised sites
		Tourist equipment		
		Means of transport		
		Social substructures		

Source: Ministério do Comércio e Turismo (1991: 69).

Table 14.5.   Typology of Portuguese cultural tourism resources.

Cultural heritage	Monuments Arts Others
Cultural activities	Religion Folklore Arts Science Traditional popular activities
Cultural resources	Religion Folklore Shows Science

Adapted from: Ministério do Comércio e Turismo (1991).

heralded a new, more serious approach to the development of cultural heritage resources for tourism.

A methodical survey of tourist resources was started in 1990 by the Direcção-Geral de Turismo. This pilot survey was later extended to the whole country by means of a comprehensive survey of resources, which is now almost complete. The inventory is based on a hierarchical classification of tourism resources (Table 14.4), which regards culture as a primary resource, which can further be divided into cultural heritage, cultural activities, and cultural resources (Table 14.5). It is interesting to note that gastronomy and wine are considered to be secondary resources, whereas religion is a primary cultural tourism resource, often considered to be a sector in its own right. In another document, the General Direction of Tourism (Direcção-Geral de

Turismo, undated a:2) refers to the sightseeing resource inventory as a 'decisive element for tourism planning, country planning and tourist definition of each region. It should also be considered as far as investments are concerned'.

Longitudinal studies of the supply of cultural attractions in Portugal are scarce. Official statistics indicate a growth in the number of museums from 255 in 1989 to 330 in 1993, in line with trends in other western European countries.

THE IMPACT OF CULTURAL TOURISM

The economic importance of tourism

Tourism is one of the branches of Portuguese economy which has enjoyed sustained growth over the last decade. Income from foreign tourism has increased from Esc 57,500 million (ECU 294 million) in 1980 to Esc 673,133 million (ECU 3.4 billion) in 1993. Tourism provided a healthy balance of payments surplus of Esc 376,902 million (ECU 1.92 billion) in 1993 (Direcção-Geral de Turismo, 1994b). Activities connected to tourism added 8% to the Gross National Income in 1993, a record value. Tourism employs 250,000 people, or 5% of the Portuguese working population.

Although the average length of stay for foreign tourists has decreased from 10.4 days in 1970 to 7 days in 1993, there is an increase in the average spend per foreign tourist in hotels, which was Esc 11,409 (ECU 58.5) a day in 1993, which means Esc 89,863 (ECU 460) per tourist and a global hotel income of Esc 59 billion (ECU 302 million). Domestic tourists spent about Esc 1468 (ECU 7.5) a day in 1993, which may be considered a low figure. This can be explained by the large proportion (39%) of people who stayed with relatives or friends (Direcção-Geral de Turismo, 1994b).

The role of direct spending on cultural services by tourists can be gauged to some extent from a study of value added in various tourism service sectors. The study reveals that the most important sectors are 'Tourist restaurants' followed by 'Air Transport Tourism'. Museums and cultural services in 1989 had a gross added value of 3.7%, a significant contribution to the economic impact of tourism in Portugal (Table 14.6).

CULTURAL TOURISM POLICY

In the last decades two important documents were drafted on the official policy of Tourism in Portugal: the *Plano Nacional de Turismo* (National Tourism Plan) and the *Livro Branco do Turismo* (White Book for Tourism) (Secretaria de Estado do Turismo, 1985; Ministério do Comércio e Turismo, 1991). The former deals

Table 14.6.   Internal structure of gross added value in Portuguese tourism, 1989.

Activities	% total value added
Hotels, restaurants and cafés	9.9
Other hotels and tourist lodging	5.7
Supplementary lodging	11.7
Private lodging	0.8
Other types of lodging	9.2
Tourist restaurants	20.2
Railway transport	2.0
Road transport	8.0
Air transport	14.7
Rent-a-car	1.2
Travel agencies	11.5
Museums and other cultural services	3.7
Non-comercial tourist services and public administration	0.9
Other	0.5
Total	100

Source: Santos (1992).

with the establishment of tourism planning and development systems and the latter presents a global analysis of the work already achieved and evaluates future prospects.

The National Tourism Plan was drawn up in the mid-1980s against a background of political uncertainty, economic instability and regional disparities. At the same time there was a cut in the sums remitted to Portugal by emigrants. Against this background tourism appeared as a dynamic sector able to promote economic activity and social stability and to attract the foreign currency necessary to finance the external deficit.

Tourism planning was necessary 'to enable the methodical development of the sector', and which 'would consider the deep and intimate interdependence and interrelation with the wider sectors of economical activity' with the aim 'of structuring decisions concerning the self-regulation and self-organization of tourism' (Secretaria de Estado do Turismo, 1985:7–8). Tourism planning would be based on the following principles:

1. Preserving the quality of Portuguese tourism;
2. Flexibility and versatility in planning approaches;
3. The promotion of cooperation between the public and private sectors;
4. Developing strategies to develop and promote regional tourism potential.

The aims of the plan were social, economic and cultural, and preservation of the environment and valorization of cultural heritage were important aspects of the plan. In order to attain these objectives the following basic aims were established:

1. Reducing the deficit in the balance of payments;
2. Reducing regional inequality;
3. Contributing to the improvement of the Portuguese standard of living;
4. Protecting the environment and the valorization of cultural heritage;
5. Strengthening the national economy;
6. Increasing the level of employment;
7. Improving leisure opportunities for the Portuguese.

The first four objectives, including the protection and valorization of cultural heritage, were due to be accomplished from 1986 to 1989. The basic objectives relating to cultural tourism during this period were:

- protection of regional architecture and typical towns;
- preservation of monuments and surrounding areas;
- development of craftsmanship and the support of folklore.

In terms of the investment required to implement the plan, the public sector was responsible for collective equipment for culture and recreation, professional education, *pousadas* (first class hotels, often located in historic buildings), social lodgings, monument conservation, public transport and in-stitutional promotion. The private sector was responsible for investment in accommodation, restaurants, and transportation. Much of the responsibility for the development of cultural tourism in Portugal therefore remained vested in the public sector.

The execution of this plan was strongly affected by external factors, includ-ing political, economic, and institutional stability, the lack of an overall development plan for the country, uncertainty as to the political will to inter-vene in the development of tourism, and a lack of data to analyse socio-economic features of tourism and to support planning. In spite of these problems, the evaluation of the achievements of the National Plan contained in the *Livro Branco do Turismo* in 1991, indicates that the Plan produced a number of positive developments, including:

1. A basic structure for national tourism planning, including the creation of *Polos de Desenvolvimento Turístico* (Poles for Tourism Development), *Regiões de Aproveitamento Turístico* (Tourist Vocation Regions) and *Eixos de Desenvolvi-mento Turístico* (Axes for Tourism Development);
2. The establishment of several rural tourism development programmes;
3. A programme for restoring and renewing spa tourism;
4. Special support was provided for tourism equipment and programmes on tourist recreation;

5. In collaboration with the *Instituto Português do Património Cultural* (Portuguese Institute for Cultural Heritage) a programme was developed to transform monuments and historic buildings into *pousadas;*
6. The *Sistema de Incentivos Financeiros ao Turismo – SIFIT* (System of Financial Incentives to Invest in Tourism) was created;
7. In the area of professional education a programme was launched to build new schools and improve others.

One of the main concerns of the Portuguese Government in the last decade has been the need to reduce the serious regional inequalities. The key role for tourism in tackling regional inequality envisaged in the National Tourism Plan was later echoed in the *Programas de Desenvolvimento Regional – PDRs* (Programmes on Regional Development) of 1989–1993 and 1994–1999 (Ministério do Planeamento e da Administração do Território, 1989, 1994). This new approach to tourism planning seems to reflect the need to structure domestic policies to meet EU legislative requirements, as well as the need to benefit from EU regional aid schemes.

In recognition of the priority given to tourism and cultural heritage in EU policy (Ministério do Planeamento e da Administração do Território,1990), the *Programa de Infraestruturas e Equipamentos Culturais – PRODIATEC* (Programme of Infrastructures and Cultural Resources) was developed. The general objectives of the PRODIATEC were the following:

1. To stimulate private sector investment and the development of tourism enterprises in the less-advanced regions;
2. To contribute to an effective use of resources and to develop the tourism potential of natural, historic and cultural aspects of the regions;
3. To contribute to employment growth;
4. To support public sector development of the productive capacity of the less-developed regions.

These programmes incorporated a set of specific goals relating to the tourist sector, some of which were directly connected with the development of cultural tourism:

1. To increase the tourist offer of inland regions, paying special attention to non-traditional hotels, *pousadas* and thermal resorts;
2. To take advantage of the resources of regions with substantial tourist potential, especially architectural and landscape features;
3. To improve the visitor potential of museums, monuments and other cultural attractions;
4. To promote the development and restoration of cultural tourism resources;
5. To contribute to the valorization of the cultural and artistic heritage of recognized tourist attractions and the promotion of traditional regional crafts and skills;

6. To contribute to promoting Portuguese history within the broader context of European culture.

PRODIATEC was exclusively concerned with cultural infrastructure and resources wholly or partly supported by public funds, which were divided into two subprogrammes. The first covered 'cultural resources of tourist interest', and aimed:

1. To create or stimulate tourist attractions, through the building, adaptation or enlargement of monuments, museums and castles to attract new visitors and increase the length of stay;
2. To create or improve resources for tourist entertainment, such as the performing arts and shows, in order to diversify Portuguese tourist products;
3. To conserve and restore monuments to foster their inclusion in tourist circuits and the valorization of local cultural skills and resources, through the project, 'Traditional Craftsmanship and Art'.

The second subprogramme on tourist accommodation aimed to restore and increase lodging capacity, contributing to increased public sector investment in non-traditional hotel lodgings. The programme, which was implemented from 1990 to 1993 had a budget of ECU 73.9 million, 60% of which came from EU structural funds and the remainder from the Government (Table 14.7).

The Cultural Resources Sub-Programme was implemented by the Portuguese Institute for Cultural Heritage, which developed tourism facilities at ten monuments and museums, carrying out restoration works, landscaping, providing visitor facilities and providing spaces for conferences, concerts, exhibitions, etc. A further 21 restoration projects were carried out at other cultural attractions, including several castles.

Portugal has also made extensive use of funding from the European Union in recent years to strengthen the competitive position of the tourism industry, and to address regional inequality. There is a general recognition that the basis of the tourism industry will remain the sun and sea product, but that this sector will grow much more slowly than in the 1980s. The source of comparative advantage for Portuguese tourism will therefore shift away from its previous climatic base, towards cultural and other 'created' sources of

Table 14.7. Investment in the PRODIATEC programme, 1990–1993.

Year	1990	1991	1992	1993	Total
Total investment	6892	22,907	27,517	16,459	73,865
European Structural funds	4251	13,994	16,272	9483	44,000

Units, Thousand ECUS at constant 1989 prices.
Source: Ministério do Planeamento e da Administração do Território (1990).

comparative advantage. The Regional Development Plans drawn up for the period 1994–99 (Ministério do Planeamento e da Administração do Território, 1994) therefore identify four main strands of development strategy in tourism, which are designed to correct the structural asymmetries created by previous policies:

1. Increasing product quality;
2. Professional development;
3. Product diversification;
4. Market diversification.

The plan therefore contains a wide range of measures designed to develop cultural tourism. These include the restoration and development of 30 historic buildings as tourist attractions, the creation of 12 new *pousadas* in historic buildings and the refurbishment of a further 11 *pousadas*. Tourism training schemes, which aim to train 40,000 tourism professionals during the five-year-plan period will pay particular attention, for the first time, to training in cultural tourism. A set of training modules will cover the following specializations: cultural heritage; religious orders and their importance in Portugal; wine growing circuits; gastronomy and regional pastry; the arts: baroque, romantic, 'manuelino' (Portuguese Gothic), etc.

A measure on the Valorization of Cultural Heritage aims to restore eight buildings designated as national monuments, and joint actions of the Ministry of Culture and the *Instituto Português dos Museus – IPM* (Portuguese Institute of Museums), the *Fundação das Descobrtas e Fundação Serralves* (Discoveries and Serralves Foundations) on museums include restoring and refurbishment of eight museums and one theatre. These measures have a global budget of ECU 1.159 billion, derived from the public and private sectors, and support from the EU (Table 14.8).

MARKETING CULTURAL TOURISM

The National Tourism Plan 1986–89 established the principle that tourism marketing should aim to reduce the dependence of Portugal on external market fluctuations, and to increase per capita tourist spending without increasing tourist numbers. The *Livro Branco do Turismo* (Ministério do Comércio e Turismo, 1991), reinforced this perspective, recognizing that survival in the increasingly competitive European Tourism market required the development of products which could meet rapidly changing market needs.

Tourist promotion was carried out by the Institute for Promotion of Tourism between 1986 and 1991. The annual activity plan for 1991, aimed to reinforce the interaction between the public and private sectors so as to:

1. attract more and wealthier tourists;

Table 14.8.   Financial planning of the sub-programme 'Tourism and Cultural Heritage' within the PRODIATEC programme.

Measures	Global cost	EU subsidies	National government	Private sector
Modernization, and diversification of tourist accommodation and entertainment	910,332	202,900	67,632	639,800
Tourist accommodation in historic buildings	65,500	49,100	16,400	
Tourism training	82,700	47,000	15,000	
Valorization of cultural heritage	83,752	47,818	15,938	
Museums and cultural resources	40,248	30,186	10,062	
Youth tourism	17,340	13,000	4,340	
Total	1,159,872	520,072	130,072	639,800

Units: Thousand ECUS.
Source: Ministério do Planeamento e da Administração do Território (1994).

2. reinforce Portugal as a European country;
3. compete effectively with other European tourist destinations;
4. promote Portugal as a holiday destination for Portuguese people.

However, by 1992 it was recognized that 'advertising campaigns were carried out in a scattered and discontinuous way'. This was one of the arguments that led to the fusion of the Institute for Promotion of Tourism with *Investimentos, Comércio e Turismo de Portugal – ICEP* (Commercial and Tourist Investment in Portugal), an organization funded by the Commerce and Tourism Ministry. This new organization has a brief to attract foreign investment, to promote national enterprises abroad and to coordinate tourism promotion in several markets, including the domestic tourism market (Investimentos, Comércio e Turismo de Portugal, 1992).

The main target markets of ICEP are Spain, the UK, Germany, France, Belgium, Italy, Sweden, and Denmark and some regions of the USA and Japan. The main target segments are families, particularly for the basic 'sea and sun' product, business groups, and sports tourism (especially the lucrative golf market).

Tourism promotion has paid special attention to cultural tourism since 1993, building on the promotion of cultural and historic events of both national and international interest. The European Capital of Culture event in Lisbon (see Richards, Chapter 2 this volume) and the sixth centenary of King Henry the Navigator's birth in 1994, added to the constant references to Portuguese History and Culture in publications aimed at tourists.

A special 'Art and Culture' brochure is now being produced for tourists, outlining the major cultural attractions of Portugal, and giving an historical background to the development of the country. The elements of culture brought to the attention of tourists in the brochure include: churches, castles, museums, art treasures, traditional cuisine, fashion and design, Manueline and Baroque architecture, *Azulejos* (blue and white ceramics), and *Fado* (traditional music). The emphasis on traditional and popular elements of culture reflects the broad approach to national culture mentioned above.

TRENDS AND PROSPECTS

Tourism has played a major role in strengthening the Portuguese economy and national identity for several decades. Between the 1960s and the 1980s, however, the development of package tourism based on a sun–sea product brought problems of over-concentration, as well as increasing the competitive pressures from comparative beach destinations in Europe and beyond. As the Government has recognized, 'Tourism in Portugal suffers from flaws and shortcomings, which must be corrected and the weak diversification of available tourist products, makes it extremely dependent on limited market segments which worsens the general vulnerability' (Ministério do Planeamento e da Administração do Território, 1990).

This is one of the major reasons that cultural tourism has taken on a new significance in Portugal during the last ten years. The growth in tourism to inland areas has outstripped the rise in coastal tourism, and placed more emphasis on the cultural aspects of the tourism resource base. Tourism policy now prioritizes diversification, thus giving to cultural tourism a higher profile. Cultural tourism is now viewed as a fruitful growth market in Portugal. 'If the cultural factors of tourism – national and international – are reinforced we may conclude there is a growing demand' (Ministério do Planeamento e da Administração do Território, 1990). Cultural tourism is a central theme of the Regional Development Plans which are due to run until 1999, ensuring that cultural tourism development will remain a key policy area for several years.

REFERENCES

Direcção-Geral de Turismo (1994a) *Inquérito de fronteira a residentes no estrangeiro: síntese de resultados para o período de 1979/92*. DGT, Lisboa.
Direcção-Geral de Turismo (1994b) *O turismo em 1993*. DGT, Lisboa.
Direcção-Geral de Turismo (undated a) *Inventário de Recursos Turísticos*. DGT, Lisboa.
Direcção-Geral de Turismo (undated b) *Ferias dos Portugueses em 1989*. DGT, Lisboa.
Investimentos, Comércio e Turismo de Portugal (1992) *Estatutos do ICEP*. ICEP, Lisboa.
Ministério do Comércio e Turismo (1991) *Livro Branco do Turismo*. MCT, Lisboa.

Ministério do Planeamento e da Administração do Território (1989) *Plano de Desenvolvimento Regional: 1989–1993*. MPAT, Lisboa.

Ministério do Planeamento e da Administração do Território (1990) *PRODIATEC: Programa de Infraestruturas Turísticas e de Equipamentos Culturais*. MPAT, Lisboa.

Ministério do Planeamento e da Administração do Território (1994) *Plano de Desenvolvimento Regional: 1994–1999*. MPAT, Lisboa.

Myerscough, J. (1995) *European Cities of Culture*. Glasgow City Council, Glasgow.

Palma, J.B. (1991) O papel do turismo cultural no quadro do desenvolvimento turístico. *Comunicações do II Encontro Ambiente, Turismo e Cultura*. Angra do Heroísmo.

Pina, P. (1988) *Portugal: O Turismo no Séclo XX*. Lucidus, Lisboa.

Pina, P. (1991) O Turismo em Portugal-O Advento, 1820–1910. *Turismo 24–26*, Ano III, Série 1, 3–43.

Poon, A. (1993) *Tourism, Technology and Competitive Strategies*. CAB International, Wallingford.

Santos, D. (1992) *O turismo na Economia Nacional-a Matriz das Actividades Turísticas de 1989*. CIDEC, Lisboa.

Secretaria de Estado do Turismo (1985) *Plano Nacional de Turismo 1986–1989*. SET, Lisboa.

Cultural Tourism in Spain   15

C. Maiztegui-Oñate and M.T. Areitio Bertolín

Estudios de Ocio, Universidad de Deusto, Apartado 1, 48080 Bilbao, Spain

INTRODUCTION

The first tourist wave which flooded the beaches of Spain in the 1970s and 1980s was stimulated by the desire for sun, sea, and sand and the relatively low price of the Spanish tourist product. The negative impacts of the development of mass tourism during this period brought the realization that a different kind of tourism was required, which in particular would move away from the readily substitutable beach tourism product. In the 1990s, therefore, Spain is hoping for a new wave of tourists who will be motivated by the unique culture and heritage of the country.

The tourist value of the cultural heritage is an asset that can complement the existing tourist supply. At the same time, tourism can support the national heritage economically. This chapter will present a general overview of the development of the supply, management, and the major policies undertaken in the realm of cultural tourism in Spain. In addition, it is interesting to reflect on how the need to broaden one's cultural background could become a spur that causes people to travel, making it a habitual social practice. It is particularly interesting to study the cultural motivations of the Spaniards. Spain has recently undergone a rapid change from a predominantly rural to a more urban society, and has industrialized rapidly in recent decades. As a consequence, interest in cultural manifestations has increased considerably in our country, and cultural tourism has become a relevant field of study and research, reflecting the varied interests of our complex society and as a phenomenon involving many key issues relating to Spanish culture and history (Fernandez Fuster, 1991).

MANAGEMENT OF CULTURAL TOURISM RESOURCES

This section presents a general overview of the major institutions that manage resources related to cultural tourism. Spain, a tourist country *par excellence*, also has a significant and rich historic and cultural heritage. Spain has six cities which have in their entirety been rated as World Heritage sites by UNESCO, as well as an array of monuments which have been awarded the same category. The Spanish Ministry of Culture alone manages a total of 130 museums and resources of historic–artistic interest, which attract approximately 11 million visitors annually.

Analysing the institutions involved in cultural tourism development in Spain is difficult given the diversity of agents concerned with these matters. Cultural tourism management involves both the tourist industry and the cultural institutions whose goal is the conservation and protection of the national cultural heritage, as well as its promotion and revitalization.

Tourism policy is the responsibility of government bodies at three distinct levels: central government, the autonomous communities or regions (e.g. the Basque region or Catalonia) and the municipalities. Since the 1960s, when the tourist sector gained considerable importance in the economic and social development of the country, the national government has regulated important tourist regions, under legislation such as the 1968 law on centres and areas of national tourist interest. Presently, the General Secretariat of Tourism, part of the Ministry of Industry, Commerce and Tourism, is in charge of tourist affairs.

The General Secretariat of Tourism is divided in three main departments.

1. The Institute of Tourism of Spain (*Instituto de Turismo de España – TUR-ESPAÑA*) whose main responsibilities are the development of tourism policy, developing relations with other public institutions and the management of specialized tourism education (Montaner Montejano, 1991).
2. The National Society of Tourist Hotels of Spain (*Sociedad Estatal Paradores de Turismo de España*) responsible for the management and operation of the network of tourist hotels and resources of the country. The *paradores* are hotels located, for the most part, in buildings of historic and artistic interest. This network was developed in the 1970s in order to create emblematic locations to foster the development of a given area or region. Currently, the Society of Paradores is undergoing a profound process of change that could lead to the privatization of the so-called 'beach paradores', that is, those resources located in tourist areas where the private sector has a significant presence.
3. The State Office of Tourism Policy (*Direccion General de Política Turística*) that conducts sociological and market studies, gathers and analyses tourist

information and organizes and keeps the national registers of tourist business, professions and activities.

Since 1978, responsibilities regarding tourist affairs (including the regulation and promotion of tourist resources) have been transferred to the 17 Autonomous Communities of the State (Marlasca, 1994). In addition, the municipalities also hold some degree of tourist responsibilities in the area of tourist promotion and information, through the Tourism Town Councils, Municipal Tourist Boards and Municipal Offices of Tourism. In managing cultural resources, reference is usually made to two important management issues: preservation and promotion. Spain's heritage is considered of importance not only by politicians but also by the civil society. National legislation on heritage reflects the interests and concerns of the civil society regarding the preservation of culture, as shown in the following statement by the Ministry of Culture (Ministerio de Cultura, 1993: 174):

> In Spain, the cultural heritage has the highest possible level of legal protection, given that it is protected by the Constitution. This means that the various public institutions, within their territorial and legal domains, have a duty to positive action towards the heritage, beyond its mere defence.

The autonomous regions therefore have exclusive responsibilities in their territories with regard to cultural heritage. In addition, Spanish law respects the principle of autonomy with regard to local institutions when it comes to issues directly relevant to them. In short, the responsibility for cultural tourism in the public sector is divided among diverse public institutions, at different levels: local, regional, and national. Besides, a significant part of the heritage is controlled by private institutions such as the Catholic Church. For instance, in terms of state museums three agents are involved in their coordination: the General Sub-directorate of Tourist Coordination, the Service of Coordination of Museums and, the General Directorate of State Museums. Despite efforts to coordinate and develop a common tourist policy involving both tourism and cultural agents, as the new strategic plan for Tourism of 1994 seeks to do, the difficulties in terms of coordination are quite evident.

STRATEGIES AND POLICIES IN CULTURAL TOURISM

One of the major difficulties encountered in the development of the cultural tourist sector in Spain has been the lack of a clear formulation of specific programmes and objectives to adequately direct its activities. The development of tourism in general has been uncoordinated and based on assumptions of unlimited market growth. This has caused structural flaws and in several instances a poor fit of the existing supply to the changing demands of national and international tourist markets. What was required was a set of generic plans that would establish certain basic principles in order to develop Spanish tourism as a whole, and stimulate cooperation in policy development between different administrative levels.

In trying to respond to this need the FUTURES Plan (Framework Plan for the Competitiveness of Spanish Tourism) was developed (Dirección General de Política Turística, 1992a). This four-year plan (1992–1995) aims to improve the competitiveness of the tourism sector by stimulating development in line with market needs, and to maximize the social benefits of tourism, while at the same time minimizing negative environmental impacts. The FUTURES Plan has not only introduced a sense of modern management to the tourist sector, but it has also presented developmental strategies for new areas of intervention, based on: a complementary offer to the typical tourism/beach product, that would promote other resources, from sports activities to cultural supply; and the development of destinations with a high level of competitiveness such as urban tourist products, tourist activities related to nature, health tourism, educational and social tourism, as well as tourism related to traditional cultural and architectural heritage.

In 1994, the Ministry of Commerce and Tourism initiated a new policy framework for tourism with the creation of the Strategic Plan for Tourism, which is currently being analysed by the autonomous regions. The main goal is administrative coordination that would entail a common policy involving all levels of government (central government, autonomous regions and municipalities). The Strategic Plan envisages joint promotional activities coordinated by TURESPAÑA, with emphasis on the development of alternative tourism areas, adventure and cultural tourism, and the coordination of infrastructure provision at different administrative levels.

In the context of this new strategy, an enormous advance has been made in the recent signing (1994) of a General Agreement for the Promotion of Cultural Tourism. This new initiative, developed jointly by the Ministry of Commerce and Tourism, and the Ministry of Culture, attempts to improve the exploitation of cultural resources for tourism. In order to do so four main areas of intervention have been established:

1. The identification of cultural tourism routes;
2. The organization of cultural events with major tourist impacts;
3. Adapting cultural attractions of tourist interest such as museums, monuments and scenic arts;
4. The promotion abroad of cultural tourism attractions.

The contribution of this ambitious and novel agreement is important because it seeks to integrate, from a management perspective, all the agents involved in cultural tourism. The project has been initiated with three pilot programmes.

1. Stimulus of cultural tourism routes. The World Heritage Cities Pilot Project aims to establish Cultural Routes in the six cities rated as World Heritage sites

(Avila, Caceres, Salamanca, Santiago de Compostela, Segovia, and Toledo). Since 1993 these cities have conducted a number of meetings to jointly address the problems caused by the costs involved in heritage maintenance.

2. Conjoint promotion of museums and monuments. The goal of the first phase of this project is the international promotion of the three main museums of Madrid: Museo del Prado (The Prado Museum), Museo Reina Sofia de Arte Moderno (Queen Sofia Museum of Modern Art) and Museo Thyssen (Thyssen Museum). In addition, the plan contemplates the computerization of the museums, as well as an analysis of demand and the development of plans for future promotion and commercialization.

3. Organization of emblematic events of special cultural and tourist significance. In terms of annual cultural events, the first is already underway in the 1995 celebration of the 175th Anniversary of the Prado Museum. This will include important exhibitions such as one devoted to the work of El Bosco.

In the context of the first pilot programme, in July 1994 the Minister of Commerce and Tourism signed a collaboration agreement with the mayors of the six World Heritage Cities in order to develop and promote cultural tourism. This programme, that will last three years, includes the creation of an integrated plan for the promotion, sign-posting, commercialization and development of tourist infrastructures as well as the adaptation of the cultural and historical resources of these cities to the needs, expectations and typologies of travellers. Research will also be undertaken in order properly to estimate, plan, conduct, and assess the effects of this growing area of cultural tourism.

CULTURAL TOURISM DEMAND IN SPAIN

The available information regarding cultural tourism in Spain indicates a general growth in demand, as has been observed in other countries. This trend was particularly strong in the 1980s, especially during the latter half of the decade. The Ministry of Tourism estimates that Spain receives about 8.3% of European cultural tourists, holding the fourth position after France, Italy, and Germany.

Cultural motives have a secondary role in the choice of holiday destination for Spanish tourists, though there are significant differences between domestic and foreign holidays (Table 15.1). Coastal destinations are most important for domestic holidays (53.7%) whereas cities and capitals are more popular when travelling abroad (25.2%). The Spanish tourist tends not to seek coastal destinations when going abroad. On the other hand, he/she seeks knowledge of different countries and cultures, as indicated by the importance of touring holidays abroad.

Even though sun and beach tourism is still important domestically, new trends seem to be emerging with regard to travel destinations. There are now

Table 15.1.   Destination of Spanish tourists, 1991.

	Destinations	
	Spain	Abroad
Coast/beach	53.7%	27.6%
Travelling through places	3.5%	29.6%
Important cities or capitals	5.1%	25.2%

Source: Dirección General de Política Turística (1992a).

some 3 million cultural trips a year, and the demand for cultural tourism is still rising. In the past, however, there has been little information on the consumption patterns of cultural tourists in Spain.

In this section data from the ATLAS cultural tourism survey in Spain in 1992 are used to give a picture of Spanish cultural tourism consumption. For this study the sites chosen were the Mosque in Cordoba, the Prado Museum in Madrid, the Art Museum in Bilbao and the UNESCO World Heritage City of Avila.

These sites gave an interesting picture of different types of cultural attractions in Spain. The Mosque in Cordoba was selected because of its singular architectural magnificence and its historical, geographical, and cultural connotations. The Prado in Madrid is possibly one of the first art galleries in the world and probably one of the greatest international cultural attractions in Spain. The Art Museum in Bilbao provided an example of a less traditional tourist destination. Finally, the walled city of Avila has an extraordinary collection of monuments, Romanic art, and palaces. The city of Avila also has a religious aspect (the extraordinary figure of Teresa de Jesus who, according to some studies, is one of the three best-known Spaniards outside Spain). One should not forget that much cultural tourism has its roots in religious pilgrimages, as exemplified by the revival of interest in the Pilgrim's Road to Santiago de Compostela.

Approximately 83% of those interviewed were visitors travelling from outside the study location, who could broadly be classified as 'cultural tourists' (Areitio *et al.*, 1993). The visitors were predominantly male (59.5%), and between the ages of 20 and 29. Visitors sampled in Cordoba and Avila tended to be older on average than visitors in Madrid, reflecting the tendency noted in other capital cities for cultural visitors to be relatively young (see Richards, Chapter 13 this volume, for example).

With regard to visitor origin, it was interesting to observe that a significant percentage were foreigners (60.5% in Cordoba, 63.5% in Avila, and 81.5% in Madrid). In Madrid, only 49% of visitors came from the EU, whereas 20% were from South America and 21% from North America. In Avila and Cordoba, however, the overwhelming majority of visitors came from other EU countries.

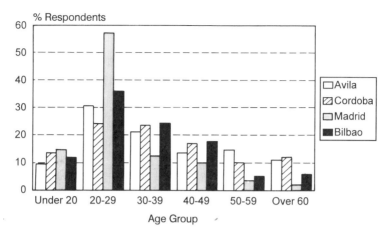

Fig. 15.1. Age profile of visitors to Spanish cultural attractions (source: ATLAS visitor surveys).

The difference between cultural consumption in Madrid and the other three cities is marked even for Spanish visitors. Spanish visitors in Madrid tended to visit performing arts and festivals in their home location, whereas for Spanish visitors in Cordoba and Avila, traditional heritage attractions and monuments were more popular. The 'cultural capital' role of Madrid is therefore reflected in both the profile of Spanish and foreign cultural visitors, and the types of cultural consumption they engage in. The Prado Museum seems to attract young, highly educated individuals, whereas Cordoba and Avila tend to attract older visitors on organized trips (Fig. 15.1).

In spite of the geographic differences in the composition of cultural visitors, there is a high degree of continuity between cultural consumption on holiday and in the region of residence. These results are in accordance with other studies such as the research conducted in 1992 by the General Secretariat of Tourism on Spaniards' holidays. About 32% of Spaniards said they visit museums, cathedrals, or monuments only in the summer, and 15% said there were no differences between the summer and the rest of the year in terms of cultural visits.

The overall conclusions derived from the survey data allow for some optimism regarding the increased interest in cultural tourism. Cultural tourism is a phenomenon not necessarily associated with a professional profile. In fact, there was little or no relationship between culture and work situation in this particular sample. The increased interest in cultural tourism is revealed in museum visits and in a renewed interest in historical monuments and heritage as if we were witnessing a rediscovery of the cultural richness of our country, leaving other activities, not related to the cultural, religious, and social heritage, for their enjoyment in the place of residence. Therefore, in terms of motivation most individuals in this group seek more of a personal enjoyment than a professional need to perform this particular type of activity.

Currently, data on Spanish cultural attractions are only available in terms of total number of visitors. Figures from 1990 to 1991 given by the Ministry of Culture show that there were 21,589,273 visitors to a total of 130 sites, exhibitions, or cities considered of relevance to cultural tourism. The figures show that there are 73 museums or cultural exhibitions and 57 sites relating to the historic–artistic heritage.

Statistics from 1993 obtained from the Ministry of Culture and the museums surveyed revealed that among the ten most visited cultural sites, the most important attractions are located in Madrid (Museo del Prado, Museo Reina Sofia and Museo Thyssen). In fact, these galleries are internationally known not only for their permanent collections but for the complementary exhibitions that represent all the artistic styles from the Middle Ages to the most ultramodern painting. The interest provoked by this art network is demonstrated by the large number of visitors. The Prado Museum alone had more visitors in 1993 than all the sites managed by the General Directorate of State Museums (Table 15.2). Figure 15.2 indicates the dominant position of Madrid in the distribution of cultural visits in Spain, and also demonstrates that the distribution of cultural visits is heavily weighted towards inland areas, providing a useful counterweight to coastal tourism.

Responding to EU legislation, in April 1994, the Ministry of Culture had to change its cultural policy with regard to entrance fees to museums, which were previously free for Spaniards but not for foreigners, including residents of the European Union. From 1994, all visitors to state museums must pay a fee of 400 pesetas. It will be interesting to see the effect of this new policy, particularly on museum visits by the Spanish. However, it should also be mentioned that the Thyssen Museum, run by a private foundation has had a compulsory fee since its opening, and has been able to place itself among the three most visited museums in Spain.

A month by month analysis of visits to cultural sites and events shows a clear increase during the months of April and May (spring and Easter period), July, August and September (summer holiday) and October and November (autumn season), showing a tendency toward higher levels of cultural visits

Table 15.2. Visitors to museums in Spain in 1993.

Museum	Number of visitors
Museo del Prado	1,567,193
Museo Reina Sofia	1,194,372
Museo Thyssen	623,326
All State Museums	1,281,528

Source: Ministry of Culture and Museums.

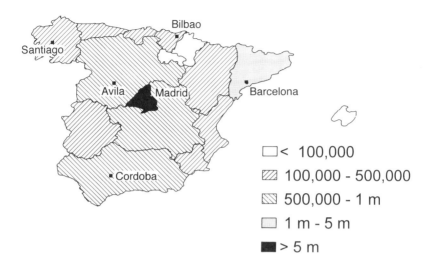

□< 100,000

▨ 100,000 - 500,000

▧ 500,000 - 1 m

▤ 1 m - 5 m

■ > 5 m

Fig. 15.2.   Regional distribution of cultural visits in Spain, 1990/91.

during holiday periods. This provides further indirect evidence of the growing importance of cultural tourism in Spain as an alternative to traditional tourist pursuits.

THE SUPPLY OF CULTURAL TOURISM

This section will present a broad description of the supply available in cultural tourism. As mentioned above, Spain is a country with a rich national heritage, including works of art representing all styles and historical periods. It has numerous important monuments, museums, cultural routes and so forth. Thus, the supply is quite varied. It is the leading country in the world in terms of total number of Declarations of World Heritage by UNESCO (Ministerio de Cultura, 1993). In addition, there is a growing number of programmed cultural events supplementing the supply of cultural attractions.

Growing competitiveness among sun, sea and sand destinations around the Mediterranean and the resulting fall in profits from tourism has stimulated a proliferation of so-called 'incentive techniques' (Marchena Gomez, 1994) that add value to the natural or historical elements of the tourist product. Cultural events have become crucial in this regard, particularly the numerous cultural festivals held throughout the country during the summer period. First, there are the classical theatre festivals such as those in Merida (Badajoz) or in Almagro, in Ciudad Real, which take advantage of heritage resources such as the famous 'Corral of Almagro' or the Ruins of the Roman Theatre in Mérida.

These events are characterized by a high quality cultural experience developed over many years of staging these events. Secondly, there are other festivals celebrated in different cities of the country which respond to the need to broaden the cultural supply for tourists and visitors. Some have gained significant renown such as the International Festivals of Santander, the 'Fortnight of Music' in San Sebastian, or 'The Grec' in Barcelona.

In 1992, three major events of international significance took place in Spain: The International Exhibition in Seville (EXPO 92), the Olympic Games in Barcelona, and Madrid Cultural Capital of Europe which captured the imagination of the nation. A measure of the scale of interest in these events is given by the calculation that 20% of the population living outside Seville travelled to the city to visit the EXPO (De Miguel, 1994). As a consequence, tourist policies incorporating culture have been given a significant boost.

In 1993, two complementary initiatives focused on culture and landscape which jointly promoted two main geographical axes in Spain were developed by several institutions.

The first was the revitalization of the Route of Santiago, the east–west axis, part of the cultural routes of the Council of Europe. Taking advantage of the celebration of the Holy Compostela Year, the autonomous regions involved, especially Galicia, made important investments in order to improve the resources and infrastructures of the route as well as developing an important marketing campaign. Especially interesting were unique events related to the route such as the celebration of medieval markets in ten cities along the route. These markets re-created the life and atmosphere of the Medieval times in order to regain the value of the culture, the artistic and monumental wealth, the gastronomy and the crafts of those towns.

The second was the restoration of the Silver Route, to disseminate the cultural richness and the beauty of the scenery in the west of the peninsula. This route crosses the country from north to south following the old roman routes and passing by places and towns (Cadiz, Seville, Gijon among others) with significant cultural resources, including important castles and monasteries.

In terms of resources managed by the Ministry of Culture, it is notable that along with the major cities such as Madrid and Barcelona which are tourist destinations in their own right, cultural attractions in the interior of the peninsula now attract the interest of cultural tourists. Autonomous regions such as Castilla-León, Castilla-La Mancha, and Andalucía, receive a high percentage of cultural visits, indicating that new initiatives in the realm of cultural tourism are attracting public interest.

In this regard, the autonomous regions of the interior and even those on the Mediterranean coast that already have a consolidated tourist product, have tried to complement their supply with additional features of cultural interest. Cultural tourism is usually seen as complementary to rural tourism, which tries to foster an image of a region of ecological importance, with a sparse population and with excellent opportunities to enjoy nature. This is the case with numerous itineraries that several regions have developed. In the Valley of Bohi (Cataluña) for example, by organizing Romanesque routes and promoting mountain sports, the agricultural economic base has been supplemented by activities linked to cultural and alternative tourism.

In rural areas the supply of cultural attractions is normally a complement to a broad tourist product that mostly includes natural, gastronomy, and folk resources. However, as cultural attractions have multiplied, each region must try to present new and unique incentives. Examples of innovative developments include the First Historical-Nature Park in Numancia (Soria) with a plan for a 'Chrono-Park' that will narrate the history from Prehistory to the present, a project for a Thematic Park in the Canary Islands promoting the historic heritage of the islands, and the Muslim Routes of Granada, commemorating the expulsion of the Moors from Spain, which has been planned for 1995 in Andalucia.

The proliferation of cultural tourism projects causes problems with coordination and the provision of adequate tourist infrastructure to enable the regions with cultural resources to benefit from the expected positive impact caused by tourism. In this regard, it is important to mention that significant areas of Spain, especially in the interior, qualify for financial assistance from the European Union, notably under the LEADER Program. There has been a rapid growth in the number of local development agencies using the tourist sector to substitute for, or at least to complement, primary sector economic activities. In several cases, educational initiatives begun in advance of tourism development *per se* have facilitated a rediscovery of the values and traditions of a region by the local population. In the sierra of La Rioja, for example, the local inhabitants have been trained as guides for the Mines and the Dinosaurs' Footprints found in the region.

In addition to these public sector initiatives to develop cultural tourism supply, the private sector is playing an increasingly important role in promoting supply through the establishment of new travel companies dedicated to cultural tourism. The traditional tour operators manage most of the demand for visits to historical sites or attendance at internationally famous cultural events. They tend to concentrate on mass products such as visits or tours in cities, mainly in Europe. Although Lisbon was European City of Culture in 1994, and the second most visited destination for Spaniards travelling abroad, there are few tour operators that offer trips to Lisbon that include cultural activities.

Currently, there are only two companies specializing in trips for culturally motivated tourists, that is, tourists who select their destination on the basis of the cultural attractions offered. These companies offer high-quality tours with cultural destinations, taken in small groups or individual trips organized according to client's needs. These commercial companies operating from Madrid and Valencia, attract a quite segmented market dispersed throughout the country. Following the typology presented by the European Union (GEATTE,1993) in a recent study on cultural tourism in Europe, the majority of these commercial products could be classified as trips with a core of a cultural interest (concerts, exhibitions, museums, festivals) and of short duration (less than a week).

Finally, one should not forget that, as in other Mediterranean countries, the Spanish population tends not to use commercial intermediaries when going on holiday. Tourism is practised in a more autonomous and personal fashion, and cultural tourism in particular is usually experienced in second vacations or weekend trips. Consequently, one can observe a progressive change in terms of the seasonal distribution of cultural tourism towards a more year-round form of tourism demand.

ECONOMIC IMPACT OF CULTURAL TOURISM

It has been shown in other countries how the rehabilitation and conservation of heritage is an important factor of economic development. The cases of cities such as Glasgow or Pittsburgh, or the cultural routes in the French and Italian regions (see Bauer, Chapter 8 this volume) demonstrate how the inclusion of the heritage in the cultural, economic and social life of the territory allows for an integrated management formula in which heritage can generate economic benefits and impact on the social life of the region. In addition, international institutions such as the Council of Europe (1993), have suggested that cultural tourism may act as an incentive that can involve the local population in the usage of such heritage. The economic and tourist exploitation of such resources can become an alternative income source for the inhabitants of the region. In this regard, cultural resources have the advantage of not having a seasonal nature so that the income can be spread throughout the year thus avoiding the precariousness characteristic of most tourist employment.

Tourism, Spain's largest industry, is a key sector in the Spanish economy. Since the 1970s, tourism production has accounted for almost 9% of the internal gross product (Dirección General de Política Turística, 1992b). Revenues due to tourism amounted to ECU 23 billion in 1990. In spite of significant problems in the Spanish tourism industry in the late 1980s and early 1990s, linked to increasing competition, falling product quality and economic recession in major source markets, signs of recovery are already apparent. According to the General Secretary of Tourism, tourism revenue in the period January to April 1994 was 9.9% higher than over the same period in the previous year. This upturn is partially due to specific short-term factors, however, such as the devaluation of the Spanish peseta and political problems in the Arab countries that compete with Spain in terms of the supply of sun and beaches. Thus, in order to maintain tourism growth on a medium and long-term basis, improvements in product quality and infrastructure are required.

Even though the proportion of Spaniards (44%) leaving the country on vacation is lower than the European average, domestic tourism is still quite important, representing more than half the total tourist expenditure in Spain, and still rising. It is estimated that the tourist sector directly employs more than half a million workers, and a further 576,000 people indirectly. In total, tourist employment represents around 11% of the employed population, even though this is a sector with a high degree of seasonality (Dirección General de Política Turística, 1992b).

The idea that every economic analysis of tourism should be complemented with a study of cultural and environmental impacts is specially relevant in the case of cultural tourism. This may help to prevent the tourist masses from participating in the inevitable destruction of the site of interest. The difficult equilibrium between the protection of the historic–artistic heritage and its exploitation as a resource of tourist interest should be achieved in such a way that the benefits derived from the visits become a source of income to cover the high cost involved in the preservation of the sites while avoiding damage to the monument or site by the tourists themselves.

CONCLUSIONS

The General Secretariat of Tourism addresses in its 1994 Strategic Plan the diversification of tourism in order to develop complementary products besides those related to the sun and beach, which account for more than 30% of the European Market. The Strategic Plan specifically attempts to promote the potential for cultural and nature tourism, given that these are areas with great resources that have not been commercialized from a tourist standpoint. One should not forget that the development of cultural tourism can help in overcoming two of the major current problems in the tourist sector in Spain. First, the concentration of tourism around a single product (sun and beaches) which causes a geographical concentration around the Mediterranean coast, and second, the seasonality of tourism. About 43% of international visitors enter Spain during the months of July to September (Dirección General de Política Turística, 1992b). Domestic tourists also travel during the summer period (76.6%) even though a change is slowly taking place.

Cultural tourism is not a remedy for all evils but it can have an important role in the new tourist strategies of the country. As a complementary resource, the diversification of markets, which would include the regions of the interior, could help to alleviate the negative effects of mass tourism. Structural changes in tourism include a tendency toward shorter vacations, more sophisticated tastes and an interest for places and events of special relevance. Thus, the multiplication of tourist destinations is a factor that favours the development of the weekend tourist market, more short breaks and weekend outings related to periodical or seasonal events such as festivals and feasts.

As an example of recent attempts to promote cultural tourism one can mention the TURESPAÑA campaigns such as 'Everything under the Sun', one of the first campaigns to emphasize the diversity of the tourist attractions of the peninsula. At regional level a recent tourist campaign in Salamanca, 'Time to live', uses a famous verse of Fray Luis de León, to recall the combination of cultural traditions and nature using two images: a stroll in the country and a snack under the shadow of the Cathedral.

Citizens reflect the times in which they live. Socio-economic changes influence the tourist sector so that the concept of a new tourist is emerging, an alternative tourist or even the post-tourist (Urry, 1990) who holds values such as self-determination, the quest for authenticity and the preservation of the environment. This type of tourist is highly aware of his/her consumption choices and of the potential impacts derived from the tourism activity. In such a context, culture can act as a catalyst that could attract the 'new tourist' of the end of the twentieth century.

Despite the challenge of coordinating the numerous institutions involved in the management of cultural tourism, one cannot avoid being optimistic with regard to the future of the Spanish market. There are two important indicators to support such optimism. First, the changes in the nature of tourist demand both nationally and internationally, and second, the importance of heritage in Spain. With regard to the former, international trends indicate that the most promising tourist destinations are multi-faceted centres combining historic and cultural attractions with natural resources (beach or countryside) which can support a wide variety of different tourist activities. In terms of heritage, and despite the fact that Spain only receives 8% of the total European cultural tourism market, the country has a significant potential that can be offered based on the diversity and richness of the historic, monumental and artistic resources that different civilizations have left in the Iberian peninsula.

DEDICATION

This chapter is dedicated J.I. Risueño, who participated in this study but could not see it completed.

REFERENCES

Areitio, T., Maiztegui, C. and Risueño, J.I. (1993) Avance de una investigación transnacional sobre turismo cultural en Europa. *Revista Letras de Deusto* 23 (57), 147–159.
Council of Europe (1993) *The Cultural Challenges for Europe's Regions.* Culture and Regions Project 10, Council of Europe, Strasbourg,
De Miguel, A. (1994) *La Sociedad Española 1993–94.* Alianza Editorial, Madrid.

Dirección General de Política Turística (1992a) *FUTURES: Plan Marco de Competitividad del Turismo Español.* Ministerio de Turismo, Madrid.

Dirección General de Política Turística (1992b) Las Vacaciones de los Españoles. *Estudios Turísticos* 116, 87–112.

Fernandez Fuster, L. (1991) *Historia General del Tourismo de Masas.* Alianza Editorial, Madrid.

GEATTE (1993) *Le tourisme culturel en Europe.* DGXXIII, European Commission, Bruxelles.

Marchena Gomez, M.J. (1994) El turismo, una experiencia de 'descubrimientos'. *Estudios Turísticos* 113, 9–24.

Marlasca, O. (1994) *Legislación Turística.* Universidad de Deusto, Bilbao.

Ministerio de Cultura (1993) *La Cultura en España y su Integración en Europa.* Ministerio de Cultura, Madrid.

Montaner Montejano, J. (1991) *Estructura del mercado turístico.* Síntesis, Madrid.

Urry, J. (1990) *The Tourist Gaze: Leisure and Travel in Contemporary Societies.* Sage, London.

Cultural Tourism in the United Kingdom   16

M. FOLEY

Glasgow Caledonian University, Park Drive, Glasgow G3 6LP, UK

INTRODUCTION

This chapter surveys some of the current issues evident in cultural tourism in the United Kingdom (UK). In particular, it examines the implications for policy and practice of debates over the nature of the 'cultural', especially with regards to 'high' and 'popular' culture. These issues are framed within the context of the tension between cultural democracy and the democratization of culture as it affects tourism policies. A key structural consideration in understanding cultural tourism in the UK is the interrelationship between England, Scotland, Wales, and Northern Ireland and the mixed economy of provision by the public, private, and voluntary sectors. These complexities in policy and provision are amplified by the range of arts, heritage, cultural, and tourism agencies with responsibilities in cultural tourism.

Within the UK, the stateless nations of Scotland and Wales have vibrant cultural lives, represented by, *inter alia*, their own languages. Notwithstanding these important differences, England continues to be the dominant tourism destination in the UK in terms of demand from overseas and domestic tourists. The relationship between England in general, and London in particular, and the rest of the UK is a prime consideration in the development of tourism policy, especially in the dispersal of demand and the benefits of tourism spending. Some of the front-line agencies involved in cultural tourism have recently introduced policies which recognize and attempt to exploit cultural tourism. However, trends in 'cultural tourism' in the UK are difficult to monitor because the concept is under constant negotiation, both in terms of its meaning and its

©1996 CAB INTERNATIONAL.
Cultural Tourism in Europe (ed. G. Richards)

ownership among a number of public sector agencies. One of the implications of this is that available statistics do not always correspond to 'cultural tourism' as defined elsewhere in this volume (see Richards, Chapter 2 this volume).

DEVELOPMENT OF CULTURAL TOURISM

Although there are many recognizable elements of cultural tourism in the UK tourism product, it is difficult to locate specific policies or initiatives aimed at this phenomenon. In part this is due to the fragmentation of public policy-making, marketing and delivery systems in both the tourism industries and in cultural services at national and local government levels. Cutting across these divisions of administrative responsibilities are the priorities of national agencies within a 'United Kingdom' which contains England, Northern Ireland, Scotland, and Wales. In each of these countries, public and voluntary sector bodies have interests in differentiated aspects of cultural tourism. The commercial sector is in turn heavily dependent on the public and voluntary sectors for the resources, finance or promotion support which provide the basis of cultural tourism products.

As an example of the complexity inherent in securing coordinated action in cultural tourism, the situation for England, in respect of major agencies, can be described as follows. Responsibility for marketing the English tourism product to residents of the UK lies with the English Tourist Board (ETB), a quasi-autonomous non-governmental organization (QUANGO) whose board members are appointed by a central government minister. Similar arrangements are in place for the British Tourist Authority (BTA) which has responsibilities for marketing Britain to visitors from non-UK nations. Regional Tourist Boards, composed on lines similar to the English body, have local responsibilities for marketing to both 'home' and 'overseas' visitors. Development of built heritage is the responsibility of English Heritage, a self-managed government agency, which has ownership of, and responsibility for, significant monuments and buildings throughout England. Surveying and recording of the historic environment is the responsibility of The Royal Commission on the Historic Monuments of England which also has grant-giving powers. Policy-making and some resourcing of the arts is the job of the Arts Council and Regional Arts Councils. The Museums and Galleries Commission funds a series of Area Museums Councils. All of these bodies relate directly, or indirectly, to the Department of National Heritage, headed by a government minister. The National Trust, a private sector organization governed by its members, owns historic buildings, gardens, parklands and other cultural artefacts 'for the nation' in England, Wales and Northern Ireland. These institutions at national and regional level are complemented by tourism, cultural and arts-related services and properties which are delivered by local government to its citizens and visitors alike. In addition, pressure and interest groups are constantly trying to influence policies, plans and actions by government and quasi-government. The recent introduction of a National Lottery in the UK has spawned two bodies to which many cultural and heritage organizations can apply for funds, namely the National Lottery (public sector) and the Foundation for Sport and the Arts (an independent trust established by the football pools companies). In both cases, arts and (possibly) museum initiatives fall within the definition of 'good causes' which can be funded by these bodies.

A major current issue for the development of cultural tourism is therefore the harmonization of approaches and coordination of efforts across a range of agencies (e.g. Scottish Tourist Board, 1994). In practice, this has meant either the appointment of staff with specific remits for coordination of the arts and tourism, at the Scottish Tourist Board (STB) and Wales Tourist Board (WTB), or the publication of guidelines and good practice, especially in relation to arts organizations improving marketing to tourist groups (English Tourist Board, 1993) or both. At a sub-national level, it can mean the inception of specific initiatives, such as the Gateway Europe Tourism Development Action Programme in Humberside, or the promotion of local liaisons, such as that introduced in Inverness, Loch Ness and Nairn.

Coordination of cultural tourism policy between different bodies is also complicated by the question of what is, and is not, to be included as 'culture' for the purposes of tourism. Where public agencies are involved, the approach to culture may reflect relationships between bodies which represent different (and possibly, conflicting) preoccupations of government. By and large, recent marketing-based initiatives have tended to concentrate on the arts and tourism, with a strong focus on established, or 'high', culture rather than 'popular' culture. Thus, manifest elements of culture which inevitably affect tourists, e.g. food and beverages, are subject to promotion and development elsewhere (e.g. Scottish Tourist Board, 1994), but not under the 'banner' of cultural tourism. Similarly, pop and rock concerts or international sporting events are effectively excluded from cultural tourism.

A further set of current issues concerns barriers to consumption of cultural products which can arise for reasons other than the rational-economic. For example, the issue of extending Sunday opening at historic sites throughout Britain and at museums, galleries and theatres in London is highlighted by the British Tourist Authority which has identified the need for 'further development of arts-based tourism' and actively pursued this end with its involvement in the national Festival of Arts and Culture in 1995. Historic houses, which could extend the cultural tourism product by introducing entertainment events, also have to navigate difficult and discouraging waters as far as licensing is concerned.

Constraints on public expenditure have also had both widespread and specific implications for cultural tourism. At the general level, this is apparent from the reduction in grant availability for arts and cultural services across the public sector and concomitant exhortations to secure funding through greater income-generation via effective uses of marketing (of which exploitation of tourism markets is but one manifestation), development of ancillary services such as retailing, attracting sponsorship and fostering mutually beneficial links with the business community. More specifically, the Arts Council has been obliged to cut funding to London orchestras and some regional arts companies, thereby introducing concerns over the quality of output from these sources. Cuts in public expenditure which have less direct connections with the tourism industries have also affected the quality of the product offered. Much that is of interest to visitors in London revolves around military and state matters. The opening of parts of Buckingham Palace to paying visitors (ostensibly to generate revenue for repairs to other royal residences) has been a significant addition to London's attractions. On the other hand, the 'peace dividend' and the associated shrinkage in defence expenditure has led to substantial reductions in summer of one of the most famous 'free' cultural experiences which London can offer, namely the Changing of the Guard ceremony.

A key decision in the recent development of cultural tourism has been the focus upon launching existing products into new (tourist) markets. This is best illustrated in the way in which some arts festivals have developed from community celebrations to include elements which will attract visitors from a wider catchment. Although established international high culture events such as the Edinburgh International Festival, the Henry Wood Promenade Concerts or the Royal National Eisteddfod have reached tourist audiences effectively in the past, popular culture events such as Mayfest in Glasgow, the Dickens Festival in Rochester and the Notting Hill Carnival in London have now extended their audiences beyond their original local community base (the last two of these events breaking the 100,000 visitor 'barrier' in 1991). An alternative and related strategy is to rely on the combination of existing products to achieve greater added value from the resulting synergy. A good example of this has been the marketing of the Chichester Festival Theatre alongside local accommodation to generate a package guaranteeing a theatre seat and a bed for the night.

THE CULTURAL TOURISM MARKET

The UK attracted 18.5 million overseas tourists and generated almost 55 million domestic holiday trips in 1992 (British Tourist Authority, 1993). Cultural activities are particularly important motivators for foreign tourists. The Overseas Visitor Survey (British Tourist Authority/English Tourist Board, 1992) indicates that aspects of cultural tourism are of considerable significance when it comes to the decision to visit Britain on holiday. Of those interviewed, 81% said that heritage, countryside or general sightseeing was either 'very important' or 'important' in their decision and 51% gave these responses for arts or entertainment. Thus, the UK tourism product is strongly associated with

Table 16.1.   Selected activites of particular importance in deciding to visit Britain, 1990.

Residence	% overseas visitors		
	Visiting heritage sites (castles, monuments, churches, etc.)	Visiting heritage exhibits (museums, galleries, etc.)	Performing arts (theatre, music, etc.)
All	37	30	19
West Europe	34	28	15
North America	44	37	26
Other English-speaking	42	29	23
Other	35	29	21
Age			
16–24	39	32	21
25–34	37	31	22
35–54	38	28	17
55–64	32	32	13
65+	24	19	15

Source: BTA Overseas Visitor Survey (1990). Based on a sample of approximately 2500 visitors to Britain.

culture, which is clearly significant in terms of product image and visitor motivations. Indeed, 73% of those interviewed had visited a museum and 37% an art gallery while in Britain; only 23% had not visited either type of attraction.

Table 16.1 shows activities of particular importance in the decisions of visitors to come to Britain in 1990 by origin and by age. The possibility of visiting heritage sites is always adjudged to be of the greatest importance (37% of all visitors gave this as an important factor in their decision) among the cultural activities offered for response. This category is especially important to visitors from countries where English is spoken and among those visitors who are less than 54 years old. These patterns are replicated among the fewer tourists who gave visiting heritage exhibits (30% of all visitors) and attending performing arts events (19% of all visitors) as being of importance in their decisions.

The proportion of visits to historic properties in the UK accounted for by overseas visitors has remained fairly steady in recent years. The number of visits to historic buildings in England by overseas visitors fell from 19.8 million (33%) in 1985 to 19.7 million (31%) in 1992 (Table 16.2). Visitors from abroad represent over two-thirds of all who go to historic properties in London (which has, by far, the largest proportion of overseas visitors of any British region). Thereafter, only Scotland had a proportion in excess of 40% in 1992, although a number of English regions had an increase in the proportion of overseas visitors between 1985 and 1992. The concentration of overseas

Table 16.2. Overseas visitors as a proportion of all visitors to historic buildings, by region in 1985 and 1992.

Region[a]	% of all visitors[b]	
	1985	1992
Cumbria	19	12
Northumbria	21	19
North West	11	22
Yorkshire/Humberside	16	19
Heart of England	41	28
East Midlands	11	14
East Anglia	9	16
London	67	68
West Country	25	24
Southern	16	18
South East	33	26
All England	33	31
Northern Ireland	..	14
Scotland	..	44
Wales	..	24
United Kingdom	..	32

[a]Tourist Board standard regions; [b]Estimated.
Source: *Sightseeing in 1985* and S*ightseeing in the UK 1992*, BTA/ETB Research Services, October 1986 and October 1992, respectively.

visitors in London has a particularly important effect on the performing arts. Overseas visitors help to keep many theatres in the capital running, and they have been responsible for a steep growth in attendances at musicals (from 28% of West End theatre visits in 1987 to 51% in 1992), because these present far less of a language barrier for tourists. The overall proportion of overseas tourists in London theatre audiences fell, nevertheless, from 40% in 1987 to 32% in 1992 (Quine, 1993).

Culture is less important as a motive for domestic tourism in the UK. Table 16.3 presents selected results from the UK Tourism Surveys of 1989 and 1993, which cover domestic tourists. About 1% of all holiday trips in the UK by British residents have their main purpose as watching performing arts in 1993 (2% if cinema is included), 3% as visiting heritage sites and 1% as visiting artistic or heritage exhibits. These last two categories have shown decreases since 1989, both in absolute terms and as a proportion of overall trips taken. A much higher proportion of tourists, however, undertake cultural activities during their holidays. This tends to confirm the importance of culture as a secondary motive for domestic tourism. The general trend in visits to heritage sites or to exhibits is, however, downwards or at least static as a proportion of total holiday trips. Table 16.4 shows levels of participation in some cultural

Table 16.3. UK residents – selected activities on domestic holiday trips, 1989 and 1993.

	Main purpose of trip		Total activities undertaken	
	1989	1993	1989	1993
Category	(millions and %)			
Watching performing arts	1.2	1.0	2.8	3.8
(theatre, cinema, concert,	2%	2%	4%	7%
opera, ballet)				
Visiting heritage sites	3.5	1.6	9.5	7.7
(castles, churches,	5%	3%	15%	14%
monuments, etc.)				
Visiting artistic or heritage	1.7	0.8	4.7	4.0
exhibits (museums, art	3%	1%	7%	7%
galleries, heritage centres)				

Source: *UK Tourism Survey* 1989 and 1993.

Table 16.4. Participation[a] in selected leisure activities away from home, by social class 1993/94.

	AB	C1	C2	DE	ALL
			(%)		
Cinema	46	39	29	24	33
Historic building	41	29	19	12	23
Theatre	33	24	16	10	19
Museum or art gallery	34	23	14	10	19
Exhibition	24	17	10	8	14
Classical concert or opera	15	9	3	3	7

[a] Percentage, aged 16 or over, participating in each activity in the 3 months prior to interview.
Source: The Henley Centre.

activities by UK residents away from home in the period 1993/94 according to their social class. It is apparent from this table that those in social classes AB (broadly professional, senior and middle managerial) and C1 (broadly, junior managerial and clerical) show above average participation in all of the activities selected.

The publication *Sightseeing in the UK, 1993* indicates that there were 367 million visits to the 5793 tourist attractions in the UK in 1993, of which 22% were to historic properties (an increase of 2% over 1992), 16% were to museums, and 5% were to art galleries (British Tourist Authority, 1994a). Attendances at consistently reporting cultural attractions grew by 8% between 1988 and 1993, with museum visits growing much faster than visits to historic properties.

A quarter of the attractions surveyed in *Sightseeing in the UK, 1993* reported that they reached their capacity on at least one day in the year. On average, full capacity was reached on 15 days only. In total, 160 attractions (almost all within the cultural tourism categories) reported that their capacity was achieved on more than 20 days but, of these, only 18 received more than 200,000 visitors in the whole year, suggesting that constraints are due to lack of capacity rather than inordinate demand (British Tourist Authority, 1994a).

Among visits to specific cultural attractions, the British Museum in London is, by far, the most popular with 5.8 million visits in 1993, coming second only to the Pleasure Beach at the Lancashire seaside resort of Blackpool (6.8 million visits in 1993) which is firmly in the popular culture arena. Visits to the British Museum have increased by 123% since 1981. The National Gallery, also in London, had 3.9 million visitors in 1993, an increase of 44% over the same period.

The Tower of London was the most popular historic property in the UK during 1993 with 2.3 million visits, an increase of nearly 10% since 1981. Next most popular was Edinburgh Castle (the subject of the case study below) with 1 million visits, showing an increase of 25% since 1981. All other top five most popular historic properties were in England and all showed increases in visits since 1981. They were the Roman Baths in Bath (0.9 million visits in 1993), Warwick Castle (0.8 million in 1993) and the State Apartments in Windsor Castle (0.8 million in 1993). Buckingham Palace, open for part of 1993, received 377,000 visits.

In spite of the importance of cultural attraction visits in the UK, there is evidence emerging that the underlying market for existing attractions is no longer growing as rapidly as in the early and mid-1980s. A recent review of museum admissions (Davies, 1995) indicates that consistently reporting attractions achieved a growth of only 2.8% in visitor numbers between 1988 and 1993 (Fig. 16.1).

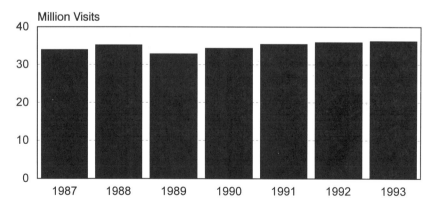

Fig. 16.1. Trends in visits to consistently reporting museums in the UK.

Events

Attendance at theatres and arts festivals is harder to monitor, but estimates by Bonink (1992) indicated that attendance at performing arts events (theatre, opera, and dance) rose from 9.8 million in 1986 to 10.1 million in 1989. There is evidence of a recent decline in theatre attendances, however, with a 13% fall in audiences in London between 1990 and 1992 (Quine, 1993).

Festivals are another difficult category to monitor because they are, by definition, packages of events, not all of which may be chargeable. In surveys of festivals (Rolfe, 1992) undertaken during 1991, four festivals reported attendance of more than 100,000 people at single, free events. These were the Edinburgh Festival Fringe, the Dickens Festival in Rochester, the Edinburgh International Festival and the Notting Hill Carnival. Over 150,000 people attended free rock concerts at 'Edinburgh's Hogmanay' on 1 January 1995 (*Edinburgh Evening News*, 2 January 1995). The survey of festivals in 1991 identified six arts festivals with ticket sales in excess of 100,000, namely the Edinburgh Festival Fringe (520,000 tickets), the BBC Henry Wood Promenade Concerts (250,000 tickets), the Edinburgh International Festival (167,000 tickets), the Brighton International Festival (130,000 tickets) and the Llangollen International Music Eisteddfod (117,000 tickets). There were 132,000 visits to the National Eisteddfod in 1993. Events which have elements of cultural tourism inherent in their attraction are often organized as military spectacles. In 1993, these included the Royal Tournament in London (235,000 visitors – a reduction of 17% from 1986), and the Edinburgh Military Tattoo held on the Esplanade of Edinburgh Castle (210,000 visitors – an increase of 9% since 1986).

The ATLAS research

Although the UK has a wealth of information on attendance at visitor attractions, specific profiles of cultural visitors are less common. The ATLAS research conducted in London and Scotland gives a picture of cultural tourists in 1992. Surveys were undertaken at two sites in London (St Paul's Cathedral and the Victoria and Albert Museum) and three sites in Scotland (the Museum of Childhood and the People's Story heritage centre in Edinburgh and Urquhart Castle, near Inverness). A third of the 1105 respondents indicated that the cultural attraction was 'important' or 'very important' in their decision to travel, although the Scottish sites tended to be less influential. Just over 50% of visitors came from overseas, with the major origin countries being the USA (29%), Germany (13%), Canada (10%) and France (9%). Most respondents had also visited other museums (57%) or monuments (60%), but in comparison with other countries the attendance at art galleries (35%) and performing arts

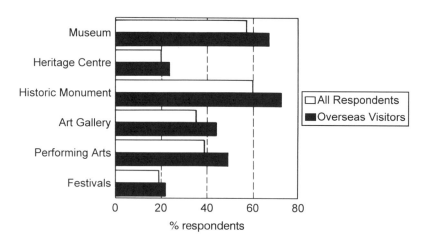

Fig. 16.2. Visits to cultural attractions in the UK by ATLAS survey respondents (source: ATLAS survey, 1992).

(38%) was relatively high (Fig. 16.2). Arts consumption by cultural tourists in Britain tends to benefit from the widespread knowledge of English among overseas visitors. Of the overseas visitors surveyed, almost 50% indicated that they had visited a performing arts event in the UK, which is far higher than the level of performing arts attendance in other countries (20%).

Tourists visiting the Scottish sites tended to be staying longer in the UK, with short-break visitors being more common in London. The more commercial base of cultural tourism in London is also reflected in the much greater use of hotel accommodation by London visitors (42%) compared with those in Scotland (20%).

Cultural visitors surveyed in the UK were more likely to be from older age groups, with 63% of respondents being over 30, compared with 56% of survey respondents overall. UK respondents were therefore also less likely to be students (17.6%) and more likely to be employed (54.3%) or pensioned (9.8%) than respondents in most other countries.

About 20% of respondents had an occupation related to culture, and there was no significant difference in levels of cultural occupation between domestic and overseas respondents. In general, the proportion of visitors with cultural occupation was higher in London (Table 16.5). Heritage sites, however, tended to have fewer visitors with a cultural occupation, emphasizing the more generalized appeal of heritage attractions compared with arts attractions.

Table 16.5. Occupations related to culture among UK cultural visitors.

Site	% respondents		
	Heritage/museums	Performing arts	Visual arts
Victoria and Albert Museum	14.4	16.4	23.7
St Paul's Cathedral	6.1	7.1	6.0
Museum of Childhood	8.9	11.8	9.5
People's Story	6.2	2.1	4.2
Urquhart Castle	10.1	6.6	9.1

CULTURAL TOURISM SUPPLY AND FUNDING

The stock of cultural tourism attractions continues to be developed in the UK by the opening of new attractions. For example, there was a growth of 22% in the number of historic properties open to the public between 1982 and 1992, a period when the number of alternative 'popular culture' attractions was also growing considerably. In 1993, 18 new museums and galleries (attracting 649,000 visits), and 11 new historic properties (565,000 visits) opened, but only two major cultural tourism attractions closed, accounting for 172,000 visits when last counted (British Tourist Authority, 1994a). The publication *Sightseeing in the UK, 1993* lists 1544 museums, 1438 historic properties and 245 art galleries, which indicates that cultural attractions account for about 56% of current attraction supply (British Tourist Authority, 1994a).

The majority of historic properties (57%) are in private ownership, which includes properties owned by the National Trust (Table 16.6). More than half of museums and galleries are in local authority ownership, with a similar proportion not making any charge for admission, presumably as a result of a desire to be seen as part of an educational rather than a recreation experience for users. Both working steam railways and industrial archaeology sites (i.e. workplaces) tend to be owned and managed by trusts.

The supply of cultural events has also grown in recent years. Of the arts festivals known to exist in the UK in 1992, only 4% originated before 1940 with a further 7% having been established between 1940 and 1959. The 1960s saw the introduction of 12% of current festivals. The 'boom' time for festival development was between 1970 and 1991 with more than three-quarters originating in that period (Eckstein, 1992). Most festivals comprise a mixture of arts forms (40%) with folk music being the largest single category of festivals available (20%). In more than half of all festivals, jazz, choral, and chamber music were offered. Between one-third and a half of festivals presented orchestral music, visual arts, drama, and literature. Less than one-third, but more than a quarter contained cabaret or comedy, folk music and folk dance, craft, and film. By far the majority of arts festivals of all types are held between May and October in any year.

Table 16.6. Selected attractions receiving a minimum of 10,000 visits in 1993.

| | Number of attractions | | |
	Historic properties	Museums and galleries	All attractions
Country			
England	429	521	1740
Scotland	94	101	356
Wales	35	38	160
Northern Ireland	11	10	77
Total United Kingdom	569	670	2333
	100%	100%	100%
Ownership			
Government[a]	157	64	272
	28%	10%	12%
Local Authority	87	344	2671
	15%	51%	29%
Private[b]	325	262	1390
	57%	39%	60%
Offering free	44	354	847
admission	8%	53%	36%
Months of opening			
Under 9 months	273	82	627
	48%	12%	27%
9 months or more	296	588	1706
	52%	88%	73%

[a] Including English Heritage, Cadw, and National Museum of Wales properties.
[b] Including properties owned by the National Trust, other trusts, religious bodies, etc.

The Policy Studies Institute (1992) discusses a number of categories of historic properties and their proportional changes in revenues earned between 1989 and 1990. Broadly, these show positive changes in admission receipts, shop trading and catering – elements of funding which are dependent upon marketing, merchandizing and visitor management rather than government grants and subsidies. Indeed, there was an increase in facilities at historic properties in England for all of the following categories between 1979 and 1992: guided tours; teas; lunches; museums or exhibitions; gardens and activities (such as sports or concerts). Many of these can be linked to the property by way of some cultural theme, but it is as likely that they may be simply commercial enterprises arising from upkeep imperatives.

English Heritage produces detailed trading accounts for 20 monuments in its ownership. Figures for 1990/91 show a range of trading circumstances from an operational contribution of £1.35 (ECU 1.71) per visit at Stonehenge to an operational loss per visit of £4.67 (ECU 5.94) at Kenwood House. The overall operating loss was seven pence per visitor across the 20 properties reported.

Grants to historic properties from English Heritage were around £30 million, expenditure on properties in care was about £23 million and staffing and administration costs nearly £41 million in a total budget of just over £100 million (ECU 127 million) in 1991/92. By far the majority of that sum is accounted for by a grant from the Department of the Environment (£90 million). Less than £8 million is received from admissions and sales on-site (English Heritage, 1993). Total expenditure by the Historic Scotland agency amounted to £31.5 million (ECU 41 million) and by Cadw (Welsh Historic Monuments) nearly £13 million (ECU 17 million) (Policy Studies Institute, 1992). In 1992, English Heritage announced its intention to seek alternative ownership of some of its 'less important' properties (many uninhabited and some in ruin) with a view to exploiting their income generation possibilities *inter alia*. A regional consultation process on this initiative is currently underway (English Heritage, 1992).

The National Trust has broadly the same range of interests as English Heritage although as a voluntary sector body it receives little government funding. Many of the sites run by the National Trust incorporate trading outlets designed to maximize merchandising opportunities for its marketing arm, National Trust Enterprises (in 1991/92, a turnover of £30 million). Not surprisingly then, its income is dependent on commercial activities, together with voluntary donations, membership subscriptions, bequests and legacies and admissions. In 1991, the Trust showed income of over £75 million (ECU 95 million), about half of which could be attributed to membership fees (members are entitled to free entry to Trust properties). Around 10% of income was received as admission fees from non-members. The National Trust for Scotland is an independent body which fulfils a similar role to that of the National Trust elsewhere in the UK. Income over the period 1990/91 was £10.5 million (ECU 14 million), about a quarter of which was from memberships.

Central government expenditure on museums and galleries in the UK was provisionally estimated to be around £280 million (ECU 356 million) in 1993/94. More than three-quarters of this figure goes to the Department of National Heritage (an increase of just less than 50% since 1985/86 in real terms) for the support of museums and galleries and other related activities within its remit. Overall distribution of grant-in-aid by the Department of National Heritage to national museums and galleries accounts for about 90% of its budget. Proportions of funding received among these institutions has remained fairly constant since 1988/89 with the British Museum receiving nearly 18% of the total, the Natural History Museum 15% and the National Gallery 9%. Most UK museums, however, are funded by local authorities.

Arts festivals receive income from a range of sources including box office, sponsorship by businesses, public sector (local authority, local arts association, Regional Arts Board or Arts Council), donations and sales of programmes,

Table 16.7.   Main sources of income by festival type.

Source	% income					
	General arts	Mixed music	Classical music	Jazz	Single art form	Folk
Box office	37	37	44	47	26	51
Business sponsorship	18	16	15	15	7	3
All public sources (local authority/local arts association, Regional Arts Board, National Arts Council)	25	17	12	17	20	14
Other[a]	30	30	29	21	48	34
Total	100	100	100	100	100	100

[a] Includes friends' associations, donations and other earned income (e.g. from catering, sales of goods, or programmes).
Source: Policy Studies Institute (1992).

Table 16.8.   Average adult admission charge for historic properties, museums and art galleries, 1991–1993.

	Historic properties (£)	% change	Museums/art galleries (£)	% change
1991	1.81	+11	1.32	+9
1992	2.00	+10	1.53	+16
1993	2.16	+8	1.71	+12

Source: Mintel (1993), British Tourist Authority (1993).

catering, etc. The proportion of these funding sources for different festival types is shown in Table 16.7. Three-quarters of festivals received some kind of local authority support in 1991 (Eckstein, 1992) including 17% which were run directly by a local authority. In the same survey, three-quarters of festivals reported receiving income from business sponsorship. Those receiving more than £100,000 (ECU 126,000) from this source in 1991 were: the Edinburgh International Festival; the Chichester Festival; the Brighton International Festival; the Aldeburgh Festival; the Bath International Festival; the Royal National Eisteddfod of Wales and Glyndebourne Festival Opera.

Admission charges for cultural attractions have risen significantly in recent years (Table 16.8). The average admission charge for historic properties rose by 8% and charges for museums and galleries rose by 12% between 1992 and 1993, at a time when retail price inflation in the UK was running at 2% (Mintel, 1993). It is worth noting, however, that just under half of museums levy no charge for visits, compared with 85% of historic properties.

THE IMPACT OF CULTURAL TOURISM

The most recent study of the economic impact of the arts and cultural services in Britain was conducted by Myerscough (1988). In tourism terms, this study concluded that tourism with an arts ingredient was worth 25% of total tourism earnings and that tourist spending specifically induced by arts events amounted to 16% of the total spend. It established that elements of the arts were especially important within tourism for those visiting from overseas, estimating that this accounted for 41% of total overseas tourism earnings. The study showed that 42% of attendance at arts-based events in London was accounted for by tourists and that museums were a major attraction throughout the UK. However, with the exception of arts festivals, theatres were important in tourism terms in London and Stratford-upon-Avon alone.

The national tourist boards in the UK observe that it is difficult to give a reliable estimate of visitor spending on attractions, but they estimate that half of the £990 million (ECU 1259 million) earned by tourist attractions in 1993 came from admission charges, and the rest from catering and the sales of gifts and souvenirs. These figures do not include revenues received by theatres and festivals for which no national data are available. However, other survey evidence indicates that British tourists whose main travel motivation was watching the performing arts spent £131 million in 1993, or 2% of all holiday expenditure. Those who visited heritage sites as the main purpose of their holiday trip in the UK spent £951 million, or 4% of all expenditure. Finally, trips which had their main motivation as the visiting of artistic or heritage exhibits accounted for £500 million, or 2% of all holiday spending in the UK (British Tourist Authority, 1994b).

A recent regional study of the economic impact of annual festivals in Edinburgh, including the Edinburgh International Festival, the Edinburgh Festival Fringe, and the Military Tattoo estimated total direct expenditure in Edinburgh and the Lothian Region of £44 million (ECU 56 million). Over 80% of total expenditure could be attributed to tourists. On average, visitors to festivals in Edinburgh spent between £10 and £30 per day if they lived locally, between £14 and £50 per day if they were on a day trip and between £30 and £100 per day if they were staying at least one night in the Lothian Region (for more details of this study, see Gratton and Richards, Chapter 4 this volume).

Expenditure by cultural tourists provides an important source of employment in the UK. The British Tourist Authority (1994a) estimated that there were a total of 49,200 full-time job equivalents (FTE) at reporting cultural attractions in 1993. There is an average of 11 jobs at gardens, 12 at museums and 14 at historic properties in the UK. Museums and galleries have the highest number of full-time, permanent jobs (estimated as 15,500 FTE), whereas historic properties have 9300 FTE. The survey also points to an increase in the percentage of seasonal jobs at attractions at the expense of permanent posts between 1992 and 1993.

Boniface (1994) draws attention to some of the social impacts of cultural tourism by attempting to identify groups, some surprising, who win and lose when culture is commodified with a view to the 'creation of a lucrative retail and leisure environment' especially using a 'heritage' theme. She observes that,

> Heritage can be damaging to communities other than those that are disadvantaged. Constant pressure of tourist visits, now often extended to be year round rather than seasonal as of old, can be wearing and intrusive on home ground and can even reduce a home's value. Bus tours enable eye-level views into first floor windows as residents of the Royal Crescent in the World Heritage City of Bath know well. In what is in effect a theme park, residents may lose, even if tourists and others are benefited. (p. 393)

CASE STUDY: EDINBURGH CASTLE

Edinburgh Castle is the most popular visitor attraction in Scotland. Perched high on the Castle Rock (the core of an extinct volcano) the castle dominates the main shopping streets lying between the 'old' and 'new' towns in Edinburgh. The silhouette of the castle on its rock has become a powerful symbol in the marketing of tourism and of Scottish produce.

Ownership and occupation

The castle belongs to the Crown and is managed on its behalf by the Historic Scotland agency. Historic Scotland was created out of the Historic Buildings and Monuments division in 1991. The mission of Historic Scotland as stated in the Corporate Plan (1992–1995) is to 'safeguard the nation's built heritage and promote its understanding and enjoyment making the best use of resources available'. In the White Paper *This Common Inheritance* (HMSO, 1990), five strands are identified to the government's approach, of which two relate directly to the castle. These are: looking after properties in government care and promoting enjoyment and understanding of heritage. The main functions of Historic Scotland can be summarized as follows:

- Protecting monuments in care and ensuring their sound conservation and maintenance;
- Encouraging visitors to monuments in care, and ensuring that they enjoy and benefit from their visits;

- Increasing public access to grant-aided historic buildings and monuments;
- Encouraging knowledge about Scotland's built heritage.

Executive agencies such as Historic Scotland were established within the government's Next Steps programme, intended to devolve ministerial responsibility for achieving objectives to managers. Ministers determine overall policy, resources and performance targets. Agencies have freedom to organize work to produce the results desired. The effect is to shift operations onto a quasi-commercial basis. Performance indicators for Historic Scotland which affect the management of the castle include:

- Increase by 4.5% the number of visitors to monuments where an admission charge is made;
- Improve presentation to visitors, in keeping with status of the monuments;
- Improve quality and variety of goods for sale to visitors;
- Increase revenue from admissions, trading and functions.

Edinburgh Castle is only one of 330 properties being looked after and presented to the public by Historic Scotland itself. A large part of the strategic management and marketing responsibilities for the castle cannot be disaggregated from the Scotland-wide programmes of the agency. Similarly, it is both impossible and (apparently seen as) undesirable to apportion expenditure to a specific cost centre such as the castle. There is a recognition of the attraction and importance of the castle. However, there is a powerful, internal belief in managing, financing and marketing it as part of a wider package.

A further complication is that the castle is not a single, homogeneous entity but a package of cultural attractions. The castle comprises several buildings that have evolved since the eleventh century. Many are in use as exhibits (e.g. the Great Hall). Others house collections of artefacts (e.g. the Scottish Crown Jewels) or belong to third parties (e.g. regimental museums). Lastly, some buildings are used as part of the military garrison. The continued location of a military garrison within the castle is said to be an attraction to tourists. For example, visitors expressed disappointment over the suspension of sentry patrols at the gates during the 'off' season. These economies were a result of expenditure restrictions on the army.

For six weeks during the summer, the esplanade is occupied by the Edinburgh Military Tattoo. This is a separate and independent commercial venture. The esplanade is rented for the duration of construction, performances, and dismantling of grandstands. In the last two years, after the final performances, Historic Scotland have entered into joint ventures with the management of the Tattoo to offer popular, musical entertainment in the unique esplanade setting. The aim is to attract a broad range of the Scottish public and to generate further revenue from the expenditure on fixed costs such as seating.

The history of Edinburgh Castle

The castle has been a residence of Scottish monarchs since the eleventh century. Construction of the fortifications in their present form began in 1356 and continued under the patronage of successive kings through to the early sixteenth century. Building and reconstruction in the early nineteenth century was driven by a shift from utilitarian and military objectives towards judgement of appropriateness for the setting and awareness of the historical importance of the castle. This period includes the rediscovery of the Scottish Honours by Sir Walter Scott and others in 1818 and the reconstruction of St Margaret's Chapel to what was thought to be its twelfth century form. The romantic associations of the castle provoked a number of unsuccessful proposals to make the castle more 'picturesque'. The last major works at the castle were in the 1920s with the construction of the Scottish National War Memorial.

During 1985 a study of visitor facilities concluded that in reception, attractions and presentation, the castle had not kept pace with visitor demands. There were problems of traffic and visitor flows, inadequate services and lack of interpretation. A proposed redevelopment failed at that time to secure public support or government resources. It was not until 1988 that work begun on improvements including a new shop (opened in 1990), a vehicle tunnel (opened in 1990), improved historical interpretation and provision for school parties. In 1991 a second phase of improvements started incorporating a new restaurant (completed in 1992) and a major exhibition of the Honours of Scotland (the Crown Jewels) was announced for 1993.

Management at Edinburgh Castle

Managers identify two issues in local site services for visitors. These are quality of staff with customer contact roles and development of the product without compromising the integrity of the castle. Both are aimed at increasing satisfaction, throughput and expenditure by visitors.

Staffing

Staff are organized under a Visitor Services Manager located on-site and responsible to an executive at Historic Scotland with central control over a range of properties. The structure is shown in Fig. 16.3.

The title of 'warder' at the castle is historically significant and, like the staffing structure, is based upon its military past. Attempts have been made to identify alternatives to the title warder, which, it is recognized, may have negative connotations. No viable alternative has been identified that describes

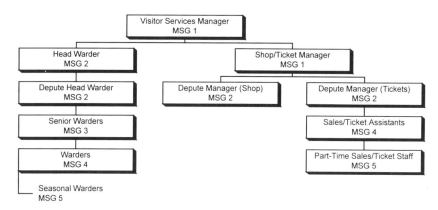

Fig. 16.3.   Visitor services staffing structure at Edinburgh Castle.

accurately the tasks undertaken. Staff are not referred to as 'warders' within public areas of the castle.

Warders on the MSG 5 grade are usually seasonal appointments and are in static posts throughout the castle. This means adopting both a security and an informational role. Warders are rotated around various points to enrich their experiences and improve their product knowledge. Although static, they are not statues: they are expected to deal with visitor enquiries about all aspects of the castle, not only the part where they are situated. In addition, they are expected to intervene in the process of a visit where behaviour may be detrimental to general enjoyment or if they can improve the experiences of visitors. MSG 4 grade warder job descriptions are identical to MSG 5, except for an additional responsibility to lead tours. Staff on the MSG 4 grade are chosen according to experience, product knowledge, communication and customer-care skills.

As well as the desire to make staff seem more approachable, a three-year training programme developed the interaction skills needed to match customers' expectations of warders. The main feature of this programme has been customer-care training. Staff are expected to improve their product knowledge by reading texts made available by management. Some staff have been supported in foreign language tuition. In accordance with the new ethos, trainers strive to change both the style and content of information imparted. Previously, delivery was felt to be unpalatable, dry and deadpan, reflecting a curatorial orientation and an assumption of visitor knowledge of architecture or history. Now, warders are encouraged to develop a more individual style, while ensuring that the basic information and itinerary are covered. This allows opportunities for personal anecdotes and tailoring of delivery to suit the audience. This is similar to the approach adopted at other government-managed heritage sites in Britain (e.g. Wood, 1990). Warders are encouraged to participate in shaping their work-environment by communicating with management. This has involved regular meetings to exchange information and a suggestions scheme for improvements to visitor services.

Nowhere is greater customer-orientation more apparent than in the recruitment policy for warders. Currently advertisements seek warders with good, applied foreign language skills. In addition, past experience in a customer-related or retail field is emphasized and if this is in tourism, then so much the better.

Product development

For most visitors, the tour is a significant part of the product. That managers want this to prevail is evidenced by the continuation of entry fees which include the price of a tour. It is not possible to pay entry excluding the tour, although it is not compulsory to join one. Managers view the style and delivery of the tour as indivisible from the experience of the castle. Product development, where this extends beyond maintenance, ensures that the tour can be enjoyed and that further expenditure will be encouraged. Tours start every 15 minutes at peak times. It is common to have 50 visitors in a tour party. Visitors are not committed to one guide, but may drift away at a point of interest and join another when ready to continue.

In developing the product, commodification (or, in their words, Disneyfication) of the castle's offerings is avoided. Modern technologies are evaluated and used in the interpretation of exhibits when considered appropriate. Thus video and simulations are both deployed. However, there is a marked differentiation by marketing management between the presentation of 'real' events that took place in the castle, verifiable by documentary sources, and the construction of stories and tales that do not attempt to represent 'actual' events. The latter type of presentation would be regarded as entirely inappropriate and unacceptable.

Finance

Sources of income are the recurring government grant, admissions, and trading revenue. The finance required to re-develop the castle has been so great as to require special grants from the Secretary of State. Table 16.9 shows income from admissions and trading since 1983.

Income from admissions is a function of pricing policies and the number of visitors attracted. Clearly, there is a direct relationship between visits and income. Trading income comprises expenditure by visitors in the cafeteria and in the shop. Although there is a connection between the number of visits and trading income, it is possible to secure growth in the latter without increasing the former, e.g. by increasing the opportunities for expenditure and by

Table 16.9.   Total visitor income for Edinburgh Castle (1983–1991).

	£ (net of VAT)		
	Admissions income	Trading income	Total
1983	889,279	346,039	1,235,318
1984	1,066,881	447,210	1,514,091
1985	1,207,216	498,943	1,706,159
1986	1,161,268	487,767	1,649,035
1987	1,337,268	629,416	1,966,684
1988	1,715,643	711,806	2,427,449
1989	1,757,921	697,201	2,455,122
1990	1,928,127	871,990	2,800,117
1991	2,186,712	987,106	3,173,818

Source: Historic Scotland.

Table 16.10.   Income per visitor at Edinburgh Castle (1983–1991).

	£ (net of VAT)		
	Visitors	Admission income per visitor	Trading income per visitor	Total income per visitor
1983	818,100	1.09	0.42	1.51
1984	847,069	1.26	0.53	1.79
1985	923,256	1.31	0.54	1.85
1986	832,485	1.39	0.59	1.98
1987	967,424	1.38	0.65	2.03
1988	957,584	1.79	0.74	2.53
1989	1,033,697	1.70	0.67	2.37
1990	1,078,120	1.78	0.81	2.59
1991	973,620	2.25	1.01	3.26

Source: Historic Scotland.

attracting visitors with a high propensity to spend or with a higher daily expenditure rate. Table 16.10 shows that much of the increase in income has been generated by improved revenue sales of merchandise. Broadly, this is commensurate with the management policy of improving opportunity and quality of trading outlets.

Visitor marketing

Data on visitor profiles are largely confined to a study carried out in 1985. These data indicated that visitors were predominantly from professional or managerial backgrounds, highly educated and mainly aged between 20 and 50. Most visitors came from the USA (29%), England (22%) or Scotland (19%), and two-thirds were first-time visitors.

Target markets being developed are based on the type of visitors to Edinburgh, 80% of whom come to the castle. Broadly, two strategies have been adopted to reach different groups. First, there is a need to attract those with disproportionately high per diem spend rates to boost trading income. This group is likely to contain a high proportion of foreign holiday-makers and business tourists. These are reached through marketing at travel trade exhibitions throughout the world (especially in Japan). The focus of activity on these trips is the quality travel market. In countries like Japan, where holidays are relatively alien to the indigenous culture, there is little to be gained from direct, personal marketing. Rather, in product life-cycle terms, the approach is to reach the 'early adopters'. It is important to stress that marketing activity is for the whole of Historic Scotland's portfolio. Similar exhibitions in Europe are used to reach tour (especially coach) operators and a package ticket is offered for entry to a number of the properties. In all cases, executives concede that the castle is used as the flagship with which it is possible to increase interest in other, less well-known properties.

Secondly, the need to increase visitation levels and to broaden visitor profiles towards a representative spread of the Scottish population drives marketing efforts. Advertisements in the *Daily Record*, a newspaper with a mainly manual-occupation readership, have led to a substantial amount of free publicity. This has taken the form of colour, 'pull-out' sections featuring Historic Scotland's properties combined with an offer of free entry. Such 'free' promotion is an active part of the marketing strategy. Travel journalists are given tours of properties and provided with ready-written copy. Historic Scotland commissioned a television advertisement to highlight their properties to Scots only. Again, the objective has been to broaden the socio-economic base and to increase visitor throughput.

Management issues

The complex situation of the castle as a symbol of Edinburgh and Scotland, as a heritage monument, as a tourist attraction and as a military facility pose a number of management problems for Historic Scotland. A careful balance must be maintained between the need for visitor access and the need for security, the need to develop income generation and the need to preserve the atmosphere of the castle, and the need to achieve a higher throughput of visitors while minimizing overcrowding at peak times. The castle managers are particularly concerned with issues of marketing and income generation, at a time when changing government policies are placing more emphasis on self-generated income. Options being assessed include the contracting out and/or franchising of some services and the use of the image of the castle for licensing and endorsement of 'quality' products and services.

CULTURAL TOURISM POLICY AND MARKETING

In 1993, the English Tourist Board produced *The Arts Tourism Marketing Handbook* which synthesizes the major marketing issues facing strategic bodies in the marketing of cultural tourism in the UK. It defines its main purposes as:

- To develop more effective communication between arts and tourism;
- To create awareness of joint marketing opportunities;
- To show arts and tourism operators the way forward from what has been achieved so far;
- To encourage new arts and tourism marketing initiatives (English Tourist Board, 1993).

Some of these issues had been identified in earlier policy documents by strategic bodies throughout the UK (e.g. Scottish Arts Council, 1992) but this new document, together with statements by the Wales Tourist Board (1993) and the Scottish Tourist Board (1993), epitomized what was to be a central thrust of policy thereafter. These were the importance of liaison and coordination among existing bodies at national, regional and local levels, exploitation of existing organization's approaches (e.g. the Arts Council's Arts 2000 festival) and operations and the centrality of 'marketing' communications techniques as the major tools for policy implementation. To a large extent, attractions such as heritage sites and exhibits are included, together with arts forms, in these documents where culture and tourism are given a push in each other's direction with assurances of mutual benefits. Interestingly, the terms 'arts tourism' or 'tourism and the arts' are being used to unify the fields discussed here as 'cultural tourism'. In itself, this may be a function of effective market segmentation in the drive to locate and label viable and reachable target groups.

The Scottish Tourist Board's (1993) publication *Tourism and the Arts in Scotland* sets out its stall even more clearly, asserting that the strategy 'would expand the business of arts organizations whilst encouraging tourism and its consequent economic benefits . . .'. Consumers of the Arts are identified as a viable and lucrative market segment for tourism businesses. Arts organizations, in the face of changing funding structures, are in need of throughput to meet performance targets and satisfy financial imperatives. The Tourist Board, however, has extended beyond the economic objectives evident in all such documents to 'broaden tourist perception of Scottish art and culture' and to 'broaden Scotland's arts tourism activities'. This approach suggests that there is a desire to erode some of the cultural stereotypes of 'Scottishness' evident in visitors' perceptions and produced by industries in whose interests commodification of a culture may lie. These sentiments are echoed by the Wales Tourist

Board (1993) in its objective to 'encourage the provision of distinctive Welsh entertainment' and its broad policy context of Wales as 'a bilingual nation, with its own cultural identity'. It announces its intention to 'use the Welsh language positively in . . . (its) . . . efforts to market Wales, especially overseas' and to 'make positive use of the linguistic and cultural traditions of Wales in tourism'. Nic Craith (1994) has pointed to the importance of language in the development of cultural tourism and opined that:

> If language is viewed as a vital component of culture, then cultural tourism will only prove successful when the local language is visible in the environment. The object of this venture, however, should not be to use the language to create a flourishing economy, but rather the creation of an environment in which the local culture and language can find expression. (p. 15)

A recent survey identified problems with the use of Gaelic at visitor attractions in the Highlands and Islands of Scotland, where, unlike Wales, there is no statutory requirement for bi-lingual signs, etc. Particular issues related to the absence of signage, interpretation, promotion or content in Gaelic, with few translation facilities compounding the problem. However, almost 80% of businesses surveyed were interested in financial assistance for the development of Gaelic facilities.

The Festival of Arts and Culture, a specific promotional campaign to provide a 'sharper focus' for the arts and culture in Britain with a view to increasing earnings from overseas tourism, will be run by the British Tourist Authority in 1995 (with a budget of £10 million for marketing promotion). It will embrace all forms of Britain's arts and culture from the past, as well as the present, and include both popular and classical forms. Marketing materials promise coverage of performing and visual arts, broadcasting, crafts and customs, literature and legends, and food and drink. With such a broad range of considerations it remains to be seen whether it will provide a 'focus'. However, it does subscribe to what appear to be the central planks of policy in this area – promoting cooperation between agencies or enterprises and increasing spending at venues to be achieved through more effective marketing.

The substantives of policies for cultural tourism cannot be divorced from wider considerations preoccupying British governments in recent years. The importance of joint public and commercial sector initiatives is evident across many policy arenas, as is encouragement for public agencies to improve their marketing approaches (Richards, 1995). Since 1979, policies to reduce or eliminate barriers to the effectiveness of tourism as an industry have affected social life across such diverse areas as Sunday trading and rules on gambling and licensing hours. The cultural tourism policies discussed above can be seen in the context of attempts to create more 'perfect' operation of markets for tourism and leisure. These include greater 'flexibility' in job markets. The tourism industries in general, and cultural tourism in particular, contain labour forces where skills are limited to on-the-job training and casual or seasonal employment is common. Also, cultural activities are areas where 'active citizenship' and voluntarism have some currency and can be encouraged.

Policies towards local government, major providers of cultural tourism opportunities in the visual and performing arts as well as in museums, have also had some effect. Local authorities are exhorted to participate in wider marketing initiatives and to spend their considerable budgets for these areas with cognisance of the economic benefits of tourism. Consideration has been given to the nature and structure of funding for museums, where professional bodies representing curatorial staff have resisted attempts to shift foci away from (broadly) education towards recreation. This has manifested itself in proposals to separate ownership and management (e.g. via competitive tendering) or introducing greater opportunities for charging (where tourists could be expected to be among those paying most heavily in any differential pricing approach). In the arts, policies of 'discouragement' such as those adopted towards the former Greater London Council and some London Boroughs in their promotion of arts aimed at, and initiated by, minority groups have been compounded by the reluctance of business sponsors to support 'marginal' groups. This has often undermined the economic viability of what may have been artistically valuable output. For those affected by these policies, initiatives designed to couple the arts and tourism will seem both inevitable and unwelcome in their implications of consumer-oriented 'cultural products'.

If cultural tourism is to satisfy consumers' needs for 'enlightening, learning and enriching experiences' (English Tourist Board, 1993) in all, or parts, of the UK, then it is fulfilling an educative role. Social groups A, B and C1 are already well represented among consumers of cultural products in the UK. If policies towards cultural tourism are to become more than the (apparent) exploitation of lucrative, high-spending market segments, then the totality of cultures evident in the UK, whether popular or 'high', will need to be represented. The approaches to British culture implicit in the policies outlined above suggest that tourists are isolated from the multicultural, multi-ethnic society which is contemporary Britain.

TRENDS AND PROSPECTS

This chapter has highlighted a number of key issues in cultural tourism in the UK. First, the development of collaborative relationships (both formal and informal) between agencies and organizations with interests in this area seem to be growing. Often, these initiatives originate from the public sector, although they are not exclusively the province of government or quasi-government. Such collaboration is associated with a greater focus on both marketing and training as tools for maximizing the potential for consumption and customer 'loyalty' at cultural tourism events and sites. Initiatives such as these offer possibilities for income generation but can lead to accusations of 'commodification' (often at the expense of educative approaches) and, sometimes, the 'invention of tradition'. Awareness of market segments and cost structures has improved recognition of the role played by ancillary services in the visitor experience. Retailing and catering at cultural tourism venues is now accepted as a fundamental expectation of visitors, as well as an opportunity to cover costs. It is likely that these will be the major growth areas in cultural tourism provision, and that stock lists, merchandising and catering techniques will assume greater prominence in the vocabulary of managers.

Lastly, the shifting nature of public sector cultural funding since 1977 has underlined the existence of a mixed economy of cultural tourism provision and consumption. One implication of this, especially with the recent availability of National Lottery funding for capital projects and acquisitions, is that planners and policy-makers will need to devote substantial efforts to assembling funding packages for specific initiatives. Another implication is that creativity and innovation among small-scale, local cultural tourism initiatives may be stifled by the prescriptive requirements of funding agencies on the one hand, and the need to generate commercial income in a competitive 'marketplace' on the other.

ACKNOWLEDGEMENTS

I am grateful to Fred Coalter at the Centre for Leisure Reseach for the opportunity to research this case. My colleague, John Flannary, at Glasgow Caledonian University ensured that I could find the time to participate in the ATLAS study.

Staff at the Historic Scotland agency were generous in the time devoted to assisting me, particularly Jenny Hess.

REFERENCES

Boniface, P. (1994) Theme park Britain. In: Fladmark, M. (ed.) *Cultural Tourism*. Donhead Publishing, London.
Bonink, C. (1992) *Cultural tourism development and government policy*. MA Dissertation, Rijksuniversiteit Utrecht.
British Tourist Authority (1990) *Overseas Visitor Survey*. BTA, London.
British Tourist Authority (1993) *Guidelines for Tourism to Britain 1993–1997*. BTA, London.
British Tourist Authority (1994a) *Sightseeing in the UK*. BTA, London.
British Tourist Authority (1994b) *UK Tourism Survey*. BTA, London.
British Tourist Authority/English Tourist Board (1992) *Overseas Visitor Survey*. BTA/ETB, London.
Davies, S. (1995) Attendance records. *Leisure Management* 15, 40–44.
Eckstein, J. (1992) Arts festivals. *Cultural Trends* 15, 1–20.
English Heritage (1992) *Visitor Trends 1991*. English Heritage, London.

English Heritage (1993) *Visitor Trends 1992*. English Heritage, London.

English Tourist Board (1993) *Arts Tourism Marketing Handbook*. ETB, London.

Historic Scotland (1992) *Corporate Plan 1992–1995*. Historic Scotland, Edinburgh.

HMSO (1990) *This Common Inheritance*. Cmd 1200, HMSO, London.

Mintel (1993) Cultural visits. *Leisure Intelligence* 3, 1–28.

Myerscough, J. (1988) *The Economic Importance of the Arts*. Policy Studies Institute, London.

Nic Craith, M. (1994) The role of language in cultural tourism. In: Munro, J. (ed.) *Cultural Tourism*. Gateway Europe, Hull, pp. 8–16.

Northern Ireland Tourist Board (1994) *Tourism in Northern Ireland – a Sustainable Approach*. NITB, Belfast.

Policy Studies Institute (1992) The built heritage. *Cultural Trends* 15, 21–57.

Quine, M. (1993) Theatre audiences in Britain: a continuing research programme. *Journal of Arts Management, Law and Society* 23, 225–239.

Richards, G. (1995) The politics of national tourism policy in Britain. *Leisure Studies* 14, 153–173.

Rolfe, H. (1992) *Arts Festivals in the UK*. Policy Studies Institute, London.

Scottish Arts Council (1992) *Charter for the Arts in Scotland*. HMSO, Edinburgh.

Scottish Tourist Board (1993) *Tourism and the Arts in Scotland*. STB, Edinburgh.

Scottish Tourist Board (1994) *Scottish Tourism – Strategic Plan*. STB, Edinburgh.

Wales Tourist Board (1993) *Tourism: a Strategy for Wales*. WTB, Cardiff.

Wood, H. (1990) The Tower of London. In: Richards, G. (ed.) *Case Studies in Tourism Management*. Papers in Leisure and Tourism Studies no. 2, University of North London, pp. 15–21.

European Cultural Tourism: **17**
Trends and Future Prospects

G. Richards

*Department of Leisure Studies, Tilburg University, PO Box 90153, 5000
LE Tilburg, The Netherlands*

The thematic and national chapters in this book have demonstrated the increasing significance of cultural tourism in Europe, and underlined the vast diversity of European cultural tourism demand and supply. The view of the European Commission that the cultural richness and diversity of Europe is one of its major tourism product strengths is amply supported by this analysis. Given such a rich source of potential cultural tourism products, it is not surprising that cultural tourism has taken on such a prominent role. What is perhaps more surprising is the widespread convergence of cultural tourism development and marketing policies which can be observed in all corners of Europe, and at all administrative levels, from local tourism plans to European Union programmes. Many have attributed this to the emergence of cultural tourism as a 'new' market segment, with enormous growth potential. Others have seen the cause in the creation of the 'heritage industry', and the rapid expansion of opportunities for cultural consumption.

What the current analysis has illustrated, is that cultural tourism is a more complex phenomenon than many previous studies have assumed. Growing interest in cultural tourism cannot simply be explained as a 'new' market trend (Myerscough, 1988), or as a response to German unification (Narhsted, 1993) or as a reflection of a growing interest in the past among those disillusioned with the present (Hewison, 1987). A more comprehensive explanation can be found in the changing relationship between cultural consumption and production in Europe.

As economic restructuring has decimated the former industrial base of most European countries, so consumption has gained an increasing role in determining the location and productivity of the new consumer-based industries of Europe, among which the cultural industries and tourism are major growth sectors. In order to maximize their productive potential, these 'new' industries rely heavily on the consumption power of the 'new middle class' or the 'service class', as was indicated in Chapter 3. Growing competition among European nations, regions and cities for a share of this consumption power has placed a greater emphasis on capturing the consumption power of the mobile consumer – the 'visitor' or 'tourist'. By attracting more consumers to a region, the consumption capacity, and thereby the production capacity of that region can be enhanced, producing more income and jobs, and therefore ensuring economic survival. Thus in place of consumption being determined by production, it is now consumption which increasingly determines production. The development of cultural tourism in a specific region also effectively allows the 'real cultural capital' locked up in the cultural resources of the region to be capitalized through tourism consumption (Zukin, 1991).

As economic competition between regions has intensified, so a number of significant changes can be observed in European cultural tourism. The need to replace manufacturing and agricultural jobs lost as a consequence of economic restructuring, for example, has led 'new' regions to join the scramble to develop cultural tourism. Thus cultural tourism is now an essential element of tourism policy from Lapland to Sicily, and from Lisbon to Vienna. Cultural attractions have multiplied, both as a response to local needs to develop cultural resources, and in response to fragmenting cultural tastes on the part of the consumer. The emergence of new cultural attractions has also begun to blur former boundaries between 'high' and 'popular' culture, which become even less distinct as attractions are made more visitor friendly to increase their commercial viability. The rapid expansion of cultural production and tourism consumption of cultural attractions has also begun to produce a segmented market for cultural tourism, between those 'specific cultural tourists' for whom culture remains the primary motive, and 'general cultural tourists' for whom culture adds spice to the usual leisure tourism diet.

This chapter examines some of the consequences of these changes in more detail, and tries to identify the major trends which have characterized European cultural tourism in recent years, and those trends which are likely to feature prominently in the near future.

TRENDS IN EUROPEAN CULTURAL TOURISM

A single Europe?

European cultural tourism is, as the European Travel Commission (1994) suggests, an essential tension between unity and diversity. At European level, there is pressure to create cultural unity which can also serve as the basis for a 'European' tourism product. At the same time, individual countries and regions are desperately seeking 'unique' and 'authentic' elements of culture which can distinguish them from their neighbours.

The national chapters in this book have painted a picture of unique national cultures and individual approaches to culture and tourism. In terms of the development and marketing of cultural tourism, however, many countries have adopted similar approaches, even if these are coloured by national or regional considerations. Many of these similarities stem from the basic distribution of cultural resources or tourism demand. In southern Europe, the legacy of classical civilizations has produced cultural tourism policies geared to monument preservation, as in Italy and Greece. In the core historical cities of northwestern Europe and Italy, tourism pressures are stimulating policies geared towards visitor management. In peripheral regions with relatively few major sites, as in Ireland and other areas of Celtic culture, the emphasis has been on the development of living culture for tourism.

Far more important than such geographic considerations, however, have been the major socio-economic changes affecting all areas of Europe during the last 20 years. The sweeping changes in production and consumption activities brought about by economic restructuring have created new roles for culture and tourism as leading sectors of the European economy. The need to turn fashionable areas of consumption into productive activity has affected the whole of Europe, and has resulted in similar policies of cultural tourism development and marketing being pursued in very different social, economic and political circumstances. The fact that these trends can be identified in other world regions, such as North America and East Asia, indicates that the basic impulse to such policy convergence is more a result of trends towards globalization than any impact of the unification of Europe, as Gratton (1992) has already demonstrated for the tourism market in general.

The broadening definition of cultural tourism

The practical problems of defining cultural tourism discussed in Chapter 2 have been amply illustrated by the different approaches to cultural tourism adopted in the various national chapters. The basic issue seems to be: what elements of 'culture' should be included in 'cultural tourism'? In some countries, a fairly narrow definition which associates cultural tourism with elements of high culture has been evident (e.g. Italy, Greece). In others, cultural tourism has always been understood to include more traditional elements, such as folk culture and gastronomy (e.g. Portugal, Belgium). In some cases, however, the meaning and scope of culture and cultural tourism have undergone considerable change, as reflected in the inclusion of rap music in the remit of the French

Ministry of Culture in the 1980s, and the designation of U2 and the Hot House Flowers as cultural tourism attractions in Ireland in the 1990s.

This widening scope for cultural tourism reflects both the blurring of boundaries between 'high' and 'popular' culture, and the increasing need to popularize the cultural tourism product to attract a wider audience. Hewison detected signs of this in the development of attractions such as the Jorvik Centre in York, which he saw as being a mixture of history and entertainment characteristic of the 'heritage industry'. Signs that such integration is increasing include the development of 'cultural theme parks' (Munsters, Chapter 6 this volume) selling a mixture of entertainment and education which has been encapsulated in the term 'edutainment' (Tourism Research and Marketing, 1994). As Rojek (1993) has suggested, the growing supply of leisure attractions means that a growing number of these are seeking to add education elements to their products as a means of differentiating themselves from the competition. Thus one might argue that one reason for the growing importance of cultural tourism is that the scope of activities which might be defined as such is constantly increasing. Such developments might suggest the need for a revision, if not the total abandonment of the 'sites and monuments' approach to defining cultural tourism.

The problem of defining cultural tourism also lies in identifying the cultural tourist. The analysis in this volume has indicated that cultural tourists must be distinguished in terms of motivation. Those whose prime motivation for travel is 'cultural' (specific cultural tourists) actually form a relatively small proportion of the total tourist market. In contrast, culture is often an important secondary motivation for tourism (general cultural tourists). The ATLAS survey data indicate that only about 9% of tourists visiting cultural attractions could be classified as specific cultural tourists. This pattern is repeated in general surveys of tourism motivation. In The Netherlands, 33% of foreign visitors cited a cultural motive in 1988, but only 8% gave culture as their prime motivation. In the UK, cultural motives were involved in over 20% of domestic holiday trips in 1993, but culture was the most important motive for only 6% of all trips (see Table 16.3).

There remains, therefore, a considerable contrast between the expansion of generalized cultural consumption, and the relatively small proportion of specialist consumers for whom culture is the basic motive for tourism consumption. Essentially, specific cultural tourists can be equated with those factions of the new middle class who distinguish themselves, as Bourdieu (1984) argues, through high levels of cultural capital and specific forms of symbolic consumption. In the context of cultural tourism, such consumers distinguish themselves through their motivations. They are not just 'doing' the major 'must-see' cultural sights, but they are adding to their own store of cultural capital through undertaking specific learning experiences. Even more significant is the fact that a high proportion of these cultural consumers are in fact also cultural producers, who are connected in some way with the cultural industries. In cultural tourism, as in other areas of the cultural industries, therefore, the links between cultural production and cultural consumption are very strong (Bevers, 1993). As Zukin (1991) suggests, therefore, cultural consumption creates employment for, and reinforces the cultural capital of the 'self-conscious critical infrastructure'.

These specific cultural tourists, who can perhaps in broad terms be equated with Bourdieu's 'new cultural intermediaries', therefore form a crucial segment of cultural tourism demand. Not only are they important consumers, with more frequent participation in cultural tourism than other segments of the population, but they have an influence on the tastes and behaviour of others, and they are often directly involved in the production process (Richards, 1996). These consumers of cultural tourism *per se* can be distinguished from the much larger group of general cultural tourists, who engage, as Urry (1990) suggests, in a culture of tourism.

Growing demand

Cultural tourism is clearly an important and growing tourism market in Europe. There has been a distinct increase in cultural attraction visits, and in the number of cultural tourists in Europe over the past 20 or 30 years. However, the data indicate that culture is often far more important as a secondary motive for tourism than as the prime motivation.

Data on cultural attraction attendances across Europe as a whole (Fig. 2.4) show that cultural visits have more than doubled in the past 20 years. It should be remembered, however, that a growth in visits does not always mean a growth in visitors. Although individual surveys have indicated a growth in the proportion of the population engaging in cultural tourism consumption in some countries has increased, the bulk of cultural visits are still accounted for by a relatively small proportion of all visitors (Schouten, 1995), often the 'specific cultural tourists'.

Growth has also been far from even, temporally or spatially. Steady increases in cultural visits across Europe in the 1970s gave way to decline in the early 1980s, reflecting the impact of economic recession. A further short period of rapid growth from the mid-1980s was in turn replaced by declining attendances in the early 1990s. The recent decline in attendance has been particularly severe in countries such as Italy, where cultural attractions rely heavily on tourists. The UK evidence also indicates that the number of specific cultural holidays fell between 1989 and 1993. The ATLAS data indicate that European cultural visits have grown no faster than the international tourism market as a whole during the past 20 years, and that in the early 1990s, cultural visits have lagged behind the growth in tourism arrivals (Fig. 2.5).

Data on cultural tourism as a proportion of all tourism trips indicate that the proportion of all European tourism trips accounted for by specific cultural tourists has probably been between 5% and 10% of tourism trips over the past 10 years. If we estimate the average to be about 7.5% of all tourism trips across Europe, this would indicate a rise in the number of specific international cultural tourism trips in Europe from about 15 million trips in 1982 to almost 22 million in 1992. These data indicate that specific cultural tourists are a more important element of the European tourism market than has previously been supposed. Estimates produced for the European Commission in 1988, for example, indicated a specific cultural tourism market of 3.5 million international trips, compared with a total cultural tourism market of 35 million trips a year (Irish Tourist Board, 1988). Data collected in the current study indicate that the total cultural tourism market, including those for whom culture is a secondary motive for travel, is about three times the size of the specific cultural tourism market. This would indicate a total European cultural tourism demand of about 60 million international trips in 1992. The development of secondary, general cultural tourism is particularly important in destinations such as Greece and Spain, where culture is an essential addition to the basic sun, sea, and sand products. Thus culture may not attract vast numbers of tourists on its own, but it provides an essential additional motivator which can help to distinguish one destination from another.

The rapid broadening of a general interest in culture is related to social developments in postwar Europe. In Chapter 3 it was pointed out that cultural tourism participation is largely determined by the distribution of cultural capital in society. A number of the national chapters have underlined the role of increasing educational levels in building cultural capital, and extending cultural participation to a wider audience (Knulst, 1989). The traditional cultural audience, whose cultural capital was nurtured by a strong social environment or 'habitus' has been joined by a much broader public, who have also developed cultural competence through education. The concurrent growth of tourism demand, fuelled broadly by the same social processes, had the effect of transforming a proportion of this growth in cultural participation into tourism consumption. The growth in cultural tourism consumption has therefore broadly kept pace with tourism consumption as a whole in recent decades.

The important role of education in building cultural capital among modern consumers also means that younger tourists form a much larger segment of the cultural tourism market than was previously thought. Over 44% of cultural visitors and 42% of tourists surveyed in the ATLAS research were aged under 30. This evidence supports other studies which indicate the high proportion of younger people among museum visitors, and the greater proportion of younger people who engage in tourism as a whole (Schuster, 1993; European Travel Commission, 1995).

Widening access to education and tourism consumption have been seen as signs of growing social equality in many countries. In recent years, however, evidence has begun to emerge that inequality is replacing equality as one of the major engines of tourism growth, and by implication of cultural tourism growth. In the UK, for example, the growing proportion of national income accumulated by those in higher socio-economic groups during the 1980s stimulated an increase in second and third holidays, which accounted for much of the growth in tourism consumption in this period (Seaton 1992), and a similar pattern of tourism consumption distribution can also be observed in Germany (Spitz and Breitenbach, 1994). It could also be argued that such developments have been particularly favourable for the growth of cultural tourism demand, since the 'money rich, time poor' higher social classes are likely to engage in a high number of short city breaks, which will also tend to have a cultural focus (Gratton, 1992).

Some of the national analyses have also pointed to a major division in the cultural tourism market between first-time and repeat visitors. First-time visitors, who accounted for about 75% of all tourists interviewed in the ATLAS survey, are far more likely to visit a large number of cultural attractions in an attempt to 'do' the cultural highlights of the destination. Evidence from national surveys suggests that the importance of cultural attractions as a motive for visiting declines after the first visit to a country, once the major sites have already been visited. This further explains why visitors from outside Europe, who are more likely to be making a first visit, are particularly drawn to the major cultural sites.

A number of conclusions concerning the development of cultural tourism demand can be drawn from this study. First, cultural tourism is not a 'new' growth market, but has been developing for a much longer period of time. Second, although the number of cultural trips may be growing, the proportion of total tourism accounted for by specific cultural tourists does not seem to be increasing. Much of the growth in cultural tourism consumption may therefore be attributable to the growth of culture as a secondary motive for travel. Third, cultural tourism is not a recession-proof market, and cultural attendances in many countries have suffered from the economic downturn at the beginning of the 1990s. Fourth, younger tourists may be a more important segment of the cultural tourism market in Europe than has previously been thought. Younger tourists are more likely to be better educated and to possess greater cultural capital than their parents, and they also engage more frequently in tourism. Finally, the demand for cultural attractions, as opposed to 'living culture' is greatest among first-time visitors. The needs of cultural tourists might therefore be expected to develop away from the consumption of sites and monuments as the market matures, and a higher proportion of repeat visitors is achieved.

Burgeoning supply of cultural attractions

The development of cultural tourism demand has always been closely linked to the supply of cultural attractions. The early development of cultural tourism was stimulated by the search for a universal European culture, a practice which was solidified by the subsequent collection and organization of the physical manifestations of European culture into museums and other cultural institutions. The role of these institutions as representations of a universal culture has been undermined by increasing de-differentiation, and the fragmentation and integration of cultural perspectives. The rise of competing cultural perspectives has helped to create a more diverse and specialized cultural tourism product, where the large national or regional museums now have to compete with a range of niche museums, offering regional, local and thematic interpretations of culture which augment and sometimes challenge European and national concepts of cultural unity.

Expansion of supply is also stimulated by the spatial fixity characteristic of tourism products, which is even more acute in the case of cultural tourism products. Culture is seen as a unique and authentic attribute of place, which can be used to distinguish the tourism products of one region or country from another. As the regions of Europe strive to create a distinctive image to attract tourists and inward investment, so the number of cultural attractions offered at regional and local level multiplies.

The supply of cultural attractions throughout Europe has grown rapidly in recent years. The pace of growth has quickened noticeably since the early 1980s, with an estimated 38% growth in the supply of cultural attractions in Europe between 1985 and 1992. This growth does not show many signs of slacking, particularly as cultural development strategies which emerged first in northern Europe are now spreading south to the Mediterranean and eastward into the restructuring economies of central and eastern Europe.

The rapid growth in cultural attraction supply, particularly in the last ten years, has created a situation where supply is outstripping demand. In many countries, the cultural attraction market is becoming increasingly polarized between a few major attractions which attract millions of visitors every year, and a growing number of smaller attractions, who must share a declining pool of visitors between them. In the UK and France, for example, much of the growth in museum attendance in recent years can be attributed to the success of major national institutions, such as the British Museum and the Louvre (see Chapters 8 and 16, this volume). The result is falling average attendance levels at cultural attractions across Europe. In some cases, lower average attendances also match a decline in the average attraction size (as in The Netherlands, for example), but the basic problem remains that fewer visitors are likely to mean less revenue, and in some cases less subsidy.

Cultural attractions must compete not just with other cultural attractions, but also with a wide range of other tourism and leisure attractions. Middleton (1989) has indicated that an overall excess in attraction supply exists in the UK. Whereas commercial attractions can be expected to adjust to demand by either product development or even ceasing operation, the same flexibility is not often available to cultural institutions such as museums, which must usually bear the burden of research, curation and other costly non-commercial functions. There is still resistance to the changes demanded of cultural institutions by new market conditions, as Schouten (1995) has observed in the case of museums. Although some may applaud this apparent resistance to increasing superficiality (Walsh, 1991), others argue that cultural institutions are not adapting fast enough to the changing political and economic climate. What we may be witnessing, in fact, is the emergence of a far more diverse landscape of cultural institutions, with new, 'postmodern' cultural attractions springing up beside the more traditional and largely state-funded institutions. It is the former group which is growing most strongly, as evidenced by the emergence of smaller, private sector museums in The Netherlands (Richards, Chapter 13 this volume), the growth in musicals tourism in the UK and Germany (see Roth and Langemeyer, Chapter 9 this volume) and the exponential growth of community festivals in the United States (Janiske, 1994). The balance of supply between the 'traditional' and the 'new' cultural attractions will not only be determined by the development of demand, but also by the shifting boundaries between state intervention and market forces in shaping European cultural supply.

Changing policies – from culture to economics

Policies relating specifically to cultural tourism have emerged relatively recently in most European countries. Even in the UK, which has provided the role model for the development of heritage tourism in many other areas, a coordinated policy for cultural tourism has only emerged in the last few years. In the past, culture and tourism were regarded as separate spheres, and cultural institutions in particular fought hard to avoid the supposedly negative impacts of visitor orientation and commercialization.

As public funding for culture has come under increasing pressure in all European countries, and the market has extended its operation into areas previously considered to be exclusively in the public domain, however, the dichotomies between culture and economy and culture and tourism have been increasingly hard to maintain. The collapse of distinction between culture and economy is marked by a growing exploitation of cultural resources for commercial ends, exemplified according to Hewison (1987) by the creation of the 'heritage industry'. The heritage attractions identified by Hewison in the UK in the mid-1980s can now perhaps be seen as the precursor of a much wider commercialization of cultural resources, which is summarized in the concept of the 'cultural industries' (Wynne, 1992).

The shifting focus of cultural policy from stimulating cultural consumption to an increasing emphasis on the economic benefits of cultural production reflects the deepening economic and political crisis caused by the restructuring of the European economy during the 1980s and 1990s. The marriage of cultural and economic goals in public policy also stimulated the growth of cultural tourism, which offers the benefits not only of jobs, income and economic support for cultural production, but also the prospect of capturing visitor spending and investment originating outside the host region or country.

Economic motives have been given further prominence by a growing dissatisfaction with traditional policies for stimulating cultural participation. Many countries which engaged in policies aiming to spread cultural participation either spatially or socially (e.g. The Netherlands, Sweden, France) have now retreated to some extent from the idea of stimulating consumption through subsidy, arguing that the market provides an effective mechanism for distributing cultural services. For example, in Rotterdam, Brouwer (1993) has noted that current cultural policies are aimed not at 'decentralization of resources, but lowering of barriers to participation. This can be achieved through marketing techniques'. Art and culture are therefore becoming increasingly interchangeable with sport and tourism, as elements in an overall destination marketing mix.

European cultural policies have essentially made a virtue out of necessity in their marriage of culture and economics. Economic justifications for cultural actions were originally forced on the EU by the Treaty of Rome, but there is now a growing realization that supporting the development of the cultural industries not only helps to create jobs, but can also have an important role in supporting local and regional cultures, as well as helping to build a European identity. The development of cultural tourism, particularly in peripheral areas, has therefore been one of the key strands of both tourism policy and cultural policy in the EU.

While state provision of culture is being increasingly supplemented by the market, there is also a growing tendency for the cultural funding gap to be filled by voluntary sector organizations. This is perhaps most obvious in the area of heritage conservation, where the escalating costs of preservation, and the growing list of structures worthy of preservation produce a serious shortage of public funding. Many organizations are now trying to follow the example set by the National Trust in England, whose large membership helps to support heritage conservation, both through subscriptions and donations, and also through voluntary labour. The use of voluntary labour in culture has grown significantly in Europe in recent years, and now voluntary workers account for over two-thirds of cultural labour in Denmark and around 50% of cultural labour in The Netherlands, for example.

Not only do volunteers provide an effective subsidy for culture (which in the case of Denmark is effectively a state subsidy), they also make the cultural workforce more flexible. A more flexible workforce, including the use of more seasonal labour, is a common strategy for public sector cultural bodies trying to cope with changing market conditions, and particularly the need to reduce labour costs, which inevitably rise faster than costs in the economy in general.

While cultural tourism development has undoubtedly had a significant economic impact in Europe, there is a growing question mark over the extent to which cultural tourism policies pursued to date have achieved their cultural goals. There is no doubt that many new facilities have been provided as a result of developments linked to cultural tourism. Unless the level of cultural participation can also be effectively broadened, however, the cultural benefits of these facilities will remain largely restricted to a small segment of the population. This is particularly problematic when the needs of the cultural tourists (at least as identified by the marketeers) differ widely from those of the host population.

The broadening aims and scope of cultural tourism policy have created considerable problems of coordination for public sector agencies. The fragmentation of cultural tourism supply, covering as it does public, private and voluntary sectors, and a wide range of tourism, heritage and arts organizations, makes it hard to ensure that all sectors of the cultural tourism 'industry' are working in concert. As funding restrictions increasingly limit the ability of public sector bodies to intervene directly in the cultural tourism market, their role will increasingly be to try and coordinate the disparate elements of cultural tourism within individual regions and countries. Policy-makers will need to ensure, however, that this coordination function is not soley dictated by the predominantly economic logic of performance indicators, but that the public sector also retains a function in ensuring access to culture and promoting a climate in which cultural creativity can flourish.

Cultural tourism as a marketing tool

Cultural tourism is viewed as a means of diversifying market demand and as a solution to the problems of very diverse areas in Europe, from declining manufacturing regions in Northern England to the crowded coastal resorts of Spain. In both cases, the motive is the same – the decline of the major economic activity of the region requires new sources of income to be found. In traditional manufacturing areas, cultural tourism (or more often heritage or industrial tourism) is seen as a way of generating tourism business from scratch. For traditional tourist destinations which rely on significant tourism flows for their survival, the development of cultural tourism is often a response to the problems of tourism itself – including overcrowding, seasonality or a decline in the number of staying visitors (Gotti and Van der Borg, 1995).

At European level, cultural tourism is also viewed as a convenient marketing solution to the problems of spatial and temporal concentration of tourism. This is one of the main driving forces behind the cultural tourism development strategies supported by the European Commission, the Council of Europe and UNESCO. Cultural tourism is seen as a way of enticing tourists to as yet undiscovered regions of Europe, releasing pressure on tourist 'honeypots', particularly in the high season. The promotion of major cultural itineraries such as the Pilgrim Route to Santiago de Compostela or the Silk Route is now being accompanied by the development of 'alternative' cultural routes to ensure more even tourist distribution on a local scale in heritage cities such as Venice and Bruges (van der Borg, 1995; Van 't Zelfde, 1995). The effectiveness of such potential marketing solutions still remains to be tested. The experience with cultural routes in Savoie in France, for example, indicates that relatively small numbers of tourists are likely to take advantage of such opportunities. Given the gulf between the small number of 'specific cultural tourists' and the larger number of less dedicated cultural tourism consumers, this is perhaps not surprising. The development of cultural tourism may, therefore, provide partial, but not total solutions to these problems.

Where cultural tourism can make a major marketing contribution is in attracting more tourists from outside the EU. The ATLAS research has shown the importance of tourists from North America and the Far East, particularly in the major cultural capitals of Europe. These tourists are more likely to be motivated by cultural attractions than European tourists, and will stay longer and generate more per capita tourism expenditure. Such markets will also be important in the future as a source of first-time visitors, as the European tourism market increasingly becomes concerned with developing repeat visits from European tourists (Bos, 1994).

The evidence from the national analyses suggests that culture has been used in the past in a fairly unsophisticated way in tourism marketing. Awareness is now beginning to emerge, however, that cultural tourists do not constitute a uniform market segment, but also have disparate needs. Cultural tourism marketing strategies will need to take more heed of the divisions between general and specific cultural tourists, between first-time and repeat cultural visitors and between cultural tourists from different countries if they are to succeed. As Foley (Chapter 16 this volume) points out, it is also important to avoid conceiving cultural tourism simply as a lucrative high-spend market segment. A successful cultural tourism marketing strategy will also have to acknowledge the cultural as well as the economic goals of cultural tourism development.

Cultural events

One of the major forms of cultural tourism marketing and development undertaken throughout Europe in recent years has been the staging of a growing number of cultural events. Cultural events are often seen as a solution to the problems of product differentiation and seasonality in an increasingly competitive tourism market. Events can help to animate static cultural attractions and create specific motivations for repeat visits, visits in the low season or in non-traditional locations (Richards 1993). Such strategies have certainly been successful in the development of festival tourism in a number of locations. In The Netherlands, for example, a policy of using major cultural events to attract foreign tourists has been pursued for several years, and there are now established guidelines for developing such events (Bos, 1994).

There are some indications, however, that many festivals and special events may be losing their novelty value as far as many visitors are concerned. As Britton (1991) has pointed out, the multiplication of events and festivals places growing emphasis on novelty and spectacle as the basic motivation for attendance. In the longer term, however, events can suffer from a 'waning effect', whereby increasing levels of investment are required to generate similar visitor numbers. This pattern is already evident in some areas, particularly where there are few 'traditional' attractions to support the development and marketing of events. This has already been illustrated in the case of Glasgow, for example.

It is important, therefore, to look beyond the pure visitor impacts of such events if they are to form a sensible part of regional development strategies. More work is needed to assess the less tangible impacts of event development, such as image and investment effects and long-term tourism development. This is often difficult in an environment in which subsidies are declining and events become increasingly dependent on sponsorship and commercial income for their success. Visitor and tourist numbers then become increasingly important, and longer-term, cultural development initiatives can be lost sight of. It is clear that organizers of many major international events are becoming aware of these problems (see Hjalager, Chapter 7 this volume, for example), but it is also clear that more careful planning and execution of cultural events is required at all levels.

Location of cultural tourism consumption and production

Cultural tourism development has often been held out as a solution to the problems of economic development in the peripheral regions of Europe. This view is also supported by some theorists, who argue that cultural tourism is a typical form of postmodern tourism, distinguished by the confusion of boundaries between high and popular culture, rural and urban, and centre and periphery. Munt (1994), for example, argues that many market trends in tourism can be attributed to a search for distinction on the part of the service class. This search, he argues, leads to the development of tourism in peripheral regions, whether on the beaches or in the jungles of South East Asia, or in the countryside of Britain. Zukin (1991), however, contends that although the dissolving boundaries between high and low culture have helped to strengthen the cultural industries, the distinction between centre and periphery in cultural consumption has been heightened by the tendency for capital to accumulate in favourable locations. In the case of cultural tourism, there is clear evidence of a continuing concentration of cultural capital production and consumption in the core regions of Europe.

On a European scale, for example, countries in north-western Europe, such as France, Germany and The Netherlands, have seen cultural attendances double since 1970. In southern Europe, Greece and Italy have also experienced growth, but at around half the rate of their northern counterparts. Spatial inequality also persists within individual countries. In the UK, for example, the failure of 'new' cultural destinations to challenge the dominant position of pre-industrial cultural centres such as London, Oxford and Edinburgh (Townsend, 1992) is partly explained by a continuing concentration of tourism investment in these locations (Richards, 1996). In France, the investment flowing from the *Grand Projets* has given Paris the Pompidou Centre, with over 7 million visits a year, and helped the Louvre to double its visitor numbers in five years. The important advantage that the 'pre-industrial' sites have is the presence of sedimented real cultural capital. It is this cultural capital which is unlocked and exploited by the 'new producers' (Zukin 1991) or the 'new cultural intermediaries' (Bourdieu 1984). This key group of cultural producers and consumers is strongly represented in the centres of old cities, close to the sites of cultural consumption and real cultural capital production (Verhoeff 1994). More than any other group, they understand that with the rise of the tourist culture,

> the meaning attributed to the traditional forms of high culture has changed. What people want is a sophisticated form of recreation and entertainment, rather than the pursuit of a personal achievement.
>
> (Claval, 1993:133)

The major urban centres of Europe have become the production centres for new cultural products which combine elements of 'high' and 'popular' culture, and it is the new cultural intermediaries who are central to this process (Wynne, 1992). The ATLAS research indicates that there is a close relationship between those with cultural occupations and cultural tourism consumption. In contrast to those who seek change or rest and relaxation in their tourism consumption (Hughes, 1987) it seems that the specific cultural tourist is very often a part of the 'self-conscious critical infrastructure' (Zukin, 1991) or the organized cultural system (Bevers, 1993), and is engaging in tourism consumption as an extension of their productive activities. It may well be that the increasing scarcity, and therefore value, of work is having the effect of blurring the distinctions between work and leisure for these groups (Gratton, 1995). Cultural tourism as a leisure practice may no longer provide sufficient grounds for distinctive consumption practices, unless it can also be linked to the distinctions imparted by cultural employment. Given the urban base of the 'cultural industries', the metropolitan focus of cultural tourism consumption and production may well increase rather than decrease in future (Richards, 1996).

TRENDS FOR THE FUTURE

Prospects for future growth

The enthusiasm of European policy-makers for cultural tourism certainly indicates great confidence in the future. Cultural tourism policies are being developed at all levels from the European Union down to local authorities, and in a wide variety of contexts. This apparent optimism is based in some cases on a lack of alternatives to cultural tourism development, but in most cases there is a conviction that cultural tourism will continue to grow in Europe. As Middleton (1989) has suggested, there seems to be a general belief in the motivating power of heritage and culture, which is supported by a lot of assertion, but few hard facts.

The evidence collected by the ATLAS Cultural Tourism Research Project indicates that cultural tourism has grown steadily over the last 20 years in response to a widening interest in culture and the general growth in tourism consumption. It seems that rising education levels have been the major engine for growth in cultural participation in general, and cultural tourism in particular. The expansion of higher education participation in northern Europe has been particularly influential in this process. On a European level, it is likely that participation in higher education will continue to grow, as living standards rise in southern and eastern Europe. In the longer term, therefore, a degree of convergence in cultural tourism participation should occur across Europe, as access to the necessary cultural competence and economic means is more evenly spread geographically. This equalization is likely to be hastened by cuts in higher education and cultural funding in many northern European countries. Spatial equalization between European nations is, however, likely to be accompanied by increasing social divergence in demand, as inequality replaces equality as the engine for cultural tourism growth (Long and Richards, 1995). The consequences of this shift are likely to include a growing segmentation of cultural tourism demand.

A shift is likely in the major source markets for cultural tourism in Europe. The ATLAS surveys have already indicated the high level of cultural motivation among tourists from southern Europe, particularly Italy and Spain. These countries are likely to become even more important in future, as the total number of tourists and the proportion of cultural tourists rise. In the longer term, there should also be a substantial growth in cultural tourism from

Eastern Europe, as visitors from these countries seek to consume the major cultural sites of Western Europe. The high level of cultural attraction visitation by first-time visitors to European countries will also hasten this process. As new visitor markets in Eastern Europe and Asia open up, these will be the most eager consumers of traditional cultural attractions. For the repeat visitor and the 'general cultural tourist', the need for authentic cultural experiences will be less pressing. For these visitors, the combination of learning and entertainment, high and popular culture, tradition and innovation will probably be most appealing.

Globalization and localization

The dialectical opposition between the forces of globalization and localization will play an even more crucial role in the development of cultural tourism in the future. On the one hand, the spread of a global culture will make elements of European culture accessible to a wider audience, both through the development of tourism and the media. One the other hand, resistance to the erosion of local identities implied by globalization will stimulate increasing use of culture as a means of local differentiation, and thus as a means of tourism development and marketing.

The globalization of the cultural tourism market has already been noted in audience research at cultural attractions across Europe. As Ashworth (1992) has pointed out, the dilemma for regions and localities wishing to tap into this globalized market is that the cultural competence of such tourists is fairly generalized. American and Japanese tourists visiting Europe, for example, are often aware of the main currents of European culture, but are not in a position to interpret or appreciate the complexities of regional or local cultural differences. It is therefore very difficult to market local cultural products to globalized cultural tourists, because the essential cultural links are missing.

This problem is seen most clearly in the smaller European countries, which often find it difficult to establish a cultural identity in the minds of tourists from outside Europe. In Denmark, as Hjalager (Chapter 7 this volume) has pointed out, it is easier to attract visitors to an exhibition of paintings by a well-known foreign artist than to an exhibition by a Danish artist. The same problem emerged recently in The Netherlands, where a major exhibition by the Dutch artist Mondriaan was organized in The Hague in 1995. The exhibition aimed to attract over 300,000 visitors, but eventually only managed to draw 185,000, the vast majority from within The Netherlands. Research on a different Mondriaan exhibition by Roetman (1994) indicated that one problem was that a relatively high degree of cultural capital was required to appreciate the abstract style of Mondriaan, and that this cultural capital was usually limited to Dutch visitors. A second problem was the location of the exhibition in The Hague, away from the more globalized, high profile attractions of Amsterdam.

This problem of linking into globalized cultural networks is likely to become even more acute in future, as the number of competing cultural products grows. Andersson (1987) for example, has linked the success of international arts festivals to the growth of the 'information society'. Those festivals able to plug into international information networks will be likely to succeed in attracting visitors, and therefore commercial support. Other events will come to depend increasingly on subsidy, and will eventually die out as public sector funding dries up. Such developments, Andersson argues, will lead to the creation of 'reticulate societies', metropolitan regions which combine competence, culture, communication and creativity, and will therefore be able to capture an increasing share of cultural activity, and the productive benefits associated with this. Therefore, cultural tourism will be increasingly concentrated in the metropolitan core of Europe, at the expense of the periphery.

This may be an extreme scenario, but it makes the point that all regions and localities will need to forge links between their local cultural base and mainstream global cultures. The growth of the cultural industries in some formerly culturally peripheral regions, such as the North of England (Wynne, 1992) or Northern Spain (Gonzalez, 1993) indicates that such links may be possible. At present, however, the cultural industries developments have been restricted largely to major urban centres with sufficient local populations to support widespread cultural activities. In the future, new solutions will have to be found to bridge the gap between urban and rural areas.

New technology, media and innovation

One of the trends often cited to support the argument that interest in cultural tourism is growing, is the increasing number of television programmes dedicated to cultural heritage. In The Netherlands, heritage television programmes have had a major role in widening awareness of, and interest in cultural heritage (Richards, Chapter 13 this volume). However, as with many other cultural forms popularized on television, such as opera or ballet, the proportion of television viewers who actually participate in these activities is relatively small.

Cultural attractions are increasingly trying to activate the currently passive impact of television and other media through the introduction of new media into the attractions themselves. The animation techniques pioneered by attractions such as the Jorvik Centre in York (UK) are now being joined by more sophisticated uses of interactive media to animate and activate static cultural attractions. Such developments will be of particular importance in two contexts. The first is in attractions where cultural artefacts are missing or need to be reconstructed. At archaeological sites, for example, three-dimensional reconstructions of buildings can be displayed interactively, allowing visitors to view the reconstructions from different angles, and perhaps even try out various 'what if' reconstructions of their own.

A second application for new technology is in attacking the problem of rising labour costs in the cultural sector. Most cultural attractions are fairly labour-intensive and, as was pointed out in Chapter 4, labour costs in the sector inevitably increase faster than costs in the economy as a whole. The use of voluntary labour, stimulated by the combination of rising unemployment and falling subsidies during the 1980s, is likely to prove a temporary fix, since the demands of commercialization in the cultural sector will actually require a greater degree of professionalization. Capital investment in labour-saving technology may at first sight seem an unlikely prospect, but the chances of attracting commercial sponsorship for such new developments are much greater than those of attracting subsidies to cover growing personnel costs. We are therefore likely to increasingly see information staff being replaced by touch-screen displays, and human animateurs by robotics.

New technology may also help cultural attractions cope with the increasing diversity of the cultural audience. In the past, cultural visitors were happy to accept the products offered to them. Today, visitors are increasingly able and willing to challenge and extend the meanings of cultural products, and this creates a need for increased diversity in cultural attractions. One means of achieving this is to use new technology to provide interpretations of cultural products aimed at specific user groups. In Europe, a particularly useful application of such technology may include the provision of interpretations in a wide range of languages, making European, national and regional culture more accessible to a global audience. A further development will almost certainly be into greater use of visual display, replacing the predominantly text-based forms of interpretation which have often constrained the cultural audience in the past (Merriman, 1991). Perhaps such developments will challenge the dominance of the existing 'high culture' based 'cultural capitals', with their dependence on text-based resources (Claval, 1993).

As Hjalager (Chapter 7 this volume) has suggested, the development of innovation systems will be particularly important in the future development of cultural tourism. To date, innovation has come mainly from the commercial sector, and mainly in the area of marketing. The product development strategies of Studiosus, for example, indicate that new markets can be created by the innovative development and marketing of cultural tourism products for specific groups (Roth and Langemeyer, Chapter 9 this volume). There are signs, however, that marketing techniques applied in the commercial sector are beginning to have a greater influence, as evidenced by the use of information technology to market art cities in Europe (Art Cities in Europe, 1995).

Policy development

The growing integration of cultural and economic policies mentioned earlier in this chapter is perhaps the precursor of a wider policy integration affecting the area of cultural tourism. As the new EU cultural programme Raphaël indicates, culture is not only viewed as an important source of economic development, but also as a means of building social cohesion and local identities. Similar broad perspectives on cultural development are being adopted by the Council of Europe, some national governments and many local governments (Corijn and Mommaas, 1995).

Such policy perspectives also recognize the changing nature of cultural consumption in Europe. With people increasingly utilizing their consumption power to shape their own identities, the ability of policy-makers to determine the forms of culture to be consumed is limited. The role of government is being reformed into that of an enabling body – the 'flexible state' (Henry, 1993) which seems happy to cede ground to the market in the spheres of culture and tourism. The extent to which the reduction of state funding also represents a willingness to relinquish state control of cultural policy is, however, called into question by a number of developments noted in this volume. In many countries it seems that the linking of funding to performance indicators will actually increase the level of state control over the content of cultural programmes, whereas in the past cultural institutions have enjoyed relative autonomy in this area (Richards, Chapter 13 this volume). There exists a danger that cultural tourism will come to be seen by many policy-makers as a convenient way of boosting visiting numbers, and thereby ensuring that cultural attractions reach a 'wider' audience.

Cultural tourism is certainly an attractive proposition from such a viewpoint, because it also offers the potential for supplementing cultural funding from the state through market mechanisms. As the current study has indicated, however, the cultural tourism market is polarized between those interested in specific forms of cultural consumption, and those for whom culture is one part of a broader leisure experience. Although the former audience (the 'specific cultural tourist') is most often targeted in cultural tourism marketing plans, it must be recognized that the size of this audience is limited, and that it is being fragmented across a growing number of competing cultural attractions. The key management task for most cultural attractions in Europe will therefore be reconciling the needs of these two basic types of cultural tourist. This will mean an increasing emphasis on combining education and entertainment, 'high' and 'popular' culture, and specialist and mass consumers. The prime need for cultural institutions will be to build the partnerships necessary to achieve this without compromising aesthetic integrity.

Popular culture is already becoming one of the major growth areas in cultural tourism. Many elements of popular entertainment are increasingly being woven into the cultural products offered to tourists (Hughes and Benn, 1994), and the initiatives in the UK and Ireland to use pop music as a 'cultural' attraction also seem likely to spread to other areas of Europe. Such new cultural tourism strategies will probably be based increasingly around events and festivals rather than static cultural attractions. Care will need to be exercised in the development of such event-based strategies, however, particularly as large-scale events likely to attract foreign tourists also require significant investment. Given the evidence that the impact of cultural events is likely to be relatively short-lived, event locations may find themselves locked into a competitive investment spiral from which it can be difficult to escape.

CONCLUSIONS

There is little doubt that cultural tourism has made a major contribution to the expansion of European tourism demand and supply in recent decades, and this contribution is likely to grow still further in future. Cultural tourism has been important in the expansion of cultural facilities, in the growth of tourism employment, and in the development of pan-European tourism and cultural policies. As Jan van der Borg has commented, however, (Chapter 12 this volume) 'having heritage is one thing, using it another'. In the past, cultural resources and the cultural tourist have largely been taken for granted, and this will have to change if the full advantages offered by cultural tourism development are to be realized. In particular, the growing segmentation of cultural tourism supply and demand requires that we stop referring to 'the cultural tourist', and start thinking about the diverse kinds of cultural tourism consumption which exist in Europe.

The prospects for a diverse European cultural tourism industry seem bright. In particular, Europe has access to an accumulation of 'real cultural capital' which, as Scitovsky (1976) has pointed out, is far in excess of that in North America, the major source market for incoming cultural tourists. In order to maintain this competitive advantage in the global tourism market, however, Europe will not only have to make effective use of traditional European culture, but will also have to extend her capacity to develop new cultural products from the stream of contemporary global culture, including popular culture from America, Japan and elsewhere. In this way, perhaps the marriage of economic and cultural policy desired by the European Union, and recognized in retrospect by Jean Monnet, may be successful.

REFERENCES

Andersson, A. (1987) *Culture, Creativity and Economic Development in a Regional Context*. Council of Europe Press, Strasbourg.

Art Cities in Europe (1995) *Cities Brochure*. Art Cities in Europe, Constance.

Ashworth, G.J. (1992) Heritage and tourism: an argument, two problems and three solutions. In: Fleischer-van Rooijen, C.A.M. (ed.) *Spatial Implications of Tourism*. Geo Pers, Groningen, pp. 95–104.

Bevers, T. (1993) *Georganiseerd Cultuur*. Dick Coutinho, Bussum.

Bos, H. (1994) The importance of mega-events in the development of tourism demand. *Festival Management and Event Tourism* 2, 55–58.

Bourdieu, P. (1984) *Distinction: a Social Critique of the Judgment of Taste*. Routledge & Kegan Paul, London.

Britton, S. (1991) Tourism, capital and place: towards a critical geography of tourism. *Environment and Planning D: Society and Space* 9, 451–478.

Brouwer, R. (1993) Het nieuwe Rotterdam: de kunst, het beleid, de zorg en de markt. *Vrijetijd en Samenleving* 11, 31–43.

Buzard, J. (1993) *The Beaten Track: European Tourism, Literature and the Ways to 'Culture' 1800–1918*. Oxford University Press, Oxford.

Claval, P. (1993) The cultural dimension in restructuring metropolises: the Amsterdam example. In: Deben, L., Heinemeijer, W. and van der Vaart, D. (eds) *Understanding Amsterdam*. Het Spinhuis, Amsterdam, pp. 111–139.

Corijn, E. and Mommaas, H. (1995) *Urban Cultural Policy Developments in Europe*. Council of Europe, Strasbourg.

European Travel Commission (1994) *Annual Report*. ETC, Paris.

European Travel Commission (1995) *Europe's Youth Travel Market*. ETC, Paris.

Gonzalez, J. (1993) Bilbao: culture, citizenship and quality of life. In: Bianchini, F. and Parkinson, M. (1993) *Cultural Policy and Urban Regeneration: the West European Experience*. Manchester University Press, Manchester, pp. 73–89.

Gotti, G. and van der Borg, J. (1995) Tourism in heritage cities. *Quaderni CISET*, 11/95.

Gratton, C. (1992) A perspective on European leisure markets. Paper presented at LSA/VVS Internationalisation and Leisure Research Conference, Tilburg, The Netherlands.

Gratton, C. (1995) A cross-national/transnational approach to leisure research: The changing relationship between work and leisure in Europe. In: Richards, G. (ed.) *European Tourism and Leisure Education: Trends and Prospects*. Tilburg University Press, Tilburg, pp. 215–232.

Henry, I.P. (1993) *The Politics of Leisure Policy*. Macmillan, Basingstoke.

Hewison, R. (1987) *The Heritage Industry: Britain in a Climate of Decline*. Methuen, London.

Hughes, H. (1987) Tourism and the arts: a potentially destructive relationship? *Tourism Management* 10, 97–99.

Hughes, H.L. and Benn, D. (1994) Entertainment: its role in the tourist industry. Paper presented at the Leisure Studies Association annual conference, Glasgow.

Irish Tourist Board (1988) *Inventory of Cultural Tourism Resources in the Member States and Assessment of Methods Used to Promote Them*. European Commission DG VII, Brussels.

Janiske, R.L. (1994) Some macroscale growth trends in America's community festival industry. *Festival Management and Event Tourism* 2, 10–14.

Knulst, W. (1989) *Van Vaudeville tot Video*. Sociale en Cultureel Planbureau, Rijswijk.

Long, J. and Richards, G. (1995) *European tourism: changing economic and cultural dimensions of tourism in a unifying Europe*. Paper presented at the European Leisure Studies Group Winter University, Bilbao, April.

Merriman, N. (1991) *Beyond the Glass Case: The Past, the Heritage and The Public in Britain*. Leicester University Press, Leicester.

Middleton, V. (1989) Marketing implications for attractions. *Tourism Management* 10, 229–234.

Munt, I. (1994) The 'other' postmodern tourism: culture, travel and the new middle classes. *Theory, Culture and Society* 11, 101–123.

Myerscough, J. (1988) *The Economic Importance of the Arts*. Policy Studies Institute, London.

Narhsted, W. (1993) Von der Kulturreise zur Reisekultur? *FVW International* 1/93, 25–26.

Richards, W.S. (1993) *How to Market Tourist Attractions, Festivals and Events*. Longman, London.

Richards, G. (1996) Production and consumption of cultural tourism in Europe. *Annals of Tourism Research* 23 (in press).

Roetman, E.E. (1994) *Motivatie in Retrospectief: een Onderzoek Naar Motivatie Voor Cultuuroerisme Tijdens de Mondriaantentoonstelling te Amsterdam*. Masters dissertation, Tilburg University.

Rojek, C. (1993) *Ways of Escape: Modern Transformations in Leisure and Travel*. Macmillan, Basingstoke.

Schouten, F. (1995) Improving visitor care in heritage attractions. *Tourism Management* 16, 259–264.

Schuster, J.M.D. (1993) The public interest in the art museum's public. In: Gubbels, T. and Hemel, A. (eds) *Art Museums and the Price of Success: an International Comparison*. Boekmanstichting, Amsterdam, pp. 45–60.

Scitovsky, T. (1976) *The Joyless Economy*. Oxford University Press, Oxford.

Seaton, A.V. (1992) Social stratification in tourism choice and experience since the war. *Tourism Management* 13, 106–111.

Spitz, S. and Breitenbach, O. (1994) Germans prize 'indispensible' annual holidays away. *FVW International – Travel Market Germany* 2/94, 1–2.

Tourism Research and Marketing (1994) *Theme Parks: UK and International Markets*. TRAM, London.

Townsend, A.R. (1992) The attractions of urban areas. *Tourism Recreation Research* 17, 24–32.

Urry, J. (1990) *The Tourist Gaze: Leisure and Travel in Contemporary Societies*. Sage, London.

van der Borg, J. (1995) *Alternative Tourism Routes in Cities of Art*. UNESCO-ROSTE Technical Report no. 23.

Van 't Zelfde, J. (1995) *Europees Toerisme in een Ander Perspectief: een Studie naar de Ontwikkeling van Alternatieve Toeristische Routes in en Tussen Europees Kunststeden*. MA Thesis, Tilburg University, Tilburg.

Verhoeff, R. (1994) High culture: the performing arts and its audience in the Netherlands. *Tijdschrift voor Economische en Sociale Geografie* 85, 79–83.

Walsh, K. (1991) *The Representation of the Past: Museums and Heritage in the Post-modern World*. Routledge, London.

Wynne, D. (1992) *The Culture Industry*. Avebury, Aldershot.

Zukin, S. (1991) *Landscapes of Power: from Detroit to Disney World*. University of California Press, Berkeley.

Index

Acropolis, the   94, 98, 183, 184, 185,
   187
Admission
   income   134, 211, 222, 239, 294,
      296, 302–303
   prices   75, 211, 222, 228, 239,
      274, 296
Adolf, S.   28
Age of cultural tourists   35, 55, 135,
      154, 167, 173, 207, 224, 241,
      254, 272, 292, 316
Agrotourism   89
Algarve   252
Almegaard, J.   142
Alps, the   159–163
Altes Museum, Berlin   9, 168, 173
American tourists   63, 188, 205, 207,
      241, 326, 330
Amsterdam   27, 32, 52, 56, 57, 77, 91,
      95, 236, 243–245
Andersson, A.   327
Andreasen, L.B.   134
Angioni, M.
Animation   157, 159, 161
Antwerp   28, 29, 65, 119–120, 124

Archaeological sites   183, 184, 185,
      186, 328
Architectural heritage   99, 101
Areitio, T.   272
Art
   cities   116–119, 217, 223, 328
   galleries   40, 192–194
   performing arts   40, 49, 60–61,
      81, 123, 239, 242, 288, 292,
      297, 307
   visual arts   189, 307
   see also Festivals
Art Cities in Europe   90, 328
ARTE (DK)   132
Arts Council of Great Britain (UK)   93,
      284, 305
Arts tourism   26, 71, 81, 93, 163, 286,
      305
Ashworth, G.J.   12, 31, 38, 64, 102,
      141, 326
Asia   4, 326
Athens   27, 94, 184, 185, 187,
      192–194
ATLAS (European Association for
      Tourism and Leisure
      Education)   24

ATLAS *contd*
  ATLAS research   32–39, 52, 53,
    55, 62, 154, 168–169,
    187–189, 207–208, 254–255,
    272–273, 291–293
Attractions
  cultural   4, 13, 22, 32, 36, 39, 40,
    41, 109–115, 150–152
  supply of *see* individual country
    entries
  typologies of cultural attractions
    22, 110, 256, 278
  visitor numbers   42, 60, 61, 135,
    152–153, 186, 289, 293, 315
Audience, cultural   31, 149, 234, 240,
    236, 324
Austria   178
Authenticity   21, 61, 63, 65, 122, 123,
    142, 280, 313
  emergent   21, 65
  staged   142, 192
Avila   272, 273

Baroque
  art   159
  architecture   264
  routes   159–163
Basque Region   66
Bauer, M.   161
Belgium   109–126
  cultural attractions   109–114
  cultural tourism policy   117–118
  demand for cultural tourism
    115–117
  management and marketing
    120–123
  product development   114–115
Benn, D.   26
Berlin   27, 91, 168–169, 174
Bernadini, G.   3
Berroll, E.   55, 62
Bevers, T.   13, 47, 49, 53, 56, 73, 84,
    236, 237, 315, 324
Bianchini, F.   60, 74, 79–80, 84, 89, 90
Bilbao   272
Bildungreisen see Study Tours
Birmingham   91

Boerjan, P.   117, 120, 121, 123
Boniface, P.   32, 298
Bonink, C.   22, 32, 33, 35, 39, 53,
    73, 74, 92, 100, 130, 234, 240,
    291
Boorstin, D.   6
Bord Failte (IRL)   200, 202, 204
  see also Irish Tourist Board
Borromée, C.   160
Bos, H.   238, 244, 322, 323
Bourdieu, P.   34, 48–49, 51, 52, 56,
    62, 152, 314, 324
Bourgeoisie   56, 62
  bourgeois notions of culture   6
Boyle, M.   28, 30, 65, 103
Bradford   64
Breitenbach, O.   317
Brent-Ritchie, J.R.   4
Briassoulis, H.   192
British Museum   94
British Tourist Authority (UK)   40, 41,
    93, 286, 290, 293
Brittany   156
Britton, S.   13, 61, 65, 323
Brouwer, R.   13, 236, 320
Bruges   59, 117, 120–123
Bruin, K.   52, 91, 238
Bruno, G.   151
Brussels   90, 116
Buckingham Palace   286
Buckley, P.J.   39, 186
Burgos   25
Butler, R.W.   64
Buzard, J.   60
Bywater, M.   24, 32, 62

Calvinism   198
Calvinist cities   57
Capacity constraints   121, 227, 290
Capital
  accumulation   57
  cities   59
Cardiff   90
Catholic Church   269
Catholicism   198
Cats (the musical)   60, 170–171
Celtic culture   197–199, 313

Centraal Bureau voor de Statistiek (NL)
      49, 236, 237, 239, 240, 241
Centres Culturel Scientifique et Industriel
      (F)   159
Cerclet, D.   160
Chateau de Blois   154
Chazaud, P.   153
Chiado (Lisbon)   98
Chios   185
Cities   88–89
      declining   79–80, 90
      see also Urban tourism
City of Culture event see European,
      Cultural Capital event
Claeys, U.   118
Clark, J.   21
Class see Social, class
Claval, P.   57, 60, 324, 328
CLIO (F)   155
Cluny, l'abbaye de   154
Coach tours   176
Coalter, F.   88
Cogneau, D.   52
Cohen, E.   21, 65
Commercial income   73, 75, 294–296
Commercialization   75–76, 93
Commodification   65, 103, 192, 298,
      302, 305, 308
Community Action Plan for Tourism   97
Consumption see Cultural, consumption
Cook, Thomas   7, 250
Coopers and Lybrand Deloitte   84
Copenhagen
      Cultural Capital   28, 29, 137–141
Cordoba   272–273
Corijn, E.   3, 27, 28, 65, 91, 103, 329
Costa, P.   66, 227
Council of Europe   99–101, 149, 150,
      153, 278
Croizé, J.C.   156
Crompton, J.   24
Cultural
      audience   13, 152, 170
      Capital
         of individuals   38, 48–49, 237,
            314, 316
         'real' cultural capital   29, 49–50,
            60, 62, 84, 312, 330

Capitals   59, 60, 80, 84, 273, 322,
      328
      see also European, Cultural Capital
      event
consumption   3, 12, 49, 50, 152,
      153, 273, 289, 312
democracy   99, 283
      see also Democratization of culture
heritage   100, 147, 149, 215,
      267, 269
      see also Heritage
industries   13, 37, 53, 76–77,
      312, 319, 324, 325, 327
infrastructure   130, 31–132
intermediaries   54, 56, 62, 162,
      324
itineraries see Cultural, routes
policy see Policy, cultural and
      individual country entries
production   8–12, 21, 22
routes   93, 98, 100, 112, 123,
      156, 159–163, 225, 228, 270,
      272, 276, 277, 322
superstructure   130
tourism
      causes of growth   5–8, 47,
         50–55, 311–312
      changing nature of   24–31
      definitions of   19–24, 35, 197,
         249
      demand   39, 41, 315–317
         see also individual country
         entries
      significance of   31–32
         see also Impact
tourists
      motivation of   24, 25, 34, 35, 38,
         39, 40, 55, 64, 102, 136, 168,
         169, 186, 193, 207, 215, 225,
         240, 242, 253–254, 267, 271,
         286–287, 288, 297, 314, 317
      profiles of   32–39, 62, 154,
         167–8, 207–208, 223–225,
         241–242, 271–273
Culture
      and tourism, convergence of
         12–14
      definitions of   20–21, 197

Culture *contd*
    spreading   127, 149, 237, 320
    see also High culture; Popular
        culture

Daman, F.J.   118, 124
DANDATA (DK)   131
Danmarks Turistråd (DK)   136, 137
Danmarks Statistik (DK)   135, 136
Darbel, A.   34, 48
Darvill, T.   99, 101
Davies, L.   55
Davies, S.   290
De Groote, P.   115
De Nicolay, R.   150
De Miguel, A.   276
De Lannoy, W.   120, 122, 123
De Roux, E.   149
Delaney, F.   199
Democratization of culture   9, 63, 149,
    283
Denmark   28, 29, 74, 93, 127–145
    cultural policy   127–128
    cultural tourism
        demand   135–137
        policy   128–130
        supply   130–134
    see also Copenhagen
Department of National Heritage (UK)
    295
Department of Tourism and Trade (IRL)
    200–203
Depondt, P.   63
Deutsche Zentrale für Tourismus (D)
    166, 175
Development *see* Regional development;
    Tourism development
Di Battista, M.   226
Direcção-Geral de Turismo (P)   256,
    257
Dirección General de Política Turística
    (E)   270, 272, 278, 279
Disneyfication   63, 148, 149, 302
    Disneyland Paris   149
Donat, O.   52
Donatos, G.   185
Dublin   28

Dubrovnik   101
Duelund, P.   127
Dunford, M.   57
DZT *see* Deutsche Zentrale für Tourismus

Eastern Europe   4, 42, 318, 326
    see also Germany, East
Eckstein, J.   11, 296
Ecomuseums   159
Economic
    development   29, 30, 71, 79, 83,
        88–89, 197, 251, 323
    impact   28–29, 77, 79–84, 236,
        244, 250, 257, 278–279,
        297–298, 320, 323
    restructuring   89
ECTARC (UK)   22, 185
Edinburgh   80–83, 297, 298–305
    Castle   298–305
    Festival   80–83, 297
Education
    influence on cultural tourism
        consumption   48, 49, 51–52,
        152, 167, 208, 224, 316,
        325
    education and training for cultural
        tourism   210, 227, 262, 301
Eiglier, P.   155
Elgin Marbles   94–95
Employment
    cultural   37, 53, 77
    impact of cultural tourism   82,
        210, 236, 257, 297–298, 330
    see also Human resources
England *see* United Kingdom
English Heritage (UK)   75, 284, 294,
    295
English Tourist Board (UK)   60, 284,
    285, 305
ENIT (IT)   221
Epidaurus Festival   187
Errington, F.   48
Ethnic tourism   23
Europalia   113, 116
European
    Commission   27, 90, 96–99, 225,
        316

DGX (Culture)   99, 191
DGXVI (Regional Policy)   99, 192
DGXXIII (Tourism)   32, 98, 225
Raphaël Programme   97, 329
see also European Regional
   Development Fund
Cultural Capital event   27–31, 65,
   80, 96, 103, 119–120,
   137–141, 191, 255, 276
   impact of   28–30
   typology of   28–29
culture   9, 11, 30, 95, 98, 100,
   102, 216, 261, 318
Regional Development Fund
   (ERDF)   99, 202, 210, 216
Social Fund (ESF)   202
Tourism Year (ETY)   97
Travel Commission (ETC)   40, 55,
   102, 312, 316
Union (EU)   3, 92, 95–99, 311,
   320, 330
Events
   arts   113, 291
   cultural   61, 90, 112, 119–120,
      157–158, 238, 270, 275, 291,
      293, 322–323
   special   172, 238, 244, 271, 276
   see also Exhibitions
Exhibitions   157, 158, 210, 227, 228,
   243–244
   'blockbuster' exhibitions   61, 90,
      238, 245
Expenditure *see* Public expenditure

Faché, W.   36, 54
FACIM (F)   161–162
FAIAT (IT)   224
Falkowska, M.   42
Fanelli, F.   3
Faucheur, P.   153
Feasts   113, 158, 192
Featherstone, M.   56
Fédération Nationale des Comités des
      Fêtes (F)   158
Feifer, M.   5
Feist, A.   73
Fernandez Fuster, L.   268

Fessy, E.   148
Festivals   83, 90–91, 113, 157, 166,
      171, 179–180, 187, 189, 203,
      275, 276, 286, 291, 293, 297,
      323
   arts   91, 295, 297
   community   9, 319
   folk   113, 158
   see also Athens; Edinburgh;
      Epidaurus; Feasts
Festival of Arts and Culture (UK)   285,
      306
Finance *see* Investment; Public
      expenditure; Sponsorship
Fisher, R.   99
Flanders   59, 110 *see also* Belgium
Florence   25, 27
Folk
   festivals   113, 158
   museums   209, 210
Folklore   190
Fowler, P.J.   32
Framke, W.   131, 133
France   5, 12, 48, 59, 77, 147–164
   cultural
      policy   149–150
      tourism demand   152–155
      tourism supply   150–152
      managment of cultural tourism
         155–163
   see also Grands Projets; Paris
French Revolution   8, 158
Frey, B.S.   72, 133
Friesland   93, 235
Funding
   cultural, in Europe   72–74
   see also Lotteries; Public
      expenditure; Sponsorship
FUTURES   270

Gachet, L.J   161
Ganzeboom, H.   48, 49
Gastronomy   112, 147
GEATTE (F)   24, 136, 278
Gender   167, 173
Germany   5, 26, 42, 77, 88, 92, 135,
      165–181, 317

Germany *contd*
   cultural tourism
      demand   167–174
      policy   166–167
      supply   174–180
      East   166–167, 172, 174
Gewertz, D.   48
Glasgow   27–28, 30, 65, 80, 83
Globalization   31, 62, 63–64, 91, 95,
      103, 168, 313, 326–327
Goeldner, R.   22
Goethe-Institut (D)   166
Gonzalez, J.   327
Gotti, G.   321
Government
   policy *see* Policy
   expenditure *see* Public expenditure
Grahn, P.   66
Grand Tour   5–6, 7, 158, 169
   definition of   5
Grands Projets   75, 147, 148, 324
Gratton, C.   36, 54, 82, 243, 244, 313,
      317, 324
Gray, C.   51, 74
Greece   94–95, 183–195, 316
   cultural tourism
      demand   185–189
      policy   189–192
      supply   184–185
      impact of tourism   192
   see also Athens
Greek National Tourist Office (G)   190
Greenwood, D.J.   66
Groen, J.   12
Grundtvig, N.   127
   Grundtviganism   127, 130
Guides   161, 176–178, 301–302
Guides Hachette   159

Habitus   48, 152, 316
Hall, C.M.   32, 65
Hamburg   171
Hannerz, U.   63
Harvey, D.   12, 49, 50, 57, 90, 103
Havas (F)   162, 163
Heilbrun, J.   51, 74
Henry, I.P.   87, 91, 329

Heritage   10, 37, 61, 88, 185, 230,
      234–235, 251, 287, 298, 330
   attractions   40, 53, 218, 287
     see also Attractions
   industries   13, 311, 314, 319
   national   94–95
   preservation   122, 190, 191, 213,
      239, 251, 254, 259, 269, 279,
      298, 320
Hermitage, the   95
Hernando, F.L.   100
Hewison, R.   13, 88, 318, 319
Hibbert, C.   5
High culture   21, 24, 26, 60, 61, 92,
      100, 152, 170, 250, 283
   relationship to popular culture   11,
      60, 152, 170, 283, 285, 307,
      312, 314, 323
   see also Popular culture
Hillman, H.   166
Historic
   buildings *see* Attractions
   monuments *see* Monuments
   Scotland (UK)   295, 298–299
Hjalager, A-M.   132, 141
Holidays
   package   7, 115, 142, 188, 226
   paid   7, 54, 157
Holland *see* Netherlands
Holloway, J.C.   20
Horne, D.   6
Hørup, I.   135
Hotels   190, 223, 242, 252, 257, 259,
      261
Hughes, G.   28, 30, 65, 103
Hughes, H.   26, 37, 324, 330
Hugot, J.P.   150
Human resources   133, 193, 203, 209,
      210, 220, 227, 229, 239, 245,
      300–302, 306–307
Hungary   42
Hut, A.   112
Hutchison, R.   73

ICARE (I)   226, 227
Identity   100, 184, 264, 329
Ikarus Reisen (D)   177

Image   118, 179, 287, 318
Impact
    of tourism on cultural heritage
        183, 279, 298
    of tourism on culture   64–66
Income, sources of   75, 239, 294, 295,
        302–303
    see also Admission, income
Industrial
    archaeology   110
    heritage   159
    Revolution   110
    tourism   14, 159
Information systems   140–141, 227,
        327
Innovation   97, 132, 141–144, 177,
        327–328
International Council on Museums and
        Sites (ICOMOS)   12
Investment   60, 83, 190, 201, 203,
        210, 235, 259, 261
Interpretation   162, 212, 213, 227, 302
Ireland   77, 92, 194–214
    cultural tourism
        demand   204–208
        policy   200–201
        supply   201–204
Irish Tourist Board (IRL)   24, 30, 35,
        57, 183, 184, 185, 316
Italy   5, 14, 57, 59, 74, 215–231, 315
    cultural tourism
        demand   220–225, 230
        management of   227–230
        policy   225–226, 230
        supply   216–220
    see also Florence

Janiske, R.L.   91, 319
Jansen-Verbeke, M.   122, 123
Januarius, M.   32
Japanese tourists   40, 241, 304, 326
Joustra, H.G.   235
Jung, B.   42, 172

Karsholt, E.   134
Kerry   208–212

Kilian, K.   245
King Baudouin Foundation (B)   124,
        125
Klein, H.-J.   173
Klingenstein (D)   177
Knops, G.   124
Knossos   184
Knulst, W.   49, 237, 240, 316
Kommunernes Landsforening (DK)   133
Kopachevsky, J.P.   65
Koprowska, T.   42
Kulturministeriet (DK)   133, 134

Landscapes, cultural   101
Lang, J.   149
Langeard, E.   155
Langsted, J.   128
Language   203, 242, 283, 288, 292,
        302, 306, 328
Lapland   66
Lascaux   156
Law, C.M.   8, 54
LEADER Programme   277
Leisure time   9, 54, 100, 317
Length of stay   37, 206, 207, 242,
        254–255
Lettl-Schröder, M.   169
Linder, S.B.   51
Lisbon   28, 255, 277
Local policy   235–236
Localization   30, 62, 63–64, 326–327
London   77, 79, 80, 91, 286, 287, 288,
        291, 292, 297, 307
Long, J.   63, 97, 325
Lotteries   88, 191, 193, 202, 285
Louvain   113
Louvre, the   8, 147, 155
Lowenthal, D.   10
Lundwall, B.-Å.   144
Luxemburg   28
Lynch, K.   57
Lyotard, J.F.   147

Maastricht   95
    Treaty (Treaty on European
        Union)   98

MacCannell, D.   6, 21, 22, 25
MacDonald, G.F.   11
MacIntosh, R.W.   22
MacNulty, P.   78, 205, 207
Madrid   28, 271, 273, 276
Maiztegui, C.   272
Mallorca   63
Malraux, A.   149
Management   137–141, 156,
         161–162, 209, 300–305
    visitor   121–123, 156, 212, 227,
         302, 304
Manchester   90
Maraite, J.   180–181
Marchena Gomez, M.J.   275
Marco Polo Reisen (D)   177
Market
    segmentation   7, 304
    size   31
    trends   12
Marketing   137–141, 161–162, 175,
         177–178, 179, 203, 21,
         262–264, 286, 303–304, 306,
         321–322, 328
    city   89
    policy   118–119, 236
Marlasca, O.   269
Mass tourism   12, 148, 156, 267, 279
Mata Hari Museum   11
Mathieson, A.   7, 64
McKenna, M.   208
Media
    multi-media   143, 302
    television   240, 327–328
Mediterranean   185, 216, 251, 275,
         278, 279, 318
Meiers Weltreisen (D)   177
Melegati, L.   101
Mercouri, Melina   27, 94, 184, 191
Merida   275
Merriman, N.   34, 49, 52, 328
Micoud, A.   151
Middleton, V.   32, 75, 318, 325
Ministère de la Culture (F)   34, 52,
         151
Ministerie van Economische Zaken
         (NL)   234
Ministerie van WVC (NL)   234, 239

Ministerio de Cultura (E)   269, 275
Ministério do Comércio e Turismo (P)
         250, 251, 258, 262
Ministério do Planeamento e da
         Administração do Território (P)
         260, 261, 262, 264
Ministero del Turismo (IT)   217, 225
Miro   142
Modernization   160, 199, 213, 250
Modernity   9, 12
Molderez, I.   115
Mommaas, H.   3, 91, 329
Mondriaan   38, 53, 238, 326
Monferrand, A.   153
Monnet, J.   3, 95, 330
Mont Saint Michel   154
Montaner Montejano, J.   268
Monuments
    designation of   11–12, 150
    supply   111, 150–155, 217–220,
         236, 237, 290
    visits to   36, 49, 153, 222–223,
         261
Mosser, F.   3
Mount Athos   98, 185
Muckross House   207, 208–212
Multi-media see Media, multi-media
Multipliers, economic   81–82
Munich   168–169
Munsters, W.   22, 109, 185, 234
Munt, I.   48, 56, 62, 323
Murphy, P.E.   33
Musee d'Orsay   75, 155
Museum of Childhood   291, 293
Museum of the Moving Image   11
Museums   6, 8, 10–11, 13, 36, 40, 48,
         49, 51, 52, 60
    Belgium   111, 121
    Denmark   133, 135
    France   151, 153, 155
    Germany   172–174
    Greece   184–185, 188
    Ireland   208–212
    Italy   219, 221–222, 226–230
    Netherlands   236, 237, 240
    Portugal   254, 257, 261
    Spain   274
    United Kingdom   290, 295

Museums and Galleries Commission
(UK) 284
Music
fado 264
music festivals 179–180, 293
musicals 60, 170–171
'Must-See' sights 38, 225, 233, 245,
314
Myerscough, J. 12, 26, 28, 29, 30, 77,
79, 80, 255, 297, 311

Narhsted, W. 24, 26, 311
National culture 63, 264, 313, 318
National Tourism Organisations 117,
235
see also Policy
National Trust (UK) 74, 284, 293,
295, 320
National Museum Accademia, Venice
227–230
National Art Gallery, Athens 188–189,
192–194
Nederlands Bureau voor Toerisme (NL)
55, 235
Nederlands Centrum Voor
Vrijetijdsvraagstukken (NL)
239
Nederlands Openluchtmuseum (NL)
239
Negrin, L. 6, 8, 11
Nelissen, N.J.M. 240
Netherlands Open Air Museum 239
Netherlands 5, 12, 14, 24, 25, 38, 49,
55, 74, 92, 93, 125, 233–247,
326
cultural funding 238–240
cultural tourism
demand 240–243
policy 233, 234–236
supply 236–238
Neue Pinakothek 168–169
New cultural intermediaries *see* Cultural,
intermediaries
New tourism, the 249, 280
New York 53
Nic Craith, M. 306
Nietzsche, F. 199

Nolan, M.L. 159
Nolan, S. 159
Nordic cultural policy model 127–128,
130
North-Rhine Westphalia 77
Norwegian tourists 136
Nostalgia 10
Notre Dame 154
Nottingham Castle 25
Novelty 24–25
NRIT (NL) 234, 238, 241

O Dwyer, B. 208
O'Carroll, C. 78, 205, 207
O'Connor, J. 63
Occupation, impact on cultural tourism
consumption 53–54, 189,
207, 273, 292–293, 324
Office de Promotion du Tourisme de la
Communaute Francais (B) 117
Office of Public Works (IRL) 202
Olympic Games 160, 276
Open monument days 114, 116, 124,
240
Opera 136
Ouvry-Vial, B. 157

Page, S.J. 200, 201, 202
Palazzo Ducale 75, 224, 225
Paleis Het Loo 25
Palma, J.B. 250
Papadopoulos, S.I. 39, 186
Paradores 268
Parent, M. 156
Paris 6, 27, 80, 150, 154
Parkinson, M. 60, 74, 84, 89
Participation
cultural 47, 49, 237
in cultural tourism 50–55
Partnership 27
Pation, V. 148
Patrimoine 147, 148, 149
Patrimony 117, 252
Paulsen, E. 129
Pavarotti 28, 142
Performance indicators 3, 14, 76, 144,
299

Perrons, D.   57
Phantom of the Opera   170–171
Pilgrims   6, 272
    see also Religious, heritage
Pina, P.   250, 251
Place   141
Poland   42
Policy
    cultural   79, 166, 319
    cultural tourism   128–130,
        189–192, 200–201, 225–226,
        230, 234–236, 255–262,
        284–286, 298, 305–307, 319,
        325
    national   91–95
        see also individual country entries
    regional *see* Regional, policy
    tourism   122, 129, 190, 234,
        268–270, 279, 283, 284
Policy Studies Institute   77, 294
Pommerehne, W.   72, 133
Pompidou Centre   147, 154
Pont du Gard   149
Poon, A.   26, 142, 249
Popular culture   9, 26, 60, 70, 254,
        283, 290, 307, 330
    relationship with high culture   11,
        60, 152, 170, 283, 285, 307,
        312, 314, 323
Porta Negra   168–169
Porto   254
Portugal   249–265
    cultural tourism
        demand   252–255
        impact of   257
        policy   257–262
        supply   255–257
    marketing   262–264
Postmodern   26, 319
Postmodernism   10, 147
Postmodernity   9–10, 12
Pousadas   259, 260, 262
Prado Museum   9, 271, 272, 273, 274
Prentice, R.   63
Privatization   75–76, 229, 245
Product differentiation   123
Product development   114–115, 130,
        177–178, 212, 262, 302

Promotion   228, 250, 262–264, 271,
        280, 304
Provincie Friesland   235
Public expenditure   29, 30, 71, 72–74,
        88, 132–138, 139, 161,
        166–167, 180, 191, 193,
        203–204, 226, 245, 285–286,
        295–296, 308, 319, 329
    see also Subsidies

Quality
    service   177, 178, 301
    tourism   124, 258
Quine, M.   13, 288, 291

Real cultural capital *see* Cultural, capital
Regional
    development   260–261, 312, 320
    policy   235–236, 268
Reina Sofia Museum   271
Religious
    buildings   150, 153
    festivals   112
    heritage   159, 162, 256
Rembrandt   52, 238, 243–244
Reservation systems   90, 132
Richard, D.   161
Richards, G.   22, 33, 35, 53, 62, 74,
        88, 90, 97, 100, 130, 306, 315,
        323, 324, 325
Richards, W.S.   323
Rietbergen, W.L.F.   240
Rijksmuseum, Amsterdam   241,
        243–245
Rioja   277
Risueño, J.I.   272
Ritzer, G.   63
Robertson, I.   4
Rock of Cashel   207
Roetman, E.E.   38, 53, 237, 238, 326
Rojek, C.   25, 314
Rolfe, H.   81
Romania   42
Roman cultural tourists   5
Rome   6
Ronchey, A.   75, 226, 229

Ronchey Act   226, 229
Ronconi, D.   100
Rotterdam   236, 320
Roukens, O.   238
Routes, cultural *see* Cultural, routes
Rubens   119
Rural tourism   124, 184, 276, 277
Russia   95

Santiago de Compostela   5, 6, 156, 272, 276
Santos, D.   258
Satie, E.   63
Savoie   159–163
Schleswig-Holstein Music Festival   179–180
Schneidermann, H.   134
Schor, J.   54
Schouten, F.   24, 315, 319
Schuster, J.M.D.   34, 51, 52, 316
Sciences en fêtes   158
Scitovsky, T.   330
Scotland   83, 287, 292, 306
   see also Edinburgh; Glasgow
Scottish Tourist Board (UK)   285, 305
Seasonality   121, 183, 205, 212, 220, 243, 252–253, 274, 279
SEAT (F)   151
Seaton, A.V.   317
Secretaria de Estado do Turismo (P)   252, 255, 257
Service Class   56, 57, 312, 323
   see also Social, class
Servuction   155
Seve, N.   161
Seville   276
Shaw, G.   6, 13, 53, 74
Short breaks   8, 36, 54, 57, 113–114, 168, 178, 317
Silk Road, the   101
Sightseeing   121
Silver Route   276
Singapore   4
Single European Market   54
Smith, V.L.   64, 66
Smith, S.L.J.   13
Social

class   48, 52, 56, 62, 135, 236, 289, 307, 314
   context of cultural tourism   47–70
   tourism   157
Socio-economic status   52–53
Sociology   47
Son et lumières   157–158, 187
Soutsos, A.   192–193
Spain   5, 24, 25, 63, 267–281
   cultural tourism
      demand   271–275
      impact of   278–279
      policy   269–27
      supply   275
   management of cultural tourism   268–269
Spatial distribution
   of demand   93, 274, 276
   of supply   50, 56, 57–61, 63, 217–219, 237, 323
Spitz, S.   317
Sponsorship   29, 75, 134, 139, 166, 180, 229, 296, 328
St Paul's Cathedral   38, 291, 293
Starlight Express   170–171
Stedelijk Museum   53
Stendhal, H.   148
Studienkreise für Tourismus   41, 167, 169
Studiosus Reisen (D)   55, 56, 176–178
Study tours   7, 24, 158, 175, 176–178
Subsidies   71, 73, 76, 144, 171, 236, 237, 245
Subsidiarity   98
Sustainable tourism   98, 102
Sweden   88
Swedish tourists   135, 136, 210
Swinglehurst, E.   7
Symbolic capital   49, 314

Tartas, P.   192
Task Force 'NRW Culture Industries Report'   77
Taylor, B.   53
Taylor, P.   82
Theatre   133, 170–171, 175, 288, 291, 297

Theatre *contd*
    audience   13, 79, 170–171
Theme years, cultural   119–120
Theme parks, cultural   112, 277, 314
Thessaloniki
    Archaeological Museum   188–189
    European Cultural Capital   191
Thomas, M.   103
Thomsen, K.   134
Thorburn, A.   3
Thyssen Museum   271, 274
Taiwan   4
Todd, J.   27
Toffler, A.   8
Tomlinson, J.   20, 21
Touring Club Italiano   217, 225–226
Tourism
    definitions of   20
    development   14, 250, 269, 284
    historical development   5–8
    industry   92, 125, 132, 144, 155
        see also Tour operators; Travel
        agents
    markets   4, 4, 185, 186
    see also Mass tourism; Holidays,
        package; Policy, tourism
Tourism Research and Marketing (UK)
    314
Tour operators   132, 155, 162,
        176–178, 240, 277, 304
Tours, cultural   115, 117, 176–178,
        240
Towner, J.   5
Townsend, A.R.   61, 324
Towse, R.   73
Traffic management   123
Transnational
    cooperation   90, 98
    research   33
Travel agents   132, 155, 178
Treaty of Rome   95, 98, 320
Trier   168–169
Tunbridge, J.E.
TURESPANA   268, 270, 270
Typology of cultural attractions *see*
    Attractions

UNESCO   95, 101–102, 184, 215, 268,
    275
United States of America   73 *see also*
    American tourists
United Kingdom   14, 24, 25, 26, 39,
    40, 41, 49, 53, 63, 72, 73, 74,
    75, 77, 87–88, 92, 207,
    283–309, 324
    cultural tourism
        demand   286–293
        impact of   297–298
        management of   300–303, 304
        marketing of   303–304, 305–307
        policy   305–307
        supply   293–296
Urbain, J.D.   152
Urban tourism   8, 54, 71, 90, 129, 175,
    184
Urry, J.   14, 21, 25, 56, 60, 315

Van den Abeele, A.   122
Van den Berg, L.   80
Van der Borg, J.   27, 57, 116, 226, 227,
    321, 322
Van der Wees, F.   236
Van der Wijk, P.   238
Van Gogh Museum   24
Vanhove, N.   115, 117, 118
Van Praet, S.   27, 28, 65
Van Puffelen, F.   77
Van 't Riet   24, 25
Van 't Zelfde, J.   322
Van Vugt, T.   243, 244
Vathia   190
Vaughan, R.   81
Venice   66, 224–245, 227–230
Verhoeff, R.   13, 38, 49, 62, 324
Vermeer   243
Victoria and Albert Museum   75, 291,
    293
Visitor management   121–123, 156,
    212, 244, 313
Visitors
    day   77, 120, 123, 241
    numbers   120, 163, 211,
        221–222, 236, 243, 245, 274,
        290

profiles   33, 116–117, 135, 193,
    211
Vlaams Commissariaat-Generaal voor
    Toerisme (B)   117, 119
Voisin, J.-C.   100
Voluntary sector   74, 246, 250, 295,
    320
Volunteers   74, 134, 161, 239, 320
Von Kieffer, R.   162
Von Molkte, H.   97, 98
Voogd, H.   141

Wales Tourist Board (UK)   285
Wall, G.   7, 64
Wallonia   110, 112
   see also Belgium
Walsh, K.   10, 56, 61, 63, 319
Way of life   21, 148, 155, 208
Weber, M.   198–199
Wheeller, B.   64
Williams, R.   19, 21, 51

Wilson, D.   66
Winkelman en van Hesse   122, 234
Wood, H.   75, 302
Wood, R.E.   23
World Heritage
    cities   272
    list   101, 268, 275
World Tourism Organization (WTO)   23
Wynne, D.   13, 26, 62, 76, 319, 324,
    327

Yzewyn, D.   125

Zago, M.   226
Zairis, P.   185
Zeppel, H.   32
Zoest, J.G.A.   241
Zukin, S.   49–50, 56, 61–62, 312, 315,
    323, 324